John Crowe Ransom:
A Descriptive Bibliography

John Crowe Ransom:
A Descriptive Bibliography

Craig S. Abbott

The Whitston Publishing Company
Troy, New York
1999

Library of Congress Catalog Card Number 97-62328

ISBN 0-87875-503-9

Printed in the United States of America

[redacted]

Contents

Acknowledgments

My research for this bibliography was supported in part by a fellowship award from the Bibliographical Society of America and by a research leave granted by Northern Illinois University. I have also had the generous assistance of colleagues, book collectors and dealers, librarians, and publishers.

Early in the project, I had the personal assistance and encouragement of Thomas Daniel Young—along with the benefit provided by his own invaluable scholarship on Ransom. For examining items in the British Library I am greatly indebted to Donald Hawes. And I owe a special debt to Stuart Wright, who freely shared with me his good advice, lent me many items from his collections, and checked my descriptions and listings.

I cannot name them all, but I must thank the many librarians who have assisted me over the several years of this project. I am especially indebted to the staff of Founders Memorial Library here at Northern Illinois University, most notably to the librarian-scholars William Baker and David Shavit and to Tobie Miller and Ron Barshinger in the Interlibrary Loan Services. Elsewhere, I am particularly indebted to Cathy Henderson, Jennifer Peters, and Barbara Smith-LaBorde of the Harry Ransom Humanities Research Center, University of Texas at Austin; Jami Peelle, Olin and Chalmers Libraries, Kenyon College; and Marice Wolfe, Jean and Alexander Heard Library, Vanderbilt University. I also thank William Cagle and Sue Presnell, Lilly Library, Indiana University; Alice R. Cotten and Libby Chenault, University of North Carolina at Chapel Hill; John Delayney, Princeton University Libraries; Rosalyn Lewis, United Methodist Publishing House, Nashville; Sandra Owens, Free Library of Philadelphia; Marilee Shore, Lanier Library Association, Tryon, North Carolina; and Nancy Turner, Ball State University Libraries.

For answering or attempting to answer my queries about the publication of Ransom's works, I thank Kristin Bryan, Louisiana State University Press; Judith B. Jones, Alfred A. Knopf, Inc.; Joanna Hitchcock, University of Texas Press; Nancy C. McGrath, Shoe String Press; Griselda J. Ohannessian, New Directions Publishing; Emily Raabe, Ecco Press; Jean Rose, Reed International Books; Charles Scribner, Scribners; and Michael Schmidt, Carcanet Press.

Introduction

This bibliography of John Crowe Ransom (1888-1974) attempts to provide a record of his published writings, from his early contributions to Vanderbilt University publications through reprintings as late as 1995.

There is, I suppose, an element of irony in preparing a bibliography of Ransom, who led criticism to triumph in its campaign to displace bibliographical and historical study as the primary focus of English departments. Yet for anyone interested in Ransom—critically, historically, or however—a bibliography would seem indispensable. Indeed, there have already been several that have proved their value, most notably and recently Thomas Daniel Young's *John Crowe Ransom: An Annotated Bibliography* (1982), which was an advance over an earlier checklist compiled by Mildred Brooks Peters. The bibliography by Young remains useful for its abstracts of Ransom's essays and for its annotated listing of works about Ransom. My aim has been to provide a fuller record of Ransom's work, mostly by adding a good number of items not in Young and by preparing bibliographical histories and descriptions of Ransom's books. While acknowledging my considerable debt to Young, I should also add that I have personally examined every item included here, except for the few noted as not seen.

A bibliography is especially important for Ransom because of his penchant for revising his texts from one publication to another. The nature and extent of his revisions cannot be determined until there is a full record of these documents and the texts they contain. Further, through the example of his own poetry (most of it written in the 1910s and 1920s and continually revised thereafter) as well as through his critical and theoretical essays and his editing of the *Kenyon Review*, Ransom exerted a great influence on succeeding generations of poets and critics. In the 1940s and 1950s, his influence was probably second only to T. S. Eliot's in shaping American poetry and in providing the basis for the critical and pedagogical practices associated with what has been called the New Criticism. My descriptive bibliography reveals the forms of publication through which he exerted this influence.

The bibliography is organized into five sections according to form of publication. *Section A* describes separate publication—that is, publication as book, pamphlet, and broadside of work written and edited by Ransom. The section is arranged chronologically by first publication of the work and with subsequent editions and impressions of a work described, also in chronological order, after the first (except that I have chosen to divide as separate works the three editions of *Selected Poems*). Preceding the description of each work is a brief introduction providing information on its publication history. Much of this information is drawn from letters in the Ransom papers in the Jean and Alexander Heard Library at Vanderbilt University (TNV), from materials in the Christopher Morley papers and Alfred A. Knopf archive at the Harry Ransom Humanities Research Center at the University of Texas (TxU), from Young's biography of Ransom and his edition of Ransom's letters (*SL*), and finally from the collection of Stuart Wright (STW).

My descriptive method is adapted from Fredson Bowers's *Principles of Bibliographical Description* and from G. Thomas Tanselle's "A Sample Bibliographical Description with Commentary," which also provides a listing of other relevant works on bibliographical theory and method. A few points of method may require emphasis or clarification. In quasi-facsimile transcriptions of title pages and other printed matter, I distinguish between roman, italic, black-letter, script, and open fonts of type. Unless otherwise indicated, the type is roman and the color black. When a color or font is indicated in brackets, it is to be understood to continue until some other color or font is indicated. In collation formulas I use italic rather than square brackets to indicated inferred signatures. I also use italic for inferred page numbers, and if there are initial pages that fall outside a book's pagination scheme, I indicate their total by an italic figure within square brackets.

In describing ink, bindings, and so forth I have used the color nomenclature of the Inter-Society Color Council and National Bureau of Standards. The parenthetical numbers after color designations are for ease of reference to the color samples in the *ISCC-NBS Color Name Charts Illustrated with Centroid Colors* (published in February 1965 as NBS Standard Sample No. 2106). It should be noted that a color sample represents the "center" of a range of color identified by the color name and number. Use of a color name and number, then, simply indicates a judgment that the color falls into the range they indicate, not that there is an exact match between the sample and the item described.

In describing typography, I have given the dimensions of a typical type-page. These, like measurements of leaves, are given as height times width. The parenthetical number, if any, is the height inclusive of any headline or direction line, or both, containing printed matter (such as running titles and page numbers). Typefaces are identified by families; samples of most may be found in W. Pincus Jaspert, W. Turner Berry, and A. F. Johnson's *The Encyclopedia of Type Faces.*

The list of copies accompanying each description provides not a census of Ransom's works in various libraries but rather the locations of the copies on which the descriptions are based. The following symbols are used:

CSA	Craig S. Abbott, DeKalb, IL
DLC	Library of Congress
I	Illinois State Library, Springfield
IAA	Aurora University, Aurora, IL
ICarbS	Southern Illinois University, Carbondale
ICIU	University of Illinois, Chicago
ICU	University of Chicago
ICN	Newberry Library, Chicago
IDanviC	Danville Area Community College, IL
IDecJ	Millikin University, Decatur, IL
IDeK	DeKalb, IL, Public Library
IDeKN	Northern Illinois University, DeKalb
IEdS	Southern Illinois University, Edwardsville
IEG	United Library, Garrett-Evangelical Theological Seminary and Seabury-Western Theological Seminary, Evanston, IL
IEN	Northwestern University, Evanston, IL
IEuC	Eureka College, IL
ILfC	Lake Forest University, IL
IMacoW	Western Illinois University, Macomb
IMonC	Monmouth College, IL

InMuB	Ball State University, Muncie, IN
INS	Illinois State University, Normal
InU-Lilly	Lilly Library, Indiana University, Bloomington
InU-Main	Main Library, Indiana University, Bloomington
IPB	Bradley University, Peoria, IL
IQ	Quincy, IL, Public Library
IQC	Quincy College, IL
IRA	Augustana College, Rock Island, IL
IRivfR	Rosary College, River Forest, IL
IRo	Rockford, IL, Public Library
ISS	Sangamon State University, Springfield, IL
ISy	Sycamore, IL, Public Library
IU	University of Illinois, Urbana
IWat	Watseka, IL, Public Library
MoSW	Washington University, St. Louis
NjP	Princeton University
OGK	Kenyon College, Gambier, OH
OO	Oberlin College, OH
RU	University of Rhode Island, Lexington
STW	Stuart Wright, Private Collection,Winston-Salem, NC
T	Tennessee State Library and Archives, Nashville
TMM	Memphis State University, TN
TNV	Vanderbilt University, Nashville
TxU-PCL	Perry-Castañeda Library, University of Texas, Austin
TxU-HRC	Harry Ransom Humanities Research Center, University of Texas, Austin
TxU-UG	Undergraduate Library, University of Texas, Austin
ViU	University of Virginia, Charlottesville
WBB	Beloit College, Beloit, Wisconsin
WM	Milwaukee Public Library
WMM	Marquette University, Milwaukee
WU	Memorial Library, University of Wisconsin, Madison
WU-Col	College Library, University of Wisconsin, Madison

After listing the locations of examined copies, I also list other descriptive bibliographies that provide descriptions (and usually locations) of the entry. Full citations of these bibliographies, as well as other works that I cite, may be found in a section preceding the indexes.

When a publisher's records, policy, and kindness have made it possible, I have supplied (with citation of the source) information as to print runs and the like. Dates of publication come, in most cases, from the copyright applications submitted to the Copyright Office of the Library of Congress and recorded in the *Catalog of Copyright Entries*. Publication prices are taken from reviews, advertisements, and catalogues. The lists of publication notices, advertisements, and reviews are not exhaustive.

Section B describes books and pamphlets by others in which works by Ransom were published for the first time or for the first time in book form. I describe the first form of the book, in most cases merely noting later forms. Within the section, I have allowed a few interlopers, books without first publication of a Ransom work but with some other particular significance.

Section C lists chronologically the appearances of Ransom's work in periodicals and provides also notes on Ransom's editorial work with periodicals.

Section D lists books and pamphlets written or edited by others that contain work by Ransom. The listing is generously representative rather than exhaustive (most anthologies of twentieth-century American poetry and most anthologies used for courses introducing students to poetry have included poems by Ransom). Items described in Section B are also listed here, with cross references to the descriptions.

Section E lists recordings of Ransom's reading of his work.

Section F lists bibliographical ghosts, items by Ransom advertised or cited as published but in fact not published. Not listed are works that were written or planned by Ransom but not, as far as I know, ever referred to as published or forthcoming, including his aborted book projects "The Third Moment" and "Land!"

To avoid obscuring somewhat the overall history of the publication of Ransom's varied work, I have resisted the temptation to create sections and subsections according to genre—that is, to have separate sections for poetry, essays, editorials, book reviews, letters, interviews, dust jacket blurbs, and translations of Ransom's work. Readers interested in the bibliographical and textual history of individual works of whatever genre should consult my indexes. The first is an index to titles of Ransom's poems, the second is an index to titles of his prose, and the third is a general index, with entries for publishers, printers, designers, editors, translators, titles of books and periodicals to which Ransom contributed, names of authors whose work he reviewed, and so on. Included in the general index are also some selected subject entries for miscellaneous genres: blurbs, editorial work, epigraphs, forewords, interviews, letters, musical settings, and translations.

I should mention some limitations of this bibliography. Although at times I indicate the presences or absence of textual variation in Ransom's works, I have not performed the extensive textual collation that would be undertaken for a variorum or critical edition. And it should be remembered that Ransom tended to revise both poetry and prose as they went from one publication to another. Cecelia Lampp Linton has provided a useful but partial record of textual variants in the poems gathered in Ransom's 1969 *Selected Poems*.

Despite my efforts to offer a thorough account of the publishing history of Ransom's works, I have no doubt missed some items. That seems especially likely for some of Ransom's early journalism and for translations of his works, and I have intentionally omitted instances in which Ransom is quoted, even if extensively, in the course of scholarly and critical studies. Finally, error has no doubt found its way into these pages from time to time. I invite additions and corrections.

POEMS ABOUT GOD

BY

JOHN CROWE RANSOM

1st Lieut. Field Artillery, A.E.F.

NEW YORK

HENRY HOLT AND COMPANY

1919

Title page:
A1.a *Poems about God*

Section A
Separate Publications

A 1 — 1919

Poems about God

Publication of *Poems about God* was facilitated by Christopher Morley, with whom Ransom had established a friendship while they were both Rhodes Scholars at Oxford in 1910-1913. On 4 June 1917, Ransom wrote Morley that three weeks earlier he had sent for his inspection and criticism a book manuscript of 29 poems that was under consideration by Doubleday, Page & Co., which had asked for Morley's "official consideration" (TxU). Ransom said he expected a decision at the end of the week. The decision was negative, and on 28 June Morley wrote to Ransom with yet another rejection, this one from Alfred Harcourt of Holt & Co., who suggested that Ransom wait until he had more poems "up to the standard" of his best (TxU). Morley had enclosed with his letter the report from Harcourt's reader, and in replying to Morley on 4 July Ransom expressed his irritation with its criticism. He agreed that some of his poems were weaker than others, but could not accept as criticism such characterizations as "incredible stupidity," "banalities," "priggish moralizing," and "commonplace." Ransom complained that the reader had failed to appreciate the fact that he was not writing "in one systematic character": "I want a lot of attitudes in there, including the conventional. I don't want it all to be 'caustic satire.'" He would do some adding, subtracting, and revising and "then take a whack at Macmillan's" (TxU). Morley agreed and returned the manuscript to him (7 July 1917, TxU).

A revised manuscript evidently went to Macmillan through Morley. On 17 September, Morley wrote Ransom, now serving with the AEF in France, that Edward C. March of

Macmillan had found in the poems "a true poetic quality which is altogether uncommon" but that Macmillan's "editorial council" had decided against publication (TNV). Morley also submitted the manuscript to the publishers B. W. Huebsch and George H. Doran, and in a letter on 31 October 1917 reported to Ransom that both "had gotten out from under" (TNV). Ransom supposed that through revision and substitutions he might yet "propitiate Henry Holt" (2 December 1917, TxU). Morley replied on 29 December that the manuscript was in the hands of Frederick A. Stokes Co., and he listed the previous refusals: "Macmillan, Holt, Knopf, Huebsch, Houghton, Mifflin and Company and Doran" (TxU). Finding himself "one of the most rejected men in literature," Ransom on 13 March told Morley that since Holt's "destructive criticisms" he had omitted a half dozen poems, revised half a dozen more, and added a dozen new ones. He wondered if he might not now "engage Holt's attention" (TxU). Meanwhile, Morley reported on 13 February 1918 that individual poems evidently from the book manuscript had been rejected by *Atlantic Monthly*, *Independent*, and *Yale Review* (TNV).

On 13 May 1918, having sent Morley additional poems, revisions of earlier ones, and an introduction, Ransom said: "The old book is clean done, I think now. That is, it's big enough as far as volume goes, and I've outgrown it till it's getting a bit artificial with me. Hence my desire to wind it up if possible" (*SL* 100). He told Morley that he was counting on his intercession with Henry Holt. On 10 September, supposing that Holt had again rejected the manuscript, Ransom wrote Morley that he was thinking of getting a leave to approach English publishers, manuscript in hand (TxU). But Holt did accept the manuscript, which had received the endorsement of Robert Frost, who at the time was on retainer with Holt as a "literary adviser." On 27 September Ransom received news of Holt's acceptance, and he told Morley that he approved of the exclusions he named (TxU). In his letter giving Ransom the good news, Morley evidently enclosed a 9 August 1918 letter from Alfred Harcourt, who was then with Holt. The letter had said that Holt did indeed "want to publish a book to be made out of the manuscript" (STW). Harcourt listed the poems they were "dead against including," namely "Sunlight," "The House," "Geometry," "What the Old Leaf Said," "The Power of God," and "Superfluity." The letter also set forth royalty terms: 10 percent after the first 500 copies. Ransom continued to tinker with the text, sending revisions through Morley, but was unable to make changes in proof. In a letter of 12 November 1918, he supposed that the proofs had been lost in the mail ("Not long ago 8,000 bags of AEF mail were lost"), and he told Morley that, if he did not receive proofs within ten days, he would send him "a list of revisions" he had made in the text—"though it isn't complete" (*SL* 103-04). On 30 November, he sent Morley the revisions, also giving him permission to make any changes he liked, asking for criticism of his possibly too garrulous introduction, and expressing a desire to see proof (TxU). On 17 March 1919, still in France, Ransom wrote Morley that he had seen publication announced in *Atlantic*, with his name over Morley's "rash endorsement"; he added that he "never saw the proof" and that he presumed Morley had entered his revisions for him (*SL* 104).

The book was published on 27 March 1919. There was but one Holt impression. In 1972, the Holt typesetting was used by Folcroft Library Editions for a photo-offset reprinting.

A1.a Holt impression (1919)

POEMS ABOUT GOD | BY | JOHN CROWE RANSOM | 1st Lieut. Field Artillery, A.E.F. | [Holt device] | NEW YORK | HENRY HOLT AND COMPANY | 1919

Copyright page (ii): 'COPYRIGHT, 1919 | BY | HENRY HOLT AND COMPANY | THE QUINN & BODEN CO. PRESS | RAHWAY, N. J.'

191 x 130 mm. *1-6*^{8}; 48 leaves. [2] *i-iv* v-vii *viii-ix* xii *1-2* 3-76 *77-84* pp. (page x is misnumbered xii).

1-2 blank; i title page; ii copyright page; iii 'THESE POEMS ARE AFFECTIONATELY | DEDICATED TO | CHRISTOPHER MORLEY'; iv blank; v-vii 'INTRODUCTION' (ending 'JOHN CROWE RANSOM. | FRANCE, | May 13, 1918.'); viii 'ACKNOWLEDGMENT' of periodical publication; ix-x 'CONTENTS'; 1 half title 'POEMS ABOUT GOD'; 2 blank; 3-76 text (ending 'THE END'); 77-78 blank; 79-84 advertisements for Holt books by Robert Frost, Louis Untermeyer, Walter de la Mare, Margaret Widdemer, Burton E. Stevenson, and Romain Rolland.

In addition to Ransom's introduction, the book contains 33 poems. Previous to publication here and with substantive variants, several of the poems had appeared in the *Independent*: "The Swimmer," "Noonday Grace," "Sunset," and "One Who Rejected Christ." One had appeared in *Contemporary Verse*: "Roses." Ransom's note of acknowledgment also lists the *Liberator* and *Philadelphia Evening Public Ledger*, but nothing by Ransom has been found in either of these (see C105 and F1).

Poems: The Swimmer
Noonday Grace
The Ingrate
Sunset
One Who Rejected Christ
Grace
Moonlight
Street Light
Darkness
Geometry
The Lover
Dumb-Bells
Overtures
Under the Locusts
Worship
The Cloak Model
By the Riverside
The Bachelor
Roses
November
A Christmas Colloquy
The Power of God
The Resurrection
Men
The Christian
Morning [The skies were jaded, while the famous sun]
April
Wrestling
Prayer
Friendship
The Four Roses
The School
Sickness

Type-page 25 lines, 123 (131) x 80 mm, 10 lines = 50 mm (e.g., p. vi); typeface Caslon with 3.7 mm face, 1.8 mm x-height. Poem titles (e.g., 'THE SWIMMER') in capitals. Running titles (e.g., '*The Swimmer*') in italic and centered in the headline but omitted from the first page of the introduction and of each poem. Pagination at the outer margin of the headline but centered in the direction line on the first page of the introduction and of each poem. White wove paper, no watermark, sheets bulk 10 mm.

Bound in moderate yellowish brown (77) paper over boards. Front, on a light brown (57) paper label in black within a double rule frame 63 x 33 mm: 'POEMS | ABOUT | GOD | JOHN |

CROWE | RANSOM'. Spine, on a light brown (57) paper label: '[17 mm double rule] | POEMS | ABOUT | GOD | RANSOM | [17 mm double rule]'. Back blank. White wove endpapers. Top edge trimmed, others unopened.

Dust jacket of moderate yellowish brown (77) wove paper printed in black. Front: 'Poems | About | God | By | Lieutenant | John | Crowe | Ransom | *See back of* | *wrapper for* | *description*'. Spine: blank. Back: 'Poems About God | By Lieutenant John Crowe Ransom | CHRISTOPHER MORLEY writes us: | [25-line quotation]'. Front flap: advertisement for Louis Untermeyer's *The New Era in American Poetry*. Back flap: advertisement for Robert Frost's *North of Boston, A Boy's Will*, and *Mountain Interval*.

Copies: ICarbS (rebound), ICN, ICU (lacking pp. 21-36), IEN (spine taped), InU-Lilly (3 copies, one rebound), STW (inscribed by Ransom to Merrill Moore on 20 February 1923, with jacket), T (inscribed by Ransom to the library on 20 July 1922), OGK (rebound), TxU-HRC (inscribed by Ransom to Morley on 31 August 1919, with jacket), TNV (2 copies, 1 rebound and 1 lacking spine), WU (spine taped).

Published at $1.25 on 27 March 1919; copyright registration A515170 (copies deposited 10 April 1919). Publication noted in "The Weekly Record," *Publishers' Weekly* 5 April 1919: 960. Advertised in *Dial* 31 May 1919: 575 and in the same issue included in "A Selected List of Poetry" (580).

Reviewed in *New York Call* 6 April 1919, Sec. 2: 11 (S. A. DeWitt); *Current Opinion* May 1919: 324; *Vanderbilt Alumnus* May 1919: 172; *Dial* 31 May 1919: 562-563 (Louis Untermeyer); *Nation* 26 July 1919: 115-116; *Bookman* October 1919: 222-223 (Maurice Francis Egan); *New York Times Book Review* 2 November 1919: 616-617; *American Oxonian* January 1920: 39-41 (R. F. H.); *Poetry* April 1920: 51-52 (Alice Corbin Henderson, signed A. C. H.); *Yale Review* April 1920: 660-667 (Charles Wharton Stork).

A1.b Folcroft Library reprint (1972)

[Within a cursive border] POEMS ABOUT GOD | BY | JOHN CROWE RANSOM | FOLCROFT LIBRARY EDITIONS / 1972

Verso of title page (2): '*Limited to 150 Copies*'. There is no Folcroft copyright notice.

216 x 155 mm. 44 leaves. [2] *i-iv* v-vii *viii-ix* xii *1-2* 3-76 pp. (page x is misnumbered xii).

This is a offset reprinting of the Holt impression, with the leaf for the Folcroft title page (and limitation notice on verso) replacing the initial blank leaf of the Holt impression and with the deletion of the blank leaf and advertisements that follow the text in the Holt impression. There is no photographic enlargement or reduction of the type-page. White wove paper, no watermark, sheets bulk 7 mm.

Bound in dark red (16) calico cloth over boards. Front and back blank. Spine stamped in gold, running down: '[ornament] POEMS ABOUT GOD [ornament] RANSOM [ornament]'. Inner-edge cut and side stitched; other edges cut as well. Light gray (264) wove endpapers. The integral leaves are preceded and followed by a white wove binder's leaf. No dust jacket.

Copies: ICIU, STW.

Chills and Fever

Poems

by

John Crowe Ransom

New York *Alfred · A · Knopf* *Mcmxxiv*

Title page:
A2.a *Chills and Fever*

A 2 **1 9 2 4**

Chills and Fever

In letter to Allen Tate on 17 December 1922, Ransom said that he had sent a manuscript of poetry to Henry Holt, who had rejected it early the previous summer; and now, he said, impatient in "waiting for the English proposition" (that is, for publication of *Grace after Meat*), he had recently sent "a better MS." to Alfred Harcourt, who in mid-1919 had left Holt to form his own publishing house (*SL* 116). By the time he wrote to Christopher Morley on 31 December 1922, however, Harcourt had already rejected the manuscript, which Ransom enclosed for Morley's examination. He asked Morley to send the manuscript to a "gullible" publisher or to send him a list of such publishers (TxU). Ransom himself later submitted the manuscript, revised, to Macmillan and received a vaguely worded rejection. Unless Morley objected, he wrote on 17 July 1923, he would now submit it to Alfred A. Knopf (TxU). He finally did so on 9 October, admitting that his *Poems about God* had "rather undistinguished sales" and now calling the manuscript "Philomela" (TxU). A month later, on 7 November, Blanche Knopf wrote Ransom to accept the manuscript but asked for reversion to the earlier title *Chills and Fever* (TxU), a phrase from his poem "Here Lies a Lady." In a 12 November letter to Louis Untermeyer, Ransom shared the good news, telling him of Harcourt's earlier rejection of the manuscript ("Harcourt was unable to 'see' my poems; an incapacity which most readers share"). But, Ransom added, "I am able since yesterday to say that Alfred A. Knopf is 'extremely enthusiastic' about my volume and offers to publish it; no earlier than 'early autumn of 1924,' however" (*SL* 123). The next day he thanked Morley for his "seasonable word" on the manuscript's behalf (TxU). The book contract, dated 16 November, was emended in Ransom's hand to allow for the publication of "a volume in England, through Hogarth Press" (STW). Knopf's acceptance of the book was announced in the December 1923 issue of the *Fugitive*: "John Crowe Ransom's second volume of poems is to be published by Alfred A. Knopf in early autumn of next year, under the title, 'Chills and Fever'" (163). In securing Knopf as publisher for *Chills*, Ransom was adding to what was already a distinguished list, one that included Ezra Pound's *Lustra* (1917), T. S. Eliot's *Poems* (1920), and Wallace Stevens's *Harmonium* (1923). For a listing of Knopf books from that period, see *The Borzoi: Being a Sort of Record of Ten Years of Publishing* (Knopf, 1925).

The manuscript first seen by Knopf must have differed considerably from that finally sent to the printer. Ransom continued to add new poems, most of which were appearing in the *Fugitive*, and to revise earlier ones. When Blanche Knopf sent the book contract to him on 15 November 1923, she asked Ransom to consult with Morley on the poems that had been added and omitted since Morley had last seen the manuscript, and she said that the final version must be delivered to the printer by 1 June 1924 for fall publication (TxU). Ransom continued to send Morley new poems and revisions of old ones. Thus, for example, on 12 February 1924, he sent three poems, including "Agitato ma non troppo," which he described as "a sort of confession of aesthetic faith" (TxU). On 27 February, he told Morley that Knopf would agree to whatever revisions Morley approved (TxU). The manuscript was due at Knopf by mid-May, and so on 1 May Ransom sent it to Morley for his final inspection. Enclosing 50 poems plus 2 or 3 extras in case Morley deleted any, Ransom explained that he had revised and arranged the poems carefully: the arrangement was "somewhat chronological" but also progressed from the more simple and romantic to the more philosophical. He began, he said, with the italicized "Agitato" as a kind of "key-note speech" and ended with his favorite poem, "Philomela" (TxU). By early July, Ransom was already reading proof (*SL* 139). Incomplete correction at this point may account for two discrepancies between the contents page and text: the contents page lists a foreword but there is none (aside from a brief note of acknowledgment); and the contents page gives the title "In Process of the Nuptials of the Duke" for the poem appearing as "In Process of a Noble Alliance" in the text.

The book was published on 29 August 1924. It was considered for that year's Pulitzer Prize for poetry. Writing to Robert Graves on 12 June 1925, Ransom passed on some news that, he said, he would not "publish to the general": "I barely missed winning the Pulitzer Prize ($1,000) for 1924, being defeated in favor of Robinson (who had already won it in 1922) because my work was offensive to one elderly committeeman who wouldn't budge to suit the others' wish, and who had his way because the decision had to be unanimous" (*SL* 143). According to John Hohenberg's history of the Pulitzer Prizes, the judges for 1924 were Richard Burton, Wilbur Cross, and Ferris Greenslet.

Setting aside E. A. Robinson's *The Man Who Died Twice* because Robinson had won previously, Cross and Greenslet voted for Ransom's *Chills and Fever;* Burton, however, argued in the committee report that Ransom's poetry was "a very mannered, freaky, morbid affair, representative of the introspective Freudian tendencies in our contemporary verse and literature" (quoted in Hohenberg 120). Faced with a divided committee, the Pulitzer advisory board decided on Robinson.

There was but one Knopf impression (perhaps of 1,500 copies, the number reported for Knopf's first edition of Wallace Stevens's *Harmonium*). It was issued over time in a series of bindings. The original typesetting was used in 1972 for a photo-offset reprinting by Folcroft Library Editions.

A2.a Knopf impression (1924)

Chills and Fever I *Poems* I *by* I *John Crowe Ransom* I [Borzoi device] I *New York Alfred • A • Knopf Mcmxxiv*

Copyright page (4): 'COPYRIGHT, 1924, BY ALFRED A. KNOPF, INC. • I PUBLISHED, AUGUST, 1924 • SET UP, AND I PRINTED BY THE VAIL-BALLOU PRESS, INC., I BINGHAMTON, N.Y. • PAPER FURNISHED BY I W. F. ETHERINGTON & CO., NEW YORK. • I BOUND BY THE H. WOLFF ESTATE, NEW YORK. I MANUFACTURED IN THE UNITED STATES OF AMERICA'.

206 x 138 mm. *1-6*^{8}; 48 leaves. *1-12* 13-95 *96* pp.

1 half title '*Chills and Fever*'; 2 list of 8 other Borzoi poetry titles (from *Come Hither*, edited by Walter de la Mare, to *Ulug Beg* by Autolycus); 3 title page; 4 copyright page; 5 '*These poems I dedicate to* I R. R. R. [i.e., Robb Reavill Ransom, his wife] I*and the summer of 1921,* I *when, if ever, came perfect* I *days.*'; 6 blank; 7 acknowledgement for poems previously published, in 11 lines and signed 'JOHN CROWE RANSOM.'; 8 blank; 9-11 'CONTENTS'; 12 blank; 13-95 text (ending 'THE END'); 96 blank. The table of contents lists, without page number, a foreword, but none appears in the book.

Of the 49 poems collected in this volume, 37 had first appeared in the *Fugitive,* 5 were published here for the first time (see titles preceded by an asterisk), and the rest had appeared in *Double Dealer*, *Literary Review of the New York Evening Post*, and *Armageddon*. The *Philadelphia Public Ledger* is also acknowledged, and it may be that "Miriam Tazewell" had appeared in it (see C105). Most of the poems underwent revision for publication here; none had appeared in *Poems about God*.

Poems: *Agitato ma non troppo*
Spectral Lovers
Bells for John Whitesides' [sic] Daughter
Winter Remembered
Triumph
*Two Sonnets (I. Yea, II. Nay)
Spring Posy
To a Lady Celebrating Her Birthday
Vaunting Oak
In Process of a Noble Alliance
Parting at Dawn
Miriam Tazewell
Here Lies a Lady
The Tall Girl
Fall of Leaf
Rapunzel Has Submitted Herself to Fashion
The Vagrant
Boris of Britain
April Treason
First Travels of Max
Grandgousier
*Miss Euphemia
*Winter's Tale
Emily Hardcastle, Spinster
Number Five
Good Ships
Youngest Daughter
Necrological
Armageddon
Epitaph
Judith of Bethulia
Conrad Sits in Twilight
Nocturne
Blackberry Winter
Lichas to Polydor
Spiel of the Three Mountebanks
Night Voices
Adventure This Side of Pluralism
On the Road to Wockensutter
Prometheus in Straits
Plea in Mitigation
Tom, Tom, the Piper's Son
Old Man Playing with Children
Captain Carpenter
*These Winters
Old Mansion
Inland City
Philomela

Type-page with variable number of lines, 136 (141) x 89 mm, 10 lines = 43 mm (e.g., p. 43); typeface Caslon with 3.2 mm face, 1.6 mm x-height. Poem titles (e.g., '*Spectral Lovers*') in italic and centered, each poem beginning on a new page. No running titles; pagination centered in the direction line. White wove paper, no watermark, sheets bulk 11 mm.

Four bindings seen.

1. Bound in paper over boards, the paper having vertical bands of moderate brown (58), dark orange-yellow (72), strong yellow (84), and light grayish olive (109). Those are the predominant colors, the bands shading into lighter and darker hues in a wash-like effect. Front and back otherwise blank. Pale yellow (89) paper label (60 x 17 mm) printed in black or dark reddish brown (44) on the spine: '[17 mm ornamented border resembling a thick-thin rule with a central scroll] | [swash C and F] *Chills* | & | *Fever* | • | [swash P] *Poems by* | JOHN | CROWE | RANSOM | [same ornamented border, inverted]'. White wove endpapers. Top edge trimmed and stained strong yellow (84), in some copies the stain having been imperfectly applied or having partially faded. Other edges unopened.

2. Bound in paper over boards, the paper having vertical bands of very light green (143) alternating with bands of red shaded from predominantly dark red (16) to light grayish red (18); very dark red (17) calico around the spine. The CSA, ICU, and ICN copies appear to have labels printed in black rather than brown. Spine, endpapers, and edges are identical to those of binding 1.

3. Bound in rainbow-like colored calico cloth over boards, the color bands running vertically and consisting of a repeated sequence of the hues purple, bluish green, and orange (almost 3 such sequences on front). Spine label, endpapers, and edges are the same as those of bindings 1 and 2.

4. Bound in pale purplish blue (203) paper over boards with grayish purplish red (262) calico cloth around the spine. Front and back blank. Spine label identical to that of other bindings except that the border consists of a series of diamond shapes, each containing a central dot, and except that the ornament after the title is a triangle resting on its hypotenuse, which is intersected centrally by a short vertical line. (The label paper appears to have been white rather than yellow, though discoloration or fading may have taken place.) Endpapers and edges are the same as those of the other bindings.

One or more of the bindings of paper over boards appear to precede the cloth binding, since the volume was listed in the *Cumulative Book Index* (July 1924-June 1925) as issued in boards. Binding 1 is probably the earliest of these. It is the binding of a review copy dated 17 August 1924 and of the earliest inscribed copy seen, with a date of September 1924. And evidently referring to binding 1, the reviewer for the November *Bookman* described the binding as "variegated paper ranging from yellow to brown to grey and resembling spectroscopic records by some astronomer." The same binding was described in a January 1925 review in the *American Oxonian* as sporting "handsome feverish yellow stripes down the board covers" (this reviewer also notes the presence of "a yellow wrapper, upon which Christopher Morley has set down two paragraphs about Ransom"). There is no evidence that these bindings represent distinct impressions of the book. Similarly colorful paper-boards bindings, followed by a cloth remainder binding, had been used for successive bindings-up of Stevens's *Harmonium* (Edelstein A1.a).

Dust jacket (seen on each binding) of white paper coated moderate yellow (87) and printed in dark brown (59). Front: '[flower border extending across whole of jacket, including flaps] | *Chills and Fever* | [swash P and B] *Poems By* | [swash C and R] *John Crowe Ransom* | CHRISTOPHER MORLEY says: | [24-line blurb] | [capitals in swash] *Alfred A. Knopf* [Borzoi Books device] *Publisher, N.Y.* | [flower border as above]'. Spine: '[border] | *Chills* | *and* | *Fever* | [swash P] *Poems by* | *JOHN* | *CROWE* | *RANSOM* | [Borzoi Books device] | ALFRED | • A • | KNOPF | [border]'. Back: between the borders at head and foot and within a rule frame ornamented with fleurs-de-lis is an advertisement for '*New* BORZOI BOOKS *Fall, 1924*' (from Dale Collins's *Ordeal* to Mildred Cram's *The Tide*). Front flap: borders at head and foot, price ('$1.50 net'), and 13-line biographical note on Ransom. (The biographical note, with some rearrangement, was that supplied Knopf by Ransom on 26 February 1924.) Back flap: borders at head and foot, and an advertisement and subscription form for the *American Mercury*. One copy seen has an unprinted glassine cover around the jacket and may have been so issued (STW).

A later dust jacket, seen on binding 4, is of light yellowish brown (76) wove paper printed in dark brown (59). Front: '[border of centrally dotted diamond shapes] | *Chills and Fever* | [swash P and R] *Poems by* | *John Crowe Ransom* | [flourish] | ALFRED • A • KNOPF [borzoi] PUBLISHER •N•Y•'. Spine: '[border continued from the front] | [swash C and F] *Chills* | *&* | *Fever* | [ornament resembling a triangle resting on its hypotenuse and intersected by a short vertical line] | *Poems by* | *John* | *Crowe* | *Ransom* | [border] | [borzoi] | ALFRED • A • | KNOPF'. Back: advertisement for 16 Borzoi books, from George W. Fuller's *A History of the Pacific Northwest* to Charles E. Crane's *Winter in Vermont*. Front flap: price ('$1.50 | net'), biographical blurb substantively identical to that of the earlier jacket. Back flap: advertisement for war savings bonds and stamps and a request that readers send the book, once read, to the U.S.O.

Copies: CSA (bindings 1 and 2), ICN (binding 2), ICU (binding 2), IEN (binding 3, spine taped), IU (binding 3, spine label partially missing), InU-Lilly (binding 2, with jacket), InU (binding 4), OGK (2 copies, binding 1), STW (4 copies, including a copy in binding 1 with jacket, Robert Penn Warren's review copy in binding 1 and signed and dated by him on 17 August 1924, a copy in binding 3 with jacket, and a copy in binding 4 but with the early jacket), T (binding 1), TNV (7 copies, including a copy in binding 1 inscribed by Ransom to Walter Clyde Curry September 1924, a copy in binding 1 inscribed to Alfred Starr September 1924, a copy in binding 1 inscribed to Louis Untermeyer 10 October 1924, a copy in binding 1 dated by owner Roberta Dillon Lyne as December 1924 and inscribed to her 10 June 1937, a copy in binding 2 and without inscription, a copy in binding 3 without inscription, and a copy in binding 4 with Ransom's autograph annotations and revisions and with duplicate leaves laid in but the title page missing), TxU-HRC (3 copies: one with binding 1 and jacket, one from the Knopf collection with binding 2 and jacket, another from Knopf with binding 4 and later jacket), WU (binding 1).

Published at $1.50 on 29 August 1924; copyright registration A801838 (copies deposited 15 September 1924). Forthcoming publication announced in *Fugitive* December 1923: 163 and August 1924: 98. Publication noted in "The Weekly Record," *Publishers' Weekly* 6 September 1924: 727 (with Ransom spelled

"Ransome"); listed in "Latest Books," *New York Times Book Review* 7 September 1924: 30, and in "Some Interesting Fall Books," *Nation* 22 October 1924: 401. Advertised in *New York Times Book Review* 7 September 1924: 26 and 14 September 1924: 28; and in *Publishers' Weekly* 20 September 1924: 863. *Chills and Fever* was still in print as late as 31 October 1949, when Ransom's royalty statement for the previous six months shows the sale of 28 copies (TNV).

Reviewed in *Borzoi Broadside* July-August 1924: 34 (Christopher Morley); *Nashville Tennessean* 31 August 1924, Firing Line section: 9 (Donald Davidson); *Saturday Review of Literature* 13 September 1924: 120 (William Rose Benét); *New York Times Book Review* 14 September 1924: 14 (Herbert S. Gorman); *Literary Review* 27 September 1924: 15 (signed W.Y., probably William Yust, a regular contributor); *Nation* 22 October 1924: 446 (Mark Van Doren); *Bookman* November 1924: 345-346 (Bernice Lesbia Kenyon); *Guardian* November 1924: 25 (Allen Tate); *Voices* November 1924: 24-25 (Robert Penn Warren); *Independent* 1 November 1924: 347 (E. A. Niles); *Saturday Review of Literature* 27 December 1924: 412 (Robert Graves; for a response to Grave's review see a letter by Edwin Mims, 28 February 1925: 570); *Double Dealer* January-February 1925: 114-116 (William Alexander Percy, signed W.A.P.); *American Oxonian* January 1925: 29; *Sewanee Review* January 1925: 105-111; *Measure* March 1925: 15-17 (Rolfe Humphries); *Dial* April 1925: 337 (Marianne Moore, unsigned); *New Republic* 27 May 1925: 23-24 (Babette Deutsch); *Yale Review* July 1925: 791-797 (Louis Untermeyer).

A2.b Folcroft reprint (1972)

[Within a border 158 x 107 mm] *Chills and Fever* | *Poems* | *by* | *John Crowe Ransom* | FOLCROFT LIBRARY EDITIONS / 1972

Verso of title page (2): '*Limited to 150 Copies*'. There is no Folcroft copyright notice.

222 x 158 mm. 49 leaves. *i-ii 1-12* 13-95 *96* pp.

This is a offset reprinting of the Knopf impression, with the addition of a leaf for the Folcroft title page (and limitation notice on verso) after the Knopf half-title leaf. The list of Borzoi poetry on the verso of the half-title leaf is not reprinted; otherwise, the entire Knopf impression is reproduced. There is no photographic enlargement or reduction of the type-page. White wove paper, no watermark, sheets bulk 7 mm.

Bound in black calico over boards, with the inner folds cut and leaves side-stitched. Front and back blank. Spine stamped in gold, running down: '[ornament] CHILLS AND FEVER [ornament] RANSOM [ornament]'. Edges cut. Light gray (264) wove endpapers. The integral leaves are preceded and followed an additional free endpaper of white wove paper thicker than the stock used for the integral leaves. No dust jacket.

Copies: ICIU, STW.

GRACE AFTER MEAT

JOHN CROWE RANSOM

With an Introduction by Robert Graves

Printed & published by Leonard & Virginia
Woolf at the Hogarth Press 52 Tavistock
Square London W.C.
1924

Title page:
A3 ***Grace after Meat***

A3 1924

Grace after Meat

Publication of *Grace after Meat* was arranged by Robert Graves, who had been introduced to Ransom's poetry through William Yandell Elliott, a graduate of Vanderbilt who was associated with the Fugitives and who was at Oxford on a Rhodes Scholarship during the years 1920-1923. On 11 July 1922 Ransom wrote Graves thanking him for his "kind words" about *Poems about God*, enclosing "some recent stuff," and telling of his plans to "submit another manuscript to the publishers" that summer (*SL* 110-111). Graves took upon himself the task of finding Ransom an English publisher. In a letter to Edward Marsh probably written in early July, Graves announced that he had "found a very good poet indeed, John Ransom, an American" and that he intended "to get him published over here as he fell completely flat in America" (*In Broken Images* 142). Ransom responded to Graves's offer of assistance on 31 August 1922: "You have my permission to use anything of mine anywhere, and at any time. And to re-entitle anything, or edit it as you please" (*SL* 112). On the assumption that he would "show it to the right publisher, for publication as early as possible," he also was sending Graves a book manuscript entitled "Philomela," consisting of poems from *Poems about God* and more recent work—a total of forty-six poems. This was probably the same (or nearly the same) manuscript that had been recently rejected by Henry Holt and later evolved into *Chills and Fever*. It is not clear precisely when Graves, with some assistance from T. S. Eliot, secured Leonard and Virginia Woolf's agreement to publish a selection from the manuscript at their Hogarth Press, but it was probably shortly before 19 November 1923, when Ransom wrote Graves to say that he was "overjoyed to hear" about "his election to British publicity through Hogarth Press" (*SL* 124). (Ransom had already had a bit of Hogarth publicity in Graves's *The Feather Bed*, published by Hogarth Press in July 1923 and containing an introduction in the form of a letter from Graves to Ransom.) In his 19 November letter, Ransom also agreed to Graves's handling of the book proofs. The next day, Ransom wrote to Blanche Knopf to ask whether publication by Hogarth of a manuscript containing some of the same poems as those in *Chills and Fever* would cause problems (TxU). She answered on

24 November that she saw no objection to Hogarth's "doing these poems" (TxU).

Ransom continued to send Graves new poems and revisions of old ones, and he repeatedly objected to the title Graves had chosen (*Grace after Meat*). But Graves served as an editor who knew his own mind. The selection of poems, their order, the introduction, and the title were his. On 20 November 1923, Ransom wrote: "More and more I like your selections. Am reconciled to them all." But he still disliked the title, which he thought drew attention to a poem he deemed an "artistic offense," and he suggested replacement titles: "Under the Locusts," "Lean Locust Branches," "Great Oak," "American Oak," "Throes of Oak," "Mortal Oak," "Vaunting Oak," "or any title poem" (*SL* 125-126). Finally, on 28 January 1924, in the same letter expressing his happiness at the book's being with the printers, he bowed to Graves's judgment on the title, asking forgiveness for his "pestiferous cavils" (*SL* 128). For some reason, publication was delayed from spring to early fall 1924. Although published later than *Chills and Fever*, this book went to the printer earlier and thus has earlier versions of the poems. Because Graves was allowed to "edit," not all of the textual variation can be attributed to Ransom.

The volume was published in late October or early November 1924. There has not been any impression or edition after the first.

GRACE AFTER MEAT | JOHN CROWE RANSOM | *With an Introduction by Robert Graves* | Printed & published by Leonard & Virginia | Woolf at the Hogarth Press 52 Tavistock | Square London W.C. | 1924

217 x 139 mm. *1-8*^{4}; 32 leaves, with the first and last leaves used as paste-down endpapers. *i-ii 1-6* 7-11 *12* 13-57 *58* pp.

i-ii blank; 1 title page; 2 blank; 3 dedication '*To* | *ROBERT GRAVES*' (swash Rs and B in first name); 4 blank; 5 'CONTENTS'; 6 blank; 7-11 'INTRODUCTION' (signed 'ROBERT GRAVES. | ISLIP, | OXFORD.'); 12 blank; 13-57 text; 58 blank.

Poems: In his introduction Graves quotes "some stanzas" (eight of them) from "The Southern Mansion," a poem which he says came to him "too late to include in the body of this book" (9). The poem is a version of "Old Mansion," which had appeared in *Chills and Fever* (A2) as "Old Mansion." In the following list, titles marked by an asterisk had appeared in *Poems about God* (A1); those not marked had all appeared in *Chills and Fever*.

An American Addresses Philomela [in *Chills* as "Philomela"]
*The School
*Grace
*By the Riverside
*Resurrection [in *Poems* as "The Resurrection"]
Winter Remembered
*Under the Locusts
*The Cloak Model
*Wrestling
*The Lover
Necrological
Adventure This Side of Pluralism
Night Voices
In Process of the Nuptials of the Duke [thus titled on the contents page of *Chills* but as "In Process of a Noble Alliance" in the text]
At Dawn [in *Chills* as "Parting at Dawn"]
Armageddon
Two Sonnets (I. Yea, II. Nay)
Judith of Bethulia
*Moonlight
Ilex Priscus [in *Chills* as "Vaunting Oak"]

Type-page 28 lines, 146 (155) x 93 mm, 10 lines = 52 mm (e.g., p. 9); typeface Caslon with 4.1 mm face, 1.9 mm x-height. Poem titles in capitals (e.g., 'WRESTLING'). No running titles; pagination centered in the direction line. White wove paper, no watermark, sheets bulk 3 mm.

Bound in paper over boards. The paper has a background of moderate orange-yellow (71) on which there are alternating columns of 24 and 23 circular leaf designs of white and moderate yellowish green (120) with a central dot of deep red (13) (across the front there are 16 such columns). Spine and back otherwise blank. Light orange-yellow (70) paper label on the front: '[within a rule frame 40 x 76 mm] GRACE AFTER MEAT | JOHN CROWE RANSOM'. Paste-down endpapers are the initial and terminal integral leaves; no free endpapers. Edges trimmed.

Copies: ICN, ICU, IEN, IU, InU, InU-Lilly, OGK, STW (2 copies, one of them inscribed to Merrill Moore on 22 February 1927),

TNV, TxU-HRC (3 copies, one with an undated inscription from Mary Nicholson and Robert Graves to Edith Sitwell), WU. Also in Higginson and Williams, *Graves* B8; Woolmer, *Hogarth Press* item 51.

Woolmer's checklist of Hogarth Press says that the volume was handprinted by the Woolfs and published October 1924 at "6s" (a misprint) and that of the 400 copies printed, only 139 were sold by 10 February 1926. Higginson and Williams report a publication date of 30 October 1924 and a price of 4s 6d. Listed in the *English Catalogue* as published November 1924 at 4s 6d net. British Library deposit 14 January 1925. Rhein's *The Handprinted Books of Leonard and Virginia Woolf at the Hogarth Press, 1917-1932* notes that the book was still in print as late as 1939 (55). For a history of Hogarth Press, see Willis's *Leonard and Virginia Woolf as Publishers*.

Publication announced in *Fugitive* December 1924: 131, where it is said that *Grace before [sic] Meat*, "which is a volume of twenty poems selected by Robert Graves from Mr. Ransom's first volume and from his later work, has just been published in England, by the Hogarth Press" (131). Publication noted (as *Grace before Meat*) in *Saturday Review of Literature* 20 December 1924: 404.

Reviewed in *Nashville Tennessean* 30 November 1924, Firing Line section: 8 (Donald Davidson); *TLS* 15 January 1925: 35, reprinted in American Writing To-Day supplement for 17 September 1954: lxxxiii; *New Statesman* 31 January 1925: 476-477 (F. L. Lucas); *Calendar of Modern Letters* March 1925: 87; *New Republic* 27 May 1925: 23-24 (Babette Deutsch); *Saturday Review of Literature* 6 June 1925: 807 (Edwin Muir); *Guardian* 2 (October 1925): 456-458 (Donald Davidson).

JOHN CROWE RANSOM

TWO GENTLEMEN IN BONDS

NEW YORK

ALFRED · A · KNOPF

1927

Title page:
A4.a ***Two Gentlemen in Bonds***

A4 1927

Two Gentlemen in Bonds

The contract for *Two Gentlemen*, signed by Alfred Knopf and dated 25 May 1926, called for delivery of the manuscript by 31 August 1926 and for payment of royalties of 10 percent (STW). On 8 August, in a letter to Donald Davidson, Ransom was able to say that he would get his manuscript for the book to Knopf "for the printer next week" (*SL* 153). At some point after that, in an undated note to Davidson, Ransom asked whether "At Sweetwater," the title of a poem he was sending him, might not also do for the book since it "defines the tone" (TNV). Although the book title remained unchanged, the poem "At Sweetwater" became "Vision by Sweetwater" and was selected as the lead poem in the volume. The selection of poems in the manuscript was probably identical or nearly identical to that of the published book, which was put together from the sonnet sequence that had appeared in *American Poetry 1925: A Miscellany* (B8) and from another 30 poems that had first appeared, for the most part during 1925, in the *Fugitive* and other periodicals. One poem, "Dead Boy," had appeared as early as February 1920, though in a very different form, and another, "Morning," as late as December 1926. Many of the poems, especially those not in the sonnet sequence, underwent revision for this volume. Nine of the poems had not been previously published. According to Young, Ransom read proofs while in Colorado, before returning to Nashville in mid-December 1926 (*Gentleman* 179).

The book was published on 21 January 1927. There was but one Knopf impression. Using a microfilm copy of that impression, University Microfilms has produced a 1970 reprint as well as on-demand reprintings.

A4.a Knopf impression (1927)

JOHN CROWE RANSOM | [88 mm rule] | [swash *T, W, G, M, N, B,* and *S* in title:] *TWO* | *GENTLEMEN* | *IN BONDS* | [Borzoi device] | [swash *N, E, R, K* in city:] *NEW YORK* | [88 mm rule] ALFRED • A • Knopf | 1927

Copyright page (iv): 'COPYRIGHT 1927, BY ALFRED A. KNOPF, INC. | MANUFACTURED IN THE UNITED STATES OF AMERICA'.

Colophon (89): 'A NOTE ON THE TYPE IN | WHICH THIS BOOK IS SET | *The type in which this book has been set (on the | Linotype) is based on the design of Caslon. It is | generally conceded that William Caslon (1692-1766) | brought the old-style letter to its highest perfection | and while certain modifications have been introduced | to meet changing printing conditions, the basic design | of the Caslon letters has never been improved. The | type selected for this book is a modern adaptation | rather than an exact copy of the original Caslon. | The principal difference to be noted is a slight short- | ening of the ascending and descending letters to ac- | commodate a larger face on a given body-size.* | [Borzoi device] | SET UP, PRINTED AND BOUND BY THE | VAIL-BALLOU PRESS, INC., BING- | HAMTON, N.Y. • ESPARTO PAPER | MANUFACTURED IN SCOT- | LAND AND FURNISHED BY | W. F. ETHERINGTON & | CO., NEW YORK.'

206 x 138 mm. *1-5*^{8} *6*^{10}; 50 leaves. *i-vi* vii-ix *x* *1-2* 3-28 *29-30* 31-64 *65-66* 67-87 *88-90* pp.

i half title 'Two Gentlemen | in Bonds'; ii advertisement for *Chills and Fever* with 8-line quotation from Mark Van Doren's review of that book; iii title page; iv copyright page; v acknowledgments in 9 lines and without heading; vi blank; vii-ix 'CONTENTS'; x blank; 1 part title 'THE INNOCENT DOVES'; 2 blank; 3-28 text; 29 part title 'THE MANLINESS OF MEN'; 30 blank; 31-64 text; 65 part title 'TWO GENTLEMEN IN BONDS'; 66 blank; 67 '*Two Gentlemen in Bonds* | A TALE IN TWENTY SONNETS | [cast of characters in 13 lines]'; 68-87 text; 88 blank; 89 colophon; 90 blank.

Poems (listed under the part titles and with asterisks marking those here published for the first time):

THE INNOCENT DOVES
*Vision by Sweetwater
Eclogue
Piazza Piece
Moments of Minnie
Husband Betrayed
*Survey of Literature
Amphibious Crocodile
Fresco
The Equilibrists
TWO GENTLEMEN
IN BONDS

Miller's Daughter
Blue Girls
*Her Eyes
Parting, without a Sequel
Hilda
*In Mr. Minnit's House
Janet Waking
Little Boy Blue
Lady Lost
THE MANLINESS OF MEN
Our Two Worthies
Dead Boy
*Puncture
Semi-Centennial
*Two in August
*Somewhere Is Such a Kingdom
*Persistent Explorer
Morning [Jane awoke Ralph so gently on one morning]
Dog
Jack's Letter
Antique Harvesters
*Man without Sense of Direction
Pink and Pale
Thinking, Drinking
In Air
Thought, Distraught
Meeting in a Garden
Epithalamion of a Peach
Swine, Wine
L'état C'est Moi
Misanthropy
Vain Protestations
Tones and Caparisons
Disappointment of a Thrall
In Bed, Not Dead
Primer of Science
Fait Accompli
Implacable Tower
Features of Creatures
Rain
Wrong
Weep or Sleep

Type-page with variable number of lines because of stanza divisions, 137 (140) x 89 mm, 10 lines = 42 mm (e.g., p. 9); typeface Caslon with 3.2 mm face, 1.6 mm x-height. Poem titles (e.g., '*Moments of Minnie*') in italic and centered, each poem beginning on a new page. No running titles; pagination centered in the direction line. White wove paper, no watermark, sheets bulk 12 mm.

Bound in paper over boards, with black calico cloth around the spine. The paper is printed in black over strong red (12) in a pattern of red gear-like designs. Front and back otherwise blank. White label (54 x 17 mm) on the spine: '[17 mm ornamented border] | [swash T, G, and B] *Two* | *Gentlemen* | *in Bonds* | [ornament resembling a letter v atop a letter u] | JOHN | CROWE | RANSOM | [same ornamented border, inverted]'. White wove endpapers. Top edge trimmed and stained strong red (12), the stain having been imperfectly applied or having partially faded or being absent in some copies. Other edges unopened.

Dust jacket of white paper coated strong red (12) and printed in black. Front: 'JOHN CROWE RANSOM | Author of *Chills and Fever* | [97 mm rule] | [swash T and W] *TWO* | [swash G, M, and terminal N] *GENTLEMEN* | [swash Ns, B, and S] *IN BONDS* | [Borzoi Books device] | [no swash] A NEW BOOK | OF POEMS | *NEW YORK* | [97 mm rule] | ALFRED A. KNOPF • PUBLISHER'. Spine: '[running down at the head] JOHN | CROWE | RANSOM [14 mm rule running across] [running down in the center, with swash letters as in the title on the front] *TWO GENTLEMEN IN BONDS* [14 mm rule running across] [running down at the foot] ALFRED | A. | KNOPF'. Back: title and author, blurb between two 105 mm rules, publisher's imprint and device. Front flap: price ('$2.00 *net*'), biographical blurb in 14 lines. Back flap: title, quotation from Christopher Morley, price.

Copies: CSA, ICN, ICU (3 copies), IEN (rebound), InU-Lilly (with jacket), InU (rebound), OGK (2 copies, one with jacket), STW (2 copies: a copy inscribed to Goldie Zaro on 30 December 1928 with jacket, a copy with the free front endpaper removed and inscribed to Robert Penn Warren on 8 April 1959 and with his annotations throughout), T, TNV (5 copies: Louis Untermeyer's copy, a copy inscribed by Ransom to Walter Clyde Curry 22 January 1927, a copy dated by Roberta Dillon Lyne March 1927 and inscribed to her 10 June 1937, an uninscribed copy with jacket, a copy with spine and title page missing and with autograph annotation and revision by Ransom), TxU-HRC (2 copies with jackets), TxU-PCL, WU.

Published at $2.00 on 21 January 1927; copyright registration A963324 (copies deposited 27 January 1927). Publication noted in "The Weekly Record," *Publishers' Weekly* 22 January 1927: 331. Listed in "Latest Books," *New York Times Book Review* 23 January 1927: 28; "Books of the Week," *New York Herald Tribune Books* 28 January 1927: 20; "Books Received," *Nashville Tennessean* 30 January 1927, mag. sec.: 2; "List of Important Spring Books," *New York Herald Tribune Books* 10 April 1927: 8; "Suggestions for Late Shoppers, *Nashville Tennessean* 11 December

1927, mag. sec.: 7. The *English Catalogue*, spelling Ransom's name with a terminal *e*, records an English publication date of March 1927 and a price of 7s 6d net.

Reviewed in *Nashville Tennessean* 23 January 1927, magazine section: 2 (Donald Davidson); *New Republic* 2 February 1927: 310 (Edmund Wilson, signed E. W.); *Literary Review* 5 February 1927: 6; *Nashville Tennessean* 13 February 1927, magazine section: 7 (Jesse Wills); *Independent* 26 February 1927: 246 (Conrad Aiken); *New York Times Book Review* 27 March 1927: 2 (Herbert S. Gorman); *Nation* 30 March 1927: 346 (Allen Tate); *Bookman* 65 (April 1927): 220-221 (Babette Deutsch); *Booklist* May 1927: 337; *New Statesman* 21 May 1927: 188; *Poetry* 30 (June 1927): 162-165 (Marie Luhrs); *New York Herald Tribune Books* 26 June 1927: 12 (Genevieve Taggard); *Criterion* 6 (August 1927): 168-172 (John Gould Fletcher); *TLS* 11 August 1927: 546; *Sewanee Review* April 1928: 211-224 (William S. Knickerbocker).

A4.b University Microfilms on-demand reprintings

University Microfilms has issued on-demand reprintings by microfilm-xerography. These evidently derive from the same microfilm copy of the Knopf impression used in 1970 for the University Microfilms reprinting (A4.c). They bear the same autograph annotations and markings of the 1970 reprinting, yet they have additional ones as well (suggesting that copy for the 1970 reprinting had been touched up). For example, on p. viii, there are underlinings of two additional titles ("Antique Harvesters" and "Survey of Literature") and there are check marks or dashes after 11 titles. Also reproduced is an autograph call number on the copyright page ('828 | R2116t') and accession note on the acknowledgment page ('English Lib. Bk fd. | [illegible word] | 1-24-33 | 27704').

The on-demand reprintings reproduce the Knopf title page and all other pages of the original. They add a note on the recto of the first leaf: thus in the 1967 copy, '[three asterisks] | This is an authorized facsimile of the original book, and was | produced in 1967 by microfilm-xerography by University | Microfilms, A Xerox Company, Ann Arbor, Michigan, U.S.A. | [three asterisks]'; and thus in the 1974 copy, 'This is an authorized facsimile of the original | book, and was produced in 1974 by microfilm- | xerography by Xerox University Microfilms, | Ann Arbor, Michigan, U.S.A.' On the page following the advertisement is a reproduction of a library catalog card for the book.

190 x 125 mm (1967 copy); 187 x 125 mm (1974 copy). Except for some leaves in the preliminaries (which show some rearrangement), each "leaf" is actually two conjugate leaves, with their fold at the fore-edge and with printing only on the two outer pages. The pattern of copying is such that odd pages have become versos and even pages rectos. White wove paper, no watermark, sheets bulk 6 mm.

Perfect bound in dark blue (183) wrappers. Front of 1967 copy, typewritten on a white paper label: '[within a vivid orange-yellow (66) border with the letters 'OP' centered in the top of the border and within a rule frame] TWO GENTLEMEN IN BONDS | John Crowe Ransom | [80 mm rule creating a second compartment of the frame] UNIVERSITY MICROFILMS | *A Xerox Company* | *Ann Arbor, Michigan, U.S.A.*' Front of 1974 copy: '[within a moderate orange-yellow (71) border lacking the letters 'OP' and within a frame as above] TWO GENTLEMEN IN BONDS | J. Ransom | [in second compartment] *Published on demand by* | UNIVERSITY MICROFILMS | *University Microfilms Limited, High Wycomb, England* | *A Xerox Company, Ann Arbor, Michigan, U.S.A.*' Spine and back blank. In the 1974 copy, there are two free endpapers at front and back, the first and last held by the flaps of the wrapper. Edges cut.

Listed at $11.90 in UMI's *Books on Demand* (1977).

Copies: IMacoW (1967 copy), INS (1974 copy).

A4.c University Microfilms reprint (1970)

This is a xerographic reprinting derived from a microfilm of the Knopf impression. The reprint adds 3 leaves before the half title—all blank except for the recto of the second leaf, which reproduces from typewritten copy: 'Authorized xerographic reprint. | UNIVERSITY MICROFILMS, A Xerox Company | Ann Arbor, Michigan, U.S.A. | 1970'. The leaves measure 209 x 131 mm, and the type-page has been slightly enlarged: 141 (146) x 91 mm, 10 lines = 44 mm. The colophon appears on p. 88, while p. 89 is blank. The copy of the Knopf impression used for the reprinting had been marked, probably in pencil, on some pages; thus, for example, the title "Man without Sense of Direction" on p. viii is underlined and the word 'possible' is written to the right of the tenth stanza of "Eclogue" (p. 5). White wove paper, no watermark, sheets bulk 5 mm.

Perfect bound in deep red (13) calico cloth over boards stamped in gold on the spine. Front and back blank. Spine, running down: 'TWO GENTLEMEN IN BONDS [open star] RANSOM'. White wove endpapers. Edges cut.

Copy: ISS.

GOD
WITHOUT
THUNDER

AN UNORTHODOX DEFENSE
OF ORTHODOXY

BY JOHN CROWE RANSOM

HARCOURT, BRACE AND COMPANY
NEW YORK

Title page:
A5a.a ***God without Thunder***

A5 **1930**

God without Thunder

In a 4 July 1929 letter Ransom described for Allen Tate the argument of "a hot & hasty book on religion" that he had been writing since February and hoped to complete that summer (*SL* 181). He had supposed then that the title would be "Giants for Gods," but on 20 January 1930, writing to Robert Penn Warren, he was calling it "Ghosts." And he had not met his completion date, at least not for a final version. He was "a little appalled" that Warren had been passing around a manuscript that still needed "considerable changes" (*SL* 190). No part of the text had seen earlier publication as a periodical essay. Ransom had, however, reviewed in the *Nashville Tennessean* (see C164, C170, C177) some of the same works discussed in the book. And it is clear that the ideas developed in it had been on Ransom's mind much earlier—as seen, for example, in a letter to Robert Graves on 2 December 1925 (*SL* 146-149).

There were two editions of the book—an American edition published by Harcourt, Brace on 16 October 1930 and an English edition published by Gerald Howe in May 1931. For the English edition, Ransom added a special preface and a new chapter. Neither publisher appears to have required any impression beyond the first. In September 1932 sluggish sales prompted the English publisher to reissue copies of its impression at a reduced price as a volume in its Olympus Library. The blurb on the front flap of this issue acknowledges that the book, despite favorable reviews, "has so far failed to find its way to that large section of the reading public which recognizes (and rejoices in) good writing and honest thinking." The blurb goes on to say that the book deserves wider recognition and that therefore the publisher is "reissuing it (little more than twelve months after first publication) at a popular price."

In 1965 Archon Books published a photo-offset reprinting from the Harcourt, Brace edition, although earlier, writing to Tate on 21 October 1960, Ransom had said that he had received "proposals to re-publish *World's Body*, and *New Criticism*, and *God Without Thunder* too" but that he felt he could not read his "old things with pleasure now" (*SL* 403).

A5a.a Harcourt, Brace edition (1930)

[Within a thick-thin double rule frame] [open face] GOD | WITHOUT | THUNDER | [not open] *AN UNORTHODOX DEFENSE | OF ORTHODOXY* | BY JOHN CROWE RANSOM | [Harcourt, Brace device] | HARCOURT, BRACE AND COMPANY | NEW YORK

Copyright page (iv): 'COPYRIGHT, 1930, BY | JOHN CROWE RANSOM | *first edition* | *Typography by Robert S. Josephy* | PRINTED IN THE UNITED STATES OF AMERICA | BY QUINN & BODEN COMPANY, INC., RAHWAY, N.J.'

215 x 145 mm. *1-21*^{8} 22^4; 172 leaves. *i-viii* ix-x *1-2* 3-162 *163-164* 165-244 *245-246* 247-315 *316-318* 319-334 pp.

i half title 'GOD WITHOUT THUNDER'; ii blank; iii title page; iv copyright page; v dedication 'TO MY FATHER'; vi blank; vii '*CONTENTS*'; viii blank; ix-x '*A LETTER*' (ending 'JOHN CROWE RANSOM | *Vanderbilt University,* | *Nashville, Tennessee,* | *June 1, 1930.*'); 1 part title 'Part One | THE DYNASTY OF HEAVEN | CHANGES'; 2 blank; 3-162 text; 163 part title 'Part Two | THE NEW GOD'S LIMITS'; 164 blank; 165-244 text; 245 part title 'Part Three' | GHOSTS: INCLUDING THE HOLY'; 246 blank; 247-315 text; 316 blank' 317 part title 'Epilogue'; 318 blank; 319-328 text; 329-334 '*INDEX*'.

After an introductory letter addressed to S.M.H. (Sidney Mttron Hirsch), the text consists of 15 chapters divided into 3 sections and an epilogue:

I. THE DYNASTY OF HEAVEN CHANGES
  1. The New God
  2. The Old God
  3. Nature and the Supernatural
  4. Principles or Gods?
  5. Religion and Magic
  6. Satan as Science
  7. Christ as Science

II. THE NEW GOD'S LIMIT
  8. What Can He Do?
  9. We His Poor Followers
  10. What Does He Know
  11. A Table and a Geographical Machine

III. GHOSTS: INCLUDING THE HOLY
12. Finite Ghosts
13. Infinite Ghosts
14. The Holy Ghost
EPILOGUE
15. By Way of a Program

Type-page 35 lines, 161 (167) x 101 mm, 10 lines = 46 mm (e.g., p. 171); typeface Caslon with 4.0 mm face, 1.9 mm x-height. Centered chapter titles (e.g., '*CHAPTER ONE* | [101 mm thick-thin double rule] | THE NEW GOD'). The text of each chapter begins with an open capital initial, 3 lines deep. Running titles centered in the headline: part title (e.g., 'THE DYNASTY OF HEAVEN CHANGES') on versos; chapter titles (e.g., 'THE NEW GOD') on rectos. No running titles on opening page of each chapter. Pagination at outer margin of headline, but centered in the direction line on the opening page of the introductory letter, each chapter, and the index. White wove paper, no watermark, sheets bulk 28 mm.

Bound in dark blue (183) calico cloth over boards. Front and back blank. Spine stamped in gold, running across: 'GOD | WITHOUT | THUNDER | ◦ | JOHN CROWE | RANSOM | HARCOURT, BRACE | & COMPANY'. White wove endpapers. Top and bottom edges trimmed. Fore-edge rough trimmed. In the STW and T copies the ornament after the title appears to be a solid bullet.

Dust jacket not seen.

Copies: ICN, IEG, IEN, InU-Lilly (Louis Untermeyer's copy), OGK, STW (inscribed to Andrew Nelson Lytle on 1 November 1930), T, TNV (2 copies: a copy inscribed to Mr. and Mrs. Alfred Starr 16 October 1930, a copy inscribed to Walter Clyde Curry 18 October 1930), TxU-HRC.

Published at $3.50 on 16 October 1930; copyright registration A30098 (copies deposited 23 October 1930). Forthcoming publication noted in *Nashville Tennessean* 3 August 1930, Firing Line section: 12; publication noted in "The Weekly Record," *Publishers' Weekly* 18 October 1930: 1870 and, along with an advertisement, in *Nashville Tennessean* 26 October 1930, Society section:

8. Listed in "Latest Books," *New York Times Book Review* 26 October 1930: 29. Earlier, reflecting the effect of the Depression on Harcourt's business, *Publishers' Weekly* 5 July 1930: 28 carried an ad in which the publisher announced 47 new books for fall (including, without titles, 22 nonfiction books, one of them by Ransom) as compared to 74 for the previous fall.

Advertised in *Publishers' Weekly* 20 September 1930: 1156; *New Republic* 22 October 1930: v, and 12 November 1930: ii; *Saturday Review of Literature* 25 October 1930: 268; *Nation* 19 November 1930: 557; *New York Herald Tribune Books* 7 December 1930: 11; *Publishers' Weekly* 20 December 1030: 2694, in an ad listing Harcourt books published in 1930 "essential to libraries."

Reviewed in *Vanderbilt Alumnus* November-December 1930: 37 (Mapheus Smith); *Nashville Tennessean* 9 November 1930, automotive section: 2 (Henry Blue Kline); *Christian Century* 3 December 1930: 1490-1491 (Lloyd C. Douglas); *Nation* 24 December 1930: 711 (Felix Morrow); *American Mercury* January 1931: 126-127 (H. L. Mencken); *Methodist Review* January 1931: 126 (Oscar L. Joseph); *Sewanee Review* January-March 1931: 103-111 (William S. Knickerbocker); *New York Herald Tribune Books* 11 January 1931: 10 (W. L. Sullivan); *World Tomorrow* February 1931: 59 (Reinhold Niebuhr, signed R. N.); *Commonweal* 4 February 1931: 385-386 (John S. Middleton); *Saturday Review of Literature* 28 February 1931: 627 (Ernest Sutherland Bates); *Bookman* March 1931: 100-101 (Francis Fergusson); *Virginia Quarterly Review* July 1931: 451-457 (Scott Buchanan); *American Oxonian* October 1931: 187-189 (A. P. Kelso).

A5a.b Archon Books reprint (1965)

[Within a thick-thin double rule frame] [open type] GOD | WITHOUT | THUNDER | [not open] *AN UNORTHODOX DEFENSE* | *OF ORTHODOXY* | BY JOHN CROWE RANSOM | ARCHON BOOKS | HAMDEN, CONNECTICUT | 1965

Copyright page (iv): 'COPYRIGHT, 1930, BY | JOHN CROWE RANSOM | PUBLISHED 1965 BY ARRANGEMENT WITH | HARCOURT, BRACE & WORLD, INC. | IN AN UNALTERED AND UNABRIDGED EDITION | LIBRARY OF CONGRESS

CATALOG CARD NUMBER: 65-17410 | PRINTED IN THE UNITED STATES OF AMERICA'.

126 x 138 mm. *1-9*^{16} *10*^{12} *11*^{16}; 172 leaves. This is a offset reprinting from the Harcourt, Brace impression. The half-title has been omitted from p. i. Aside from that change and the changes to the title and copyright pages, the contents (and their pagination) are identical to those of the Harcourt, Brace impression. The type-page has been slightly reduced to 160 (166) x 100 mm. White wove paper, no watermark, sheets bulk 19 mm.

Bound in dark yellowish green (137) calico cloth over boards stamped in gold on the spine. Front and back blank. Spine, running across, 'RANSOM | [25 mm rule] | GOD | WITHOUT | THUNDER | [25 mm rule] | ARCHON'. White wove endpapers. Top and bottom edges cut; fore-edge trimmed. No dust jacket.

Published at $9.00 on 23 April 1965. One impression of 1,000 copies (letter, Nancy C. McGrath, Shoe String Press, 6 September 1995).

Copies: IDeKN, IMacoW, OGK, STW, TNV (2 copies).

A5b.(1) Gerald Howe edition, first issue (1931)

GOD WITHOUT | THUNDER | AN UNORTHODOX DEFENCE | OF ORTHODOXY | By | JOHN CROWE RANSOM | [Howe device] | GERALD HOWE LTD | 23 SOHO SQUARE LONDON | 1931

Copyright page (iv): 'ALL RIGHTS RESERVED | PRINTED IN GUERNSEY, C.I., BRITISH ISLES, | BY THE STAR AND GAZETTE COMPANY LTD.'

199 x 132 mm. *A*^{16} B-I^{16} K-M^{16}; $1,5 signed (-A1), $5 with an added asterisk (e.g., 'M*'). 192 leaves. *i-v* vi-viii *ix-xi* xii *1-3* 4-26 *27* 28-52 *53* 54-74 *75* 76-93 *94* 95-111 *112* 113-142 *143* 144-167 *168-171* 172-191 *192* 193-213 *214* 215-231 *232* 233-253 *254* 255-274 *275-277* 278-304 *305* 306-328 *329* 330-346 *347-349* 350-358 *359-361* 362-368 *369-372*.

i half title 'GOD WITHOUT THUNDER'; ii blank; iii title page; iv copyright page; v-viii 'PREFACE TO THE ENGLISH EDITION' (ending 'JOHN CROWE RANSOM | *Vanderbilt University,* | *Nashville, Tennessee*'); ix 'CONTENTS'; x blank; xi-xii 'A LETTER | *To S.M.H.* (ending 'J.C.R.'); 1 part title 'PART ONE | THE DYNASTY OF HEAVEN | CHANGES'; 2 blank; 3-167 text; 168 blank; 169 part title 'PART TWO | THE NEW GOD'S LIMITS'; 170 blank; 171-274 text; 275 part title 'PART THREE | GHOSTS: INCLUDING THE HOLY'; 176 blank; 177-346 text; 347 part title 'EPILOGUE'; 348 blank; 349-358 text; 359 part title 'INDEX'; 360 blank; 361-368 'INDEX'; 369-371 advertisements for Howe books (Lawrence Hyde's *The Prospects of Humanism* and *The Learned Knife*, and the second impression of *Science and Religion: A Symposium*); 372 blank.

This is a resetting of the text, with the addition of the "Preface to the English Edition" and with the addition to Part Two of a new chapter entitled "XII. God as a Mathematician" (the subsequent chapters then being renumbered). The selection of terms for the index seems to have been independent from that for the American edition. Ransom's preface mentions the publication and reception of the American edition, points out the addition of "God as a Mathematician" as a reply to Sir James Jean's *The Mysterious Universe*, says that he has "not thought it proper to make many alterations in the text for the benefit of the British reader" (v), and welcomes the recent publication of *A New Commentary on Holy Scripture*.

Type-page 34 lines, 143 (151) x 92 mm, 10 lines = 42 mm (e.g., p. 21); typeface Granjon with 4.4 mm face, 1.9 mm x-height. Centered chapter titles (e.g., 'CHAPTER I | THE NEW GOD'). Running titles centered in the headlines: part titles on versos (e.g., 'THE DYNASTY OF HEAVEN CHANGES'); chapter titles on rectos (e.g., 'THE NEW GOD'). No running titles on first page of each chapter. Pagination at outer margin of headline; signatures in the direction line and indented 8 mm from outer margin. White wove paper, no watermark, sheets bulk 24 mm.

Bound in black fine-grain calico cloth over boards. Front blank. Spine, stamped in gold: '[running across] GOD | WITHOUT | THUNDER | RANSOM | HOWE'. Back: Howe monogram device blind stamped in lower left corner. White wove endpapers.

Edges trimmed. (Because the one copy examined has evidently been rebound in blue cloth; this binding description is based on the assumption that the binding of the first issue was identical to that of the second.) Dust jacket not seen.

Copies: British Library (rebound; examined for me by Donald Hawes).

Listed in the *English Catalogue* as published in May 1931 at 12s. 6d. net. British Library deposit 21 May 1931. Advertised at 12s 6d in *TLS* 12 November 1931: 882; *New Statesman and Nation* 5 December 1931: xxix.

Reviewed in *Criterion* October 1931: 127-131 (John Gould Fletcher); *Blackfriars* December 1931: 760-764 (Gerald Vann); *TLS* 24 December 1931: 1036; *New Freeman* 10 December 1930: 21-22 (James Rorty).

A5b.(2) Gerald Howe edition, second issue (1932)

This issue is identical to the first except that it has an added initial leaf tipped in on the verso of the front free-endpaper and that it has a new dust jacket.

The recto of the tipped-in leaf is blank; the verso lists the five '*First Volumes*' in the Olympus Library, from *God without Thunder* to Geoffrey West's *The Life of Annie Besant*.

Dust jacket of light greenish gray (154) laid paper with vertical chainlines 27 mm apart and watermark 'Abbey Mills | Greenfield'; printed in dark brown (59). Front: '[within a panel on a design consisting of a mountain peak and a Greek temple] The Olympus Library | GOD WITHOUT | THUNDER | AN UNORTHODOX DEFENCE OF ORTHODOXY | JOHN CROWE RANSOM | [quotation from review in *Adelphi*] | [on a step of the temple] JOHN FARLEIGH'. Spine: '[within a panel on a Greek column] OLYMPUS | LIBRARY | God | Without | Thunder | JOHN | CROWE | RANSOM | 4'6 | NET [at the foot] HOWE'. Back: design like that of the front, with an advertisement for Olympus Library books ('books of exalted aim and wide | appeal'), Ransom's *God without Thunder* and Geoffrey West's

H. G. Wells being listed as the first titles in the series, to be followed by Count Harry Kessler's *Walter Rathenau*, Geoffrey West's *The Life of Annie Besant*, and Lawrence Hyde's *The Prospects of Humanism*. Front flap: title, author, and 16-line blurb with a 14-line note citing favorable reviews. Back flap: 32 line blurb.

Copies: ICN, ICarbS (spine repaired in coarse black calico cloth, preserving author and title from original as a label), InU-Lilly (with jacket), OGK, STW (Ransom's copy with autograph revisions in Chapters X and XV), TxU-HRC (with jacket), TNV (3 copies, 1 with jacket), WMM, WU (rebound, lacking initial 2 leaves and terminal 2 leaves and thus possibly a copy of the first issue).

Listed in the *English Catalogue* as published in September 1932 at 4s 6d net.

A 6 **1933**

Shall We Complete the Trade?

Ransom's essay "Shall We Complete the Trade?" first (or simultaneously) appeared in the April-June 1933 issue of *Sewanee Review* (C188), which was edited at the time by William S. Knickerbocker and published by the University of the South, Sewanee, Tennessee. This pamphlet is an offprint from that publication, printed from the same typesetting but repaginated and supplied with a wrapper. The essay proposes allowing European nations to pay off war debts by supporting Americans studying abroad.

[Front wrapper] SHALL WE COMPLETE | THE TRADE? | A Proposal for the Settlement of Foreign | Debts to the United States | BY | JOHN CROWE RANSOM | [device of the University Press of Sewanee] | [within a thick-thin rule frame] *"I propose, then , that we convert war credits, otherwise | worthless, into a fund for higher education on an unheard-of | scale; the place of study to be Europe; the beneficiaries to | be those Americans who seem likeliest to use their oppor- | tunities wisely and patriotically."* | [below the frame] Reprinted from the April Number of | THE SEWANEE REVIEW | 1933

No copyright page or notice.

233 x 152 mm. *1-3* 4-11 *12* pp.

1 front wrapper; 2 blank; 3 '*by John Crowe Ransom* | SHALL WE COMPLETE THE TRADE? | [text begins]'; 4-11 text; 12 blank.

Type-page 39 lines, 169 (177) x 101 mm, 10 lines = 44 mm (e.g., p. 8); typeface Caslon with 3.4 mm face and 1.6 mm x-height. The text begins with an initial capital 2 lines deep. Running titles centered in the headline on rectos and versos: 'SHALL WE COMPLETE THE TRADE?' Pagination at the outer margin of the headline. White wove paper.

Bound in paper wrappers. Front: see above. Edges trimmed.

Copy: ViU (seen in photocopy).

Probably published at about the same time as the April 1933 *Sewanee Review*. Reviewed in *American Oxonian* July 1933: 188-189 (B.B.).

A 7 **1934**

Happy Farmers

For this publication of his essay "Happy Farmers," which had been rejected by *Hound and Horn* (Young, *Gentleman* 243) and which first appeared in *American Review* in October 1933 (C193), Ransom made numerous revisions. Many are primarily stylistic. The most extensive revision consists of the addition of eight consecutive sentences to section IV of the essay. The two other Tryon Pamphlets advertised on the wrappers of Ransom's were in fact published, both in 1934. Blackmur's is a critique of Southern Agrarianism, including a discussion of *I'll Take My Stand*, and Winters's is a group of poems preceded by a critical introduction. I have located no other Tryon Pamphlets. Ransom's essay, responding to Louis M. Hacker's *The Farmer Is Doomed*, argues that Agrarian farmers who, as "economic dualists," engage primarily in subsistence farming and secondarily in "money farming" are not doomed. There was apparently but one impression of Ransom's pamphlet.

[Front wrapper] HAPPY FARMERS | by | JOHN CROWE RANSOM | [123 mm thick-thin double rule] | Is the farmer doomed? | Professor Ransom shows | the way the farmer *must* | take to achieve indepen- | dence and avert economic | annihilation | 25c | *The Tryon Pamphlets : : Tryon, N.C.*'

180 x 124 mm. 1^{14}; 14 leaves. *1* 2-27 *28* pp.

1 'Happy Farmers | *By* JOHN CROWE RANSOM | [text begins]'; 2-26 text; 27 '[text ends] | (Reprinted from THE AMERICAN REVIEW of October, | 1933 in revised form.)'; 28 blank.

Type-page 29 lines, 143 (150) x 89 mm, 10 lines = 50 mm (e.g., p. 13); typeface Caslon, with 4 mm face, 1.8 mm x-height. Text begins with 8 mm initial capital. Running title ('HAPPY FARMERS') centered in the headline on versos and rectos. Pagination enclosed in square brackets at the outer margin of the headline. White laid paper with vertical chainlines 18 mm apart, watermark '*Champion* | *Garamond* Text', sheets bulk 2 mm.

Bound in moderate orange (53) wove paper wrappers printed in black. Front: see above. Back: '*OTHER TRYON PAMPHLETS* | [advertisement for Yvor Winters's *Before Disaster* and R. P. Blackmur's *Psyche in the South*] | New titles will appear in this | series at frequent intervals | THE TRYON PAMPHLETS — — TRYON, N.C. | WOOD'S PRESS — TRYON NC'. No endpapers. Edges cut.

Copies: STW, TxU-HRC, MoSW (seen in photocopy). At the head of the front wrapper of the MoSW copy is rubber-stamped the date 'JUN 29 1934', perhaps indicating a date of receipt shortly after publication.

A 8 1935

Topics for Freshman Writing

At Vanderbilt University, where Ransom held teaching positions during the periods 1914-1917 and 1919-1937, he regularly taught courses in composition. This textbook not only reflects that experience but also incorporates readings from several of Ransom's essays. The contract for the book, then entitled "Progressive Writing," was signed and dated by Richard W. Thornton on 6 June 1934 (STW). It granted Ransom an advance of $500 against royalties of 15 percent and, if year-end sales reached 5,000 copies, an additional royalty of 3 percent.

It is uncertain how many impression of the single edition were made. In addition to the first impression (prepared for July 1935 publication but without a printing date on the copyright page, in accordance with Holt's practice at the time), I have seen copies bearing the printing dates of September 1935 and November 1935 and thus copies of three impressions altogether. The supplemental handbook section was later revised and extended to become *A College Primer of Writing* (A11).

A8.1 First impression (1935)

TOPICS FOR | FRESHMAN WRITING | TWENTY TOPICS FOR WRITING | WITH APPROPRIATE MATERIALS FOR STUDY | SELECTED AND EDITED | BY | JOHN CROWE RANSOM | VANDERBILT UNIVERSITY | [Holt device] | NEW YORK | HENRY HOLT AND COMPANY

Copyright page (ii): 'COPYRIGHT, 1935, | BY | HENRY HOLT AND COMPANY, INC. | PRINTED IN THE | UNITED STATES OF AMERICA'.

187 x 125 mm. *1-16*^{16} *17*^{8}; 264 leaves. *i-ii* iii-ix *x* xi-xiv 1-415 *416-418* 419-509 *510* 511-514 pp.

i title page; ii copyright page; iii-ix 'PREFACE | TO THE INSTRUCTOR' (ending 'J.C.R. | Vanderbilt University, | December 15, 1934.'); x blank; xi-xiv 'CONTENTS'; 1-415 text divided into 20 sections; 416 blank; 417 part title 'SUPPLEMENT | A HANDBOOK IN BRIEF | A: SENTENCE STRUCTURE | B: PUNCTU-

ATION | C: COMPOSITION'; 418 blank; 419-506 text of handbook; 510 blank; 511-514 'INDEX'.

The twenty sections, with a writing assignment for each, are as follows:

I. The Making of a Freshman
II. The Function of the College
III. A Magazine Study
IV. The Planned Society
V. Co-Education
VI. A Course Paper
VII. Machinery, Overproduction, and Unemployment,
VIII. Intercollegiate Football
IX. Machinery and Civilization
X. A Bibliography and a Short Paper
XI. Literature and Science
XII. A Book Review
XIII. The Land
XIV. The Sideshows and the Main Tent [on extracurricular activities]
XV. Nationalism and Foreign Trade
XVI. Religion and Morals on the Campus
XVII. A Bibliography and a Long Paper
XVIII. The Movies
XIX. Reforming the College
XX. A Book Review

Among the readings for the assignments are four from Ransom's own works: in IX he reprints, under the title "Acceleration and Enjoyment" (187-193), a portion of *God without Thunder* (A5); in XIII, a portion of "Happy Farmers" (272-283) from the pamphlet version of this essay (A7); in XV, a portion of "Shall We Complete the Trade" (324-333) from his *Sewanee Review* essay (C188); and in XVI, under the title "Myths Are Still Good" (341-349), another portion of *God without Thunder*. His comments introductory to the readings also touch upon these selections from his work. Thus, for example, he says that "Happy Farmers" may "be sound in theory yet not be documented closely enough as a work of science, and is here tossed among the pronouncements of the authorities by way of creating a diversion" (254-255).

Type-page 34 lines, 144 (152) x 93 mm, 10 lines = 43 mm (e.g., p. 195); typeface Old Style with 3.4 mm face, 1.9 mm x-height. Running titles centered in the headlines on rectos and versos (e.g., 'LITERATURE AND SCIENCE'); pagination at outer margin of headlines (but centered at the foot on initial pages of sections). White wove paper, no watermark, sheets bulk 26 mm.

Bound in moderate reddish brown (43) calico cloth over boards stamped in pale yellow (89) on front and spine. Front: circular Holt device within a 185 x 117 mm rule frame. Spine: '[thick rule, 4 mm x 32 mm] | [32 mm rule] | TOPICS | FOR | FRESHMAN | WRITING | • | RANSOM | HENRY HOLT | AND COMPANY | [rules as above, with order reversed]'. Back blank. White wove endpapers. On the back paste-down endpaper is printed a 'QUICK GUIDE TO THE HANDBOOK' consisting of page numbers that instructors may use as correction symbols in marking students' papers. Edges trimmed. Probably not issued in a dust jacket.

Copies: STW, TNV.

Published at $2.00 on 22 July 1935; copyright registration A84831 (copies deposited 3 August 1935). Reviewed in *English Journal* (college edition) January 1936: 87.

A8.2 Second impression (1935)

Added to the copyright page after the publisher's imprint: 'September, 1935'. Copies: INS, OGK.

A8.3 Third impression (1935)

The printing notice on copyright page is changed to 'November, 1935'. Sheets bulk 24 mm. Copies: InU (rebound), STW, T, TNV.

JOHN CROWE RANSOM

The

World's

Body

1938

Charles Scribner's Sons · New York
Charles Scribner's Sons · Ltd · London

Title page:
A9.a ***The World's Body***

A 9 **1938**

The World's Body

The World's Body was put together from fifteen essays previously published in *American Review*, *Southern Review*, *Virginia Quarterly Review*, and *Yale Review*, the earliest having appeared in May 1933 and the latest in winter 1938. In his acknowledgements, Ransom says: "These essays, minus perhaps some joints and sticking-plaster with which I have now put them together, have all had periodical publication. The present arrangement of them does not quite conform to the order of original publication" (xv). Three of the essays underwent changes of title: "Forms and Citizens" had been published as "A Poem Nearly Anonymous: The Poet and His Formal Tradition" in *American Review*; "A Cathedralist Looks at Murder" had appeared in *Southern Review* as a portion of a review entitled "Autumn of Poetry"; and "Contemporaneous Not Contemporary" had appeared in *Southern Review* as a portion of a review entitled "Fiction Harvest."

On 22 April 1938, Ransom thanked Allen Tate for moving him "in the general direction of publication" and for having "put in the determining word to [Maxwell] Perkins of Scribner's"—also for "having collaborated, often unintentionally, in the preparation of the content" (*SL* 238). The extent of Tate's epistolary collaboration, on this work as on others, is suggested by the frequency with which Ransom's letters thank Tate for his criticism during these years. (Because Ransom did not routinely save letters from his correspondents, the substance of Tate's criticism must be inferred from Ransom's response to it.) Ransom's dedication of the book to his "friends and former colleagues on the staff of the College of the South West of England" may imply also an indebtedness incurred during his Guggenheim Fellowship at Exeter in academic year 1931-1932.

The original contract for "A Work of Criticism—Title Later" was signed and dated by Charles Scribner on 28 May 1937 and set royalty payment at 10 percent of retail price (STW). On 17 June Ransom mentioned to Tate that he had a "big but congenial job" working on his "Scribner's manuscript" (*SL* 225). He was engaged in more than revising and ordering essays already written. He was continuing to write additional essays, notably "Shakespeare at Sonnets," which he described to Tate on 10 October 1937 as "the first fruits of the Kenyon dispensation," referring to his having left Vanderbilt the previous month for his new position at Kenyon College (*SL* 226). As late as 18 October 1937, Ransom was sending Tate a draft of the preface and was still uncertain as to the book's title. He asked Tate to "meditate" on the title and supposed that he could "always fall back on 'Poets without Laurels,'" as Tate had suggested. On 29 October, he thanked Tate for his criticism, saying that he would use all his comments, which he found "just and useful" (*SL* 228). He may, then, have met or come close to meeting his commitment to get the manuscript of the book to Scribner's by 31 October. On 1 January 1938, Ransom told Tate that he had sent Scribner's the galley proofs and was expecting the page proofs soon. Even at this point there was to be collaboration. Ransom told Tate that he would get him "to look over a few matters" when he came to visit (*SL* 237). It is not known when he settled on *The World's Body* as the title for the book. It should be noted that the dust jacket supplies a subtitle, *Foundations for Literary Criticism*, not present elsewhere in the book.

The book was published by Scribner's on 22 April 1938. It has been reprinted by Kennikat Press and Louisiana State University Press. On 2 December 1958, Richard Huett of George Braziller wrote Ransom about the possibility of re-publishing the book, along with *God without Thunder*, but supposed that it "might need extensive revision" (TNV). That proposal came to nothing, but on 12 May 1964 Cornell Jaray of Kennikat informed Ransom that they had obtained license from Scribner's for a reprint. Evidently Ransom had already corresponded with them, since Jaray addressed Ransom's ideas about adding material to the book. Jaray explained that Kennikat would simply reprint about 750 copies by photo-offset and that revision would be "impractical," though he added that he would inform Scribner's of Ransom's desire to revise (TNV). (A somewhat differing version appears in a letter of 8 December 1966, when Kennikat had completed negotiations to reprint *Kenyon Critics*. In that letter, Jaray reminds Ransom that he had said that *World's Body* reflected his views at the time the book was published and that "no apologies are required" [TNV].) The publishing agreement between Kennikat and Scribner's granted Kennikat license to publish for 5 years, at a price no less than $7.50 and royalties of 10 percent on the list price, as many hardback copies of the book as it wished. Scribner's retained license to publish in paperback but agreed not to exercise that right for 2 years (30 April 1964, TNV).

About two years later, on 9 December 1966, L. H. Brague, Jr., of Scribner's wrote Ransom that LSU Press had informed them of Ransom's agreement to write a foreword for a paperback reprinting. He said that Scribner's had hoped to issue a revised *World's Body* in its Scribner's Library but that it now seemed more practical to allow LSU Press to go ahead with its "edition" and then, after the expiration of LSU's license in 5 years, to prepare their own revised edition (TNV). To the LSU Press reprint, Ransom did add a prefatory note and a "Postscript." The book has not been subsequently re-published by Scribner's.

A9.a Scribner's impression (1938)

[Within a slightly and irregularly wavy single-line frame (145 x 88 mm)] *JOHN CROWE RANSOM* | [42 mm rule] | *The* | *World's* | *Body* | *1938* | *Charles Scribner's Sons • New York* | *Charles Scribner's Sons • Ltd • London*

Copyright page (iv): 'COPYRIGHT, 1938, BY | CHARLES SCRIBNER'S SONS | [9 mm rule] | Printed in the United States of America | *All rights reserved. No part of this book* | *may be reproduced in any form without* | *the permission of Charles Scribner's Sons* | A | [Scribner Press device]'. The letter 'A' along with the Scribner device, or seal, was Scribner's code for a first impression.

204 x 131 mm. *1-23*^{8}; 184 leaves. *i-vi* vii-xi *xii* xiii-xiv *xv-xviii* 1-350 pp.

i half title '*The World's Body*'; ii blank; iii title page; iv copyright page; v dedication '*To my friends and former colleagues* | *on the staff of the College of the* | *South West of England, at Exeter.*'; vi blank; vii-xi '*Preface*' (ending 'JOHN CROWE RANSOM'); xii blank; xiii-viv '*Contents*'; xv '*Acknowledgments*'; xvi blank; xvii bastard title '*The World's Body*'; xviii blank; 1-350 text.

Contains Ransom's preface and 15 essays. Previous periodical publication of the essays is indicated after each title.

A Poem Nearly Anonymous [C190]
Forms and Citizens [C192, as "A Poem Nearly Anonymous: The Poet and His Formal Tradition"]
Poets without Laurels [C206]
The Poet as Woman [C228]
Poetry: A Note in Ontology [C198]
A Psychologist Looks at Poetry [C213]
A Cathedralist Looks at Murder [from "Autumn of Poetry," C215]
The Cathartic Principle [C208]
The Mimetic Principle [C212]
Sentimental Exercise [C225]
The Tense of Poetry [C211]
Contemporaneous Not Contemporary [from "Fiction Harvest," C223]
Shakespeare at Sonnets [C233]
Art and Mr. Santayana [C229]
Criticism, Inc. [C230]

Type-page 30 lines, 148 (157) x 89 mm, 10 lines = 50 mm (e.g., p. 23); typeface Caslon with 4.2 mm face, 1.9 mm x-height. Essay titles (e.g., '*A Poem Nearly Anonymous*') centered and in italic. Texts of essays and preface begin with capital initial, 3 lines deep. Running titles in the headline indented 4 mm from the inner margin: '*The World's Body*' on versos; essay titles (e.g., '*A Poem Nearly Anonymous*') on rectos. But '*Preface*' on rectos and versos of pp. viii-xi and '*Contents*' on verso p. xiv; and no running titles on opening page of each essay. Pagination in the headline and indented 4 mm from the outer margin (but, on the first page of preface and table of contents, thus indented in the direction line and, on first page of each essay, centered in the direction line). White wove paper, no watermark, sheets bulk 28 mm.

Two bindings seen.

1. Bound in very dark green (147) calico cloth over boards stamped in gold on the front and spine. Front: '*JOHN CROWE RANSOM* I [42 mm rule] I *The* I *World's* I *Body*'. Spine: '*The* I *World's* I *Body* I [8 mm rule] I *RANSOM* I *SCRIBNERS*'. White wove endpapers. Top and bottom edges trimmed, fore-edge rough trimmed.

2. Bound in dark blue (183) calico printed in white; otherwise identical to binding 1.

Dust jacket (seen on both bindings) of light bluish green (163) paper printed in moderate blue (182). Front: 'JOHN CROWE RANSOM | [within a circle that is on a background of blue horizontal lines] The | World's Body | [63 mm swelled rule] *Foundations for* | *Literary* | *Criticism* | [without the circle, in light bluish green on a background of moderate blue] Presenting the critical system of one of the most inter- | esting minds of our time. The ideas developed here have refer- | ence to literature, past and contemporary, but, more | specifically, they outline a system of doctrine relating to | the meaning and psychology of poetry. As a whole, the | book defines a new position in philosophical criticism.' Spine: '[on a bluish green panel that is on a background of blue lines extending from the front] The | World's | Body | * | Foundations | for | Literary | Criticism | * | JOHN | CROWE | RANSOM | * | [at the foot in bluish green on moderate blue] SCRIBNERS'. Back: advertisement headed '*Poetry and Belles Lettres*' and listing 7 Scribner titles, from *The Selected Poems of Conrad Aiken* to Charles Townsend Copeland's *The Copeland Reader*. Front flap: '$2.75 | The | World's Body | *by* | John Crowe Ransom | *author of "Chills and Fever," "Two* | *Gentlemen in Bonds," etc.* | [29-line blurb]'. Back flap: blurb for Mary M. Colum's *From These Roots*. Also seen on binding 1 (TNV copy inscribed to Roberta Lyne) is a jacket with a blank back and back flap.

Copies: CSA (binding 1), ICN (binding 1), ICU (rebound), IEN (binding 2), INS (lacking half title leaf, title page loose, binding 1), IU (binding 2), InU-Lilly (two copies in binding 1, one with jacket), OGK (one copy in binding 1 with jacket, one in binding 1 without jacket, one in binding 2 with jacket), STW (one copy in binding 1 inscribed to Randall Jarrell on 28 April 1938 with jacket, another in binding 2 with jacket), T (binding 1), TNV (four copies in binding 1, including one belonging to Allen Tate and one with jacket and inscription to Roberta Dillon Lyne 1 September 1938), TxU-HRC (two copies in binding 1 and with jackets, including one inscribed to L. W. Payne, 10 August 1938), WU (binding 2).

Published at $2.75 on 22 April 1938; copyright registration A118302 (copies deposited 4 June 1938). Published in England at 8s 6d in May 1938 (*English Catalogue*). Scribner's manufacturing record card at Princeton shows but one impression of 2,620 copies. It appears that of these, 1,500 were bound at that time (and probably represent binding 1) and that the remainder were "bound for outlet" on 22 January 1941 (and represent binding 2). The plates for the book were melted on 22 August 1940, and the book was noted as out of print on 2 August 1948. The record card has no information on the two dust jackets. The evidence of the dates of the books advertised suggests that the jacket without the advertisements is later.

Advertised in *New York Times Book Review* 22 May 1938: 18; *New York Herald Tribune Books* 29 May 1938: 11. Advertised as "ready shortly" at 8s 6d in *TLS* 26 March 1938: 217. Listed in "A Selected List of Important Spring Books," *New York Herald Tribune Books* 3 April 1938: 8, and in "The Weekly Record," *Publishers' Weekly* 30 April 1938: 1785.

Reviewed in *New Yorker* 30 April 1938: 63 (unsigned); *New York Herald Tribune Books* 8 May 1938: 10 (Thomas Merton); *Time* 9 May 1938: 67 (unsigned); *Kenyon Collegian* 18 May 1938: 2 (John Nerber); *Saturday Review of Literature* 21 May 1938: 8-9 (Henry Seidel Canby); *Booklist* 15 June 1938: 360; *Twentieth Century Verse* July 1938: 72-74 (Kenneth Allott); *New Republic* 10 August 1938: 27-28 (Theodore Spencer); *Nation* 13 August 1938: 160-162 (Louis Kronenberger); *TLS* 13 August 1938: 532 (unsigned; in the same issue Ransom is discussed in an unsigned editorial entitled "Exclusive Critics" [531]); *Yale Review* September 1938: 183-185 (Frederick A. Pottle); *Criterion* October 1938: 152-154 (Michael Roberts); *Hika* October 1938: 17-18 (Robert T. S. Lowell); *Vanderbilt Alumnus* October 1938: 14; *New York Times Book Review* 18 December 1938: 12 (Percy Hutchison); *Virginia Quarterly Review* Summer 1938: 446-450 (R. P. Blackmur); *American Oxonian* 1939: 74-75 (T. Brooks); *Scrutiny* June 1939: 2-10 (H. B. Parkes); *Southern Review* Autumn 1939: 376-400 (Arthur Mizener); *Poetry* October 1939: 51-54 (Kenneth Burke).

A9.b Kennikat Press reprint (1964)

[Within a frame identical to that of the Scribner's impression] *JOHN CROWE RANSOM* | [42 mm rule] | *The* | *World's* | *Body* | [beneath the frame] KENNIKAT PRESS, INC./PORT WASHINGTON, N.Y.

Copyright page (iv): 'THE WORLD'S BODY | Copyright 1938 by Charles Scribner's Sons | This edition published by Kennikat Press by arrangement with | Charles Scribner's Sons, 1964 | Library of Congress Catalog Card No: 64-24465 | Manufactured in the United States of America'.

215 x 137 mm. *1-10*^{16} *11*^{8} *12*^{16}; 184 leaves. This is an offset reimpression from the Scribner's typesetting. Pagination, contents, and typography identical to those of the Scribner's impression. White wove paper, no watermark, sheets bulk 28 mm.

Bound in very deep purplish red (257) calico cloth over boards stamped in gold on the spine. Front and back blank. Spine: '[double rule 41 mm] | The | World's | Body | [ornament resembling a stick-figure with fleur-de-lis head and long inwardly curled arms] | Ransom | KENNIKAT | [double rule 41 mm].' White wove endpapers. Top and bottom edges cut, fore-edge trimmed. Probably issued without a dust jacket.

Copies: IDeKN, STW (Ransom's copy).

A9.c Louisiana Paperbacks revised impression (1968)

[Within a frame identical to that of the Scribner's impression] *JOHN CROWE RANSOM* | [42 mm rule] | *The* | *World's* | *Body* | [beneath the frame] LOUISIANA STATE UNIVERSITY PRESS • BATON ROUGE

Copyright page (iv): 'Copyright 1938 by Charles Scribner's | Sons; renewed 1965 | New material copyright © 1968 by Louisiana State University Press | Paperback edition manufactured by | Kingsport Press, Inc., Kingsport, Tennessee'.

216 x 135 mm. 208 leaves. [4] *i-vi* vii-xi *xii* xiii-xiv *xv-xviii* 1-390 *391-394* pp.

This is an offset reprinting from the Scribner's typesetting, without alteration of the type-page but with added, newly set text. The additional two front leaves and two back leaves are blank. On p. xii, previously blank, is a note by Ransom saying that the fifteen essays "must stand here just as they were in the original edition of 1938" but that he has added a postscript to "do justice to the reputations" of two poets—Shakespeare and T. S. Eliot—whose treatment in the original edition he has since noted as the book's "two most odious errors." Thus pp. 351-90 contain his corrective "Postscript," consisting of variant versions of "T. S. Eliot: A Postscript" and "A Postscript on Shakespeare's Sonnets" that appeared in 1968 in, respectively, *Southern Review* and *Kenyon Review* (see C357 and C359). The textual variation is substantial. The periodical version of the Shakespeare portion, for example, has several paragraphs absent from the book version, including a final paragraph on the need to look "into the dark immoralities which abound in literature just as they do in the conduct of our actual lives." For the periodical version, Ransom put together a manuscript consisting in part of revised page proofs from the book (OGK).

The type-page of this added "Postscript" is slightly shorter (155 mm) and narrower (88 mm) than that of the original part of the book. Slightly smaller type is used for its running titles (a 3.9 mm rather than 4.1 mm face). White wove paper, no watermark, sheets bulk 32 mm. On p. 380, line 12, is a misprint 'strained' for 'stained'.

Perfect bound in white paper printed with swirling black brushstroke designs on a strong greenish blue (169) background on the front, spine, and back, and lettered in white, black, and vivid orange (48). Front: '[white] JOHN CROWE RANSOM | [orange] THE | WORLD'S | BODY | [white] The first paperback edition of a major | book by one of America's leading critics, | with a new afterword by the author | $2.95'. Spine, running across: '[white] Ransom | THE | WORLD'S | BODY | L 28 | LOUISIANA | PAPERBACKS'. Back: 3-line blurb, quotations from *Saturday Review, New York Times, Yale Review,* and *TLS;* publisher's address, Louisiana Paperbacks imprint and number, price. Inside covers blank. No endpapers. Top and bottom edges cut; fore-edge trimmed.

Copies: CSA (2 copies), OGK, STW (with undated inscription to Peter Taylor and with Ransom's autograph revisions on 5 pages of text), WU.

Published at $2.95 on 18 August 1968; copyright registration A68802. One impression of 4,000 copies (letter, Kristin Bryan, LSU Press, 23 August 1995). Listed in "Reprints and New Editions," *Virginia Quarterly Review* Spring 1969: xliii. Advertised in *Southern Review* April 1968: ii as available in July; in *American Literature* May 1968: n.p. for August publication; in *Southern Review* October 1968: ii; and in *Virginia Quarterly Review* Winter 1969: vii.

Reviewed in *New York Review of Books* 22 May 1969: 41-44 (Denis Donoghue); *Sewanee Review* July-September 1969: 508-516 (George Core).

THE NEW CRITICISM

by John Crowe Ransom

NEW DIRECTIONS

Norfolk, Connecticut

Title page:
A10.a ***The New Criticism***

A10 **1941**

The New Criticism

The contract for "'A Group of Literary Studies' (title still to be chosen)" was signed and dated June 1940 by James Laughlin, president of New Directions, and then signed by Ransom (STW). It set royalties at 10 percent of the retail price, granted a $150 advance against royalties (to be paid in three equal installments), and called for delivery of the book manuscript before 1 November 1940, a deadline Ransom did not quite meet. In a 14 November 1940 letter quoted in Young's *Gentleman in a Dustcoat*, Ransom remarked: "I am sweating gore finishing off my book for New Directions" (345). Earlier, as he explained to Tate in a letter of 19 November 1940, he had sent the manuscript to Laughlin, with whom he had arranged for an additional chapter on his "own doctrine" (*Gentleman* 345, OGK). This chapter, he said, will "almost save myself from writing another book." In a later letter to Tate, on 16 January 1941, Ransom acknowledged that he "owed the suggestion" for the chapter to Delmore Schwartz, who "said it was a pity" that he "couldn't find an 'ontological' critic" (*SL* 275). Ransom finished the chapter in November 1940 and probably had the complete manuscript to Laughlin shortly after his 14 November letter to Tate. The manuscript incorporated several essays and parts of essays that had been published during the previous two years in *Hika*, *Kenyon Review*, and *Southern Review*, along with other essays still to be published during winter and spring 1941 in *Accent* and *Southern Review*. On 14 April 1941, he told Tate that he expected the book to be out "within a couple of weeks," adding that he was "far from satisfied" with his performance (*SL* 280).

New Directions published the book on 10 May 1941 and probably never required an impression beyond the first. Subsequently, reprints of the book have been available in limited numbers through on-demand reprinting by University Microfilms, Ransom himself having evidently expressed his wish for no further publication. On 21 April 1961, Laughlin acknowledged in a letter to Ransom the author's desire that the book not be reprinted "in its entirety" (TNV). But on 18 July 1969, Laughlin wrote that he was pleased to hear that Ransom, thinking "more kindly" of the book, was preparing to make revisions and add some essays. Laughlin asked about the possibility of receiving the manuscript before the end of August, in time for the spring 1970 list (TNV). This project seems to have evolved into or was displaced by *Beating the Bushes*. Although New Directions did not re-publish *New Criticism*, it was reprinted in 1979 by Greenwood Press.

A10.a New Directions impression (1941)

THE NEW | CRITICISM | by John Crowe Ransom | [device of man with animal] | NEW DIRECTIONS | Norfolk, Connecticut

Copyright page (iv): 'COPYRIGHT 1941 BY | NEW DIRECTIONS | MANUFACTURED IN THE UNITED STATES OF AMERICA'.

202 x 138 mm. *1-20*^{8} *21*^{10} *22*^{8}; 178 leaves. *i-vi* vii-xiii *xiv 1-2* 3-131 *132-134* 135-208 *209-210* 211-275 *276-278* 279-339 *340-342* pp.

i half title 'THE NEW | CRITICISM'; ii blank; iii title page; iv copyright page; v dedication 'To | PHILIP BLAIR RICE'; vi blank; vii-xii 'Preface' (ending 'JOHN CROWE RANSOM'); xiii 'CONTENTS'; xiv blank; 1 part title 'I | I. A. Richards: | THE PSYCHOLOGICAL CRITIC'; 2 blank; 3-131 text; 132 blank; 133 part title 'II | T. S. Eliot: | THE HISTORICAL CRITIC'; 134 blank; 135-208 text; 209 part title 'III | Yvor Winters: | THE LOGICAL CRITIC'; 210 blank; 211-275 text; 276 blank; 277 part title 'IV | Wanted: | AN ONTOLOGICAL CRITIC'; 278 blank; 279-336 text; 337-339 'Index'; 340-42 blank.

Contains, in addition to Ransom's preface, the four essays indicated by the part titles. The essay on Empson incorporates, with revision, "Mr. Empson's Muddles" from *Southern Review* (C234); a portion of that on Eliot appeared with the title "Eliot and the Metaphysicals" in *Accent* (C256); that on Winters appeared in an pre-publication "abridgement" in *Southern Review* (C255); the final essay goes over some of the same ground as Ransom's "Pragmatics of Art" in *Kenyon Review* (C246) without, it seems, being textually related, and it does incorporate text from "The Thing about Poetry" from *Hika* (C249).

Type-page 28 lines, 139 (151) x 93 mm (e.g., p. 141) or, more often, 29 lines, 144 x (156) x 93 mm (e.g., p. 13), 10 lines = 50 mm; typeface Baskerville with 3.7 mm face, 1.8 mm x-height. Texts of essays and preface begin with capital initial, 2 lines deep. Essay numbers, titles, and subtitles centered (e.g., 'II | T. S. Eliot | THE HISTORICAL CRITIC'). Running titles centered in the headline: book title on versos ('THE NEW CRITICISM'); preface and essay titles on rectos (e.g., 'T. S. ELIOT'); 'INDEX' on verso and recto. No running titles on first page of essays, preface, or index. Pagination centered in the direction line. White wove paper, no watermark, sheets bulk 24 mm.

Bound in dark blue (183) calico cloth over boards. Front and back blank. Spine label of grayish yellowish brown (80) paper printed in dark brown (59): 'John | Crowe | Ransom | ★ | THE NEW | CRITICISM | ★ | New | Directions'. White wove endpapers. Edges trimmed.

Dust jacket of grayish yellowish brown (80) wove paper printed in dark brown (59). Front: 'John Crowe Ransom | ★ | THE NEW | CRITICISM | AN EXAMINATION | OF THE CRITICAL THEORIES OF | I. A. RICHARDS, | T. S. ELIOT, YVOR WINTERS, | WILLIAM EMPSON | ★ | New Directions'. Spine: '[running across] John | Crowe | Ransom | ★ | [running down] THE NEW | CRITICISM | [running across] | ★ New | Directions.' Back: 'NEW DIRECTIONS BOOKS | [list of novels, stories, criticism, poetry, anthologies, and history titles published by New Directions]'. Front flap: title, author, 42-line blurb, price ('$2.50'). Back flap: advertisements for Yvor Winters's *Maule's Curse* and for the Makers of Modern Literature series in preparation, including a volume by Ransom on Emily Dickinson (see F2).

Copies: ICU (rebound), IU, InU-Lilly (with jacket), STW (Ransom's copy with autograph revisions, and a copy inscribed to Philip Wheelwright on 9 July 1942 with jacket), TNV (2 copies, one with jacket), TxU-HRC, WU (rebound).

Published at $2.50 on 10 May 1941. Copyright registration A155125.; renewed 30 December 1968, R451813. Griselda Ohannessian, New Directions, believes that there was only one printing and that of perhaps 1000 copies (letter, 5 August 1995). Listed in "The Weekly Record, *Publishers' Weekly* 24 May 1941: 2094, and in "Latest Books Received," *New York Times Book Review* 25 May 1941: 24. Also listed in "A List of Books Published by

New Directions, 1936-1963," *A New Directions Reader*, ed. Hayden Carruth and James Laughlin (Norfolk: New Directions, 1964), where book and jacket design are credited to Albert Erskine Jr. and where the printer is noted as Colonial Press, Clinton, MA. Advertised in *New Directions in Prose & Poetry* 1941: 763, in *Direction* Summer 1941:45, and in *PMLA* December 1942, part 2: 35.

Reviewed in *New York Herald Tribune Books* 15 June 1941: 11 (Babette Deutsch); *Saturday Review of Literature* 5 July 1941: 13 (Alexander Cowie); *Nation* 12 July 1941: 37 (Louise Bogan); *Common Sense* August 1941: 249-250 (Harry Roskolenko); *Accent* Autumn 1941: 51-55 (Richard Eberhart); *Rocky Mountain Review* Fall 1941: 15 (Ray B. West Jr., signed R. B. W.); *Sewanee Review* October-December 1941: 520-536 (William S. Knickerbocker); *American Oxonian* 1942: 97-102 (F. O. Matthiessen); *Kenyon Review* Winter 1942: 126-132 (Kenneth Burke); *Thought* March 1942: 138-140 (William J. Grace); *Yale Review* March 1942: 608-611 (Herbert Muller); *Poetry* January 1943: 575-579 (J. V. Healy); *American Literature* March 1943: 82-84 (Fred B. Millett).

A10.b University Microfilms on-demand reprintings

There have been on-demand xerographic reprintings by University Microfilms, these being bound in the typical yellowish gray (93) or dark blue (183) paper wrappers and front label used by UM. Copies: TxU, WMM (rebound), WU. In Ransom's papers is a carbon copy of letter dated 27 April 1959 from Robert M. MacGregor of New Directions to Eugene Power of University Microfilms, extending from 10 to 20 the contracted limit on copies that could be made until October of that year, at which time the limit could be reviewed. MacGregor added: "I am sure you understand why we and Mr. Ransom want to limit so severely the circulation of this work. I expect that I earlier explained that he no longer feels that this is an adequate statement of his ideas" (TNV). MacGregor wrote at least one more such letter extending the limit—this one on 6 July 1961 (TNV).

A10.c Folcroft Library impression (1971)
Not seen. Listed in *National Union Catalog, 1976.*

A10.d1 First Greenwood reprint (1979)

THE NEW | CRITICISM | by John Crowe Ransom | [publisher's device] | GREENWOOD PRESS, PUBLISHERS | WESTPORT, CONNECTICUT

Copyright page (iv): '[LC cataloging-in-publication data] | ISBN 0-8371-9079-7 | PUBLISHER'S NOTE | *Because of the scholarly importance of this work and its | unavailability through antiquarian and other book sources, we | have reprinted this volume from a photocopy of the original | edition.* | Copyright 1941 by New Directions Publishing Corporation. | Copyright © 1968 by John Crowe Ransom. | Published in 1941 by New Directions, Norfolk, Connecticut | Published under agreement with New Directions Publishing | Corporation. | Reprinted in 1979 by Greenwood Press, Inc. | 51 Riverside Avenue, Westport, CT 06880 | Printed in the United States of America | 10 9 8 7 6 5 4 3 2 1'.

214 x 139 mm. *1-11*^{16}; 176 leaves. *iii-vi* vii-xiii *xiv 1-2* 3-131 *132-134* 135-208 *209-210* 211-275 *276-278* 279-339 *340* pp.

This is a photo-offset reprinting from a photocopy of the New Directions impression. The copyright page has been reset. The typepage has been reduced, measuring 133 (144) x 89 mm (e.g., p. 141) or 139 x (145) x 89 mm (e.g., p. 13). White wove paper, no watermark, sheets bulk 20 mm.

Bound in moderate reddish brown (43) calico cloth over boards. Front and back blank. Spine stamped in black: '[running down] RANSOM [22 mm vertical rule] THE NEW CRITICISM [running across] [Greenwood device]'. White wove endpapers. Edges trimmed. No dust jacket.

Copies: STW, WU.

A10.d2 Second Greenwood reprint

Identical to the first Greenwood impression except in the following points.

The copyright page has been reset: '[LC cataloging-in-publication data] | ISBN 0-8371-9079-7 | PUBLISHER'S NOTE | *Because of the scholarly importance of this work and its* | *unavailability through antiquarian and other book sources, we have* | *reprinted this volume from a photocopy of the original edition.'* | Copyright 1941 by New Directions Publishing Corporation. | Copyright © 1968 by John Crowe Ransom. | Published in 1941 by New Directions, Norfolk, Connecticut | Published under agreement with New Directions Publishing | Corporation. | [LC card number and ISBN] | Reprinted in 1979 by Greenwood Press | 88 Post Road West, Westport, CT 06881 | An imprint of the Greenwood Publishing Group, Inc. | Printed in the United States of America | [recycle symbol] | [3-line note on paper permanence] | 10 9 8 7 6 5 4 3 2'.

The leaf size is 209 x 130 mm. Sheets bulk 21 mm. Side-stitched and perfect bound in deep blue (179) calico cloth over boards. Front and back blank. Spine stamped in silver: '[running down] Ransom The New Criticism [running across] [Greenwood device]'. The integral leaves are preceded and followed an additional free endpaper of white wove paper thicker than the stock used for the integral leaves and evidently of the same stock as the conjugate leaves used as the primary free and paste-down endpapers. Edges cut.

Copies: CSA, TNV.

A11 1943

A College Primer of Writing

Ransom's *College Primer* is a revised and extended version of the handbook portion of his *Topics for Freshman Writing*. In *The House of Holt*, Ellen D. Gilbert cites a 1 December 1942 letter (from the Holt archive at Princeton) in which Robert H. Elias, a professor at the University of Pennsylvania, told the publisher that he found *Topics* unsuitable for his composition courses but praised its supplemental handbook. "Following up on this lead," Gilbert says, "College Department Editor Robert MacMurphey asked Ransom if he could add some exercises to the handbook to make it suitable for publication as a separately bound pamphlet." In an undated letter, Ransom agreed to the project, saying that he himself could use such a handbook for an impending class of 200 Navy reservists (Gilbert 233). The original contract, for "A Handbook in Brief," was signed and dated by MacMurphey on 9 December 1942 (STW). It called for submission of the manuscript within two months and set royalties at 15 percent "on the Publishers' gross receipts per copy which, for the purposes of this agreement, shall be reckoned as seventy-five per cent of the published price for the Educational edition or fifty-eight per cent of the published price for the Trade edition, if any." On 20 March 1943 Ransom wrote Tate that he had been "struggling with an unpalatable undertaking, revision of a Freshman handbook for Holt." He explained that Holt had been after him for "a couple of months" but that he had not "the time or mood to get down and finish it up," something he would now do "within the week" (OGK).

In the 1970s it seemed for a time as if the book might gain further life in a new edition. In a letter to Ransom on 31 December 1970, Phillip W. Leininger (editor-in-chief of Holt's college department) proposed asking Robert Graves to write an introduction for a new edition of *College Primer*, one with a text unchanged except for updated examples (TNV). On 11 February 1971 he wrote again, saying that they had in hand Graves's "Preface," asking for a brief introduction by Ransom, and explaining that the examples would be left as they were because Graves opposed substituting contemporary ones (TNV). The new edition did not appear. The only edition is the one that was published on 20 July 1943 and that I have seen in only two impressions.

A11.1 First Holt impression (1943)

A | COLLEGE PRIMER | OF WRITING | *by* | JOHN CROWE RANSOM | *Kenyon College* | [Holt device] | *NEW YORK* | HENRY HOLT AND COMPANY

Copyright page (ii): 'COPYRIGHT, 1943 | BY | HENRY HOLT AND COMPANY, INC. | PRINTED IN THE | UNITED STATES OF AMERICA'.

186 x 125 mm. *1-9*^{8}; 72 leaves. *i-ii* iii-vi 1-137 *138* pp.

i title page; 2 copyright page; iii-iv 'Preface' (ending 'J.C.R. | *Kenyon College, April 25, 1943*'); v-vi 'CONTENTS'; 1-30 'Sentence Structure'; 31-79 'Punctuation'; 80-134 'Composition'; 135-137 'INDEX'; 138 blank.

Type-page 37 lines, 145 (151) x 97 mm, 10 lines = 39 mm (e.g., p. 64), but 41 lines with 10 lines = 36 mm for pages occupied by examples (e.g., p. 128); typeface Old Style with 3.2 mm face, 1.6 mm x-height (but, for text of examples, 2.9 mm face, 1.6 mm x-height). Running titles at the inner margin of the headline: part titles on versos (e.g., 'PREFACE' and 'SENTENCE STRUCTURE'); section heads on rectos (e.g., 'THE WRITING OF NUMBERS'). Pagination at outer margin of headlines (but centered in the direction line on first page of each part). White wove paper, no watermark, sheets bulk 7 mm.

Bound in moderate reddish brown (43) calico cloth over boards. Front and back blank. Spine, running down, stamped in silver: 'RANSOM [square brace mark] A COLLEGE PRIMER OF WRITING [closing square brace mark] HOLT'. White wove endpapers. Edges cut. Probably issued without a dust jacket.

Copies: CSA, ICN, IDeKN, STW (2 copies, including Ransom's copy in the publisher's presentation binding of brown half-leather stamped in gold and with gilt top edge and marbled endpapers), TNV, TxU-HRC.

Published at $1.10 on 20 July 1943; copyright registration A174799; renewed 1 February 1971, R498477. Listed in "The Weekly Record," *Publishers' Weekly* 7 August 1943: 435. Briefly noted in

College English December 1943: 171. Advertised in *PMLA* March 1945: viii.

A11.2 Later Holt impression (1945)

Added to the copyright page after the Holt imprint is the date '*September, 1945.*' Bound in blackish blue (188) calico cloth (InU) or dark blue (183) calico cloth (WU). Otherwise identical to the earlier impression. Copies: InU, WU.

SELECTED

POEMS

BY

JOHN CROWE RANSOM

1945

ALFRED A KNOPF

NEW YORK

Title page:
A12a.1 ***Selected Poems,*** **1945**

SELECTED POEMS

BY

JOHN CROWE RANSOM

1947

EYRE & SPOTTISWOODE

LONDON

Title page:
A12b ***Selected Poems*, 1947**

A 12 1945

Selected Poems

In a letter to Tate, 27 February [1943?], Ransom said that he would return to poetry "shortly by publishing Collected Poems with some revisionary touches here and there"; then, correcting himself, he added parenthetically, "I mean: Selected Poems" (*SL* 305). Of the 42 poems gathered for this collection, 20 had appeared in *Chills and Fever* and 17 in *Two Gentlemen*. The remaining five poems, put last in the text, had all had periodical publication. Ransom's "revisionary touches" were extensive and in some cases radical (e.g., in "Blue Girls," "Spectral Lovers," and "Vaunting Oak").

The Knopf manuscript-record form shows receipt of the manuscript on 2 October 1944 and, after a reading by Herbert Weinstock, its acceptance on 10 October. At Alfred Knopf's suggestion, Weinstock wrote his report in the form of publicity or catalogue copy; indeed, with some alteration in its last sentence, his report appears as the dust jacket blurb on the published book (TxU). The galley proofs for the book were date-stamped 21 February 1945 and bear, in addition to proofreader's marks, some further revision by Ransom (STW). The book may have still been at the printer in April 1945, since it was on 13 April that Ransom okayed changing the date of his introduction from 28 September 1944 to 10 April 1945 (TxU).

On 2 June 1945 Ransom wrote Alfred Knopf that it was "a beautiful book" (TxU). Designed by W. A. Dwiggins, the book is listed in Dwight Agner's *The Books of WAD* as item 45.19. Dwiggins (1880-1956) had begun designing for Knopf in 1926. He was noted for his unconventional use of ornament and for designing several typefaces, including Electra, Caledonia, Arcadia, Eldorado, Stuyvesant, Tippecanoe, and Winchester.

The Knopf edition was published on 11 June 1945, and a second impression was not required until June 1952. The English edition, published by Eyre & Spottiswoode, was delayed until 30 April 1948. On 14 July 1948, having just received copies of the Eyre & Spottiswoode edition, Ransom wrote to William Koshland at Knopf, implying that he was unaware of any arrangements for it. In reply on 19 July 1948, Koshland explained that the contract for the Eyre & Spottiswoode edition had been made in fall 1945 but that "British publishing difficulties" delayed publication until "now" (TxU).

A12a.1 Knopf edition, first impression (1945)

SELECTED | POEMS | BY | JOHN CROWE RANSOM | [drawing of a seated angel with a bird resting on its right hand] | 1945 | ALFRED A KNOPF | NEW YORK

Copyright page (iv): 'COPYRIGHT 1924, 1927, 1934, 1939, 1945 BY ALFRED A. KNOPF, INC. | [reservation of rights in 3 lines] | *Manufactured in the United States of America* | *Published simultaneously in Canada by The Ryerson Press* | FIRST EDITION'.

Colophon (77): 'A NOTE ON THE TYPE | *This book was set on the Linotype in Janson, a recutting made* | *direct from the type cast from matrices made by Anton Janson* | *sometime between 1660 and 1678.* | *Of Janson's origin nothing is known. He may have been a rela-* | *tive of Justus Janson, a printer of Danish birth who practised in* | *Leipzig from 1614 to 1635. Some time between 1657 and 1668* | *Anton Janson, a punch-cutter and type-founder, bought from the* | *Leipzig printer Johann Erich Hahn the type-foundry which had* | *formerly been a part of the printing house of M. Friedrich Lan-* | *kisch. Janson's types were first shown in a specimen sheet issued* | *at Leipzig about 1675.* | *The book has been composed, printed, and bound by The* | *Plimpton Press, Norwood, Mass. Typography and binding design* | *by W. A. Dwiggins.* | THIS BOOK HAS BEEN PRODUCED IN FULL COMPLIANCE WITH ALL | GOVERNMENT REGULATIONS FOR THE CONSERVATION OF PAPER, METAL, | AND OTHER ESSENTIAL MATERIALS.'

212 x 140 mm. *1-6*^{8}; 48 leaves. [2] *i-vi* vii-ix *x-xiv* 1-75 *76-80* pp.

1 blank; 2 advertisement headed '*DISTINGUISHED POETRY*' and listing 7 titles published as Borzoi Books (from William Rose Benét's *The Dust Which Is God* to Jon Beck Shank's *Poems*); i half title 'SELECTED POEMS'; ii blank; iii title page; iv copyright page; v dedication '*To HELEN*' his daughter; vi blank; vii-ix '*Contents*'; x blank; xi '*Preface*' (ending 'JOHN CROWE RANSOM | *April 10, 1945.*'); xii blank; xiii bastard title 'SELECTED POEMS'; xiv blank; 1-75 text; 76 blank; 77 colophon; 78-80 blank.

Ransom's brief preface acknowledges prior publication of the poems and offers "two items of information": "It would be difficult for me to recover exactly the order in which the poems were composed, but I believe the present arrangement is substantially in that order. And some of the earlier poems I have felt impelled to trim and revise a little."

Poems:
Winter Remembered
Miriam Tazewell
Dead Boy
Spectral Lovers
Necrological
Bells for John Whiteside's Daughter
The Tall Girl
Good Ships
Emily Hardcastle, Spinster
Parting at Dawn
Vaunting Oak
Spiel of the Three Mountebanks
Here Lies a Lady
Tom, Tom, the Piper's Son
Conrad in Twilight
Armageddon
Judith of Bethulia
Blue Girls
Philomela
Old Man Playing with Children
Captain Carpenter
Old Mansion
Piazza Piece
Eclogue
Her Eyes
Parting, without a Sequel
Janet Waking
Lady Lost
Two in August
Somewhere Is Such a Kingdom
Antique Harvesters
Our Two Worthies
Puncture
Dog
Man without Sense of Direction
Survey of Literature
The Equilibrists
What Ducks Require
Prelude to an Evening
Of Margaret
Painted Head
Address to the Scholars of New England

Type-page of irregular line length because of verse, 160 (167) x 101 mm, 10 lines = 49 mm (e.g., pp. 50 and 52); typeface Janson with 4.2 mm face, 1.9 mm x-height. Poem titles (e.g., '*Here Lies a Lady*') centered and in italic, each poem beginning on a new page. No running titles. Pagination centered in the direction line. White wove paper, no watermark, sheets bulk 5 mm.

Bound in black diagonal fine-rib cloth over boards, stamped in gold. Front: '*SELECTED POEMS | JOHN CROWE RANSOM*'.

Spine: [running up] '*SELECTED POEMS* [ornament] *JOHN CROWE RANSOM* [running across at the foot] KNOPF'. Back: Borzoi Books device blind stamped in relief at the lower right. White wove endpapers. Top edge cut and stained very light bluish green (162). Bottom and fore-edge trimmed.

Dust jacket of yellowish gray (93) paper printed in black. Front: '[within a thick-thin double rule frame ornamented with fleurs-de-lis at the inner angles] SELECTED | POEMS | BY | JOHN CROWE | RANSOM | [floral ornament] | [swash A] *All the poems that the author thinks most | representative of his work over a period of | twenty-five years.*' Spine, running up: '*Alfred • A • Knopf* [Borzoi device] *SELECTED POEMS by JOHN CROWE RANSOM*'. Back: within a thick-thin double rule frame, a list of 7 Borzoi poetry titles for 1945 (from William Rose Benét's *The Dust Which Is God* to Jon Beck Shank's *Poems*). Front flap: price ('$2.00 | net'), 34-line blurb, book design credit (to W. A. Dwiggins). Back flap: photograph of Ransom and a 17-line biographical blurb ending with this sentence: "At the time of writing, New Directions has in press a fourth volume of prose, *Essays in Poetics*" (see F3).

Copies: CSA (with jacket), ICN, ICU, IDeKN, IEN, INS, IU (3 copies), InU, InU-Lilly (with jacket), OGK (2 copies), STW (4 copies: Ransom's copy in publisher's presentation binding of green full leather stamped in gold and with marbled endpapers, Ransom's copy with autograph revisions, a copy inscribed to Randall Jarrell on 14 July 1945 with jacket, a review copy inscribed to Robert Penn Warren on 9 July 1959 with jacket), TNV (6 copies, including a copy with jacket and inscription to Allen Tate 1 June 1945 and a copy with jacket and inscription to Frances and Lon [Cheney] 2 August 1958), TxU-HRC (with jacket), WBB, WMM, WU (with jacket).

Published at $2.00 on 11 June 1945; copyright registration A188132.

Advertised in *Publishers' Weekly* 5 May 1945: 1795 and in *New York Times Book Review* 17 June 1945: 16. Listed in "The Weekly Record," *Publishers' Weekly* 9 June 1945: 2312; *Sewanee Review* Summer 1948: 349.

Reviewed in *Kirkus* 15 March 1945: 121; *Nashville Tennessean* 17 June 1945: 15 (E. H. Duncan); *New Yorker* 7 July 1945: 67-68; *New York Times Book Review* 8 July 1945: 6 (Howard Moss); *Saturday Review of Literature* 14 July 1945: 30-31 (Theodore Spencer); *Nation* 11 August 1945: 138-139 (F. W. Dupee); *New Republic* 13 August 1945: 196-198 (Jean Wahl); *America* 29 September 1945: 525 (Anna Beatrice Murphy); *New Mexico Quarterly Review* Winter 1945: 512-516 (Alan Swallow); *Living Church* 25 November 1945: 11-12 (James Dyar Moffett); *Quarterly Review of Literature* 2.4 (1945): 366-370 (Arthur Mizener); *Books on Trial* December 1945-January 1946: 134; *American Oxonian* 1946: 63-67 (Donald A. Stauffer); *Wings* Winter 1946: 25-26 (Robert Avrett); *Poetry* January 1946: 212-215 (Richard Eberhart); *Accent* Spring 1946: 206-207 (Robert Richman); *Virginia Quarterly Review* Summer 1946: 438-447 (Dan S. Norton); *Furioso* Fall 1946: 65-66 (Howard Nemerov).

A12a.2 Knopf edition, second impression (1952)

Title page date changed to 1952. Copyright page (ii): 'COPYRIGHT 1924, 1927, 1934, 1939, 1945 BY ALFRED A. KNOPF, INC. | [reservation of rights in 3 lines] | *Manufactured in the United States of America* | *Published in Canada by McClelland & Stewart Limited* | PUBLISHED JUNE 11, 1945 | SECOND PRINTING, JUNE 1952'. Colophon (77) omits conservation statement.

Also differs from the first impression in arrangement of contents and pagination and in paper and binding cloth, and in dust jacket. [4] *i-vi* vii-ix *x-xii* 1-75 *76-80* pp. *1-2* blank (no advertisement); *3* half title; *4* blank; i title page; ii copyright page; iii dedication; iv blank; v preface; vi blank; vii-ix contents; x blank; xi bastard title; xii blank; 1-75 text; 76 blank; 77 colophon; *78-80* blank.

White laid paper with vertical chainlines 23 mm apart; watermark 'WARREN'S | OLDE STYLE'. Sheets bulk 7 mm. Bound in black calico cloth, with lettering and top-edge stain identical to those of the first impression.

Dust jacket of very light bluish green (162) paper printed in moderate reddish brown (43). Front and spine are identical to those of the first impression (aside from color). Back: '[within a rule frame is an advertisement for 'THE BOOKS OF | WALLACE STEVENS'. Front flap: price changed to '$3.00 | net' and blurb has been slightly revised (so that, for example, Ransom's voice has been "distinguishable" for "more than three decades" rather than for "more than twenty-five years"). Back flap: the blurb omits reference to *Essays in Poetics*; added after the blurb: 'PRINTED IN U.S.A.').

Copies: IDeKN, STW (with jacket), TxU-HRC (with jacket), TNV, WU-Col.

The Knopf planning card for the 1963 *Selected Poems* records total sale of the 1945 edition at 3380 copies as of 20 February 1963 (TxU).

A12b Eyre & Spottiswoode edition (1948)

[Strong reddish orange (35)] SELECTED POEMS | [black] BY | JOHN CROWE RANSOM | 1947 [sic] | EYRE & SPOTTISWOODE | LONDON

Printer's imprint (4): 'THIS BOOK IS PRINTED FOR EYRE & SPOTTISWOODE | (PUBLISHERS) LTD., 14, 15, AND 16 BEDFORD STREET, | LONDON, W.C. 2, BY T. & A. CONSTABLE LTD., | HOPETOUN STREET, EDINBURGH'. No copyright notice.

215 x 138 mm. π^6 A-C^8 D^{10}; first leaf of gatherings signed, plus leaf D2 as 'D*'; 40 leaves. *i-vi* vii-ix *x-xi* xii 1-67 *68* pp.

i half title 'SELECTED POEMS'; ii blank; iii title page; iv printer's imprint; v dedication '*To HELEN*'; vi blank; vii-viii 'CONTENTS'; ix 'PREFACE' (ending 'JOHN CROWE RANSOM. | *April 10, 1945.*'); x blank; xi bastard title 'SELECTED POEMS'; xii blank (except page number); 1-68 text.

Contains the same preface and the same poems in the same order as the American edition. There are, however, textual variants in the poems. Most are changes to British spelling, so that for example 'center' in line 8 of "Wintered Remembered" becomes 'centre', 'pretense' in line 10 of "Dead Boy" becomes 'pretence', and 'honor' in line 57 of "Here Lies a Lady" becomes 'honour' (although "The Equilibrists" retains 'Honor' throughout). There are at least two substantive variants: in line 31 of "Tom, Tom, the Piper's Son," the reading is 'a far greater kingdom' rather than Knopf's 'a far great kingdom'; in line 23 of "Eclogue," the reading is 'ravage cried' rather than 'ravage cries'.

Type-page of irregular line length because of verse, 177 (182) x 101 mm, 10 lines = 42 mm (e.g., pp. 19 and 67); typeface Fournier with 4.2 mm face, 1.9 mm x-height. Poem titles (e.g., 'HERE LIES A LADY') centered and in capitals, each poem beginning on a new page. No running titles. Signatures at inner margin of direction line; pagination centered in direction line. White laid paper, no watermark, vertical chainlines 22-24 mm apart; sheets bulk 6 mm.

Bound in dark yellowish green (137) calico cloth over boards, lettered in dark red (16). Front: 'JOHN CROWE RANSOM I SELECTED I POEMS'. Spine, running across: '[border ornament resembling four pine trees on a double rule] I Selected I POEMS I [fleury cross ornament] I John I Crowe I Ransom I [same border ornament but inverted]' I E. & S.' Back blank. White laid endpapers. Edges cut.

Dust jacket of white laid paper (horizontal chainlines 23 mm apart) lettered in black and strong reddish orange (35). Front: '[orange] SELECTED I POEMS I [black] BY I JOHN I CROWE RANSOM I [drawing of three blossoms and six buds, each on a stalk symmetrically arranged in a vase]'. Spine blank. Back: advertisement for Allen Tate's *Poems, 1920-1945*, said to be 'UNIFORM WITH THIS VOLUME'. Front flap: '[orange] SELECTED POEMS I [black] *By* JOHN CROWE RANSOM'; 23-line blurb; '9*s. net*'. On some copies (WU and CSA), the price is covered by a paper label with a price of '10/6 I NET'. Back flap blank.

Copies: CSA (2 copies with jackets), InU-Lilly (with jacket), IQC, OGK, STW (2 copies: one with jacket and one with holograph text of "Vision by Sweetwater" on the recto of the back free endpaper), TNV (with jacket), TxU-HRC (3 copies with jackets, including one from the library of Edith Sitwell and one from the library of Richard Church with a tipped-in review copy notice), WU (with jacket).

Published on 30 April 1948 at 9s (TxU-HRC review copy). The *English Catalogue* gives a publication date of April 1948; *Whitaker's Cumulative Book List* gives a date of May 1948. British Library deposit 4 May 1948. Number of copies unknown; print-run ledgers for Eyre & Spottiswoode no longer exist (letter, Jean Rose, Reed International Books Library, 15 August 1995). Advertised at 9s. in *Poetry Quarterly* Spring 1948: 63 and again, as "now ready," in *Poetry Quarterly* Summer 1948: 128; also in *TLS* 17 September 1954: 592

Reviewed in *Poetry Quarterly* Summer 1948: 122-126 (Derek Stanford); *Poetry London* May 1949: 29-30 (Anne Ridler).

A13 1951

The Kenyon Critics

Ransom selected the contents of *Kenyon Critics* from essays and reviews that had been published in the first twelve volumes (1939-1950) of *Kenyon Review*, which he had founded and edited after moving to Kenyon College in September 1937. There are 33 contributions by as many contributors; there is at least one item from each volume, the 1948 volume being represented by more (seven) than any other. The book was published by World Publishing on 23 February 1951. There appears to have been no impression after the first.

In a letter to Ransom on 8 December 1966, Cornell Jaray of Kennikat Press said that his firm had successfully concluded negotiations with World Publishing to "reissue" *Kenyon Critics*. He asked Ransom if he wanted to add a new preface or foreword (TNV). The Kennikat photo-offset reprinting appeared late the following year, without any such addition.

A13.a World impression (1951)

[101 mm slightly swelled rule] | The Kenyon Critics | STUDIES IN MODERN LITERATURE FROM | THE Kenyon Review EDITED BY | *John Crowe Ransom* | [101 mm rule] | [World device] | *The World Publishing Company* | CLEVELAND AND NEW YORK | [101 mm slightly swelled rule]

Copyright page (iv): 'Published by THE WORLD PUBLISHING COMPANY | *First Edition* | HC151 | Copyright 1951 by the *Kenyon Review* | [reservation of rights and statement of U.S. manufacture in 4 lines]'.

208 x 140 mm. *1-11*^{16}; 176 leaves. *i-iv* v-x *1-2* 3-251 *252-254* 255-342 pp.

i half title '[101 mm slightly swelled rule] | The Kenyon Critics'; ii blank; iii title page; iv copyright page; v-vi '[identical rule] | 'CONTENTS'; vii-x '[identical rule] | Introduction' (ending 'JOHN CROWE RANSOM | *Gambier, Ohio* | *January 15, 1951*'); 1 part title '[identical rule] | Essays'; 2 blank; 3-251 text; 252 blank; 253

part title '[identical rule] | Book Reviews'; 254 blank; 255-340 text; 341-342 'Bibliography'.

Edited and introduced by Ransom, who otherwise includes nothing of his own in this selection of 33 items from the first twelve volumes (1939-1950) of the *Kenyon Review*. The entries are arranged chronologically by order of appearance within two divisions—essays and reviews. The critics: W. H. Auden, William Barrett, Eric Bentley, John Berryman, John Peale Bishop, R. P. Blackmur, Cleanth Brooks, Jr., Richard Chase, Eleanor Clark, Richard Eberhart, Richard Ellmann, William Empson, Dudley Fitts, R. W. Flint, Paul Goodman, Irving Howe, Randall Jarrell, Vivienne Koch, Martin Lebowitz, Robie Macauley, Adrienne Monnier, Donat O'Donnell, Philip Rahv, Philip Blair Rice, Isaac Rosenfeld, Delmore Schwartz, Lionel Trilling, Parker Tyler, Eliseo Vivas, C. G. Wallis, Austin Warren, Robert Penn Warren, and Harold Whitehall.

Type-page 38 lines, 162 (168) x 101 mm, 10 lines = 43 mm (e.g., p. 9); typeface Granjon with 3.8 mm face, 1.7 mm x-height. Each essay begins with a capital initial 2 lines deep. Running titles centered in the headline: half title on versos ('KENYON CRITICS'); authors on rectos (e.g., 'PHILIP RAHV'); except 'INTRODUCTION' on verso and recto and 'CONTENTS' on verso. No running titles on pages that begin with a title. Pagination at the outer margin of the headline, except centered in the direction line of pages that begin with a title. White wove paper, no watermark, sheets bulk 24 mm.

Bound in black calico cloth over boards stamped in silver. Front: list of 33 contributors in 33 lines (from 'John Peale Bishop' to 'W. R. Flint', the latter's initial being mistakenly reversed here and on the contents page). Spine: '[running across] [thick rule, 20 mm] [running down] [110 mm rule] | THE KENYON CRITICS [thick vertical rule, 20 mm] JOHN CROWE RANSOM | [98 mm rule] [running across] WORLD'. Back blank. White wove endpapers. Top edge stained brilliant yellow (83). Top and bottom edges trimmed, fore-edge rough trimmed.

Dust jacket of white wove paper with lettering in black and white on a background of dark greenish yellow (103) on front and back, of dark greenish yellow and white on spine; lettered in black on white on flaps. Front: 'The | Kenyon | Critics | [white rule] | Studies in Modern Literature | from the *Kenyon Review* | Edited, with an Introduction, | by [white] JOHN CROWE RANSOM'. Back has advertisements for *Ernest Hemingway*, ed. John K. M. McCaffery, and *Letters of Emily Dickinson*, ed. Mabel Loomis Todd. Front flap has a price of $4.00 and a blurb continued on the back flap.

Copies: CSA (2 copies, 1 with jacket), ICN, IDeKN, INS, InU-Lilly (with jacket), OGK, STW (with jacket and Ransom's autograph emendations), TNV (with jacket), TxU-HRC, WBB. Also in Wright, *Jarrell* B16; Stefanik, *Berryman* B12.

Published at $4.00 on 23 February 1951; copyright registration A54100.

Forthcoming publication noted in an announcement of Ransom's receiving the Bollingen Award, *Publishers' Weekly* 3 February 1951: 799. Advertised in *New York Times Book Review* 4 March 1951: 31 and in *Hika* Spring 1951: inside front cover. Listed in "Weekly Record," *Publishers' Weekly* 24 February 1951: 1080.

Reviewed in *Kirkus* 15 January 1951: 47; *Chicago Sunday Tribune Books* 18 March 1951: 15 (Paul Engle); *Saturday Review of Literature* 9 June 1951: 15 (Louis L. Martz); *New Republic* 18 June 1951: 18 (Raymond Mortimer); *Arizona Quarterly* Summer 1951: 175-177 (Charles I. Glicksberg); *New York Times Book Review* 5 August 1951: 9 (Granville Hicks); *American Oxonian* 1952: 60-61 (J. N. Yarnall); *Western Review* Summer 1952: 325-328 (Murray Krieger).

A13.b Kennikat press reprint (1967)

This is a photo-offset reprinting from the World typesetting. The World imprint on the title page is replaced with Kennikat's: 'KENNIKAT PRESS, INC./PORT WASHINGTON, N.Y.' The copyright page has been reset: 'THE KENYON CRITICS | Copyright 1951 by The Kenyon Review | Reissued in 1967 by Kennikat Press by arrangement with | The World Publishing Company | Library of Congress Catalog Card: 67-25258 | Manufactured in the United States of America | Analyzed in the ESSAY AND GENERAL LITERATURE INDEX | under Main Entry: The Kenyon Review'.

215 x 137 mm. Collation and pagination are identical to those of the World impression. The type-page has been slightly enlarged to 163 (169) x 101 mm. White wove paper, no watermark, sheets bulk 24 mm.

Bound in blackish blue (188) calico cloth over boards. Front and back blank. Spine stamped in silver: '[35 mm rule] | THE | KENYON | CRITICS | *Edited by* | John C. | Ransom | KENNIKAT | [35 mm rule]'. White wove endpapers. Edges trimmed.

Copies: IPB, STW.

A 14 **1 9 5 5**

Poems and Essays

In a letter of 21 January 1955, following a meeting with Ransom, Herbert Weinstock of Knopf summed up their agreement as to a collection of poems and essays: it should include the entire contents of *Selected Poems* (A12) plus about 30,000 words of essays, and publication would be set for about April 1956 (TxU). On 2 February, he told Ransom that Knopf would like to do the book under the Vintage imprint, and he asked when he might receive the copy (TxU). On 5 February Ransom offered 1 April 1955 for the submission date but on 29 March had to say that his editorial duties for the *Kenyon Review* were preventing him from meeting it (TxU). Meanwhile, on 8 February, Alfred Knopf had sent Ransom the Vintage contract, which called for a royalty of 5 percent of the catalog retail price on domestic sales, two-thirds of that for foreign sales. Ransom was to receive $250 advance against royalties (TxU). (Ransom's royalties for *Selected Poems* were 10 percent.)

There was then a series of reminders from Weinstock and delays by Ransom, caused in part by his revisions of both the poetry and prose. By 25 May Weinstock evidently had all of the manuscript (and had copy-edited it) except the final essay, "The Concrete Universal" (TxU). And on 10 June Harry Ford notified Ransom that this essay too was sent along to the printer (TxU). At the last minute, on 19 June, Ransom sent Ford the poem "Dog," which Ford had asked him not to cut and which Ransom agreed to reinstate after "Puncture" (TxU). On 19 July Ford acknowledged receipt of the proofs that he had sent Ransom nine days before, he noted that Ransom had not read proof against the manuscript, and he said that most errors were the fault of the printer, since Ransom's secretary had done "a beautiful job in the preparation of copy" (TxU).

The book was published in August or September 1955. There were at least two subsequent impressions.

A14.1 First impression (1955)

[On facing pages] [verso] *VINTAGE* | *BOOKS* | ■ | *NEW YORK* | *1955* [recto] POEMS | AND | ESSAYS | *SELECTED,* | *EDITED,* |

AND | *ARRANGED BY* | *THE AUTHOR* | JOHN | CROWE | RANSOM

Copyright page (iv): '[acknowledgements in 13 lines] | PUBLISHED BY VINTAGE BOOKS, INC., | BY ARRANGEMENT WITH ALFRED A. KNOPF, INC. | *Copyright, 1924, 1927, 1934, 1939, 1945, 1947, 1952, 1953, 1955, by* | *Alfred A. Knopf, Inc. All rights reserved.* [reservation of rights continued for 4 lines] | *Manufactured in the United States of America. Published* | *simultaneously in Canada by McClelland and Stewart Limited.* | FIRST VINTAGE EDITION'.

Colophon (186): '*THIS BOOK was set on the Linotype in Janson, an excellent* | *example of the influential and sturdy Dutch types that prevailed* | *in England prior to the development by William Caslon of his* | *own designs, which he evolved from these Dutch faces. Of* | *Janson himself little is known except that he was a practising* | *typefounder in Leipzig during the years 1660 to 1687. Com-* | *posed, printed, and bound by* THE COLONIAL PRESS INC., *Clinton,* | *Massachusetts. Paper manufactured by* S. D. WARREN COMPANY, | *Boston, Massachusetts. Cover design by* BRADBURY THOMPSON.'

184 x 107 mm. 96 leaves. *i-iv* v-vi *1-2* 3-76 *77-78* 79-86 *87* 88-185 *186* pp.

i half title '*POEMS* | *AND* | *ESSAYS* | ■ | *JOHN* | *CROWE* | *RANSOM*'; ii-iii title pages; iv copyright page; v-vi '*CONTENTS*'; 1 part title '*POEMS* | ■ | *JOHN* | *CROWE* | *RANSOM*'; 2 blank; 3-76 text; 77 part title '*ESSAYS* | ■ | *JOHN* | *CROWE* | *RANSOM*'; 78 blank; 79-185 text; 186 biographical note in 13 lines and colophon.

The volume contains, with revision, all of the poems from the 1945 *Selected Poems* (A12) and adds to them "Vision by Sweetwater" and "Persistent Explorer" from *Two Gentlemen* (A4).

Poems:
Winter Remembered
Miriam Tazewell
Dead Boy
Spectral Lovers
Eclogue
Vision by Sweetwater
Her Eyes
Parting, without a

Necrological
Bells for John Whiteside's Daughter
The Tall Girl
Good Ships
Emily Hardcastle, Spinster
Parting at Dawn
Vaunting Oak
Spiel of the Three Mountebanks
Here Lies a Lady
Tom, Tom, the Piper's Son
Conrad in Twilight
Armageddon
Judith of Bethulia
Blue Girls
Philomela
Old Man Playing with Children
Captain Carpenter
Old Mansion
Piazza Piece
Sequel
Janet Waking
Lady Lost
Two in August
Persistent Explorer
Somewhere Is Such a Kingdom
Antique Harvesters
Our Two Worthies
Puncture
Dog
Man without Sense of Direction
Survey of Literature
The Equilibrists
Prelude to an Evening
What Ducks Require
Of Margaret
Painted Head
Address to the Scholars of New England

Also contains these essays, all first collected in this volume and all substantively revised for the occasion. Previous periodical publication is indicated following each title.

Old Age of an Eagle [C315 as "Hardy—Old Poet]
Humanism at Chicago [C316]
More Than Gesture [C319 as "The Shores of Criticism"]
The Communities of Letters [C317]
On Shakespeare's Language [C292, see also B33]
Empirics in Politics [C322]
Why Critics Don't Go Mad [C312]
The Concrete Universal: Observations on the Understanding of Poetry [C327]

Type-page 37 lines, 157 (165) x 84 mm, 10 lines = 43 mm (e.g., p. 80); typeface Janson with 3.8 mm face, 1.7 mm x-height. Running titles only for prose, at outer margin of the headline: 'JOHN CROWE RANSOM' on versos; essay titles on rectos (e.g., 'OLD AGE OF AN EAGLE'). Pagination at outer margin of the direction line. Poem and essay titles at right margin (e.g., '*GOOD SHIPS*'); essays begin with an initial capital 11 mm high. White wove paper, no watermark, sheets bulk 12 mm.

Perfect bound in white paper printed on front, spine, and back with an abstract design in black on a rainbow-like pattern of strong pink (2), brilliant yellow (83), and light greenish blue (172). Front: '[black on rainbow] John | Crowe | Ransom | [white on black] A Vintage Book K-24 [vertical rule] 95¢ [vertical rule] Canada $1 [to the right of the previous line] Poems | And | Essays'. Spine, running down in black on pink: 'John Crowe Ransom Poems and Essays [thin vertical rule] Vintage K-24'. Back: author and title in white on black, blurb ('John Crowe Ransom has made his own selection for | [underscored] Poems and Essays [not underscored] from among his published works. | The terminal essay, "The Concrete Universal: | Observations on the Understanding of Poetry," was | written in 1955 especially for this book, and | it might be called a distillation of the central | interests and patterns of John Crowe Ransom's work.'), quotation from Randall Jarrell, publisher's imprint ('A Vintage Book'), cover design credit (to Bradbury Thompson). Edges cut.

Copies: ICU (rebound, preserving front and back covers), IU (rebound, preserving front and back covers), InU-Lilly, STW (4 copies), TNV (2 copies), TxU-HRC (2 copies), TxU-PCL, WU.

Published at $0.95 on 29 August 1955 according to copyright application but on 12 September 1955 according to copyright page of 2nd impression; copyright registration A204292.

Advertised in *Atlantic* September 1955: 83; *Publishers' Weekly* 10 September 1955: 966; *New York Times Book Review* 11 September 1955: 13; *Saturday Review* 17 September 1955: 7; *Kenyon Review* Autumn 1955: 667. Listed in "Weekly Record," *Publishers' Weekly* 17 September 1955: 1327. Reviewed in *Sewanee Review* October-December 1963: 642-644 (Roger Hecht).

A14.2 Second impression (1962)

Identical to the first impression except for changes to the title and copyright pages reflecting the fact that, as of 1 January 1961,

Vintage Books began operating as a division of Random House. A misprint in the first edition has not been corrected: line 16 of "Eclogue" reads 'I till you' (p. 39).

[On facing pages] [verso] *VINTAGE* | *BOOKS* | [Vintage device] | *A DIVISION OF* | *RANDOM HOUSE* | *NEW YORK* [recto] POEMS | AND | ESSAYS | *SELECTED,* | *EDITED,* | *AND* | *ARRANGED BY* | *THE AUTHOR* | JOHN | CROWE | RANSOM

Copyright page (iv): 'VINTAGE BOOKS | *are published by* ALFRED A. KNOPF, INC. | *and* RANDOM HOUSE INC. | © Copyright, 1924, 1927, 1934, 1939, 1945, 1947, 1952, 1953, 1955, | by Alfred A. Knopf, Inc. | All rights reserved under International and | Pan-American Copyright Conventions. | Published in New York by Random House, Inc., | and in Toronto, Canada, by Random House of Canada, Limited. | *Vintage edition published September 12, 1955, second printing* | *May, 1962.* | Reprinted by arrangement with Alfred A. Knopf, Inc. | MANUFACTURED IN THE UNITED STATES OF AMERICA'.

Copies: INS (rebound, preserving front and back covers), STW.

A14.3 Later impression (n.d.)

Identical to the second impression except for changes to copyright page, colophon, and binding. The text on the copyright page appears in the top half of the page; the copyright symbol '©' appears before the date '1955' rather than before the word 'Copyright'; and the two lines of printing history have been omitted. The colophon omits the paper manufacturer. On the front cover, the book number and price have been changed to read 'Vintage Book V-24 $1.45'; on the back, the word 'LITERATURE' has been added at the upper left. Copy: IEN (rebound, preserving front and back covers).

A15 1961

Selected Poems of Thomas Hardy

On 20 May 1938, Ransom wrote Allen Tate: "For the time being I have gratified an old impulse and written to Macmillan (as the copyright holders) to see if they want an anthology of Hardy, with a critical introduction. It's a shame that he is accessible to unacquainted students only through his *Complete Poems*, and some very bad general anthology selections, and no decent criticism at all. Haven't heard from them yet" (*SL* 241). Then, on 28 May 1938, Ransom informed Tate of the result of his proposal: "Your cynicism is amply justified in the matter of Macmillan's wanting to publish Hardy freshly and intelligently—though the last adjective may seem to beg the question on my part. To tickle your vanity as a prophet I enclose the letter of the young man who wrote me. His name is not even included on the stationery of the house, though I observe he rates a secretary, or at least some of her time" (*SL* 242). Ransom's "old impulse" endured, and on 24 April 1961 Macmillan published Ransom's edition of 127 of Hardy's poems, along with an introduction that is a variant version of his essay on Hardy that had appeared the previous year in *Kenyon Review*. Macmillan issued the book in both cloth and paper binding. After this initial impression, the book went through at least 10 impressions in paperback under Macmillan's Collier Books imprint. Ransom evidently also received and may have signed a Collier Books contract, dated 11 April 1962, for a volume entitled *Selected Poems of Tennyson* (STW), but he did not in fact complete such an edition.

A15.a(1) Macmillan impression, cloth-bound issue (1961)

Selected Poems | *of* | [swash T] *Thomas Hardy* | [flourish] | EDITED | AND WITH AN INTRODUCTION BY | JOHN CROWE RANSOM | THE MACMILLAN COMPANY | NEW YORK *1961*

Copyright page (iv): '© The Macmillan Company 1960, 1961 | [acknowledgments and reservation of rights in 11 lines] | First Printing | Printed in the United States of America | Library of Congress catalog card number: 61-7054'.

209 x 138 mm. *1-3*^{16} *4*^{6} *5-6*^{16}; 86 leaves. *i-iv* v-xxxiii *xxxiv-xxxvi* 1-131 *132* 133-134 *135-136* pp.

i half title '*Selected Poems* | *of* | [swash T] *Thomas Hardy*'; ii blank; iii title page; iv copyright page; v-viii 'CONTENTS'; ix-xxxiii 'INTRODUCTION' (ending 'JOHN CROWE RANSOM'); xxxiv blank; xxxv bastard title identical to half title; xxxvi blank; 1-131 text of poems; 132 blank; 133-134 'INDEX OF TITLES'; 135-136 blank.

Ransom's introduction is a variant version of his essay "Thomas Hardy's Poems, and the Religious Difficulties of a Naturalist," *Kenyon Review* Spring 1960 (C342). According to the introduction, Ransom selected 125 poems from Hardy's *Collected Poems* and 2 poems from the posthumous *Winter Words*.

Type-page 38 lines, 166 (174) x 105 mm, 10 lines = 43 mm (e.g., p. xx); typeface Caledonia with 3.5 mm face, 1.7 mm x-height. No running titles; pagination centered in the direction line. White wove paper, no watermark, sheets bulk 12 mm.

Bound in black calico cloth over boards stamped in silver. Front: '*Selected Poems* | *of* | [swash T] *Thomas Hardy*'. Spine, running down: 'RANSOM [flourish] *Selected Poems of* [swash T] *Thomas Hardy* [identical flourish reversed] MACMILLAN'. Back: blank. White wove endpapers. Top and bottom edges cut; fore-edge trimmed.

Dust jacket of white paper printed with a dark grayish yellow (91) background on front and spine and with lettering and designs in black, white, and moderate red (15). Front: '[thick, black, rectangular frame within which are three contiguous frames of stippled black and to the right of which is a thick vertical line of red] | [white] *Selected Poems* | *of Thomas Hardy* | EDITED BY | JOHN CROWE RANSOM'. Spine: '[the rectangular frame extends from the front and its left side is extended down the spine] | [on a panel of red] [black] RANSOM [white] SELECTED POEMS OF THOMAS HARDY [black] MACMILLAN'. Back: list of other '*Poetry from Macmillan*' (from Hardy's *Collected Poems* to Vachel Lindsay's *Collected Poems*). Front flap: price ('$4.50'), blurb, jacket design credit to Riki Levinson. Back flap: 20-line biographical note on Ransom

Copies: ICU, IDeKN, IU, STW (2 copies, including one inscribed to Robert Penn Warren in June 1961 with jacket), WBB.

Published at $4.50 on 24 April 1961; copyright registration A498468. Listed in "Weekly Record," *Publishers' Weekly* 22 May 1961: 64. Advertised in *College English* April 1961: n.p., in *American Literature* May 1961: n.p., and in *Kenyon Review* Summer 1961: [iv] as "now available" and "long-awaited."

Reviewed in *Criticism* (Wayne State UP) Spring 1962: 162-165 (James Wright); *Library Journal* 1 April 1961: 1468 (Burton A. Robie); *Booklist* 1 September 1961: 15; *Prairie Schooner* Winter 1962-63: 371-372 (Marjorie Leafdale Loehlin).

A15a.1(2) First Macmillan impression, paperbound issue (1961)

The paperbound issue is otherwise identical to the hardbound except that the leaves measure 209 x 135 mm and that in place of the printing notice are the words 'Macmillan Paperbacks Edition 1961'.

Perfect bound in white paper printed with a dark grayish yellow (91) background with lettering and designs in black, white, and moderate red (15). Front: identical to that of the jacket of the hardbound issue, except that above the rectangular frame appears '[black] $2.25 MACMILLAN PAPERBACKS [white script] mp'. Spine: '[the rectangular frame extends from the front and its left side is extended down the spine] [reddish orange on black] RANSOM [white on black] SELECTED POEMS OF THOMAS HARDY [grayish yellow] MACMILLAN [running across at the foot in black on grayish yellow] [script] mp | [roman] 57'. Back: quotation from Ransom's introduction in 8 lines, 7-line blurb, cover design credit (to Riki Levinson), design like that on front but with red line at the left. No endpapers. Edges cut.

Copies: CSA, STW.

Published at $2.25, evidently simultaneously with the hardbound copies.

A15.b1 First Collier Books impression (1966)

Selected Poems | *of* | [swash T] *Thomas Hardy* | [flourish] | EDITED | AND WITH AN INTRODUCTION BY | JOHN CROWE RANSOM | COLLIER BOOKS, NEW YORK

Copyright page (iv): '© The Macmillan Publishing Company 1960, 1961 | [reservation of rights in 6 lines] | [LC catalog card number] | First Collier Books Edition 1966 | [acknowledgments in 6 lines] | The Macmillan Company, New York | Printed in the United States of America'.

203 x 134 mm. Two additional blank leaves appear at the end; otherwise, this impression is identical to the Macmillan hardbound impression in collation and pagination. Printed by offset from the typesetting of the hardbound impression, without reduction or enlargement of the type-page. White wove paper; no watermark; sheets bulk 11 mm.

Perfect bound in white paper printed with a vivid yellow (82) background and with lettering and design in black and white. Front: '[within a frame of two black rules, a white rule, and another black rule] [on a black rectangle] [white] $2.25 | [white open-face type] SELECTED POEMS OF | [yellow, not open] THOMAS HARDY | [ornament] | [white open-face] EDITED BY | [yellow, not open] JOHN CROWE RANSOM | [on yellow] [oval black-and-white photograph of Hardy within a black oval frame] | [black] 125 representative works by the last of the great Victorians | and the brooding precursor of modern poetry'. Spine: '[running across] [Collier device of a C containing a globe-like design] | [running down] [open face] RANSOM [not open] SELECTED POEMS OF THOMAS HARDY 07049'. Back: '[within rule frames like those on the front] POETRY | [open face] THE SEARCH FOR | AN UNKNOWN GOD' followed by an ornament, 31-line blurb, Collier device and imprint, book number. No endpapers. Edges cut.

Copies: CSA, STW.

A15.b2 Second Collier Books impression (1968)

Added to the copyright page: '*2nd Printing 1968*'. On the back cover, the publisher's address ('866 THIRD AVENUE, NEW YORK, NEW YORK 10022') is added, and the book number omitted. Copy: CSA.

A15.b3 Third Collier Books impression (1969)

Omits city from title page and copyright page, and adds '*Third Printing 1969*' to copyright page. Copy: INS (rebound, preserving covers).

A15.b4 Fourth Collier Books impression
Not seen.

A15.b5 Fifth Collier Books impression (1972)

Publisher's imprint on title page reads: 'COLLIER BOOKS, NEW YORK, NEW YORK'. Changes printing notice on copyright page (to 'FIFTH PRINTING 1972') and adds publisher's address. Copy: INS (rebound, preserving covers).

A15.b6-9 Sixth-ninth Collier Books impressions
Not seen.

A15.b10 Tenth Collier Books impression (n.d.)

Publisher's imprint on title-page reads: 'COLLIER BOOKS | *Macmillan Publishing Company* | NEW YORK'. Copyright page (iv): '© Macmillan Publishing Company | a division of Macmillan, Inc., 1960, 1961 | [reservation of rights in 6 lines] | [LC catalog card number] | First Collier Books Edition 1966 | 17 16 15 14 13 12 11 10 | ISBN 0-02-070490-9 | [acknowledgments in 6 lines] | Macmillan Publishing Company | 866 Third Avenue, New York, N.Y. 10022 | Printed in the United States of America'.

202 x 135 mm. Added to p. 132 are three additional stanzas of Hardy's "New Year's Eve" that the Macmillan impression and the 1st, 2nd, 3rd, 4th (probably), and 5th and posssibly other earlier Collier impressions had omitted from p. 32, where there is now also a note to that effect. A misprint in the earlier impressions has been corrected: at p. 6, line 3, 'unfingered, with,' has been corrected to 'upfingered, with'. Sheets bulk 12 mm.

The binding closely resembles that of the 5th impression, except that no price appears on the front, the Collier device is a circle containing a dot, the partial ISBN number does not appear on the spine, the inner black rule frame is absent on the back, the price appears on the back at the upper right ('>> $8.95'), a line reading 'Macmillan Publishing Company' appears before the address on the back, and 'ISBN 0-02-070490-9' is running down at the lower right on the back.

Copy: CSA.

SELECTED POEMS

John Crowe Ransom

A REVISED AND ENLARGED EDITION

New York · Alfred · A · Knopf

1963

Title page:
A16.1 ***Selected Poems,*** **1963**

A16 1963

Selected Poems, revised and enlarged

When Ransom revised his poems for *Poems and Essays* (A14), his editor at Vintage, Harry Ford, asked him whether he would like the changes to be incorporated in the 1945 edition of *Selected Poems* (A12) when it was reprinted (10 July 1955, TxU). As it turned out, though, there was no revised printing of that edition. On 13 September 1961, an internal memorandum at Knopf, from Lucy DeMaine to Sidney Jacobs, indicated plans for a new printing, but DeMaine noted that the Vintage "corrections" had not been made in the *Selected Poems* plates and that making them would seem "to involve a great deal of trouble" for a printing of 1,000 copies. Earlier, on 14 July, William Koshland had written another editor at Knopf, William T. Loverd, that a visit to a library had turned up only one new poem by Ransom since 1945 or 1946 but a great deal of criticism. He suggested approaching Ransom about the possibility of a new book of essays or possibly a new collection of poems (TxU). During October 1961, then, there was a series of letters between Koshland and Ransom about these prospects (TxU). In a letter to Tate on 21 October 1961, Ransom said that Knopf had asked "for a new book of essays, or another *Poems and Essays* if I have a further version of the poems." He explained that he had promised himself "to bring [his] selection of poems up to 50, adding a few others (revised vitally) of the old ones" and perhaps adding "two or three new ones" (*SL* 403, where this letter is conjecturally dated 1960 rather than 1961).

With plans for a revised edition of some sort, the new printing of the 1945 *Selected Poems* was not made, and the edition would remain out of stock. Reminded by Koshland that he was to supply new text, Ransom wrote on 12 March 1962 that he had been "starting fresh on some new verse," and he enclosed "Master's in the Garden Again" as an "exercise" that produced "a new poem out of an old one more than a revision of the old one" (the old one being "Conrad in Twilight"). He told Koshland that he would like to take the rest of the year to assemble 50 or so poems for "a definitive edition" (TxU). In October Knopf learned that Ransom was to be awarded a $5,000 fellowship from the Academy of American Poets for distinguished poetic achievement, the announcement of which was to be made in December. That fact added urgency to the plans for a new edition. Congratulating Ransom for the award on 31 October, Koshland again reminded Ransom that he was to supply a new manuscript for a "definitive selected or collected volume of verse and miscellaneous material." He raised the possibility of reprinting the old edition if Ransom could not meet his December deadline (TxU). In reply on 12 November, Ransom proposed what in effect would be a sort of compromise between reprinting the old edition and publishing a definitive edition. He would have revisions and a few additions (TxU).

In preparing this new manuscript, Ransom used *Poems & Essays*, which, he wrote Koshland on 5 December 1962, "contains the best versions of the old poems" (TxU). The Knopf manuscript-record form for the new edition indicates that the manuscript was received on 11 December and was read by Judith B. Jones, who would see the book through the press (TxU). Ransom continued to add new material—for example sending the poem "Hilda," which Jones inserted by retrieving from production the setting copy. When Ransom returned page proofs (there were no galleys) on 17 March 1963, he explained that he had omitted the last stanza of "The Vanity of the Bright Young Men" ("as introducing too much special history"); he asked for the addition of "Old Man Pondered," on page 68 if possible; he sent a new version of "Prelude to an Evening"; and he called for more spacing between the three "movements" of "Master's in the Garden Again" (TxU). A strike by the printers at Kingsport Press gave Jones time to have these changes made. And Ransom continued to request changes, notably to the poem "*Agitato ma non troppo*," until 15 April, when Jones wrote him that this was "positively the last correction" to be allowed (TxU). On 17 June, Ransom wrote Koshland that he was "much pleased" with the book; his poems, he said, "do *look* well in that lovely type and page-form" (TxU). (It was an entirely new setting of type, not a revision of the 1945 setting.) The publisher's "planning card" for the book set advance distribution at 500 copies and projected twelve-month sales to be between 500 and 1,000 copies with a later prospect of slow, steady sales until the copies were exhausted. Evidently unaware of the extent of Ransom's revisions and not anticipating the notice the book would receive, whoever prepared the planning card noted that the list of review copies was to be kept down because, it said, the book was not "new" except for the addition of a prose piece and two revised poems. Initially the plan called for an impression of only 1,500 copies, but this figure was later doubled. The book was published on 21 June 1963. As was announced on 10 March 1964, the book won the National Book Award for poetry. There were two additional impressions in that year. There was no English edition or impression.

A16.1 First impression (1963)

SELECTED | POEMS | John Crowe Ransom | [abstract leaf design] | [76 mm slightly swelled rule] | A REVISED AND ENLARGED EDITION | [Borzoi device] | [capitals in swash] *New York* • *Alfred* • [no swash] *A* • *Knopf* | 1963

Copyright page (iv): 'L. C. catalog card number: 63-12791 | [50 mm swelled rule] | THIS IS A BORZOI BOOK, | PUBLISHED BY ALFRED A. KNOPF, INC. | [50 mm swelled rule] | Copyright 1924, 1927, 1934, 1939, 1945, © 1962, | 1963 by Alfred A. Knopf, Inc. All rights reserved. | No part of this book may be reproduced in any | form without permission in writing from the pub- | lisher, except by a reviewer, who may quote brief | passages in a review to be printed in a magazine or | newspaper. Manufactured in the United States of | America, and distributed by Random House, Inc. | Published simultaneously in Toronto, Canada, by | Random House of Canada, Limited. | Published June 11, 1945 | Reprinted June 1952 | Second edition, revised, enlarged, reset, | and printed from new plates, June 1963'.

Colophon (112): '[capitals in swash] *A Note on the Type* | [no swash] THIS BOOK is set in ELECTRA, a Linotype face de- | signed by W. A. Dwiggins (1880-1956). This face | cannot be classified as either modern or old-style. It | is not based on any historical model, nor does it | echo any particular period or style. It avoids the ex- | treme contrasts between thick and thin elements | that mark most modern faces, and attempts to give | a feeling of fluidity, power, and speed. | *Composed, printed, and bound by* | *Kingsport Press, Inc., Kingsport, Tennessee.* | *Binding based on an original design* | *by W. A. Dwiggins.* | *Typography by Vincent Torre* | [leaf ornament]'.

212 x 136 mm. *1-8*^{8}; 64 leaves. [2] *i-iv* v *vi* vii *viii* *1-2* 3-110 *111-118* pp.

1 blank; 2 '[swash capital] *New* [no swash] *Poetry from Knopf'*, listing 6 books (from John Logan's *Spring of the Thief* to *Six Poets of Modern Greece*); i half title 'SELECTED POEMS'; ii blank; iii title page; iv copyright page; v-vi 'Preface'; vii-viii 'Contents'; 1 bastard title 'SELECTED POEMS'; 2 blank; 3-111 text; 112 colophon; 113 '[capitals in swash] *A Note about the Author*' (dated '*May 1963*'); 114-118 blank.

This edition contains all the poems present in the 1945 *Selected Poems* (A12), many of them revised. Ransom says in his preface that he has added, "at the places where they seem to belong chronologically," a few poems from his earlier volumes. Actually, one of the added poems, "Old Man Pondered," had never been collected in one of his volumes. It had first appeared in *Saturday Review* in 1929 (C172) and had had its first book publication in Louis Untermeyer's 1930 *Modern American Poetry* (B16) Ransom also adds at the end two reworkings of earlier poems, the last accompanied by a commentary on its revision. In this listing, those poems preceded by an asterisk have been added:

Winter Remembered
Miriam Tazewell
Dead Boy
Spectral Lovers
**Agitato ma non troppo*
Necrological
Bells for John Whiteside's Daughter
The Tall Girl
*First Travels of Max
Good Ships
Emily Hardcastle, Spinster
Parting at Dawn
Vaunting Oak
*In Process of a Noble Alliance
Spiel of the Three Mountebanks
Here Lies a Lady
*Hilda
Janet Waking
Lady Lost
Two in August
*Persistent Explorer
*Morning [Jane awoke Ralph so gently on one morning]
Somewhere Is Such a Kingdom
*Old Man Pondered
Antique Harvesters
Our Two Worthies
Puncture
Dog
Man without Sense of Direction
Survey of Literature
The Equilibrists

The Vanity of the Bright Young Men [earlier entitled "Tom, Tom, the Piper's Son"]
Conrad in Twilight
Armageddon
*Prometheus in Straits
Judith of Bethulia
Blue Girls
Philomela
Old Man Playing with Children
Captain Carpenter
Old Mansion
Piazza Piece
Eclogue
*Vision by Sweetwater
Her Eyes
Parting, without a Sequel
Prelude to an Evening
What Ducks Require [the order of this and the previous poem has been reversed]
Of Margaret
Painted Head
Address to the Scholars of New England
*Master's in the Garden Again [revision of "Con- in Twilight"]
*Prelude to an Evening [revised and explicated]

Type-page 35 lines, 161 (168) x 88 mm, 10 lines = 46 mm (e.g., p. 110); typeface Electra with 3.7 mm face, 1.8 mm x-height. Poem titles (e.g., 'Captain Carpenter') centered and above an 88 mm slightly swelled rule. No running titles. Pagination at the outer margin of the direction line. White laid paper with vertical chainlines 30 mm apart, watermark '*Utopian*', sheets bulk 10 mm.

Bound in blackish blue (188) calico cloth over boards stamped in gold on front and spine. Front: '*SELECTED POEMS* | *JOHN CROWE RANSOM*'. Spine: '[running down] *SELECTED POEMS* [pinnate leaf ornament] *JOHN CROWE RANSOM* [running across] *Knopf*'. Back: Borzoi device blind-stamped in relief. White wove endpapers. Top edge cut, fore-edge rough trimmed, bottom edge trimmed. Top edge stained brilliant yellow (83).

Dust jacket of white paper with lettering and design in white and dark blue (183) on a background of moderate blue (182) on front, spine, and back. Front: '[dark blue] SELECTED POEMS BY | [white] JOHN CROWE RANSOM | [petal-like design extending onto spine and back] | [dark blue] A REVISED AND ENLARGED EDITION [Borzoi device]'. Spine, running down: '[white] JOHN

CROWE RANSOM SELECTED POEMS [dark blue] ALFRED • A • KNOPF'. Back: text of "Piazza Piece" in dark blue, Borzoi device in white, publisher in dark blue. Front flap: '[dark blue on white] $4.00 | S.P.J.C.R. | A.A.K. | [petal-like design in moderate blue] | [13-line blurb in dark blue] | [moderate blue] JACKET DESIGN BY HERBERT BAYER | 6/63'. Back flap: photograph of Ransom attributed to James R. Deaver, 17-line biographical blurb in dark blue, '[running up from the foot, in moderate blue] PRINTED IN U.S.A.'

Copies: CSA (with jacket), ICU, IEN, IRo (with jacket), IU, InU-Lilly (with jacket), InU, OGK, STW (4 copies in jackets, including one with Ransom's undated inscription to Robert Penn Warren and Warren's annotations and another dated 17 June 1963), TxU-HRC (with jacket), WBB, WU (2 copies, 1 with jacket).

Published at $4.00 on 21 June 1963; copyright registration A634352. Undated publicity and production forms in the Knopf archive note a total of 1,500 copies of the first impression, but a "planning card" dated 20 February 1963 has that figure crossed out and 3,000 written in its place (TxU).

Advertised in *Kenyon Review* Autumn 1963: 564. *Kenyon Review* Winter 1964: 1 carried a full-page advertisement of this "extensively revised and enlarged edition," the publication of which "coincides with the 25th anniversary of this review which he founded in 1939"; this issue also includes an unsigned tribute to Ransom by Robie Macauley (p. 23) as well as "a collection of new writing by his old friends."

Announced in *Saturday Review* 8 February 1964: 28 and *Publishers' Weekly* 2 March 1964: 16 as one of the "leading contenders" for the National Book Awards. In the category for poetry, Ransom's *Selected Poems* appeared along with volumes by W. S. Merwin, Louis Simpson, May Swenson, and Mark Van Doren. The judges for this category are listed as Jean Garrigue, Anthony Hecht, and John Hall Wheelock. The winners, Ransom among them, were officially announced on 10 March; see *New York Times* 11 March 1964: 36, *Publishers' Weekly* 185 (16 March 1964): 10 and 28, *Publishers' Weekly* 185 (23 March 1964): 21-25, this last item quoting from Ransom's acceptance speech.

The full text of the speech appeared in *Sewanee Review* (see C350).

Reviewed in *Library Journal* July 1963: 2709 (Ray Smith); *Christian Science Monitor* 1 August 1963: 11 (Philip Booth); *New Leader* 5 August 1963: 17-18 (Stanley Edgar Hyman); *New York Herald Tribune Books* 11 August 1963: 6 (Stephen Stepanchev); *Sewanee Review* October-December 1963: 642-644 (Roger Hecht); *New York Review of Books* 31 October 1963: 8-9 (G. S. Fraser); *Saturday Review of Literature* 1 February 1964: 36-37 (Robert D. Spector); *Time* 3 April 1964: 102 (also on Ransom's receiving the National Book Award); *Booklist* 15 April 1964: 780; *Minnesota Review* Winter 1964: 272-275 (Michael Balzer); *Southern Review* Spring 1966: 453-463 (Thornton H. Parsons).

A16.2 Second impression (1964)

Differs from the first impression in the following points. The title-page date is '1964'. Added to the copyright page: 'Second Printing, April 1964'. The printer's imprint is omitted from the colophon. Leaf measures 212 x 138 mm. Paper is wove, without watermark. Dust jacket of pale yellow (89) paper, with same lettering and design as the first impression but with yellow replacing white and light blue replacing moderate blue. There is an uncorrected misprint in line 14 of "Dog" (p. 77): 'years'. Copies: IDeK (with jacket), STW (with jacket), TNV.

A16.3 Third impression (1964)

The British Library catalogue lists a copy of a third printing dated 1964. Not seen. A Knopf production form dated 12 December 1966 indicates that the last "run," or impression, of the book had been made on 28 July 1964 and had consisted of 1,820 copies. It also notes that as of the date of the form, there were 904 copies still on hand (TxU).

A 17 **1965**

The Poets Go Along

This brief tribute to Alfred A. Knopf was printed in 1965 by Harry Duncan at the Cummington Press for a collection of keepsakes by various presses. Duncan sent proofs to Ransom on 12 February 1965, adding "You still haven't let me know whether you might use some copies" (STW). The collection of keepsakes was completed by 29 June 1965, when Duncan wrote Ransom that Charles Antin had delayed its distribution because of Knopf's illness (STW).

JOHN CROWE RANSOM | THE POETS GO ALONG

Colophon (8): 'Cloister Old Style type on Rives paper. | The Cummington Press: West Branch, Iowa.'

177 x 113 mm. *1*^{4}; 4 leaves. *1-8* pp.

1 title; 2 blank; 3-7 text of Ransom's tribute to Alfred A. Knopf; 8 colophon.

Type-page 25 lines, 105 x 62 mm, 10 lines = 38 mm (e.g., p. 4); typeface Cloister Old Style, with 4 mm face, 1.7 mm x-height. The text begins with a moderate reddish orange (37) open capital 2 lines deep. No running titles or pagination. White wove paper, watermark 'RIVES', sheets bulk 1 mm.

The initial and terminal leaves of this twice folded sheet serve as its "wrappers." The top edge is unopened. The keepsake was issued, together with other keepsakes by 49 small presses, in a dark reddish purple (242) box, 288 x 124 x 22 mm, with a label of white paper printed in deep purplish red (256) and wrapped around the spine. Front: 'A *KEEPSAKE* | for | Alfred • A • Knopf | *Written and printed* | *by various hands* | *celebrating his* | *fiftieth year as a* | *book publisher* | 1965'. Spine: title between two ornaments. Back: '1915 [within a circular device, in white on red] BORZOI | BOOKS | [borzoi] | FIFTY | YEARS [to the right of the device, in red] 1965'. The first keepsake in the box bears the same wording as the front of the box and contains a foreword by Charles Antin, who arranged for the portfolio of keepsakes and asked each press to provide 150 copies of its contribution.

Copies: ICN, STW (Ransom's copy with 2 letters from the printer, Harry Duncan, laid in), TxU HRC (seen in photocopy). The collection of keepsakes is listed in *Private Press Books 1965* (1966): 48. For a brief history and a checklist of Cummington Press, see Mary L. Richmond's "The Cummington Press," where *The Poets Go Along* is listed as item 76. The text of Ransom's tribute also appeared in *Portrait of a Publisher* (D263).

A18 **1969**

Selected Poems, third edition

On 10 August 1966, almost precisely three years before it would see publication, Ransom wrote William Koshland at Knopf to say that he was thinking of a new *Selected Poems,* "a final Selected volume" (TxU). Aside from Koshland's 19 August letter thanking Ransom for the good news, however, I have found no exchange of letters for the rest of 1966 or for 1967 relating to a new edition. In the Knopf archive is a form showing that a fifth printing of the 1945 *Selected Poems* (1,820 copies) had been run on 28 July 1964 and that as of the end of November 1966, the publisher still had on hand 1,160 copies and as of the end of 7 May 1967, 904 copies (TxU). (The form is misleading in that it does not take account of the new typesetting for the 1963 edition. Thus its reference to the fifth impression of the 1945 edition actually applies to the third impression of the 1963 edition.) At any rate, the publisher may not have been eager to produce another edition at that time. On 24 February 1968, Ransom again wrote Koshland, saying that he was at work on a "final" edition of his poems, which he planned in three parts: "Apprentice Poems" including some from *Poems about God* and some from *Chills and Fever*; "Fugitive Poems" from the early 1920s; and "Late or Later Poems," which Ransom called "some of my best" and which would also include some rewritten Fugitive poems. He also wanted to add his explication of the revision of "Conrad in Twilight." He supposed that he could get a completed manuscript to Koshland by early summer (TxU).

His letter was answered by Judith B. Jones, who told him that she would be his editor for the new book (19 March 1968, TNV). There followed a fruitful correspondence in which Jones played an important role in developing the edition. She suggested that the edition contain both original and revised forms of the poems and commentary on the changes (2 and 20 August 1968), and she had queries (e.g., on 17 October) that Ransom considered in his commentaries and revision (TxU). This revision also delayed publication. Ransom sent Jones portions of the manuscript and then wanted them returned for further revision. On 28 August, for example, he asked her to return the eight pairings of old and new versions because he was "distinctly in a changing and bettering mood" (TxU). On the Editorial Fact Sheet she prepared on 15 November 1968, Jones had projected a publication date of April 1969 (perhaps to coincide with Ransom's 81st birthday), but at some point that date was canceled and replaced by May; on the publicity review list, a publication date of 22 May is canceled and replaced by 21 July (TxU). Finally, on 30 December 1968, Jones was able to acknowledge receipt of the final section of the manuscript (TxU). On 6 January 1969, though, Ransom was still offering revisions, especially on the spacing of "*Agitato ma non troppo,*" and he asked for the same "modernized Caslon type" as had been used for *Two Gentlemen in Bonds*. Jones sent Ransom page proofs (there were no galleys) on 15 April, suggesting that Ransom might want to add commentary on the visual arrangement of "Agitato," and asking for return of the proofs by 25 April to meet a tight schedule (TxU). On 22 May Jones told Ransom that his proof corrections were good and that she was able to have the printer incorporate his "latest touching up" of "Agitato" (TxU). (Cecelia Lampp Linton's dissertation, "A Textual Variorum of John Crowe Ransom's *Selected Poems*, 1969," usefully presents textual variants in printed appearances of each poem in the 1969 edition, although the record of variants is incomplete because Linton did not examine all authoritative or possibly authoritative appearances of each poem.)

The new edition was finally published on 4 August 1969. The British sub-edition was published in January 1970 by Eyre & Spottiswoode. Writing to Ransom on 29 January 1970, Koshland said that copies of it had just arrived and that he was sending a batch on to him, pointing out that, as was customary, Knopf had had sheets printed for Eyre & Spottiswoode, which then had the sheets bound and jacketed in England (TNV).

Ransom did not see the new edition as final after all. On 31 December 1970, he wrote Jones to ask if there were any chance of "a Fourth and Final Edition" that would contain 80 poems. He had, he explained, gone back and revised some of "the lesser poems" from his earlier editions, taken four poems ("quite refurbished") from *Poems about God*, rewritten poems from the 1969 edition, and discarded the prose commentary except for a few appended items of explanation (TxU). Jones replied on 13 January 1971 that she would be interested in seeing what he had done but also that no new edition could be published until the old had been sold out, probably in two years (TxU). Before Ransom's death on 3 July 1974, some of the revised and refurbished poems did appear in periodicals (see C363, C364, C365). And in

1976 the possibility of a new edition was again raised. On 29 November 1976, Jones wrote to Helen Forman, Ransom's daughter, that in his last year, Ransom had sent 30 or so poems that would either make a new book or a new section of the previous one. She explained that after considerable correspondence she had put together a manuscript and, she thought, had returned it to him for a final look. Jones asked Forman if she could retrieve the manuscript and if she would approve of Robert Lowell's guiding, selecting, and putting his name to the new collection, Lowell having already agreed to the project (TNV). This edition never appeared.

In 1978, the book being out of print at Knopf, a photo-offset reprinting was issued in paperback by Ecco Press. In 1991, Knopf brought the book back into print, publishing a fifth impression in a redesigned binding and dust jacket (letter, Judith B. Jones, Knopf, 14 September 1995). That same year, in England, Carcanet Press issued a reprinting in paperback.

A18.a1 First Knopf impression (1969)

John Crowe Ransom | [ornament] | Selected Poems | Alfred A. Knopf New York 1969 | [Borzoi device] [on facing page] Third Edition, Revised and Enlarged

Copyright page (iv): 'THIS IS A BORZOI BOOK | PUBLISHED BY ALFRED A. KNOPF, INC. | Copyright 1924, 1927, 1934, 1939, 1945, | © 1962, 1963, 1969 by Alfred A. Knopf, Inc. | Copyright renewed 1952, 1954 by John Crowe Ransom | [reservation of rights and notice of simultaneous publication in Canada by Random House and of distribution by Random House] | Library of Congress Catalog Card Number: 69-14732 | First published June 1945, reprinted June 1952. | Second edition revised, enlarged, reset, and printed | from new plates, June 1963, reprinted May 1964 and September 1964. | Third edition newly revised, enlarged, reset, and | printed from new plates, July 1969. | Manufactured in the United States of America'.

Colophon (163): 'A Note on the Type | This book was set in Monticello, a Linotype revival of the | original Roman No. 1 cut by Archibald Binny and cast in | 1796 by the Philadelphia Type foundry Binny & Ronald- | son. The face was named Monticello in honor of its use in | the monumental fifty-volume *Papers of Thomas Jefferson,* | published by Princeton University Press. Monticello is a | transitional type design, embodying certain features of | Bulmer and Baskerville, but it is a distinguished face in | its own right. | The book was composed, printed, and bound by Kingsport | Press, Inc., Kingsport, Tennessee. Typography and bind- | ing design by Betty Anderson.'

228 x 151 mm. *1-4*^{16} *5*^{8} *6*^{16}; 88 leaves. [4] *i-iv* v-viii *1-2* 3-34 *35-36* 37-92 *93-94* 95-106 *107-108* 109-159 *160-164* pp.

1-4 blank; i half title 'Selected Poems'; ii 'Third Edition, Revised and Enlarged'; iii title page; iv copyright page; v-viii 'Contents'; 1 part title 'The Innocent Doves'; 2 blank; 3-34 text; 35 part title 'The Manliness of Men'; 36 blank; 37-92 text; 93 part title 'Two Gentlemen in Bonds | (in twelve sonnets)'; 94 blank; 95-106 text; 107 part title 'Sixteen Poems in Eight Pairings | with original and final versions studied comparatively'; 108 blank; 109-159 text; 160 blank; 161 'A Note About the Author | John Crowe Ransom | [note in 11 lines]'; 162 blank; 163 colophon; 164 blank.

For this edition, Ransom has revised poems from the previous edition, deleted two poems ("In Process of a Noble Alliance" and "Old Man Pondered"), added poems from his early volumes, reorganized the order of presentation, and provided commentary for revisions of paired poems. In his sixteen pairings of "original" and "final" versions of poems, the so-called originals are for the most part not originals, their texts having been revised since first publication. Indeed, some of that revision evidently took place for this edition, so that Ransom presents as pairs revised "originals" and revisions of the revised originals. It should be noted that in his preface to these pairings, Ransom refers to them as "pairings or couplings of poems," not as pairings of variant texts or even versions of the same poem. In the following listing, poems not present (in some form) in the 1963 edition are preceded by an asterisk.

[Under the part title "The Innocent Doves"]

Miriam Tazewell
Spectral Lovers
*The Rose
*Moments of Minnie
Somewhere Is Such a Kingdom

Bells for John Whiteside's Daughter
The Tall Girl
Piazza Piece
Lady Lost
Blue Girls
Janet Waking
Eclogue
Vaunting Oak
Two in August
Emily Hardcastle, Spinster
Parting at Dawn
Good Ships
*Romance of a Youngest Daughter
Vision by Sweetwater
*April Treason
Judith of Bethulia
Her Eyes
Parting, without a Sequel
Hilda

[Under the part title "The Manliness of Men"]

Winter Remembered
Dead Boy
First Travels of Max
Necrological
Captain Carpenter
Spiel of Three Mountebanks [previously "Spiel of the Three Mountebanks"]
*Nocturne
Dog
*Blackberry Winter
Armageddon
Old Man Playing with Children
Prometheus in Straits
Our Two Worthies
Philomela
*Crocodile
Survey of Literature
Old Mansion (After Henry James) [previously without parenthetical element]
*On the Road to Wockensutter (A Western)
Morning [Jane awoke Ralph so gently on one morning]
*Jack's Letter
Persistent Explorer
Puncture
Man without Sense of Direction
Antique Harvesters
The Equilibrists
To the Scholars of Harvard [previously "Address to the Scholars of New England"]
What Ducks Require
Painted Head

[Under the part title "Two Gentlemen in Bonds (In Twelve Sonnets)" and numbered I through XII]

*Pink and Pale
*Thinking, Drinking
*Epithalamion of a Peach
*In Bed Not Dead
*Primer for Statesmen
**Fait Accompli*

*Bad News
*L'état c'est moi
*Misanthrope
*Kingdom Come ["To an honest knight . . ."]
*Rain
*Injured Sire

[Under the part title "Sixteen Poems in Eight Pairings with Original and Final Versions Studied Comparatively," the pairs, accompanied by commentary, are numbered I through VIII, and within each pair the "original" is designated *A* and the "final" version designated *B*]

I *A* *Overtures, *B* *Two Gentlemen Scholars (A Pastoral)

II *A* Conrad Sits in Twilight [previously also "Conrad in Twilight"], *B* Master's in the Garden Again

III *A* Agitato man non troppo, *B* Agitato ma non troppo

IV *A* Tom, Tom, the Piper's Son, *B* The Vanity of the Bright Boys [previously "The Vanity of the Bright Young Men"]

V *A* *Semi-Centennial, *B* *Birthday of an Aging Seer

VI *A* Here Lies a Lady, *B* Here Lies a Lady

VII *A* Of Margaret, *B* Of Margaret

VIII *A* Prelude to an Evening, *B* Prelude to an Evening

Type-page 38 lines, 175 (185) x 109 mm, 10 lines = 46 mm (e.g., p. 116); typeface Monticello with 3.8 mm face, 1.8 mm x-height (but Bell typeface for half title, title page, table of contents, part titles, and poem titles). Beneath the poem titles (e.g., 'Miriam Tazewell') is a 63 mm swelled rule. No running titles; pagination centered in the direction line. White laid paper with vertical chainlines 23 mm apart; watermark 'WARREN'S | OLDE STYLE'; sheets bulk 12 mm.

Bound in bluish gray (191) calico over boards. Front, stamped in dark gray (266): 'J | [ornament] | C | [ornament] | R'. Spine, stamped in silver: '[running down] Selected Poems [running across] [ornamented double rule] | Third | Edition | [ornament] | Knopf | [ornamented double rule] | [running down] John Crowe Ransom'. Back, stamped in dark gray: Borzoi device. Yellowish gray (93) endpapers. Top edge cut; fore- and bottom edges trimmed.

Dust jacket of white paper lettered in white, light blue (181), and strong yellowish green on a background of dark grayish blue (187) on front, spine, and back; in light blue and strong yellowish green on pale yellow (89) background on flaps. Front: '[script] [green] SELECTED | POEMS | [blue] JOHN | CROWE | RANSOM | [white] THIRD EDITION, REVISED AND ENLARGED'. Spine: '[script] [running down] [white] SELECTED POEMS | [green] THIRD EDITION, REVISED AND ENLARGED [Borzoi device running across] [blue, running down] ALFRED • A • KNOPF'. Back: photograph captioned '[blue] *John Crowe Ransom with his granddaughter'*. Front flap: price in green ('$5.00'); 30-line blurb in dark blue but beginning with a script capital 'W' in light blue; '[green] *Jacket design by Golda Fishbein*'. Back flap: Ransom's name in light blue script; 19-line biographical note in dark blue, publisher's device in green and imprint in light blue; and date ('8/69') in light blue.

Copies: ICU (with jacket), IDeKN, IEN, INS, IRo (with jacket), IU (2 copies), InU, OGK, STW (with jacket), TNV (Ransom's copy with autograph revisions), TxU-HRC (2 copies with jackets), WMM, WU (2 copies, 1 with jacket), WU-Col.

Published at $5.00 on 4 August 1969. Copyright registration A117815. The Knopf manuscript transmittal sheet, dated 16 January 1969, tentatively set the first impression at 4,000 copies (TxU).

Advertised in *Kenyon Review* 1969: 578. Listed in "Weekly Record," *Publishers' Weekly* 13 October 1969: 72. Reviewed in *Library Journal* July 1969: 2620 (Dorothy Curley); *Washington Post Book World* 7 September 1969: 9 (Chad Walsh); *Christian Science Monitor* 18 December 1969: 9 (Victor Howes); *Saturday Review* 17 January 1970: 34 (Robert Wallace); *Poetry* January 1971: 275-276 (Jerome Mazzaro).

A18.a2 Second Knopf impression (1973)

Differs from the first impression in the following points. On the copyright page, the printing history has been changed to read: 'Published June 1945. | Reprinted one time | Second edition revised, enlarged, reset, and printed | from new plates, June 1963. | Reprinted two times | Third edition newly revised, enlarged, reset, and | printed from new plates, July 1969. | Second printing, October 1973 | Manufactured in the United States of America'. (The title page, biographical note, and colophon are unchanged.)

The leaf measurement is 226 x 152 mm. The paper is laid, with chainlines 29 mm apart and without watermark; sheets bulk 14 mm.

Bound in medium gray (265) calico cloth. Top edge stained pale blue (185). On the front flap of the dust jacket the price is now '$5.95'. (The date on the back flap,'8/69', is unchanged.)

Copy: STW (A. R. Ammons's copy, dated spring 1974, with jacket).

A18.a3-4 Third and fourth Knopf impressions
Not seen.

A18.a5 Fifth Knopf impression (1991)

For this impression, the book's binding and jacket were redesigned, and there were other changes as well. The title page date reads '1991'. The copyright page adds Library of Congress cataloging-in-publication data, and replaces the earlier printing notice with 'Fifth printing, June 1991'. The colophon omits credit for manufacture and design.

225 x 145 mm. *1-3*^{16} *4*^{8} *5-6*^{16}. Pagination unchanged. Added to the recto of the second unpaginated leaf: 'Also by John Crowe Ransom | [rule] | Poems and Essays | Two Gentlemen in Bonds | Chills and Fever'. The note on Ransom (161) has been revised, chiefly to reflect his death in 1974 and to add this final sentence: 'Near the end of his life he | wrote that "intellectually there has

been no period of my life | happier than this late one, where I am in the verse patch | again.'" Otherwise, the contents are unchanged, without revision or resetting. White laid paper with vertical chainlines 20 mm apart; no watermark; sheets bulk 14 mm.

Bound in black calico cloth over boards. Front blank. Spine blind stamped, running down: '*John Crowe Ransom • Selected Poems* [ornament] *Knopf'*. Back, stamped in white: '[running down' R [running across] *Selected Poems* | [running down] ANSOM'. White endpapers. Edges trimmed.

Dust jacket of white translucent paper printed in black, strong red (12), light gray (264), and very light greenish blue (171). A panel of greenish blue extends from the front, around the spine, and onto the back. A red rule and gray rule extend across the whole width of the jacket, including the flaps. Front: SELECTED | [red rule] | POEMS | [gray rule] | JOHN | CROWE | RANSOM'. Spine: lettered like the binding but in red and with a borzoi replacing the ornament. Back: bar code and ISBN ('ISBN 0-679-40257-8') in black. Front flap, in black: 'FPT U.S.A. $22.00 | Canada $29.00 | [red rule] | This reissue of the work of one of the century's most | important and influential American poets introduces to a | new audience a major figure who was an inspiration to an | entire generation of American poets, as well as to such | contemporaries as Robert Graves and Robert Penn Warren. | [gray rule] | [16-line blurb including a quotation from Randall Jarrell]'. Back flap: biographical note on Ransom, jacket design credit (to Barbara de Wilde), publisher's imprint, date ('6/91'), borzoi.

Copies: CSA (2 copies, with jackets), IRo (with jacket), OGK (with jacket), STW (with jacket), TxU-HRC (with jacket).

A18.b Eyre & Spottiswoode impression (1970)

John Crowe Ransom | [ornament] | Selected Poems | Eyre & Spottiswoode : London [on facing page] Third Edition, Revised and Enlarged

Copyright page (iv): 'Copyright 1924, 1927, 1934, 1939, 1945, | © 1962, 1963, 1969 by Alfred A. Knopf, Inc. | First published in Great Britain 1970 | by Eyre & Spottiswoode (Publishers) Ltd. | 11 New Fetter Lane, EC4 | Printed in United States of America'.

223 x 139 mm. Collation, pagination, typography, and paper are identical to those of the first Knopf impression. The colophon, however, is omitted (leaving p. 163 blank).

Bound in black paper over boards, patterned to resemble calico cloth. Front and back blank. Spine stamped in gold: '[running down] SELECTED POEMS John Crowe Ransom [running across] E & S'. Yellowish gray (93) wove endpapers. Top and bottom edges cut; fore-edge trimmed.

Dust jacket of white paper printed in black, vivid greenish yellow (97), and strong green (141). Front: '[in black on a greenish yellow background enclosed by a green band and a black line] JOHN | CROWE | RANSOM | [102 mm rule] | Selected Poems | Third Edition, Revised and Enlarged'. Spine, running down: '[black] JOHN CROWE RANSOM Selected Poems | [running across] E&S'. Back: '[black] JOHN CROWE RANSOM | [greenish yellow rule, 101 mm] | [photograph of Ransom smoking a pipe]'. Front flap: 39-line blurb, 'PRICE NET | £2 | IN UK ONLY.' Back flap: 'Author's Photograph James R Deaver | [63 mm rule] | PRINTED IN GREAT BRITAIN'.

Copies: IRivfR (with jacket), STW (Donald Davie's copy with jacket and Ransom's copy with autograph revisions), TxU-HRC (with jacket).

Published at 40s (£2.00) in January 1970. British Library deposit 12 January 1970. *BNB* B70-04800. Advertised in *TLS* 29 January 1970: 99, and 26 February 1970: 215.

Reviewed in *New Statesman* 13 February 1970: 224 (Alan Brownjohn); *Spectator* 14 February 1970: 213 (Ashley Brown); *TLS* 23 April 1970: 446; *Listener* 23 July 1970: 122 (John Fuller); *Stand* [Summer] 1973: 66-67 (Jon Glover).

A18.c Ecco Press impression (1978)

John Crowe Ransom | [ornament] | Selected Poems | The Ecco Press New York | [publisher's device] [on facing page] Third Edition, Revised and Enlarged

Copyright page (iv): 'Copyright 1924, 1927, 1934, 1939, 1945, | © 1962, 1963, 1969 by Alfred A. Knopf, Inc. | Copyright renewed 1952, 1954 by John Crowe Ransom | All rights reserved | Issued in 1978 by The Ecco Press, | 1 West 30th Street, New York, N.Y. 10001 | The Ecco Press logo by Ahmed Yacoubi | Cover design by Cynthia Krupat | Printed in the United States of America | Library of Congress Catalog Card Number: 69-14732 | ISBN 0-912-94654-7 | This edition published by arrangement with | Alfred A. Knopf, Inc.'

225 x 148 mm. *1-3*^{16} *4*^{8} *5-6*^{16}; 88 leaves. Pagination identical to that of the first Knopf impression.

This is an offset reprinting from the Knopf typesetting. The contents are identical to those of the Knopf first impression, except that the third initial unnumbered page, which is blank in the first Knopf impression, here bears a list of titles in 'The American Poetry Series' (from volume 1, Sandra McPherson's *Radiation*, to volume 16, Ransom's *Selected Poems*) and except for the production information in 'A Note on the Type' (p. 63), which here reads: 'The book was composed by Kingsport Press, Inc., | Kingsport, Tennessee and printed an bound by Had- | don Craftsmen Inc., Scranton, Pennsylvania. Typog- | raphy and binding design by Betty Anderson.' The note on the author (p. 161) has not been revised to reflect Ransom's death. The type-page has been slightly reduced, to 173 (183) x 108 mm. White wove paper, no watermark, sheets bulk 13 mm.

Bound in white paper printed in black, light gray (264), and deep orange (51). Front: '[on a gray background within a double rule frame] [orange] SELECTED | POEMS | [black] [118 mm rule] | [reproduction of an engraving of a Doric temple in ruins, with a cottage, farm animals, and three human figures before it] | [118 mm rule] | [orange] JOHN | CROWE | RANSOM | [black] THIRD EDITION, REVISED AND ENLARGED'. Spine, running down: 'SELECTED POEMS • JOHN CROWE RANSOM • *ECCO*'.

Back, within a double rule frame and on a gray background: price ('$3.95'), title, rule, author, series title ('THE AMERICAN POETRY SERIES, 16'), blurbs from Randall Jarrell, Delmore Schwartz, and 1964 National Book Award Citation, publisher's device in orange, address and notice of distribution by Viking Press, cover design credit, SBN. No endpapers. Edges trimmed.

Copies: CSA, IQ, STW, TxU-PCL, WMM (rebound), WU (rebound).

Publication noted in *Washington Post Book World,* 24 December 1978: 2. Advertised at $3.95 with a quotation from Randall Jarrell in *Kenyon Review* Spring 1979: 124. There was only this one impression of 2,300 copies (Emily Raabe, Ecco Press, 11 August 1995).

A18.d Carcanet impression (1991)

John Crowe Ransom | [ornament] | Selected Poems | CARCANET [on facing page] Third Edition, Revised and Enlarged

Copyright page (iv): 'First published in Great Britain in 1991 by | Carcanet Press Limited | 208-212 Corn Exchange Buildings | Manchester M4 3BQ | Copyright 1924, 1927, 1939, 1945, | © 1962, 1963, 1969 by Alfred A. Knopf, Inc. | Copyright renewed 1952, 1954 by John Crowe Ransom | All rights reserved | [BL cataloguing-in-publication data in 6 lines] | ISBN 0 85635 948 3 | The publisher acknowledges financial assistance | from the Arts Council of Great Britain | Printed and bound in England by SRP Ltd, Exeter'.

213 x 134 mm. 84 leaves. *i-iv* v-viii *1-2* 3-34 *35-36* 37-92 *93-94* 95-106 *107-108* 109-159 *160* pp.

This is a photo-offset reproduction, reduced in size, of the original Knopf typesetting. Omitted are the initial blank leaf and the leaves containing the list of other works by Ransom, the note on the text, and the note on the author. Type-page 165 (175) x 102 mm. White wove paper, no watermarks, sheets bulk 11 mm.

Perfect bound in white paper. Front: '[on a background of a photograph of part of a house and tree, in white, pale blue (185), bluish black (193), and shades of bluish gray] [white] JOHN CROWE RANSOM | Selected Poems | [black] CARCANET'. Spine, running down: 'JOHN CROWE RANSOM [brilliant blue (177)] SELECTED POEMS [black] CARCANET'. Back: statement by Randall Jarrell, 22-line blurb, Carcanet address, ISBN, bar code, price (£6.95), and, running down at the right in brilliant blue, cover photo credit (to '*John P Raw*'). No endpapers. Edges cut.

Copies: CSA, STW, WU.

Published at £6.95 on 21 November 1991. There has been one impression of approximately 1,000 copies (letter, Michael Schmidt, Carcanet, 22 August 1995).

A19 **1970**

Wanted: An Ontological Critic

Got up in wrappers, this item is an offprint, or *Sonderdruck*, from *Moderne englische und amerikanische Literaturkritik*, edited by Willi Erzgräber (D334).

[On the front wrapper] Sonderdruck | aus | Moderne englische und amerikanische Literaturkritik | Seiten 65-90 | [104 mm rule] | WANTED: AN ONTOLOGICAL CRITIC | by | JOHN CROWE RANSOM | 1970 | WISSENSCHAFTLICHE BUCHGESELL-SCHAFT | DARMSTADT

No copyright notice.

210 x 139 mm. 13 leaves. *65* 66-90 pp.

65-90 text.

Contains, in English only, a portion of Ransom's essay "Wanted: An Ontological Critic" (i.e., section 4 through the end), reprinted from *The New Criticism* (A10).

Type-page 38 lines, 156 (162) x 103 mm, 10 lines = 41 mm (e.g., p. 66); typeface Garamond with 3.3 mm face and 1.5 mm x-height. Running titles centered in the headline: 'John Crowe Ransom' on versos, 'An Ontological Critic' on rectos. Pagination at the outer margin of the headline. White wove paper, no watermark, sheets bulk 1 mm.

Perfect bound in white paper, with moderate reddish brown (43) tape around the spine. Front wrapper printed in black (as above). Back blank. Edges cut.

Copies: CSA, OGK, STW.

A20 **1971**

Le Donne e i cavalieri

John Crowe Ransom | LE DONNE | E I CAVALIERI | Scelta, traduzione e introduzione | di Giovanni Giudici | ARNOLDO MONDADORI EDITORE

Copyright page (6): '© *Alfred A. Knopf, Inc. 1962-1963* | © *Arnoldo Mondadori Editore 1971* | *Titolo dell'opera originale* | *Selected Poems by J. C. Ransom* | *I edizone marzo 1971'*.

Colophon (176): '*Stampato in Italia - Printed in Italy* | *Questo volume è stato impresso* | *nel mese di marzo dell'anno 1971* | *presso le Arti Grafiche delle Venezie* | *di Vicenza'*.

194 x 124 mm. *1-11*^{8}; 88 leaves. *1-8* 9-18 *19* 20-167 *168* 169 *170-176* pp.

1-2 blank; 3 'LO SPECCHIO | I poeti del nostro tempo'; 4 blank; 5 title page; 6 copyright page; 7 part-title 'INTRODUZIONE'; 8 blank; 9-18 introduction (ending '*Gionanni Giudici* | Milano, dicembre 1966'); 19 bastard title 'LE DONNE E I CAVALIERI'; 20-167 text; 168 blank; 169 'NOTE'; 170 blank; 171 part-title 'INDICE'; 172-175 index; 176 colophon.

Contains the following poems, chosen from Ransom's 1963 *Selected Poems*, with the texts in English on versos and with Italian translations on rectos.

Winter Remembered
Miriam Tazewell
Bells for John Whiteside's Daughter
Good Ships
Emily Hardcastle, Spinster
Parting at Dawn
In Process of a Noble Alliance
Here Lies a Lady
Conrad in Twilight
Armageddon
Prometheus in Straits
Judith of Bethulia
Hilda
Janet Waking
Two in August
Persistent Explorer
Somewhere Is Such a Kingdom
Antique Harvesters
Man without Sense of Direction
Survey of Literature
The Equilibrists
Prelude to an Evening
Painted Head

Blue Girls
Captain Carpenter
Old Mansion
Piazza Piece
Vision by Sweetwater
Parting, without a Sequel
Master's in the Garden Again
Prelude to an Evening [revised, with commentary]

Type-page 34 lines, 153 (161) x 82 mm, 10 lines = 45 mm (e.g., p. 11); width of verse lines is greater, e.g., 100 mm on p. 20); typeface Dante with a 3.9 mm face and 1.8 mm x-height. No running titles. Pagination centered in the direction line. White wove paper, no watermark, sheets bulk 14 mm.

Two bindings seen.

1. Bound in white calico cloth over boards. Front and back blank. Spine printed in black between two vertical rules: '[at the foot, running across, is the publisher's device] [running up] LE DONNE E I CAVALIERI RANSOM'. Light gray (264) endpapers, with an extra white free-endpaper at front and back. Bound up with the leaves is a dark orange-yellow (72) paper wrapper that is blind-embossed with a horizontal rib pattern and lettered on the front in orange-yellow on a panel of dark purplish red (259) and beneath that in black. Edges cut.

2. Probably later bound in dark red (16) fine linen cloth. Front and back blank. Stamped in gold on the spine: '[27 mm rule] | RANSOM | [4 mm rule] | LE DONNE | E I | CAVALIERI | [27 mm rule]'. White wove endpapers. Edges cut so that leaves measure 189 x 121 mm.

Copies: STW (Ransom's copy in binding 1 and with an undated inscription from the translator), RU (binding 2), TNV (binding 1).

Published at L. 2500 in March 1971 (*Bibliografia nazionale Italiana*, November-December 1971).

A21 **1972**

Beating the Bushes

As early as 1942, in *New Directions* 7, James Laughlin had advertised a volume by Ransom entitled *Poetics* in his "Checklist of New Directions Books in Print." And the biographical note on the dust jacket of Ransom's 1945 *Selected Poems* said that New Directions had in press *Essays in Poetics*. Neither ever appeared (see F3 and F4), but clearly Laughlin was interested in publishing another volume of Ransom's prose. In a letter to Allen Tate, 18 April 1966, Ransom mentioned "a big book of essays long promised to Jay [i.e., James] Laughlin" (*SL* 417). Not until 24 September 1969, however, was Laughlin able to acknowledge receipt of a box of essays, with the promise of more to come and with the title still to be settled (TNV). Laughlin continued to prod Ransom for the additional essays, as on 23 October 1969, 22 July 1970, and 3 February 1971 (TNV). By 1971 the problem seemed to be the completion of the final essay, a revision of Ransom's "Blake Triumphant" from the *New York Review of Books* (C361), which was to be entitled "Blake's Eternal Man." On 30 June 1971 Frederick R. Martin of New Directions told Ransom that he hoped to have the Blake essay in early July, at the same time asking Ransom about the title for this new collection and wondering if "Poetics: A Study of Language" was the title of what Laughlin called "the book that never was" (TNV). Evidently unable to meet the deadline, Ransom was reassured by Martin on 16 September that he need not return his $250 advance—indeed that Laughlin was still enthusiastic about the book and would send the $250 balance upon receipt of the essay (TNV). The Blake essay evidently never was completed. The book was published on 20 April and contained the essays Martin listed in his 16 September letter, minus the Blake essay. The book was issued simultaneously in cloth and paper bindings. There was only one impression.

A21(1) Hardbound issue (1972)

JOHN CROWE RANSOM | [floral ornament] | Beating the Bushes | *Selected Essays 1941-1970* | A NEW DIRECTIONS BOOK

Copyright page (iv): 'Copyright © 1941, 1972 by New Directions Publishing Corporation | Copyright 1942, 1943, 1945, 1947, 1952 by Kenyon College | Library of Congress Catalog Card Number: 79-159738 | [reservation of rights and acknowledgments in 8 lines] | Manufactured in the United States of America | First published clothbound and as New Directions Paperbook 324 | in 1972 | Published simultaneously in Canada by McClelland & Stewart, Ltd. | Designed by Gertrude Huston | New Directions Books are published for James Laughlin | by New Directions Publishing Corporation, | 333 Sixth Avenue, New York 10014'.

203 x 135 mm. *1-6*^{16}; 96 leaves. *i-viii 1* 2-46 *47* 48-71 *72* 73-79 *80* 81-92 *93* 94-118 *119* 120-127 *128* 129-135 *136* 137-148 *149* 150-156 *157* 158-169 *170* 171-176 *177-184* pp.

i half title '[floral ornament] | Beating the Bushes'; ii blank; iii title page; iv copyright page; v '*Contents*'; vi blank; vii bastard title '[floral ornament] | Beating the Bushes'; viii blank; 1-176 text; 177-184 blank.

Contains 11 essays, all from the *Kenyon Review* except "Wanted: An Ontological Critic," which had concluded *New Criticism* (A10), and "The Concrete Universal," which appears here for the first time and may stand as the continuation of two earlier essays with that title (the second essay having ended with a note that it was "to be continued"). All of the previously published essays are revised. "The Iconography of the Master" is a revised portion of "Poetry: II, The Final Cause" (C295 and B58). For his text of "Why Critics Don't Go Mad," Ransom apparently went to *Kenyon Review* (C312) rather than to the revised text in the later *Poems and Essays* (A14). The essays:

Wanted: An Ontological Critic
An Address to Kenneth Burke
Positive and Near-Positive Aesthetics
Art Needs a Little Separating
Art Worries the Naturalists Who in Turn Worry the Arts with Organism, Fusion, Funding
Beating the Naturalists with the Stick of Drama
Art and the Human Economy
The Iconography of the Master
Poets and Flatworms

Why Critics Don't Go Mad
The Concrete Universal

Type-page 33 lines, 141 (147) x 97 mm, 10 lines = 43 mm (e.g., p. 75); typeface Times New Roman with 3.6 mm face, 1.7 mm x-height. Essay titles in italic (e.g., '*Wanted: An Ontological Critic (1941)*') beneath a floral ornament. No running titles; pagination at outer margin of direction line; no pagination on the first page of each essay. White wove paper, no watermark, sheets bulk 13 mm.

Bound in moderate red (15) calico cloth stamped in black on the spine. Front and back: blank. Running down the spine: 'JOHN CROWE RANSOM Beating the Bushes NEW DIRECTIONS'. White wove endpapers. Top and bottom edges cut, fore-edge trimmed.

Dust jacket of white paper with lettering and design in black. Front: 'JOHN CROWE RANSOM | Beating | the Bushes | [floral ornament] | Selected Essays 1941-1970'. Spine, running down: 'JOHN CROWE RANSOM Beating the Bushes NEW DIRECTIONS'. Back: list of 'Some Other Books of Criticism' (7 titles, from Edward Dahlberg's *Can These Bones Live* to Martin Turnell's *The Art of French Fiction*; publisher's imprint and address. Front flap: author, title, beginning of blurb in 16 lines, imprint, price ('$7.95'). Back flap: blurb continued for 20 lines, jacket credit (to Gertrude Huston), publisher's imprint and address.

Copies: IDeKN, INS, IRo (with jacket), InU-Lilly (with jacket), OGK (2 copies), STW (2 copies, 1 with jacket), WBB, WU (with jacket).

Published at $7.95 on 20 April 1972. Copyright registration A340561. There was one impression of 5,000 copies, 1,000 of these bound in cloth for this issue (letter, Griselda Ohannessian, New Directions, 8 August 1995). Advertised in *New York Review of Books* 18 May 1972: 30 and in *Sewanee Review* Fall 1974: lxxvi.

Reviewed in *Library Journal* 1 January 1972: 89, for March publication by New Directions and distribution by Lippincott; *Library Journal* 1 March 1972: 877 (John R. Willingham), for April publication; *Christian Century* 26 April 1972: 488; *Choice* September

1972: 916; *Southern Literary Journal* Fall 1972: 177-186 (George Core); *Modern Age* Fall 1972: 440-442 (Robert Buffington); *Commentary* November 1972: 79-82 (David Bromwich); *New York Times Book Review* 10 December 1972: 4-5, 12 (Edward W. Said); *Georgia Review* Summer 1973: 275-282 (Thomas Daniel Young); *Carleton Miscellany* Fall-Winter 1973-74: 111-118 (Richard Foster).

A21(2) Paperbound issue (1972)

Aside from its binding, this issue of 4,000 copies of the sole impression of 5,000 copies differs from the hardbound only in having a smaller leaf size (201 x 130) and in printing on pp. 177-178 a listing of New Directions Paperbooks.

Perfect bound in white paper with lettering and design in black. Front: identical to the front of the hardbound issue's dust jacket. Spine: identical to the dust jacket except that 'NDP324' replaces the publisher's imprint. Back: 'LITERATURE | JOHN CROWE RANSOM | Beating the Bushes | Selected Essays 1941-1970 | [24-line blurb] | *Cover design by Gertrude Huston* | A NEW DIRECTIONS PAPERBOOK NDP324 $3.45'.

Copies: CSA (2 copies), InU-Lilly, STW.

Published at $3.45, simultaneously with hardback issue.

A22 **1973**

Cloak Model

In a letter of 25 August 1972 Ransom replied to an invitation from Pomegranate Press, saying that would send in a week "a new poem" for a series that the press was undertaking. Somewhat later than promised, he sent his poem "Cloak Model." Its receipt was acknowledged on 18 September by the proprietor of the press, Stephen M. Savage, who said that he planned for December publication and would send Ransom proofs in November. Ransom was then to receive payment of $50.00 and 15 complimentary copies of the broadside. For some reason not disclosed in this correspondence (at Ball State University), publication was delayed until April 1973. The poem was an old one made new by heavy revision. On this broadside the poem is accompanied by a lithograph by Karyl Klopp.

CLOAK MODEL | [text in 6 quintets] | *John Crowe Ransom* | [to the right of the poem is a lithograph in blue, predominantly deep blue (179), which is signed and dated in pencil] K Klopp iv • 1973 | [printed in black] This poem is here printed for the first time in an edition limited to 65 copies | of which this is No. [number handwritten in black]. Issued April, 1973, by The Pomegranate Press, | 1713 Massachusetts Avenue, Cambridge, Massachusetts 02138. | Text Copyright 1973 by John Crowe Ransom.

The poem "Cloak Model" had previously appeared, in variant texts, in *Poems about God* (A1) and *Grace after Meat* (A3). The text here differs substantively from those two versions.

Broadside. 492 x 320 mm. Typeface Deepdene with 6.3 mm face, 2.5 mm x-height. White wove paper. The IEN and InU copies have a watermark at lower right resembling an open-face M surmounted by a cross.

Copies: IEN, ICU (copy 58), InU-Lilly (copy 43), STW (Ransom's unnumbered copy, also proofs of text and lithographs).

A23 **1984**

Selected Essays

In editing this collection, Thomas Daniel Young and John Hindle gathered 24 essays and arranged them in chronological order according to the date of first publication, those dates ranging from 1924 through 1959. Seventeen of the essays had not previously appeared in a volume by Ransom. The editors indicate the sources of the texts, but in at least one case they have drawn on a source other than that cited: they have taken "Criticism as Pure Speculation" not from *Intent of the Critic* (B30) but from the 1951 edition of *Literary Opinion in America* (D126), where the first two paragraphs of the essay are "condensed" into one and where six words are missing from the next paragraph.

Selected Essays of | JOHN CROWE RANSOM | [swelled rule 63 mm, with central gap] | *Edited, with an Introduction, by* | THOMAS DANIEL YOUNG *and* JOHN HINDLE | *Louisiana State University Press* | *Baton Rouge and London*

Copyright page (vi): 'Copyright © 1984 by Louisiana State University Press | *All rights reserved* | Manufactured in the United States of America | Designer: Barbara Werden | Typeface: Linotron Primer | Typesetter: G & S Typesetters, Inc. | Printer and binder: Vail-Ballou Press'; LC cataloging in publication data; 'ISBN 0-8071-1130-9'.

227 x 150 mm. *1-8*^{16} *9*^{8} *10-12*^{16}; 184 leaves. *i-xiv* 1-337 *338* 339-354 pp.

i series imprint 'SOUTHERN LITERARY STUDIES | Louis D. Rubin, Jr., *Editor*'; ii blank; iii half title '*Selected Essays of John Crowe Ransom*'; iv blank; v title page; vi copyright page; vii dedication '*For* | HELEN RANSOM FORMAN'; viii blank; ix '*Contents*'; x blank; xi '*Acknowledgments*'; xii blank; xiii bastard title '*Selected Essays of John Crowe Ransom*'; xiv blank; 1-24 '*Introduction*'; 25-337 text of essays; 338 blank; 339-341 '*Appendix A* | *From a Letter to Allen Tate, September 5, 1926*'; 342-344 '*Appendix B* | *Chronology*'; 345-348 '*Appendix C* | *A Checklist of Ransom's Critical Essays*'; 349-354 '*Index*'.

Essays (the first four are grouped under the title "Four Short Pieces from *The Fugitive*"):

The Future of Poetry
Mixed Modes
Thoughts on the Poetic Discontent
Prose: A Doctrine of Relativity
Classical and Romantic
The Aesthetic of Regionalism
Forms and Citizens
Poetry: A Note in Ontology
Criticism, Inc.
The Arts and the Philosophers
Honey and Gall
Criticism as Pure Speculation
Wanted: An Ontological Critic
Artists, Soldiers, Positivists
Art and the Human Economy
Poetry: I, The Formal Analysis
Poetry: II, The Final cause
The Literary Criticism of Aristotle
William Wordsworth: Notes toward an Understanding of Poetry
Humanism at Chicago
The Concrete Universal: Observations on the Understanding of Poetry, I.
The Concrete Universal: Observations on the Understanding of Poetry, II.
New Poets and Old Muses
The Idea of a Literary Anthropologist and What He Might Say of the *Paradise Lost* of Milton

In addition, the editors quote from several of Ransom's letters in their introduction and transcribe in an appendix a large portion of a 5 September 1926 letter to Allen Tate.

Type-pages of various sizes: 162 (169) x 105 mm, 39 lines (e.g., p. 278); 167 (173) x 105 mm, 40 lines (e.g., p. 48); 170 (177) x105 mm, 41 lines (e.g., p. 22). In each, 10 lines = 42 mm; typeface Primer with 3.2 mm face, 1.7 mm x-height. Essay titles (e.g., 'FORMS AND CITIZENS') are centered, and the text of the introduction and each essay begins with an capital initial in a 14 mm ornamented square, 4 lines deep. Running titles at the inner margin of the headline: half title on versos ('SELECTED ESSAYS OF JOHN CROWE RANSOM'); essay titles or section heads on rectos (e.g., 'FORMS AND CITIZENS' and 'APPENDIX A'). No running titles on opening pages of essays or sections. Pagination at the outer margin of the headlines, except centered in the direction line on first page of essays and sections. White wove paper, no watermark, sheets bulk 22 mm.

Bound in grayish yellow (90) calico cloth over boards. Front and back blank. Spine, running across and stamped in gold on three black rectangles with gold borders at top and bottom of each: '[within 1st rectangle] YOUNG | AND | HINDLE | [within 2nd] *Selected* | *Essays* | *of* | JOHN | CROWE | RANSOM | [within 3rd] *Louisiana*'. Light yellowish brown (76) wove endpapers. Edges cut.

Dust jacket with pale green (149) background for front, spine, and back and very light greenish blue (171) background for flaps; lettering in black. Front: photograph of Ransom (his hand extending onto the spine) in very light greenish blue, '*Selected* | *Essays* *of* | JOHN | CROWE | RANSOM | [57 mm greenish blue rule] | EDITED, WITH AN | INTRODUCTION, BY | Thomas Daniel Young | AND | John Hindle'. Spine: title, 30 mm greenish blue rule, editors' last names, LSU Press device. Back: advertisement for Young's *Gentleman in a Dustcoat*, publisher's address, ISBN. Front flap: title, editors, blurb. Back flap: blurb continued, biographical notes on editors, series title and editor, publisher's address.

Copies: CSA (with jacket), ICU, INS, IU, OGK, STW (with jacket), TxU-PCL, WU.

Published at $30.00 in February 1984, and in England at £28.50 in May 1984. One impression of 1,500 copies (letter, Kristin Bryan, LSU Press, 23 August 1995).

Advertised for March publication in *Library Journal* 15 February 1984: 247 and in *Choice* March 1984: 909; also advertised in *Southern Review* April 1984: ii.

Reviewed in *Library Journal* 15 February 1984: 376 (T. F. Smith), for March publication; *Virginia Quarterly Review* Winter 1985:

16; *New York Times Book Review* 20 May 1984: 11 (Donald Davie); *New Republic* 25 June 1984: 32 (Christopher Ricks); *Choice* July-August 1984: 1608-1609; *Resources for American Literary Study* Autumn 1985: 252 (Mark Royden Winchell); *South Atlantic Quarterly* Spring 1986: 205-206 (George Core).

A 24 **1985**

Selected Letters

This edition, prepared by Thomas Daniel Young and George Core, presents full texts of Ransom's letters ranging from 16 July 1911 through 9 July 1968, with many of the early letters addressed to members of his family and the later to such correspondents as R. P. Blackmur, Cleanth Brooks, Andrew Lytle, Arthur Mizener, Wallace Stevens, Lionel Trilling, Robert Penn Warren, and, especially, Allen Tate. Six of the letters were first published with the title "Art as Adventure in Form" in *Southern Review* (C366). In addition to the letters, the volume prints a previously unpublished poem beginning "Minerva had no pride of pedigree" (105) and the poem "The Eye Can Tell," which the editors annotate as having been "written in the late winter of 1973." The poem is a revision of "Old Man Pondered," which had been first published in 1929 (C172) and had been collected in Ransom's 1963 *Selected Poems* (A16). In 1973 it had appeared as "Four Threesomes; or Three Foursomes" in *Sewanee Review* (C365).

Core's introductory essay is revised from its appearance in *Virginia Quarterly Review* 53 (Summer 1977): 455-474. Stevens's essay from which book's epigraph was taken first appeared in *Sewanee Review* 56 (Summer 1948): 367-379 and was collected in his *Opus Posthumous* (New York: Knopf, 1957).

Selected Letters of | JOHN CROWE RANSOM | [swelled rule 63 mm, with central gap] | *Edited, with an Introduction, by* | THOMAS DANIEL YOUNG *and* GEORGE CORE | *Louisiana State University Press* | *Baton Rouge and London*

Copyright page (vi): 'Copyright © 1985 by Louisiana State University Press | *All rights reserved* | Manufactured in the United States of America | Designer: Barbara Werden | Typeface: Linotron Primer | Typesetter: G & S Typesetters, Inc. | Printer and Binder: Edwards Brothers, Inc. | Vanderbilt University and the Mellon committee of the College of Arts and Sciences, University | of the South, furnished subventions toward defraying the production costs of this book.'; acknowledgment of previous publication of Core's introduction, of six letters, and of the poem "The Eye Can Tell"; LC cataloging in publication data; 'ISBN 0-8071-1168-6'.

229 x 150 mm. *1-14*^{16}; 224 leaves. *i-xvi* 1-15 *16* 17-28 *29-30* 31-106 *107-108* 109-183 *184-186* 187-263 *264-266* 267-345 *346-348* 349-421 *422* 423-430 *431-432* pp.

i series imprint 'SOUTHERN LITERARY STUDIES | *Louis D. Rubin, Jr., Editor*'; ii blank; iii half title '*Selected Letters of John Crowe Ransom*'; iv blank; v title page; vi copyright page; vii '*To the memory of Allen Tate | and for Louis D. Rubin, Jr.*'; viii blank; ix excerpt from Wallace Stevens's "John Crowe Ransom: Tennessean"; x blank; xi 'CONTENTS'; xii blank; xiii 'ACKNOWLEDGMENTS'; xiv blank; xv bastard title '*Selected Letters of John Crowe Ransom*'; xvi blank; 1-15 'INTRODUCTION | A Naturalist Looks at Sentiment', concluding with a 'BIBLIOGRAPHICAL NOTE'; 16 blank; 17-22 'EDITORIAL NOTE | A Mask and an Unveiling'; 23-28 'A CHRONOLOGY | John Crowe Ransom, 1988-1974'; 29 part title '1911-1920'; 30 blank; 31-106 text; 107 part title '1921-1929'; 108 blank; 109-183 text; 184 blank; 185 part title '1930-1939'; 186 blank; 187-263 text; 264 blank; 265 part title '1940-1949'; 266 blank; 267-345 text; 346 blank; 347 part title '1950-1968'; 348 blank; 349-420 text; 421 'APPENDIX' (text of "The Eye Can Tell"); 422 blank; 423-430 'INDEX'; 431-432 blank.

Type-pages of two sizes: 44 lines, 168 (175) x 105 mm (more common, e.g., p. 239); 45 lines, 172 (179) x 105 mm (e.g., pp. 245 and 352). In each, 10 lines = 42 mm; typeface Primer with 3.1 mm face, 1.6 mm x-height. The text of the introduction, editorial note, and editorial comment of each part begins with an capital initial in a 14 mm ornamented square, 4 lines deep. Beneath the heading of each letter (e.g., '*To Edwin Mims* | June 8, 1937') is a thick rule running the width of the type-page. Running titles in the headline, flush with the inner margin: on versos, 'SELECTED LETTERS OF JOHN CROWE RANSOM'; on rectos, part titles or section heads (e.g., '1930-1939' and 'INDEX'). No running titles on pages with part titles or on first pages with text of parts or sections. Pagination at the outer margin of the headlines, except centered in the direction line on initial pages of parts and sections. White wove paper, no watermark, sheets bulk 23 mm.

Bound in light olive gray (112) calico cloth over boards. Front and back blank. Spine, running across and stamped in gold on three dark red (16) rectangles with gold borders at top and bottom of each: '[within 1st rectangle] YOUNG | AND | CORE | [within 2nd] *Selected* | *Letters* | *of* | JOHN | CROWE | RANSOM | [within 3rd] *Louisiana*'. White wove endpapers. Edges cut.

Dust jacket with dark red (16) background for front, spine, and back and light gray (264) background for flaps; lettering in black. Front: photograph of Ransom (his hand extending onto the spine) in light gray, '*Selected* | *Letters of* | JOHN | CROWE | RANSOM | [57 mm light gray rule] | EDITED, WITH AN | INTRODUCTION, BY | Thomas Daniel Young | AND | George Core'. Spine: title, 25 mm light gray rule, editors' last names, LSU Press device. Back: advertisement for *Selected Essays* and Young's *Gentleman in a Dustcoat*, publisher's address, ISBN. Front flap: title, editors, blurb. Back flap: blurb continued, biographical notes on editors, series title and editor, publisher's address.

Copies: CSA (with jacket), ICU, INS, IU (2 copies), InU, OGK, STW (with jacket), TxU-PCL, WU.

Published at $32.50 in January 1985, and in England at £30.80 in February 1985. One impression of 1000 copies (letter, Kristin Bryan, LSU Press, 23 August 1995).

Advertised in *Southern Review* January 1985: ii and in *Virginia Quarterly Review* Winter 1985: 15.

Reviewed in *Library Journal* January 1985: 82 (Daniel L. Guillory), for January publication; *New York Times Book Review* 17 March 1985: 22 (Robert Phillips); *Choice* June 1985: 1496 (W. Pratt); *Christian Science Monitor* 17 July 1985: 23 (Thomas D'Evelyn); *Virginia Quarterly Review* Autumn 1985: 708-713 (Ashley Brown); *World Literature Today* Autumn 1985: 601 (George Hendrick); *TLS* 16 August 1985: 894 (Dick Davis); *Partisan Review* Winter 1986: 126-132 (Denis Donoghue); *Sewanee Review* January-March 1986: 143-148 (J. Mazzaro); *Southern Humanities Review* Summer 1987: 279-281 (Carroll Y. Rich).

Section B
First Appearance Contributions to Books

B 1 **1913**

American Rhodes Scholars, Oxford, 1910-1913

AMERICAN RHODES SCHOLARS | OXFORD | 1910-1913

No copyright notice or colophon.

249 x 157 mm. *A-B*^{8} *C*^{4}; 20 leaves. *1-6* 7-8 *9* 10-23 *24* 25-26 *27* 28-31 *32* 33-34 *35* 36-38 *39* 40 pp.; 6 unnumbered plates.

1-2 blank; 3 title page; 4 'Contents.'; plate 1 (frontispiece photograph of Sir Francis J. Wylie, the Oxford Secretary of the Rhodes trustees during 1903-1931); 5 'Caveat Lector.'; 6-8 'Colin Clout on Oxford.'; plates 2-5 (photographs of Rhodes scholars); 9-23 'Biographical.' (biographies of scholars); 24 'The American Club.'; plate 6 (photograph in, presumably, the American Club); 25-26 text continued; 27-31 'Wayfaring in England.'; 32-34 'North Oxford.'; 35-38 'Letters of R. K. B.'; 39-40 'Oxford.'

In his copy (TxU-HRC), Christopher Morley wrote '(John Ransom)' at the end of "The American Club," evidently indicating Ransom's authorship of that essay. The copy of F. Wallis Armstrong, Jr. (NjP), has on its first page an autograph annotation dated January 1934 and signed by Christopher Morley:

> As far as I can remember (since you ask) I wrote *Caveat Lector*, *Colin Clout*, *Letters of R. K. B.*, and the *Poem* ("Oxford")—*Wayfaring in England* was written, I think, by Roger Loomis (now of the faculty of Columbia

> Univ.) The others who were supposed to toil in this venture were John Crowe Ransom, Elmer Davis, and (I think) Elmer D. Keith—Probably Johnny Ransom wrote the piece about the American Club; or perhaps Elmer Davis wrote that & John Ransom the *North Oxford*—
> It's a long time ago—

Both Davis and Ransom had served as presidents of the American Club. But there is further evidence for attributing "The American Club" to Ransom: in the upper margin of "Caveat Lector," there is an annotation in Morley's hand identifying the "two incompetents" who hastily compiled this yearbook as himself and Ransom (p. 5), and the author of "The American Club" refers to himself as "this editor" (p. 25). Since Morley lays no claim to the piece, it would seem to fall to Ransom as the other editor. Furthermore, in Ransom's copy (TNV) there is an autograph correction of a word in the essay (p. 25, line 18, 'obliterated' is changed to 'obviated').

Type-page 53 lines, 181 (187) x 101 mm, 10 lines = 34 mm (e.g., p. 25); typeface Old Style. White wove paper, no watermark, sheets and plates bulk 3 mm.

Bound in dark purplish blue (201) diagonal dotted-line cloth over boards. Front, stamped in gold within a blind-stamped rule frame: 'AMERICAN RHODES SCHOLARS | 1910-1913 | [seal]'. Spine and back blank. White wove endpapers. Edges trimmed. No dust jacket seen.

Presumably published in 1913.

Copies: NjP (from Armstrong's library, examined in photocopy), TNV (from Ransom's library), TxU-HRC (from Morley's library).

B 2 **1 9 2 3**

The [Winter] Owl

[Reproduced from hand drawing] *The* [an owl] *Owl.* | [on drawing of a scroll]—*Contents*— | [beneath the scroll is a list of contents in 29 lines of type]

Printer's imprint (p. 2): 'THE PRINTERS | The Illustrations by | Vincent Brooks, Day & Sons Ltd. | Parker Street, Kingsway | The Letterpress by | The Westminster Press | 11 Henrietta Street, Covent Garden | 1923'.

311 x 243 mm. *A*^{2} B-H^4; 30 leaves. $1 signed. *1-2* 3-60 pp., with 9 plates, inserted singly after pp. 4, 14, 18, 22, 26, 28, 46, 48, 58.

Contains the first book publication of Ransom's poems "Winter Remembered" (14), which had appeared in the January 1922 *Sewanee Review* (C47), and "An American Addresses Philomela" (46-47), which had appeared as "Philomela" in the February-March 1923 *Fugitive* (C55). Both differ textually from their earlier appearances. Robert Graves, the editor, later included both poems in *Grace after Meat* (A3), where the text of the first differs only in spelling and punctuation and where the text of the second has, in addition, minor substantive variants.

Type-page 38 lines, 226 (234) x 150 mm, 10 lines = 60 mm (e.g., p. 53); typeface Caslon, italic for poetry, roman for prose. White laid paper with horizontal chainlines 23 mm apart; watermark '[crown] | [black-letter] Abbey Mills | Greenfield'; sheets and plates bulk 7 mm.

Bound in white paper over boards printed in dark bluish gray (192) for background and with lettering (reproduced from hand-drawing, not type) and design in black and white. Front: '*The* | *Winter Owl* | [drawing of a large owl surrounded by 7 owls and perched on a white panel listing the surnames of contributors, from Beerbohm to Turner and with Ransom's spelled with a terminal *e*] | 12/6'. Spine blank. Back: '[owl perched on a scroll] | [on the scroll, in a cursive hand] Athenian fowl with feathered legs | Stand emblem of our will | To hunt the rat that sucks the eggs | Of virtue, joy, and skill. | [beneath the scroll, in a cursive hand] Published by | Cecil Palmer | 49 Chandos Street | Covent

Garden. | Edited by Robert Graves and William Nicholson.' White wove endpapers. Edges trimmed.

Copies: ICN, TxU-HRC (2 copies).

Published at 12s 6d in November 1923 (*English Catalogue*). Reviewed in *TLS* 20 December 1923: 898. *Winter Owl* is the third and, as it turned out, final issue of Graves's *Owl*. There had been two previous issues: numbers 1 (May 1919) and 2 (October 1919), neither of which contained any contributions by Ransom.

B 3 **1923**

Armageddon

ARMAGEDDON | BY JOHN CROWE RANSOM | A FRAGMENT | BY WILLIAM ALEXANDER PERCY | AVALON | BY DONALD DAVIDSON | [pegasus device] | PUBLISHED BY | THE POETRY SOCIETY OF SOUTH CAROLINA | CHARLESTON, S.C. | MCMXXIII

Copyright page (2): 'COPYRIGHT, 1923 | BY THE POETRY SOCIETY OF | SOUTH CAROLINA, U.S.A.'

Colophon (18): circular device with a tree in the center and around it at the top in black-letter type the words 'The State Co.' and at the bottom in roman the words 'PRINTERS-BINDERS-ENGRAVERS [last word barely legible]'. Limitation notice (3): A LIMITED EDITION, FOR MEMBERS, | CRITICS, AND LOVERS OF VERSE.'

216 x 126 mm. 1^{10}; 10 leaves. *1-8* 9-17 *18-20* pp.

Contains the first appearance of Ransom's poem "Armageddon" (9-12), the Southern Prize Poem for 1923 (the first poem to receive that prize of $100). The poem was later revised for *Chills and Fever* (A2). The poems by Percy and Davidson received honorable mention.

Type-page with irregular number of lines, 157 (166) x 76 mm, 10 lines = 42 mm (e.g., pp. 11 and 13); typeface Old Style. White laid paper with horizontal chainlines 24 mm apart, no watermark, sheets bulk 2 mm.

Bound in moderate yellowish brown (77) wove paper wrappers. Front: 'ARMAGEDDON | BY JOHN CROWE RANSOM | THE SOUTHERN PRIZE POEM | AND THE HONORS OF | 1923 | [society device] | PUBLISHED BY | THE POETRY SOCIETY OF SOUTH CAROLINA | CHARLESTON, S.C. | MCMXXIII'. Back blank. No endpapers. Edges trimmed.

Copies: ICU, InU-Lilly, STW (with W. A. Percy's bookplate), TNV, TxU-HRC (2 copies).

Published 5 November 1923 for distribution to members of the Poetry Society of South Carolina (there were 341 members listed in the society's 1923 *Year Book*); copyright registration A763201 (copies deposited 8 November 1923).

B 4 **1923**

Anthology of Magazine Verse for 1923

Anthology of Magazine Verse | for 1923 | and | Yearbook of American Poetry | Edited by | WILLIAM STANLEY BRAITHWAITE | [line-cut drawing of a boy under a tree, a crane in flight, goats, and a sailing ship, the boy holding a curled paper with the book title and editor's name] | BOSTON | B. J. BRIMMER COMPANY | 1923

Copyright page (vi): '*Copyright, 1923,* By B. J. BRIMMER COMPANY | *Copyright, 1923,* By THE BOSTON TRANSCRIPT COMPANY | [9 mm rule] | FIRST IMPRESSION, NOVEMBER, 1923 | PRINTED IN THE UNITED STATES OF AMERICA | PRESS OF THE GOODMAN BROS., INC. | BOSTON'.

210 x 136 mm. *1*^{10} 2-*24*^{8} *25*^{4} *26-36*^{8} *37*^{6}; 292 leaves. Part I (anthology): *i-viii* ix *x* xi-xix *xx 1-2* 3-376 pp.; Part II (yearbook): *1-4* 5-165 *166-168* 169-188 pp.

Contains Ransom's poems "In Process of a Noble Alliance" (288), "Philomela" (289-290), "Conrad at Twilight" (290-291), and "Here Lies a Lady" (291-292)—the first three reprinted from *Fugitive* (C56, C55), the last from *Literary Review* (C58), and all published here for the first time in book form. The only substantive variant occurs in "Conrad at Twilight," where Ransom's 'wraith' is misprinted as 'wrath' (line 5).

Type-page 39 lines, 137 (143) x 85 mm, 10 lines = 36 mm (e.g., p. xiii); typeface Scotch Roman. White laid paper with vertical chainlines 20 mm apart, no watermark, sheets bulk 36 mm.

Bound in brownish gray (64) paper over boards, with moderate brown (58) calico cloth around the spine. Front: on a white paper label, '[within a double rule frame] BRAITHWAITE'S ANTHOLOGY | OF MAGAZINE VERSE | FOR 1923 | YEARBOOK OF AMERICAN POETRY | [double rule forming a second compartment] WILLIAM STANLEY BRAITHWAITE'. Spine: on a white paper label, '[double rule 38 mm] Anthology *of* | Magazine | Verse | 1923 | [8 mm rule] | BRAITHWAITE | [double rule 38 mm]'. White wove endpapers. Top edge trimmed; fore- and bottom edges untrimmed. Dust jacket of white paper printed in black.

Copies: CSA, ICU (2 copies), IDecJ, InU-Lilly (with a portion of the jacket mounted on recto of front free-endpaper), IU, STW, TNV. Also in Edelstein, *Stevens* B15; Hogan, *Robinson* p. 66.

Published at $3.00 on 26 November 1923; copyright registration A766919 (copies deposited 28 January 1924). Hogan reports one impression of 3375 copies; Edelstein reports that of those copies, 245 constituted a special issue that had a colophon (p. *iv*), was numbered and signed, and had cloth also at the corners of the boards and a gilt top edge.

Reviewed in *New York Times Book Review* 20 January 1924: 22; *Nation* 6 February 1924: 147.

B 5 **1924**

The Bowling Green

[Within a double-rule frame, 131 x 80 mm, the outer frame in strong reddish orange (35)] *The Bowling Green* | *An Anthology of Verse* | *Selected by* | *Christopher Morley* | [engraving of a reddish orange device: an open book and the words 'FRUCTUS QUAM FOLIA'] | *Garden City New York* | *Doubleday, Page & Company* | *1924* [All initial capital letters are swash type, except those of the words '*Selected*', '*Garden*', and '*Page*' and those in the device.]

Copyright page (iv): 'COPYRIGHT, 1924, BY | DOUBLEDAY, PAGE & COMPANY | PRINTED IN THE UNITED STATES | AT | THE COUNTRY LIFE PRESS, GARDEN CITY, N.Y. | *First Edition*'.

179 x 115 mm. 1^8 $(1_1 + 1)$ 2-13^8; 105 leaves. *i-vi* vii-xxi *xxii* xxiii-xxv *xxvi-xxviii* 1-182 pp.

Contains Ransom's poems "Sonnet of a Sure Heart" (125), "They Praise the Sun" (126), "They Hail the Sunrise" (127-128), published here for the first time in book form. The anthology is made up of poems selected from those appearing in "The Bowling Green," a column Morley conducted for the *New York Evening Post* from 9 February 1920 to 31 December 1923. The texts are identical to those in the *Evening Post* (C34, C39, C41) except that in "They Praise the Sun" 'sinks' replaces 'sink' (line 10).

Type-page 27 lines, 122 (134) x 80 mm, 10 lines = 45 mm (e.g., pp. xi and 52); typeface Caslon Old Style. The title page is on an inserted leaf, presumably because of the additional presswork required for the engraving. White wove paper, no watermark, sheets bulk 14 mm.

Bound in light yellow-green (119) paper over boards, with moderate blue (182) linen cloth around the spine and lettering in black. Front: '[within a rule frame] The Bowling Green'. Spine: 'The | Bowling | Green | DOUBLEDAY | PAGE & CO.' Back blank. Top edge trimmed; fore-edge untrimmed; bottom edge unopened.

Dust jacket of yellowish green (135) paper printed in black. Front: '[within a double rule frame] THE BOWLING GREEN | [captioned 17th-century print of Man and Love bowling against Sin and Folly] | *An Anthology of Verse* | *Selected by* | CHRISTOPHER MORLEY'. Spine: title, editor, publisher. Back: blurb between double rules. Front flap: '*The Bowling Green* | *Price, net, $1.75*'. Back flap: advertisement for works by Morley.

Copies: IDeKN, TNV (from Ransom's library), TxU-HRC (2 copies, with jackets), WMM.

Published at $1.75 on 30 April 1924; copyright registration A792331 (copies deposited 10 May 1924).

Advertised in *Literary Review* 3 May 1924: 736 and 17 May 1924: 768 ("This little green-bound volume is just the size to tuck in a pocket, or a week-end bag, or in thc small, intimate bedside shelf by the night light"). Reviewed in *Bookman* July 1924: 606; *New York Times Book Review* 6 July 1924: 12; *Outlook* 12 November 1924: 415.

B 6 **1924**

Modern Essays (Second Series)

MODERN ESSAYS | (SECOND SERIES) | SELECTED BY | CHRISTOPHER MORLEY | [publisher's device] | NEW YORK | HARCOURT, BRACE AND COMPANY | 1924

Copyright page (ii): 'COPYRIGHT, 1924, BY | HARCOURT, BRACE AND COMPANY, INC. | PRINTED IN THE U.S.A. BY | THE QUINN & BODEN COMPANY | RAHWAY, N.J.'

187 x 125 mm. *1-30*^{8}; 240 leaves. [2] *i-ii* iii-ix *x* xi-xiv *xv-xvi 1-2* 3-457 *458-462* pp.

Contains Ransom's essay "Waste Lands" (346-359), reprinted from the 14 July 1923 *Literary Review* (C61) and published here for the first time in book form and introduced by Morley (345-346).

Type-page 27 lines, 142 (149) x 89 mm, 10 lines = 53 mm (e.g., p. 351); typeface Old Style. White wove paper, no watermark, sheets bulk 32 mm.

Bound in moderate orange (53) calico cloth over boards, stamped in black. Front: '[44 mm thick-thin double rule] | MODERN | ESSAYS | SECOND SERIES | *Selected by* | CHRISTOPHER | MORLEY — — | [44 mm rule]'. Spine: '[thick-thin double rule] | MODERN | ESSAYS | SECOND | SERIES | *Selected by* | CHRISTOPHER | MORLEY — — | [rule] | HARCOURT | BRACE & CO.' Back blank. White wove endpapers. Edges trimmed. Dust jacket not seen.

Copies: InU, OGK, STW, TxU-HRC (2 copies).

Published at $2.00 on 8 May 1924; copyright registration A792458 (copies deposited 17 May 1924).

Advertised in *New York Times Book Review* 6 July 1924: 24 and in *Saturday Review of Literature* 9 August 1924: 30. Reviewed in *New York Times Book Review* 18 May 1924: 14; *Independent* 21 June 1924: 344 (D.R.); *Outlook* 2 July 1924: 364 (Edmund Lester

Pearson); *Bookman* August 1924: 742-743 (Richardson Wright); *Nation* 13 August 1924: 168-169 (Johan J. Smertenko); *Saturday Review of Literature* 27 September 1924: 140 (Joseph Wood Krutch).

B 7 **1924**

The Best Poems of 1924

THE BEST POEMS | OF 1924 | EDITED BY | L. A. G. STRONG | Author of "Dublin Days" | Editor of "The Best Poems of 1923" | [within a bouquet device] SCIRE • QVOD | SCIENDVM | [below the device] BOSTON | SMALL, MAYNARD & COMPANY | PUBLISHERS

Copyright page (iv): 'COPYRIGHT, 1924 | By SMALL, MAYNARD & COMPANY | (Incorporated) | Printed in the United States of America | PRINTED BY THE MURRAY PRINTING COMPANY | CAMBRIDGE, MASS. | BOUND BY THE BOSTON BOOK-BINDING COMPANY | CAMBRIDGE, MASS.'

164 x 110 mm. *1-15*^{8} *16*^{4}; 124 leaves. *i-iv* v-vii *viii* ix-xv *xvi* xvii-xxviii *1-2* 3-211 *212* 213-218 *219-220* pp.

Contains Ransom's poems "Captain Carpenter" (165-167), reprinted from the February 1924 *Fugitive* (C69), and "Emily Hardcastle, Spinster" (168), reprinted from the 3 November 1923 *Literary Review* (C67). The texts are those of the periodical appearances, not those of *Chills and Fever* (A2), which had appeared three months earlier.

Type-page 36 lines, 126 (130) x 76 mm, 10 lines = 35 mm (e.g., p. 20); typeface Modern. White laid paper with vertical chainlines 20 mm apart, no watermark, sheets bulk 19 mm.

Bound in dark blue (183) calico cloth stamped in gold. Front: '[within an ornamental border] The Best Poems | of | 1924'. Spine, running across: '[between rules of border ornaments at head and foot] The Best | Poems | of | 1924 | SMALL | MAYNARD | AND | COMPANY'. Back blank. White wove endpapers. Edges trimmed. Dust jacket not seen.

Copies: ICU, IMonC, OGK, STW, TNV. Also in Hogan, *Robinson* p. 68.

Published at $2.00 on 29 November 1924; copyright registration A814506 (copies deposited 2 January 1925). Hogan records one impression of 1500 copies.

Reviewed in *New York Times Book Review* 28 December 1924: 31; *Nashville Tennessean* 4 January 1925, Firing Line sec.: 12 (John Crowe Ransom); *Saturday Review of Literature* 7 February 1925: 515; *Booklist* March 1925: 227; *Bookman* May 1925: 364.

B 8 **1925**

American Poetry 1925

AMERICAN POETRY | 1925 | [42 mm rule] | A MISCELLANY | [Harcourt, Brace device] | NEW YORK | HARCOURT, BRACE AND COMPANY

Copyright page (ii): 'COPYRIGHT, 1925, BY | HARCOURT, BRACE AND COMPANY, INC. | *First edition, August,* 1925 | PRINTED IN THE U.S.A. BY | THE QUINN & BODEN COMPANY | RAHWAY, N.J.'

188 x 125 mm. *1-16*^{8} *17*^{4}; 132 leaves. *i-ii* iii-xiv *1-2* 3-26 *27-28* 29-49 *50-52* 53-64 *65-66* 67-69 *70-72* 73-87 *88-90* 91-102 *103-104* 105-119 *120-122* 123-136 *137-138* 139-142 *143-144* 145-164 *165-166* 167-172 *173-174* 175-180 *181-182* 183-187 *188-190* 191-198 *199-200* 201-206 *207-208* 209-222 *223-224* 225-241 *242-244* 245-248 *249-250* pp.

Contains the sonnet sequence "Two Gentlemen in Bonds" (145-164), consisting of "Pink and Pale," "Thinking, Drinking," "In Air," "Thought, Distraught," "Meeting in a Garden," "Epithalamion of a Peach," "Swine, Wine," "L'état C'est Moi," "Misanthropy," "Vain Protestations," "Tones and Caparisons," "Disappointment of a Thrall," "In Bed, Not Dead," "Primer of Science," "Fait Accompli," "Implacable Tower," "Features of Creatures," "Rain," "Wrong," "Weep or Sleep."

This is the first publication of all the poems except "Rain," which had appeared as "Proud Heart Rained Upon" in *Measure* in June 1925 (C138). The table of contents (xii) incorrectly lists "Tones and Caparisons" as following "Fait Accompli." There are a total of twenty sonnets (one per page), precisely meeting one of the four rules for contributors enumerated by Louis Untermeyer in his foreword: "No editor. Each contributor is to have twenty pages completely at his disposal; he is free to fill all or as many of them as he wishes" (iii). There was some incentive to fill them, since according to rule 1 the royalties were "to be divided in proportion to the length of each poet's contribution" (iii). The other contributors were Conrad Aiken, William Rose Benét, H. D., T. S. Eliot, John Gould Fletcher, Alfred Kreymborg, Vachel Lindsay, Amy Lowell, Edna St. Vincent Millay, Edwin Arlington Robinson, Carl Sandburg, Wallace Stevens, Sara Teasdale, Jean Starr

Untermeyer, Louis Untermeyer, and Elinor Wylie. This is Ransom's only appearance in this "biennial" anthology. The first appeared in 1920, the second in 1922; this was the third (followed by one in 1928).

Type-page 30 lines, 127 (138) x 84 mm, 10 lines = 43 mm (e.g., p. 24); typeface Linotype Old Style. White wove paper, no watermark, sheets bulk 21 mm.

Bound in moderate blue (182) calico cloth over boards. Spine, stamped in gold, running across: 'Miscellany | of | American | Poetry | 1925 | HARCOURT | BRACE & CO.' White wove endpapers. Edges trimmed. Gallup reports a mottled blue dust jacket printed in blue.

Copies: ICU, IRA, STW, TxU-PCL. Also in Bonnell, *Aiken* B18; Boughn, *H.D.* B8; Gallup, *Eliot* Ba2.

Published at $2.00 on 3 September 1925; copyright registration A864536 (copies deposited 11 September 1925). One impression of 2765 copies (Gallup). Reprinted by photo-offset by Granger Books, Miami, FL, in 1977.

Listed in "The Weekly Record," *Publishers' Weekly* 5 September 1925: 752; advertised in the same issue (p. 722). Reviewed in *Independent* 19 September 1925: 331 (C.S.); *Nashville Tennessean* 20 September 1925: Book Review and Literary Page (Donald Davidson); *New York Herald Tribune Books* 29 November 1925: 11 (Newton Arvin); *American Mercury* December 1925: lxxii; *Tower* (Dartmouth College) 12 December 1925: 16 (Richard Eberhart, signed R. G. E.).

B9 **1925**

Modern American Poetry

MODERN AMERICAN | POETRY: [swash initial letters] *A Critical* | *Anthology,* [no swash] *Edited by* | LOUIS UNTERMEYER | THIRD REVISED EDITION | [Harcourt device] | [swash initial letter] *New* [no swash] *York* | HARCOURT, BRACE AND COMPANY

Copyright page (ii): 'COPYRIGHT, 1919, BY | HARCOURT, BRACE AND HOWE, INC. | COPYRIGHT, 1921, 1925, BY | HARCOURT, BRACE AND COMPANY, INC. | PRINTED IN THE U.S.A. BY | THE QUINN & BODEN COMPANY | RAHWAY, N.J.'

206 x 140 mm. *1-41*^{8}; 328 leaves. [2] *i-ii* iii-xi *xii* xiii-xxix *xxx 1-2* 3-29 *30* 31-601 *602* 603 *604-606* 607-621 *622-624* pp.

Contains Ransom's poems "Spiel of the Three Mountebanks" (468), "Here Lies a Lady" (470-471), "First Travels of Max" (471-473), "Piazza Piece" (473), "Antique Harvesters" (474-475). Introduced by Untermeyer's bio-critical headnote (466-468). This is the first book appearance only of "Antique Harvesters." Its text here is the same as that of its publication in the April 1925 *Southwest Review* (C132). The text of "First Travels of Max" seems intermediate between those of *Chills and Fever* (A2) and the 1963 *Selected Poems* (A16), its first line, for example, agreeing with former while its sixty-first agrees with the latter.

Type-page 37 lines, 143 (150) x 89 mm, 10 lines = 39 mm (e.g., pp. v and 272); typeface Caslon. White wove paper, no watermark, sheets bulk 36 mm.

Bound in dark blue (183) linen cloth over boards. Blind-stamped on front: 'MODERN | AMERICAN | POETRY | [eagle] | LOUIS UNTERMEYER'. Spine: title, editor, and publisher stamped in gold. Back blank. White wove endpapers. Top edge cut, fore-edge lightly trimmed, bottom edge trimmed. Dust jacket not seen.

Copies: CSA (2 copies), ICU, IU (rebound), STW.

Published at $3.00 on 17 September 1925; copyright registration A861950 (copies deposited 24 September 1925). Advertised in *New Republic* 9 September 1925: ii. Published in London by Jonathan Cape at 15s. in April 1926.

Reviewed in *American Mercury* December 1925: lxx; *New Republic* 2 December 1925: 42-43 (Edmund Wilson); *New York Herald Tribune Books* 6 December 1925: 1-3 (Stuart Sherman).

B10 **1925**

The Best Poems of 1925

THE BEST POEMS | OF 1925 | EDITED BY | L. A. G. STRONG | Author of "Dublin Days" | Editor of "The Best Poems of 1923" and | "The Best Poems of 1924" | [within a bouquet device] SCIRE • QVOD | SCIENDVM | [below the device] BOSTON | SMALL, MAYNARD & COMPANY | PUBLISHERS

Copyright page (iv): 'Copyright, 1924, by Alfred A. Knopf, Inc., and Sheamas O'Sheel. | Copyright, 1925, by D. Appleton and Company, George H. Doran | Company, Harper and Brothers, Houghton Mifflin Company, B. W. | Huebsch, Inc., The Macmillan Company, Robert M. McBride and Com- | pany, and Charles Scribner's Sons. | Copyright, 1925, by Small, Maynard & Company. | Printed in the United States of America | THE MURRAY PRINTING COMPANY | CAMBRIDGE, MASS. | THE BOSTON BOOKBINDING COMPANY | CAMBRIDGE, MASS.'

164 x 110 mm. $\mathit{1\text{-}14^{8}\ 15^{4}\ 16\text{-}18^{8}}$; 140 leaves. *i-vi* vii-xxix *xxx-xxxiii* 1-241 *242* 243-248 pp.

Contains Ransom's poem "Eclogue" (177-180), reprinted from the *Fugitive* (C129) and published here for the first time in book form, and his poem "Parting at Dawn" (181), reprinted from *Chills* (A2).

Type-page 30 lines, 128 (132) x 76 mm, 10 lines = 43 mm (e.g., p. xix); typeface Bodoni. White laid paper with vertical chainlines 20 mm apart, no watermark, sheets bulk 19 mm.

Bound in dark blue (183) calico cloth stamped in gold. Front: '[within an ornamental border] The Best Poems | of | 1925'. Spine, running across between border ornaments at head and foot: 'The Best | Poems | of | 1925 | SMALL | MAYNARD | AND | COMPANY'. Back blank. White wove endpapers. Edges trimmed. Gallup records a blue dust jacket printed in gold.

Copies: IU, STW, WU. Also in Gallup, *Eliot* Ba3.

Published at $2.00 on 18 November 1925; copyright registration A875165 (copies deposited 20 November). Listed in "Books of the Week," *New York Herald Tribune Books* 29 November 1925: 17, and in "Latest Books," *New York Times Book Review* 29 November 1925: 32. Reviewed in *New York Herald Tribune Books* 6 December 1925: 1-3 (Stuart Sherman); *Nation* 10 February 1926: 162; *Bookman* March 1926: 103; *Booklist* April 1926: 285; *Dial* May 1926: 428.

B11 **1925 (1926?)**

Anthology of Magazine Verse for 1925

Anthology of Magazine Verse | for 1925 | and | Yearbook of American Poetry | Edited by | WILLIAM STANLEY BRAITHWAITE | [line-cut drawing of a boy under a tree, a crane in flight, goats, and a sailing ship, the boy holding a curled paper with the book title and editor's name] | BOSTON | B. J. BRIMMER COMPANY | 1925

Copyright page (iv): 'Copyright, 1925 by | William Stanley Braithwaite | B. J. Brimmer Company | Selling Agents | Copyright, 1925 by | The Boston Transcript Company | Printed in the United States of America'.

207 x 138 mm. 1^{18} 2-16^{16} 17^{8}; 314 leaves. Anthology: [2] *i-iv* v *vi* vii-xxi *xxii* xxiii-xxxiv *1-2* 3-383 *384*; yearbook: *1-2* 3-5 *6* 7-163 *164* 165-169 *170* 171-181 *182* 183-208 pp.

Contains Ransom's poems "The Miller's Daughter" (253-254), "Piazza Piece" (254), "The Last Judgment (A Fresco)" (254-256), "Eclogue" (256-259)—all reprinted from *Fugitive* (C137, C129, C119, C129) and all but "Eclogue" and "Piazza Piece" published here for the first time in book form. There are several misprints (e.g., in the last line of "The Miller's Daughter," 'most' is misprinted as 'mose') but no evident authorial revision.

Type-page (for poetry) 41 lines, 147 (154) x 85 mm, 10 lines = 36 mm (e.g., p. 283); typeface Century. White wove paper, no watermark, sheets bulk 35 mm.

Bound in brownish gray (64) paper with moderate brown (58) calico cloth around the spine. Front: on a white paper label, '[within a double rule frame] BRAITHWAITE'S ANTHOLOGY | OF MAGAZINE VERSE | FOR 1925 | YEARBOOK OF AMERICAN POETRY | [double rule forming a second compartment] WILLIAM STANLEY BRAITHWAITE'. Spine: on a white paper label, '[double rule 37 mm] Anthology *of* | Magazine | Verse | 1925 | [6 mm rule] | BRAITHWAITE | [double rule 37 mm]'. White wove endpapers. Edges trimmed.

Dust jacket of pale yellow wove paper (89) printed in black. Front quotes May Lamberton Becker ("'*BRAITHWAITE'S ANTHOLOGY IS A NATIONAL INSTITUTION.*'") and has title and editor and the same drawing as the title page. Back advertises Edna St. Vincent Millay's *Complete Poems and Plays* and other volumes published by Harper & Brothers. Front flap lists price as $3.00. Back flap asks readers to vote for the best poems in the anthology.

Copies: CSA, ICU (2 copies), IU, STW, TNV (2 copies, 1 with jacket).

Published at $3.00 late in 1925 (Braithwaite's introduction is dated 2 November 1925) or early in 1926. Not found in the *Catalog of Copyright Entries*.

Reviewed in *New York Herald Tribune Books* 14 February 1926: 48 (Allen Tate); *Booklist* July 1926: 408; *Virginia Quarterly Review* July 1926: 442-450 (Howard Mumford Jones).

B12 **1926**

In Memoriam: Herbert Cushing Tolman

IN MEMORIAM | Herbert Cushing Tolman | [drawing of Vanderbilt Phi Beta Kappa Key] | PUBLISHED BY | Alpha of Tennessee | Vanderbilt Chapter of Phi Beta Kappa | NASHVILLE, TENNESSEE | 1926

No copyright notice.

217 x 138 mm. *1-7*^{8}; 56 leaves. *i-ii 1-4* 5-107 *108-110* pp. Plates opposite pp. 1, 13, 30, 53, and 88.

Ransom was a member of the publications committee for this volume in memory of Tolman, who died 24 November 1923 and who had been a classical scholar on the Vanderbilt faculty and founder of Vanderbilt's Phi Beta Kappa chapter. The volume includes Ransom's poem "Nostri in Memoriam Doctissimi" (70), which had appeared in *Vanderbilt Alumnus* (C65) and which he had read at the memorial meeting of the chapter on 5 December 1923.

Type-page 44 lines, 161 (169) x 93 mm, 10 lines = 37 mm (e.g., p. 52); and 37 lines, 10 lines = 44 mm (e.g., p. 50); typeface Century. White wove paper, watermark 'Buckeye', sheets bulk 11 mm.

Bound in dark grayish green (151) diagonal fine-rib cloth stamped in gold. Front: '[within a border of intersecting double lines] IN MEMORIAM | HERBERT CUSHING TOLMAN | [Phi Beta Kappa key within an adjacent border with two pairs of double lines on each side and one pair at the foot]'. Spine: '[swash N] IN | [no swash] MEMORIAM | H.C. | TOLMAN | VANDERBILT | CHAPTER | ΦBK'. Back blank. White wove endpapers. Edges trimmed. No dust jacket seen.

Published in 1926; not recorded in *Catalog of Copyright Entries*.

Copies: STW (inscribed to Ransom by Charles E. Little, who edited the volume), TNV (3 copies).

B13 **1926**

The Best Poems of 1926

THE BEST POEMS | OF 1926 | EDITED BY | L. A. G. STRONG | Editor of "The Best Poems of 1923," | "The Best Poems of 1924," "The | Best Poems of 1925" | [publisher's device] | DODD, MEAD & COMPANY | NEW YORK 1926

Copyright page (iv): 'Copyright, 1926, by Centaur Press, Harcourt, Brace and | Company, Inc., Harper & Brothers, Houghton Mifflin Company, | The Macmillan Company and Yale University Press. | Copyright, 1926, by Dodd, Mead & Company, Inc. | Printed in the U.S.A. | MANUFACTURED IN THE UNITED STATES OF AMERICA |BY THE VAIL-BALLOU PRESS, INC., BINGHAMTON, N.Y.'

163 x 112 mm. *1-16*^{8} *17*^{4}; 132 leaves. *i-iv* v-vii *viii* ix-xvii *xviii* xix-xxv *xxvi-xxviii* 1-234 *235-236* pp.

Contains Ransom's poems "History of Two Simple Lovers" (172-174) and "Lady Lost" (175), both appearing here for the first time in book form. The text of the first is identical to that in *Fugitive*, September 1925 (C146), except that its final stanza is not set in bold-face type. The text of the second poem differs from that in *Fugitive*, December 1925 (C148). In addition to a misprint in line 19 ('soft-jaired' for 'soft-haired'), it has variants in word division and punctuation suggesting that the printer's copy may not have come from the *Fugitive*.

Type-page 30 lines, 128 (132) x 76 mm, 10 lines = 43 mm (e.g., p. 137); typeface Bodoni. White wove paper, no watermark, sheets bulk 20 mm.

Bound in dark purplish blue (201) calico cloth over boards stamped in gold. Front: '[within an ornamental border] The Best Poems | of | 1926'. Spine, running across between border ornaments at head and foot: 'The Best | Poems | of | 1926 | DODD, MEAD | & COMPANY'. Back blank. White wove endpapers. Edges trimmed. Dust jacket not seen.

Copies: ICU, STW, TMM, WU. Also in Higginson and Williams, *Graves* B11.1.

Published at $2.00 on 11 December 1926; copyright registration A958529 (copies deposited 22 December).

Reviewed in *New York Times Book Review* 30 January 1927: 2 (Herbert S. Gorman); *New York Herald Tribune Books* 27 February 1927: 21 (Genevieve Taggard); *Saturday Review of Literature* 7 May 1927: 804 (Louis Untermeyer).

B14 **1928**

Fugitives: An Anthology of Verse

[Within a light grayish red (10) double-line border (135 x 88 mm), the outer line having a circle at each corner and the inner line having circles at intervals of 3 mm] [open face type] FUGITIVES | [not open face] [70 mm rule] | [swash *A*s] *An Anthology of Verse* | [light grayish red heron in flight and two stars] | [71 mm rule] | [swash initial letters] *New York* | [no swash] HARCOURT, BRACE & COMPANY

Copyright page (ii): 'COPYRIGHT, 1928, BY | HARCOURT, BRACE AND COMPANY, INC. | PRINTED IN THE U.S.A. BY | QUINN & BODEN COMPANY, INC. | RAHWAY, N.J.'

190 x 130 mm. *1-11*^{8} χ1.2; 90 leaves. [2] *i-ii* iii-vii *viii* ix-xii *1-2* 3-17 *18-20* 21-24 *25-26* 27-28 *29-30* 31-42 *43-44* 45-58 *59-62* 63-83 *84-86* 87-100 *101-102* 103-116 *117-118* 119-133 *134-136* 137-150 *151-152* 153-164 *165-166* pp.

Contains Ransom's poems "The Lover" (63-64), "Under the Locusts" (65-66), "Necrological" (67-68), "Bells for John Whitesides' [sic] Daughter" (69), "Judith of Bethulia" (70-72), "Captain Carpenter" (73-75), "Our Two Worthies" (76-78), "The Equilibrists" (79-81), "What Ducks Require" (82-83). These poems in this order are what Ransom suggested for his section of the anthology (letter to Tate, 25 June 1927, *SL* 174-175). All but the last of them had appeared in at least one of his own volumes. "What Ducks Require" is here first published in book form and in a text differing substantively from that of its appearance in *New Republic* (C157). In *The Fugitive Group* Louise Cowan provides an account of the preparation, publication, and reception of the anthology (247-257). The foreword was written by Donald Davidson, revised somewhat by Tate, and vetted by the other contributors. In addition to Ransom, Tate, and Davidson, the contributors were William Yandell Elliott, James Marshall Frank, Stanley Johnson, Merrill Moore, Laura Riding, Alec Brock Stevenson, Robert Penn Warren, and Jesse Wills.

Type-page typically has 31 lines, 134 (145) x 88 mm (e.g., pp. v and 92); typeface Garamond. White laid paper with vertical chain-lines 18 mm apart; watermark 'WARREN'S | OLDE STYLE'; sheets bulk 15 mm.

Bound in paper over boards and dark violet (212) calico cloth around the spine. The paper is white with horizontal zig-zag patterns of light violet (210) and moderate reddish brown (43). Front: on a white paper label printed in light grayish red (10), '[67 mm rule] | [68 mm rule resting on 14 circles] | [open face] FUGITIVES | [not open, swash *A*s] *An Anthology of Verse* | [two rules as above, but reversed]'. Spine: on a white paper label printed in light grayish red, '[23 mm double rule] FUGITIVES | [swash *A*s] *An* | *Anthology* | *of Verse* | [23 mm rule] | [no swash] HARCOURT, BRACE | AND COMPANY | [23 mm double rule]'. Back blank. White wove endpapers. Top edge trimmed; others rough trimmed.

Dust jacket of pale orange-yellow (73) wove paper printed in moderate brown (58) and dark reddish purple (242). Front: '[inline script] *fugitives* | [heron and 4 stars in purple] | [not script] AN ANTHOLOGY OF VERSE'. Back has order form for Harcourt, Brace volumes. Front flap has a blurb. Back flap advertises *American Poetry 1927: A Miscellany* (mistakenly listing Ransom as among its contributors).

Copies: IEdS, STW (3 copies, 1 with jacket), TNV (3 copies, 1 with jacket), TxU-HRC (with jacket).

Published at $2.50 on 26 January 1928; copyright registration A1061501 (copies deposited 1 February 1928). Announced "for early publication" in *Nashville Tennessean* 15 January 1928, mag. sec.: 7. Not advertised by Harcourt among its 39 books in "Selections of Spring Titles," *Publishers' Weekly* 10 March 1928: 928-929.

Reviewed in *Nashville Tennessean* 26 February 1928, magazine section: 7 (William S. Knickerbocker); *New Republic* 7 March 1928: 103-104 (Edmund Wilson); *Nation* 14 March 1928: 296 (Mark Van Doren); *Sewanee Review* April 1928: 211-224 (William S. Knickerbocker); *Poetry* May 1928: 102-107 (Yvor Winters); *Bookman* June 1928: 441-443 (Babette Deutsch); *Dial* 84 (June 1928): 523 (Marianne Moore, unsigned); *Saturday Review of Literature* 23 June 1928: 994 (William Rose Benét). Merrill Moore's *The Fugitive: Clippings and Comment* (B26) reprints most of these reviews and, in addition, one from the *Nashville Banner* 2 February 1928.

B15 **1929**

The Noise That Time Makes

THE NOISE THAT TIME MAKES | BY MERRILL MOORE | WITH A FOREWORD BY JOHN CROWE RANSOM | [drawing of a clock] | HARCOURT, BRACE AND COMPANY | NEW YORK

Copyright page (iv): 'COPYRIGHT, 1929, BY | HARCOURT, BRACE AND COMPANY, INC. | PRINTED IN THE UNITED STATES OF AMERICA | BY QUINN & BODEN COMPANY, INC., RAHWAY, N.J. | TYPOGRAPHY BY ROBERT S. JOSEPHY'.

197 x 134 mm. *1-8*^{8} *9*^{4}; 68 leaves. *i-viii* ix-xiii *xiv* xv-xix *xx 1-2* 3-27 *28-30* 31-56 *57-58* 59-83 *84-86* 87-111 *112* 113 *114-116* pp.

Contains a foreword (ix-xiii) by Ransom (ending 'JOHN CROWE RANSOM | *Nashville, Tennessee,* 1929').

Type-page 23 lines, 130 (135) x 92 mm, 10 lines = 57 mm (e.g., p. xi); typeface Bodoni. White wove paper, watermark 'WARREN'S | OLDE STYLE', sheets bulk 11 mm.

Bound in paper over boards and black calico cloth around the spine. The paper has a diagonal design in moderate yellow (87) and in black shaded to gray and then white. Spine, stamped in gold, running across: 'THE | NOISE | THAT | TIME | MAKES | • | MOORE | HARCOURT | BRACE&CO'. White wove endpapers. Edges trimmed.

Dust jacket of pale orange-yellow (73) wove paper printed in black and dark reddish orange (38). Front: title in orange-yellow on black; drawing of a shell, lightning, and telephone; and author's name. Back: order form for Harcourt, Brace books. Front flap: a blurb. Back flap advertises Helen Hoyt's *Leaves of Wild Grape.*

Copies: ICU (inscribed by Moore to the University of Chicago, May 1932), INS, InU-Lilly (inscribed by Moore to Max Eastman, October 1929), STW (2 copies, one inscribed to William Stanley Braithwaite in October 1929, the other inscribed to Ransom in

October 1929 with jacket and having a x-ray photograph of Moore's skull and cervical vertebrae pasted to the front pastedown endpaper and with a publicity photograph), TNV (2 copies, one with jacket and inscription by Moore to Alfred and Elizabeth [Starr], October 1929), TxU-HRC (2 copies, one inscribed by Moore to Idella Purnell, October 1929, and with x-ray photograph as above and with a photograph of Moore, in the flesh and clothed, pasted to the back pastedown, and the other copy, with jacket, inscribed by Moore to Christopher Morley, October 1929).

Published at $2.00 on 10 October 1929; copyright registration A14209 (copies deposited 17 October 1929).

Reviewed in *Saturday Review of Literature* 9 November 1929: 364 (Louis Untermeyer); *New York Herald Tribune Books* 17 November 1929: 4 (Babette Deutsch); *New York Times Book Review* 24 November 1929: 35; *Virginia Quarterly Review* January 1930: 151-160 (James Southall Wilson); *Hound & Horn* January-March 1930: 285-287 (Dudley Fitts); *New Republic* 29 January 1930: 280 (Robert Penn Warren); *Poetry* May 1930: 104-106 (Yvor Winters).

Ransom's foreword also appears (reset, with textual variation) on pages 3-5 of a 32-page undated (1939?) pamphlet privately printed for Moore (TNV). The front of its moderate blue (182) wrapper is used as a title page: 'Foreword | BY JOHN CROWE RANSOM | TO | The Noise That Time Makes | A FIRST VOLUME OF 101 SONNETS | BY | MERRILL MOORE | AND SOME REVIEWS OF THIS BOOK'. A copy of this pamphlet was also bound up with others in a volume without a title page but with a spine title stamped in gold on a black leather label: '[rule] | POEMS | AND | COMMENT | [rule] | MERRILL | MOORE | [rule]' (TNV). So too was a copy bound up with other pamphlets and off-prints in a volume with a title page reading 'MERRILL MOORE | A MISCELLANY | First Series | I-X | Boston, Massachusetts | 1939' and, as Part VI, in a volume entitled *Poems and Sonnets of Merrill Moore with Reviews and Comments: Seven Pamphlets in One Volume* (Boston, 1949) (WBB). The foreword was also reprinted as a foreword to Moore's *Fugitive Sonnets* (D139).

B16 **1930**

Modern American Poetry

MODERN | AMERICAN POETRY | *A CRITICAL ANTHOLOGY* | *Edited by Louis Untermeyer* | [circular design of two Pegasuses drinking from a trough] | FOURTH REVISED EDITION | HARCOURT, BRACE AND COMPANY | *NEW YORK*

Copyright page (iv): 'COPYRIGHT, 1919, BY | HARCOURT, BRACE AND HOWE, INC. | COPYRIGHT, 1921, 1925, 1930, BY | HARCOURT, BRACE AND COMPANY, INC. | *Typography by Robert S. Josephy* | PRINTED IN THE UNITED STATES OF AMERICA | BY QUINN & BODEN COMPANY, INC., RAHWAY, N.J.'

203 x 139 mm. *1-27*^{16} *28*^{8} *29*^{4}; 444 leaves. *i-iv* v-xiii *xiv* xv-xxxviii *1-2* 3-832 *833-834* 835-850 pp.

Contains Ransom's poems "Bells for John Whitesides' Daughter" (574), "Spiel of the Three Mountebanks" (575-577), "Here Lies a Lady" (577), "First Travels of Max" (577-579), "Lady Lost" (579), "Antique Harvesters" (580-581), "Piazza Piece" (581-582), "Captain Carpenter" (582-584), "Blue Girls" (584), "Old Man Pondered" (584-585). This is the first book publication of "Old Man Pondered," reprinted from the 15 June 1929 *Saturday Review* (C172). In a letter to Untermeyer on 7 July 1931, Ransom said that he had used this edition of *Modern American Poetry* in his "course on Modern Literature at Vanderbilt in the spring" and that he was using it also that summer in a course at West Tennessee Teachers College (*SL* 203-204).

Type-page 41 lines, 146 (152) x 93 mm, 10 lines = 36 mm (e.g., p. 25); typeface Bodoni. White wove paper, no watermark, sheets bulk 38 mm.

Bound in moderate blue (182) calico cloth over boards. Front: blindstamped circular design like that on title page. Spine stamped in gold, running across: 'MODERN | AMERICAN | POETRY | [37 mm rule] | UNTERMEYER | HARCOURT, BRACE | & COMPANY'. White wove endpapers. Top and bottom edges trimmed; fore-edge rough trimmed. Edelstein reports a cream dust jacket printed in black and blue.

Copies: STW, TxU-HRC, WU-Col (rebound). Also in Bonnell, *Aiken* B30; Edelstein, *Stevens* B18

Published at $3.50 on 16 July 1930; copyright registration A25648 (copies deposited 26 July 1930). Edelstein reports a first impression of 6800 copies; Bonnell, who like Edelstein gives a publication date of 14 June 1930, reports copies in a textbook binding for sale at $2.50 and copies in three-quarter morocco for sale at $10.00.

Reviewed in *Saturday Review of Literature* 2 August 1930: 24 (William Rose Benét); *New England Quarterly* October 1930: 772-773 (Frederic I. Carpenter); *American Mercury* November 1930: xii, xiv; *Poetry* December 1930: 164-171; *American Literature* March 1931: 115-116 (David Cornel DeJong), with a response by Untermeyer in the May 1931 issue (319-320).

B17 **1930**

I'll Take My Stand

B17.a Harper impression (1930)

[84 mm ornamental rule] I'LL TAKE MY STAND | [swash *T*s and *A*] *The South and the Agrarian Tradition* | [no swash] By TWELVE SOUTHERNERS | [84 mm ornamental rule] | [Harper device] | [84 mm ornamental rule] HARPER & BROTHERS PUBLISHERS | 19•*New York and London*•30 | [84 mm ornamental rule]

Copyright page (iv): '*FIRST EDITION* | I'LL TAKE MY STAND: *Copyright, 1930, by* | *Harper & Brothers. Printed in the U.S.A.* | K-E'. The code 'K-E' indicates a printing date of October 1930.

205 x 137 mm. *1-24*^{8}; 192 leaves. *i-vi* vii-xx *xxi-xxii* 1-359 *360-362* pp. Grimshaw records a collation of "[1^{10} ($+1_1$) 2-19^{10}]" and pagination ending "359 [360]," for a total of 191 leaves.

Contains an unsigned "Introduction: A Statement of Principles" (ix-xx), for which Ransom had primary responsibility, and his signed essay "Reconstructed but Unregenerate" (1-27). The essay is in large part a revised version of "The South Defends Its Heritage," which had appeared in the June 1929 issue of *Harper's Magazine* (C171), with additions from "The South—Old or New?", which had appeared in the April 1928 issue of *Sewanee Review* (C166) and which itself has portions used in the *Harper's* essay. In a letter to Tate on 4 July 1929, Ransom explained that "Reconstructed by Unregenerate" had been his own title for the essay in *Sewanee Review* but had been changed to "The South—Old or New?" by its editors (*SL* 182). In *Waking Their Neighbors Up*, Thomas Daniel Young quotes from Ransom's unpublished "Articles of an Agrarian Reform," an early draft of an introductory statement for the collection (11-13), as well as from unpublished correspondence relating to it and to the Agrarian movement generally. For the history of the volume, see also Virginia Rock's "The Making and Meaning of *I'll Take My Stand.*" Donald Davidson received and edited the essays from the contributors. For Davidson's account of the venture, see his "*I'll Take My Stand*: A History."

Type-page 30 lines, 148 (159) x 97 mm, 10 lines = 49 mm (e.g., p. 9); typeface Granjon. White wove paper, no watermark, sheets bulk 36 mm.

Bound in dark grayish green (151) calico over boards. Front: [stamped on a gold band] 'I'LL TAKE MY STAND | [on another gold band] BY TWELVE SOUTHERNERS'. Spine, running across: '[stamped on a gold band] I'LL TAKE | [on another gold band] MY STAND | [stamped in gold] BY TWELVE | SOUTH-ERNERS | [30 mm rule ornamented at each end with a dot] | HARPERS'. Back blank. White wove endpapers. Edges trimmed. Top edge stained brownish orange (54). Grimshaw reports a dust jacket in gray and blue.

Copies: ICIU (top-edge stain faded or absent), IU (rebound), STW (3 copies, including one with jacket and one inscribed by Donald Davidson to his father on 7 November 1930), TNV. Also in Grimshaw, *Warren* B2.

Listed in the "Fall Book Index," *Publishers' Weekly* 20 September 1930: n.p., as by "Eleven Southerners" and with a probable price of $3.00. Publication forecast for 15 October in *Nashville Tennessean* 3 August 1930, Firing Line section: 12.

Published at $3.00 on 12 November 1930; copyright registration A31038 (copies deposited 12 November 1930). Publication noted in "The Weekly Record," *Publishers' Weekly* 15 November 1930: 2335. Advertised in *Nation* 3 December 1930: 629.

Reviewed in *Hound & Horn* 1930: 436-439 (Thomas D. Mabry); *Vanderbilt Alumnus* November-December 1930: 37 (Mapheus Smith); *Nashville Tennessean* 16 November 1930, society section: 8 (James I. Finney); *Saturday Review of Literature* 20 December 1930: 467-468 (William S. Knickerbocker; for a response to this review, see a letter by Helen Hill, 24 January 1931: 556); *Sewanee Review* January-March 1931: 97-103 (W. B. Hesseltine); *Annals of the American Academy of Political and Social Sciences* January 1931: 268 (F. C. James); *Symposium* January 1931: 145-149 (James Southall Wilson); *Virginia Quarterly Review* January 1931: 152-157 (Gerald W. Johnson); *New York Times Book Review* 4 January 1931: 3 (Arthur Krock); *Nation* 14 January 1931: 48-49 (Henry Hazlitt); *Nation* 21 January 1931: 67-68

(Stringfellow Barr); *Yale Review* March 1931: 611-613 (Ulrich B. Phillips); *Booklist* April 1931: 359; *Criterion* April 1931: 483-485 (T. S. Eliot); *Management Review* May 1931: 158 (W. J. Donald, signed W. J. D.).

B17.b Peter Smith reprint (1951)

[84 mm ornamental rule] I'LL TAKE MY STAND | [swash *T*s and *A*] *The South and the Agrarian Tradition* | [no swash] By TWELVE SOUTHERNERS | [84 mm ornamental rule] | [84 mm ornamental rule] NEW YORK | PETER SMITH | 1951 | [84 mm ornamental rule]

Copyright page (iv): 'I'LL TAKE MY STAND: *Copyright, 1930, by | Harper & Brothers. Printed in the U.S.A. | Reprinted, 1951 | By permission of Harper and Brothers*'.

This is an offset reprinting of the original Harper typesetting, with no alteration in pagination, collation, or typography. The leaf size is 203 x 134 mm, and the sheets bulk 22 mm.

Bound in moderate blue (182) calico cloth over boards. Front and back blank. Spine, running across: 'I'LL TAKE | MY STAND | PETER SMITH'. White wove endpapers. Edges trimmed. No dust jacket seen.

Copies: IDeKN, STW, TxU-UG, WU-Col.

B17.c Harper Torchbook revised impression (1962)

I'LL | *THE SOUTH* TAKE | *AND THE AGRARIAN TRADITION* | MY | STAND | *BY TWELVE SOUTHERNERS* | *Introduction by Louis D. Rubin, Jr.* | *Biographical Essays By Virginia Rock* | [thick rule extending left from fore-edge to the fore-edge of the facing page] | [facing page] *HARPER TORCHBOOKS* [torch device] *THE ACADEMY LIBRARY* | *HARPER & BROTHERS, NEW YORK*

Copyright page (iv): '[eight line dedication to Walter L. Fleming] | I'LL TAKE MY STAND | COPYRIGHT, 1930, BY HARPER &

BROTHERS. RENEWED COPYRIGHT | 1958 BY DONALD DAVIDSON. INTRODUCTION TO THE TORCHBOOK | EDITION COPYRIGHT © 1962 BY LOUIS D. RUBIN, JR. BIOGRAPHICAL | ESSAYS TO THE TORCHBOOK EDITION COPYRIGHT © 1962 BY | VIRGINIA ROCK. | PRINTED IN THE UNITED STATES OF AMERICA. THIS BOOK WAS | ORIGINALLY PUBLISHED BY HARPER & BROTHERS IN 1930. | FIRST HARPER TORCHBOOK EDITION PUBLISHED 1962 | [6-line reservation of rights] | [thick rule extending from the facing page to the fore-edge]'.

203 x 135 mm. 208 leaves. *i-v* vi-xxx 1-384 *385-386* pp.

This is an offset reprinting of the original Harper typesetting, without photographic reduction or enlargement but with alterations in the preliminaries (including new half title, title page, copyright page, and contents page) and with reset titles for each of the essays. Also added to the original are Rubin's introduction (vi-xviii) and Rock's "Twelve Southerners: Biographical Essays." The wavy dashes separating paragraphs in Ransom's "Introduction: A Statement of Principles" (now on pp. xix-xxx) have been omitted. There is also some textual revision that either first appears here or perhaps derives from a Harper impression later than the first. At p. 43, a sentence in lines 18-20 reads in the first impression: 'Political | democracy becomes allied with industrialism can it be con- | unrealized.' At some point, as is seen in the Torchbook impression, the garble was changed to this: 'Political | democracy, as Mr. Laski has shown, left social democracy | unrealized.' Also, at p. 238, line 8, the misprint 'They are' has been corrected to 'There are'. White wove paper, no watermark, sheets bulk 22 mm.

Perfect bound in stiff white paper lettered in black and moderate yellow-green (120), the design on front resembling a large vivid orange sun on a white background and above a yellow-green ploughed field. No endpapers. The front cover indicates that the book is Torchbook TB1072, with a price of $2.25.

Copies: IDeKN (spine obscured by tape), INS (rebound), STW (Robert Penn Warren's copy with his autograph emendations), TxU-UG (rebound).

Published at $2.25 in 1962. Reviewed in *Sewanee Review* 71 (Winter 1963): 133-142 (Edward M. Moore)

B17.d Peter Smith reprint from the Harper Torchbook impression (1976)

I'LL | THE SOUTH TAKE | *AND THE AGRARIAN TRADITION* | MY | STAND | *BY TWELVE SOUTHERNERS* | *Introduction by Louis D. Rubin, Jr.* | *Biographical Essays By Virginia Rock* | GLOUCESTER, MASS. | PETER SMITH | 1976

Reprinted from the Harper Torchbook impression. Bound in light gray calico cloth over boards, spine lettering stamped in black. Copies: CSA, STW, TNV.

B17.e LSU impression from the Harper Torchbook impression (1977)

I'LL | TAKE | MY | STAND | *The South and the* | *Agrarian Tradition* | BY TWELVE SOUTHERNERS | *Introduction by Louis D. Rubin, Jr.* | Biographical Essays by Virginia Rock | [thick rule, 137 mm] | LOUISIANA STATE UNIVERSITY PRESS | *Baton Rouge and London*

Copyright page (vi): 'Copyright 1930 by Harper & Brothers | Copyright renewed 1958 by Donald Davidson | Introduction copyright © 1962, 1977 by Louis D. Rubin, Jr. | Biographical essays copyright © 1962, 1977 by Virginia Rock | Manufactured in the United States of America | All rights reserved | [LC cataloging-in-publication data] | ISBN 0-8071-0357-8'.

210 x 137 mm. 232 leaves. *i-x* xi-xxxv *xxxvi* xxxvii-xlviii *xlix-l* 1-359 *360* 361-410 *411-414* pp.

Reprinted from the Torchbook impression, with revised preliminaries (including the addition of another introduction by Rubin) and with updating and resetting of Rock's biographies. Ransom's introduction now occupies pp. xxxvii-xlviii. White wove paper, no watermark, sheets bulk 23 mm.

Perfect bound in stiff wove paper, lettered in moderate reddish brown (43) and white on a background of vivid yellow (82) and white on front and spine and background of white on back. No endpapers. Back bears the price of $5.95.

Copies: CSA, STW, TxU-UG (rebound, preserving covers).

Published at $5.95 in 1977 as a title in the Library of Southern Civilization series edited by Lewis P. Simpson.

Reviewed in *Sewanee Review* 86 (October-December 1978): 595-604 (Thomas Daniel Young).

B18 **1934**

Daemon in the Rock

[Swash D and R] *Daemon in the Rock* | [89 mm wavy rule] | *BY* | *EDWIN RICHARDSON FROST* | [Putman monogram device] | [89 mm wavy rule] | *G. P. PUTMAN'S SONS* | *NEW YORK* | *1934*

Copyright page (iv): 'COPYRIGHT, 1934, BY EDWIN RICHARDSON FROST | [reservation of rights in 2 lines] | PRINTED IN THE UNITED STATES OF AMERICA'.

197 x 131 mm. *1-4*^{8}; 32 leaves. *i-vi* vii-xi *xii 13-14* 15-61 *62-64* pp.

Contains a foreword by Ransom (ix-x).

Type-page with varying number of lines, 139 (150) x 89 mm, 10 lines = 43 mm (e.g., pp. ix-x); typeface Granjon. White wove paper, no watermark, sheets bulk 6 mm.

Bound in vivid purplish blue (194) diagonal fine-rib cloth over boards, stamped in strong reddish orange (35). Front: '[swash D, Es, and T] *DAEMON IN THE ROCK* | [96 mm triple rule] | [swash Es and T] *EDWIN RICHARDSON FROST'*. Spine: title, ornament, author, and publisher. White wove endpapers. Edges trimmed. Top edge stained moderate reddish orange (37).

Dust jacket of pale orange-yellow (73) wove paper printed in blackish blue (188). Front: title, author, quotation from Sidney Mttron Hirsch. Back blank. Front flap: blurb. Back flap: biographical note, price.

Copies: CSA, STW (2 copies, one with jacket and another inscribed by Frost to Ransom on 28 April 1934), TNV (with jacket).

Published at $1.50 on 27 April 1934; copyright registration A72359 (copies deposited 3 May 1934). Reviewed in *New York Times Book Review* 17 June 1934: 12; *New York Herald Tribune Books* 29 July 1924: 13.

B19 **1936**

Modern American Poetry

[Within a thick-thin rule frame] [open face] Modern | American Poetry | [not open face] *A CRITICAL ANTHOLOGY* | EDITED BY LOUIS UNTERMEYER | [circular line drawing of two winged horses drinking from a trough] FIFTH REVISED EDITION | *Harcourt, Brace and Company, New York*

Copyright page (iv): 'COPYRIGHT, 1919, 1921, 1925, 1930, 1936, BY | HARCOURT, BRACE AND COMPANY, INC. | [reservation of rights in 3 lines] | PRINTED IN THE UNITED STATES OF AMERICA | BY QUINN & BODEN COMPANY, INC., RAHWAY, N.J.'

228 x 154 mm. *1-21*^{16} 22^{4}; 340 leaves. *i-iv* v-xxv *xxvi 1-2* 3-641 *642* 643-654 pp.

Contains Ransom's poems "Bells for John Whitesides' Daughter" (437-438), "Lady Lost" (438), "Blue Girls" (438), "Here Lies a Lady" (439), "Janet Waking" (439-440), "Spiel of the Three Mountebanks" (440-441), "First Travels of Max" (441-442), "Antique Harvesters" (442-443), "Piazza Piece" (443-444), "Captain Carpenter" (444-445), "Old Man Pondered" (445-446), "Parting, without a Sequel" (446), "Prelude to an Evening" (447), "Painting: A Head" (447). This is the first book publication of "Prelude to an Evening," which had appeared in the May 1934 *American Review* (C198), and of "Painting: A Head," which had appeared in the 26 December 1934 *New Republic* (C204). The texts here are those of the periodical publication, with the exception of the title of "Painting: A Head" (which in all previous appearances is "Painted Head").

Type-page 47 lines, 184 (190) x 118, 10 lines = 39 mm (e.g., p. 436); typeface Caslon. White wove paper, no watermark, sheets bulk 36 mm.

Bound in moderate reddish brown (43) calico cloth over boards. Front: stamped in silver within a frame formed by four intersecting blind-stamped rules, 'MODERN | AMERICAN | POETRY'. Spine: title, author, and publisher stamped in silver. Back: intersecting blind-stamped rules like those on the front. White wove endpapers. Edges trimmed. Top edge stained yellow (fading and soiling prevent a more specific designation). Dust jacket not seen.

Copies: ICU, IDeK, STW, WU (rebound). Also in Hogan, *Robinson* p. 71.

Published at $3.50 on 5 March 1936; copyright registration A92370 (copies deposited 19 March 1936). Hogan reports a first impression of 10,000 copies, 3000 of which were issued as a text edition without top-edge stain but otherwise identical to the trade issue. Also issued in a "combined edition," that is, bound up with the 1936 edition (4th ed.) of *Modern British Poetry* and sharing with it a single title page.

Reviewed in *Christian Century* 1 April 1936: 507; *Booklist* May 1936: 264; *Saturday Review of Literature* 9 May 1936: 19 (William Rose Benét); *Commonweal* 15 May 1936: 84; *New York Herald Tribune Books* 17 May 1936: 11 (Ben Ray Redman); *New England Quarterly* March 1937: 189-190 (John Finch).

B20 **1936**

Southern Poets

[Script] Southern Poets | [roman] REPRESENTATIVE SELECTIONS, WITH | INTRODUCTION, BIBLIOGRAPHY, AND NOTES | BY | EDD WINFIELD PARKS | [ornament] AWS [ornament] | [84 mm rule] AMERICAN BOOK COMPANY | *New York • Cincinnati • Chicago | Boston • Atlanta*

Copyright page (iv): 'COPYRIGHT, 1936, BY | AMERICAN BOOK COMPANY | *All rights reserved* | [13 mm rule] | PARK'S SOUTHERN POETS | W.P.I. | MADE IN U.S.A.'

178 x 110 mm. *1-33*^{8} *34-35*^{10}; 284 leaves. *i-iv* v-cxxix *cxxx* cxxxi-cxlviii *1-2* 3-319 *320* 321-375 *376* 377-399 *400* 401-419 *420* pp.

Contains Ransom's poems "Spectral Lovers" (270-271), "Here Lies a Lady" (271), "Judith of Bethulia" (271-273), "Blue Girls" (273), "Our Two Worthies" (273-275), and "Autumn Love" (275-276), this last poem appearing here for the first time in book form but in a text identical to that of its earlier appearance in the 20 February 1929 *New Republic* (C169).

Type-page (for verse) 37 lines, 142 (149) x 84 mm, 10 lines = 38 mm (e.g., p. 290); typeface Fournier. White wove paper, no watermarks, sheets bulk 20 mm.

Bound in dark blue (183) calico cloth over boards, stamped in gold. Front: '[triple rule, 103 mm] | ★ | Southern Poets | ★ | [triple rule, 103 mm]'. Spine: '[triple rule, 30 mm] | Southern | Poets | ★ | Parks | [ornament] | AWS | [ornament] | American | Book | Company | [triple rule, 30 mm]'. Back: blind-stamped publisher's device. White wove endpapers. Edges trimmed. Dust jacket not seen.

Copies: IDeKN, STW, TNV, TxU-HRC, WBB.

Published at $1.00 on 10 March 1936 in the American Writers Series edited by Harry H. Clark; copyright registration A92212 (copies deposited 13 March 1936). Reprinted in 1970 by Phaeton Press, Inc., New York.

Reviewed in *South Atlantic Quarterly* April 1936: 233-234 (David K. Jackson); *Commonweal* 5 June 1936: 168; *Sewanee Review* October-December 1936: 507-509 (Merrill Moore); *American Literature* November 1936: 347-348; *William and Mary Quarterly* January 1937: 126-127 (Charles T. Harrison)

B21 **1936**

Who Owns America?

WHO OWNS AMERICA? | *A New Declaration of Independence* | EDITED BY | HERBERT AGAR & ALLEN TATE | [92 mm rule] | [Houghton Mifflin device] | [92 mm rule] | BOSTON Houghton Mifflin Company NEW YORK | [black letter] The Riverside Press Cambridge | [roman] 1936

Copyright page (iv): 'COPYRIGHT, 1936, BY HOUGHTON MIFFLIN COMPANY | ALL RIGHTS RESERVED INCLUDING THE RIGHT TO REPRODUCE | THIS BOOK OR PARTS THEREOF IN ANY FORM | [black letter] The Riverside Press | [roman] CAMBRIDGE • MASSACHUSETTS | PRINTED IN THE U.S.A.'

205 x 138 mm. *1-22*^{8}; 176 leaves. *i-v* vi *vii* viii-x *1-3* 4-109 *110-113* 114-214 *215-217* 218-279 *280-283* 284-342 pp. (but no pagination on initial page of each of the 21 essays).

Contains Ransom's essay "What Does the South Want?" The text differs substantively from the version published in the April 1936 *Virginia Quarterly Review* (C218). The introduction by Herbert Agar defines the "common ground" of the 21 contributors as "a belief that monopoly capitalism is evil and self-destructive, and that it is possible, while preserving private ownership, to build a true democracy in which men would be better off both morally and physically, more likely to attain that inner peace which is the mark of a good life" (ix). Eight of the contributors had also appeared in *I'll Take My Stand* (B17).

Type-page 37 lines, 155 (163) x 93 mm, 10 lines = 42 mm (e.g., 185); typeface Caslon. White wove paper, no watermark, sheets bulk 30 mm.

Bound in moderate blue calico cloth over boards. Front, stamped in blackish blue (188): 'WHO OWNS | AMERICA?'. Spine, stamped in blackish blue: 'WHO OWNS | AMERICA? | [16 mm rule] | [14 mm rule] | AGAR & TATE | HOUGHTON | MIFFLIN • CO'. Back blank. Edges trimmed. White wove endpapers.

Dust jacket of white wove paper. Front: '[on a background progressing from light greenish gray (154) at the top to blackish blue (188) at the foot] [black] WHO OWNS | *America*? | [white] *A* NEW DECLARATION *of* | INDEPENDENCE | [moderate reddish orange (37) star] | [white] *Edited by* HERBERT AGAR | *and* ALLEN TATE | [reddish orange rule] | *Democracy yesterday; Plutocracy today;* | *Fascism perhaps tomorrow. It can happen* | *here unless we act at once.*' On the back are quotations from the book, within a rule frame. Front flap: price, blurb. Back flap: photograph of Agar and biographical note.

Copies: IDeKN, OGK, STW, TNV (2 copies), WMM.

Published at $3.00 on 28 April 1936; copyright registration A94339 (copies deposited 8 May 1936).

Listed in "The Weekly Record," *Publishers' Weekly* 2 May 1936: 1801. $3.00; in "Latest Books Received," *New York Times Book Review* 3 May 1936: 25; and in *Booklist* June 1936: 280. Advertised in *New Republic* 27 May 1936: 82, and included in "A Check List of Summer Books," 24 June 1936: 212

Reviewed in *New York Times Book Review* 10 May 1936: 1, 13 (John Corbin); *Current History* June 1936: 3; *Review of Reviews* June 1936: 12-13 (Herschel Brickell); *Commonweal* 12 June 1936: 191-193 (R. A. McGowan); *Southern Review* Summer 1936: 15-21 (Crane Brinton); *Virginia Quarterly Review* July 1936: 476-480 (Stringfellow Barr); *New Republic* 1 July 1936: 245-246 (Kenneth Burke); *Saturday Review of Literature* 25 July 1936: 17 (John Chamberlain); *Harvard Business Review* Autumn 1936: 131 (Dan Throop Smith); *American Review* October 1936: 601-604 (Seward Collins); *Foreign Affairs* October 1936: 208; *TLS* 3 October 1936: 792.

B22 **1936**

Announcement

November 1, 1936. | *Announcement* | To Persons Interested in Agrarian, Distributist and Homestead Principles | [text begins]

No copyright notice. The leaflet is signed on the final page: 'Committee for the Alliance of Agrarian and Distributist Groups: | Lyle H. Lanier | John Crowe Ransom | Rev. John C. Rawe | Chard Powers Smith | James M. Waller, Secretary, | 124 Twenty-first Avenue, South, | Nashville, Tenn.'

235 x 159 mm. *1*^{2}; 2 leaves. *1-4* pp.

Contains a report on the conference of Agrarians and Distributists held in Nashville on 4-5 June 1936, definitions of the two groups, announcement of plans for a monthly publication, an invitation to membership in the Alliance, and a "Statement of Agrarian and Distributist Principles Adopted on June 5, 1936." For a brief account of the conference, see Conkin 124-126. The plans for a monthly publication eventually produced the magazine *Free America*, to which Ransom contributed once (see C247).

Type-page 202 x 127 mm, 10 lines = 44 mm; typeface Century. White wove paper, no watermark.

No binding. Edges cut.

Copy: STW.

B23 **1937**

Southern Treasury of Life and Literature

[102 mm crenellated rule] | SOUTHERN | TREASURY | *of* LIFE *and* | LITERATURE | [102 mm crenellated rule] | SELECTED BY | STARK YOUNG | *Author of* | SO RED THE ROSE | FELICIANA • THE THREE FOUNTAINS | HEAVEN TREES | [102 mm crenellated rule] | CHARLES SCRIBNER'S SONS | NEW YORK CHICAGO BOSTON | SAN FRANCISCO DALLAS ATLANTA

Copyright page (iv): 'COPYRIGHT, 1937, BY | CHARLES SCRIBNER'S SONS | [8 mm rule] | Printed in the United States of America | [reservation of rights in 3 lines] | A | [Scribner press device]'.

196 x 131 mm. 1^8 $2\text{-}24^{16}$ 25^8; 384 leaves. *i-iv* v-xviii *xix-xx* 1-742 *743-744* 745-748 pp.

Contains Ransom's poems "Autumn Love (English Sonnet of Italian Parts)" (478-479), in a text identical to that in the 20 February 1929 *New Republic*, where it first appeared (C169); "Spectral Lovers" (479-480), in a unique text; "Blue Girls" (480), in a text identical to that of *Two Gentlemen in Bonds* (A4); and "Judith of Bethulia" (480-481), in a unique text. The text of "Spectral Lovers" appears to have been slightly revised from that of *Chills and Fever* (A2) and misprints 'wishing' for 'swishing' in line 20. The text of "Judith of Bethulia" is that of *Fugitives: An Anthology of Verse* (B14), except that in line 8 'Gray' replaces 'Grey' and that in line 41 the reading is 'that thought' while other published texts read 'the thought'. None of the poems appears here for the first time in book form.

Type-page 41 lines, 160 (166) x 102 mm, 10 lines = 39 mm (e.g., p. 161); typeface Linotype Old Style. White wove paper, no watermark, sheets bulk 32 mm.

Bound in moderate orange (53) calico cloth over boards, printed in dark brown (59) and light yellow (86). Front: '[within a brown rule frame, a yellow rule frame, and a compartment formed by intersecting yellow rules interrupted above and below by brown ornaments] *A Southern* | TREASURY | *of Life* | *and Literature* | BY | STARK YOUNG'. Spine: title, editor, ornament, and publisher between yellow and brown rules Back: blank. White wove endpapers. Edges trimmed. Dust jacket not seen.

Copies: INS, InU-Main, STW, TxU-HRC (2 copies).

Published at $1.48 on 1 February 1937; copyright registration A104307 (copies deposited 24 March 1937). Reviewed in *Commonweal* 5 March 1937: 536; *Booklist* April 1937: 238.

B24 **1937**

Literary Opinion in America

LITERARY OPINION | IN AMERICA | *Essays Illustrating the Status, Methods, | and Problems of Criticism in the | United States Since the War* | EDITED, WITH AN INTRODUCTION BY | MORTON DAUWEN ZABEL | [Harper device] | 1937 | HARPER & BROTHERS | NEW YORK LONDON

Copyright page (ii): 'LITERARY OPINION IN AMERICA | *Copyright, 1937, by Harper & Brothers* | *Printed in the United States of America* | [reservation of rights in 5 lines] | FIRST EDITION | H-M'. Harper's code 'H-M' indicates a printing date of August 1937.

215 x 141 mm. *1-21*^{16} *22*^{12}; 348 leaves. [2] *i-ii* iii-liv *1-2* 3-141 *142-144* 145-466 *467-468* 469-611 *612* 613-637 *638-640* pp. Tipped-in on p. 638 of some copies is a 6-item errata slip (not affecting Ransom's essay).

Contains Ransom's essay "The Esthetic [sic] of Regionalism" (106-121), reprinted from *American Review* January 1934 (C195) and published here for the first time in book form. The revised edition of 1951 and its Harper Torchbook "edition" of 1962 omit this essay and add "Criticism as Pure Speculation" (see D126).

Type-page 36 lines, 165 (172) x 101 mm, 10 lines = 46 mm (e.g., p. 107); typeface Granjon. White wove paper, no watermark, sheets bulk 31 mm.

Bound in grayish reddish brown (46) calico over boards, stamped in gold on front and spine. Front: 'LITERARY OPINION | IN AMERICA | MORTON DAUWEN ZABEL | [flourish]'. Spine, running across: 'LITERARY | OPINION | IN | AMERICA | • | ZABEL | [flourish] | HARPERS'. White wove endpapers. Edges trimmed.

Dust jacket of light yellowish brown (176) paper printed in dark red (16). Front: title, subtitle ('A BOOK OF MODERN CRITICAL ESSAYS'), subjects and authors of essays. Back lists titles in Harper's Modern Classics series. Front flap: price ('$2.50'), blurb, and at the foot 'No. 3466'. Back flap advertises Jay B. Hubbell's *American Life in Literature.*

Copies: CSA (with jacket, without errata slip), IDeKN, IRo (rebound), STW (2 copies, 1 with jacket), TNV (with jacket), TxU-HRC (without errata slip). Also in Abbott, *Moore* B10; Gallup, *Eliot* Ba12.

Published at $2.50 on 8 September 1937; copyright registration A108679 (copies deposited 8 September 1937).

Reviewed in *Commonweal* 18 February 1938: 475; *Nation* 19 February 1938: 216, 218-219 (Harry Levin); *Booklist* 15 March 1938: 265; *New York Herald Tribune Books* 20 March 1938: 25 (Bookwright); *New Republic* 13 July 1938: 285 (F. O. Matthiessen); *New York Times Book Review* 18 September 1938: 26 (Edward Larocque Tinker).

B25 **1938**

America through the Essay

AMERICA | THROUGH THE ESSAY | *An Anthology for English Courses* | EDITED BY | A. THEODORE JOHNSON | Professor of English | Southwestern at Memphis | AND | ALLEN TATE | Professor of English | The Woman's College of the University of North Carolina | *New York* | OXFORD UNIVERSITY PRESS | 1938

Copyright page (iv): '*Copyright,* 1938, *by Oxford University Press, New York, Inc.* | *Printed in the United States of America*'.

213 x 138 mm. 1^8 2^2 3^4 $4\text{-}32^8$ 33^8 34^2; 256 leaves. *i-xii* *1-2* 3-500 pp.

Contains Ransom's essay "Poets without Laurels" (348-361), reprinted from the 1935 *Yale Review* (C206) and published here one day before its appearance in *World's Body* (A9).

Type-page 39 lines, 166 (172) x 101 mm, 10 lines = 42 mm (e.g., p. 352); typeface Janson. White wove paper, no watermark, sheets bulk 30 mm.

Bound in dark red (16) calico cloth over boards. Front and back blank. Spine, stamped in gold, running across: 'AMERICA | THROUGH | THE | ESSAY | *An Anthology* | JOHNSON | & | TATE | OXFORD'. White wove endpapers. Edges trimmed. Gallup reports a glassine dust jacket.

Copies: ICU, IEdS (missing front free endpaper), STW, TNV. Also in Gallup, *Eliot* Ba13.

Published at $1.75 on 21 April 1938; copyright registration A116652 (copies deposited 6 May 1938). (Gallup reports a price of $2.00.) Reviewed in *English Journal* November 1938: 796.

B26 **1939**

The Fugitive: Clippings and Comment

[Within a rule frame] The Fugitive | Clippings and Comment | about the magazine and the members of the group | that published it | COLLECTED BY | MERRILL MOORE | with | A POSTSCRIPT | by | JOHN CROWE RANSOM | BOSTON, MASSACHUSETTS | *1939*

Copyright page (4): 'Copyright, 1939, by Merrill Moore | Printed in the United States of America.'

229 x 152 mm. *1-9*^{4}; 36 leaves. *1-6* 7-11 *12* 13-70 *71-72* pp.

Contains Ransom's "Postscript" (11) to Moore's prefatory "Personal Memorandum." The postscript is dated 25 June 1939.

Type-page 46 lines, 167 (175) x 110 mm, 10 lines = 37 mm (e.g., p. 10); typeface Century. White wove paper, no watermark, sheets bulk 5 mm.

Bound in moderate blue (182) wove paper wrappers printed in black. Front: 'THE FUGITIVE | Clippings and Comment | Collected by | MERRILL MOORE'. Spine and back blank. Inside front cover: 15-line blurb. No endpapers. Edges cut. Copies of the pamphlet, in their wrappers, were also bound up with other pamphlets and offprints and with a title page reading: 'MERRILL MOORE | *A MISCELLANY* | First Series | I-X | Boston, Massachusetts | 1939'.

Copies: ICarbS (original wrappers), ILfC (in *A Miscellany*)), STW (2 copies, each in *A Miscellany*), TNV (4 copies, 1 rebound and 1 in *A Miscellany*).

B27 **1940**

Contemporary Southern Prose

CONTEMPORARY | SOUTHERN | [floriated type] PROSE | [not floriated] Edited By | Richmond Croom Beatty | AND | William Perry Fidler | 1940 | [71 mm rule with square ornament at each end] | D. C. HEATH AND COMPANY | *BOSTON*

Copyright page (ii): 'Copyright, 1940, By D. C. Heath and Company | NO PART OF THE MATERIAL COVERED BY THIS COPY- | RIGHT MAY BE REPRODUCED IN ANY FORM WITH- | OUT WRITTEN PERMISSION OF THE PUBLISHER. | PRINTED IN THE UNITED STATES OF AMERICA. 4HO | OFFICES: Boston New York Chicago | San Francisco Dallas Atlanta London'.

217 x 136 mm. *1*^{8} 2-*19*^{16} *20-21*^{8}; 312 leaves. [2] *i-v* vi-vii *viii* *1-4* 5-255 *256-260* 261-293 *294-296* 297-320 *321-324* 325-595 *596* 597-614 pp.

Contains the essay "Happy Farmers" (150-166), reprinted (with a few substantive variants) from the October 1933 *American Review* (C193) rather than from the version published as a Tryon pamphlet (A7).

Type-page 37 lines, 171 (178) x 101 mm, 10 lines = 45 mm (e.g., p. 151); typeface Electra. White wove paper, no watermark, sheets bulk 30 mm.

Bound in moderate bluish green (164) calico cloth over boards. Front and back blank. Spine: '[in dark red (16) on a pale orange-yellow (73) paper label] Contem- | porary | *Southern* | PROSE | [32 mm rule] | *Edited by* | R. C. BEATTY | *and* | W. P. FIDLER | [32 mm rule] | [32 mm ornament] | [32 mm rule] | *HEATH*'. White wove endpapers. Edges trimmed.

Dust jacket of yellowish gray (93) laid paper, with vertical chain-lines 18 mm apart, watermark '*A Tru-Colour Text*'; printed in dark red. Front: title in red on gray, names of contributors in gray on red.

Copies: IDeKN, STW (with jacket), TNV (2 copies, 1 with jacket).

Published at $2.00 on 26 August 1940; copyright registration A144924. Reviewed in *College English* December 1940: 303.

B28 **1940**

A Voyage to the British Isles

[Within a double rule frame] *A Voyage* | [deep reddish orange (36)] to the British Isles | [black] [a line of seven dish-like ornaments] | Being the Journal of | [reddish orange] Charles McKinley, [black] Gent. | *The first edition* [three italic hyphens] | CM | Printed privately for the Author | at the Kokosing Press, near | St. Paul's Church, Mt. Vernon, Ohio | [reddish orange] MDCCCCXL

Copyright page (iv): '*First Edition* | COPYRIGHT, 1940, BY CHARLES MCKINLEY, JR. | PRINTED IN THE UNITED STATES OF AMERICA'.

177 x 124 mm. 51 leaves. *i-viii* 1-94 pp.

Contains "A Prefatory Note" (vii-viii) signed 'John Crowe Ransom | October 5, 1940'. In the note, Ransom says that he became acquainted with McKinley's writings three years previous, when McKinley used to read them in his "group of collegiate writers at Kenyon" (viii). Much of the text of *Voyage* appeared first in academic year 1939-1940 in *Hika*, the student literary magazine at Kenyon College.

Type-page 28 lines, 128 (140) x 80 mm, 10 lines = 46 mm (e.g., p. 6); or, especially after p. 26, 27 lines, 127 (140) x 80 mm, 10 lines = 47 mm. Typeface Garamond. White wove paper, no watermark, sheets bulk 6 mm.

Perfect bound in light gray (264) laid paper with vertical chainlines 23 mm apart. Front: '*A Voyage* | to the British Isles | [line of seven dish-like ornaments] | Charles McKinley, Gent. | CM'. Spine and back blank. No endpapers. Edges trimmed.

Copy: DLC (rebound, preserving front and back covers), OGK, STW (inscribed to Ransom by McKinley on 1 November 1940).

Published at $1.50 on 26 October 1940; copyright registration A147396. Reviewed in *Hika* November 1940: 11.

B29 **1941**

New Poems 1940

[Six 102 mm rules] | NEW POEMS: | 1940 | An Anthology of British and American Verse | Edited by Oscar Williams ◆ A Living Age Book | The Yardstick Press ◆ New York ◆ 1941 | [six 102 mm rules]

Copyright page (2): 'COPYRIGHT, 1941, BY THE YARDSTICK PRESS | FIRST PRINTING | PRINTED IN THE UNITED STATES OF AMERICA | BY J. J. LITTLE & IVES COMPANY, NEW YORK'.

203 x 139 mm. *1-16*^{8} *17*^{4} *18*^{8}; 136 leaves, with four additional leaves of plates paged 263-270 (i.e., gathering 17). [2] *1-8* 9-13 *14* 15-18 *19-20* 21-250 *251-252* 253-261 *262-270* 271 *272* 273-276 *277-278* pp.

Contains the poem "Address to the Scholars of New England" (152-154), reprinted from the autumn 1939 *Kenyon Review* (C245) and published here for the first time in book form.

Type-page 31 lines, 143 (147) x 93 mm, 10 lines = 46 mm (e.g., p. 11); typeface Janson. White laid paper with vertical chainlines 28 mm apart, watermark '[device resembling a scale within a round bottle arising from which is a line with a diamond shape surmounted by a cross mark] | [script] *Utopian*', sheets bulk 27 mm. Also issued in white wove paper, no watermark, sheets bulk 27 mm.

Bound in yellowish gray (93) calico cloth over boards. Front and back blank. Spine stamped in gold on a dark reddish orange (38) panel: '[thick-thin double rule] | NEW | POEMS | 1940 | Edited by | OSCAR | WILLIAMS | [thin-thick double rule]'. White wove endpapers. Top edge cut and stained dark reddish orange, fore-edge untrimmed, bottom edge trimmed.

Dust jacket of yellowish white (92) paper printed with a deep reddish orange (36) background on front, spine, and back and with lettering in black. Front: 'Recent Work by the Leading Poets | [within a white frame of single rules top and bottom and five rules right and left and on a background of contributors' names in white] NEW POEMS | 1940 | edited by | Oscar Williams | [below the frame] 30 PORTRAITS OF THE POETS'. Front flap lists price as $2.50. Back flap advertises Williams's *The Man Coming toward You.*

Copies: CSA (wove paper), ICU, IWat, STW (with jacket), TNV (with jacket). Also in Abbott, *Moore* B12; Bonnell, *Aiken* B48; Edelstein, *Stevens* B26; MacMahon, *Bishop* B6; Stefanik, *Berryman* B5; Wallace, *Williams* B38.

Published at $2.50 on 17 April 1941; copyright registration A154642.

Advertised for 17 March 1941 publication in *Kenyon Review* Spring 1941: 137; also advertised on the final unnumbered page of the March through April 1941 issues of *Living Age.*

Reviewed in *Living Age* May 1941: 299 (Willard Maas); *Decision* June 1941: 83-85 (Marya Zaturenska); *Poetry* July 1941: 215-219 (Leon Edel); *New York Times Book Review* 14 September 1941: 2, 19 (Peter Monro Jack); *New York Times Book Review* 26 October 1941: 41 (Edward Larocque Tinker).

B30 **1941**

The Intent of the Critic

[Swash Ts and Ns] *THE INTENT* | *OF THE CRITIC* | [no swash] BY | Edmund Wilson | Norman Foerster | John Crowe Ransom | W. H. Auden | EDITED, WITH AN INTRODUCTION, BY | Donald A. Stauffer | [80 mm swelled rule] | PRINCETON | PRINCETON UNIVERSITY PRESS

Copyright page (iv): 'COPYRIGHT, 1941 | BY PRINCETON UNIVERSITY PRESS | PRINTED IN | THE UNITED STATES OF AMERICA | BY PRINCETON UNIVERSITY PRESS | AT PRINCETON, NEW JERSEY | ◆ | LONDON: HUMPHREY MILFORD | OXFORD UNIVERSITY PRESS'.

217 x 138 mm. *1-10*^{8}; 80 leaves. *i-vi 1-2* 3-38 *39-40* 41-62 *63-64* 65-88 *89-90* 91-124 *125-126* 127-147 *148-154* pp.

Contains the first appearance of Ransom's essay "Criticism as Pure Speculation" (91-124), which had been delivered as a lecture at Princeton University, along with those by Wilson, Foerster, and Auden, in winter 1940-1941.

Type-page 28 lines, 149 (163) x 93 mm, 10 lines = 53 mm (e.g., p. 95); typeface Electra. White wove paper, no watermark, sheets bulk 16 mm.

Bound in moderate yellowish pink (29) calico cloth over boards. Front and back blank. Spine decorated with a pattern of 7 silver rules repeated 11 times and having a medium gray paper label (32 x 24 mm) lettered in white: '[swash Ts and Ns] *THE* | *INTENT* | *OF THE* | *CRITIC*'. White wove endpapers. Edges trimmed.

Dust jacket of white wove paper with lettering in black and white on a background of strong red (12) and dark gray (266) on the front, of dark grayish reddish brown (47) on the spine, and of white on the back. Front flap: price ('$2.50') and biographical notes on the authors. Back flap: biographical notes continued and advertisement for *The Intent of the Artist*, which is offered as a companion volume.

Copies: ICIU, INS, InU-Lilly (with jacket), STW (with jacket), TNV (with jacket). Also in Bloomfield and Mendelson, *Auden* B27.

Published at $2.50 on 16 September 1941; copyright registration A156973. Publication in England was by Oxford University Press (at 15s 6d on 12 February 1942). The book was reprinted by photo-offset by Peter Smith, Gloucester, MA, in 1963, and was reset for a paperback Matrix edition (SM 1051) published by Bantam Books, New York, in November 1966.

Advertised in *Nation* 18 October 1941: 379. Reviewed in *Saturday Review* 11 October 1941: 3-4, 20 (Howard Mumford Jones); *Nation* 18 October 1941: 376-378 (Jacques Barzun); *New York Times Book Review* 26 October 1941: 16 (George S. Hellman); *Partisan Review* November-December 1941: 512-513 (Frederick Wilcox Dupee); *Kenyon Review* Winter 1942: 126-132 (Kenneth Burke); *TLS* 22 August 1942: 418; *Review of English Studies* July 1943: 317-318 (B. E. C. Davis).

B31 **1942**

War Letter

WAR LETTER | [71 mm rule] | THE KENYON REVIEW, | Gambier, Ohio | June 5, 1942 | To Our Loyal Supporters: | [text begins]

No copyright notice. The letter is signed 'John Crowe Ransom, | *Editor;* | Philip Blair Rice, | *Managing Editor;* | Robert A. Weaver, Jr., | *Business Representative.*'

268 x 178 mm. 1 leaf. *1*-2 pp.

Consists of a letter on the discontinuation of the *Southern Review* and on a campaign to raise funds for the continued publication of the *Kenyon Review,* which takes over the subscription list of *Southern Review.* The letter was reprinted in the July 1942 issue of *American Oxonian* (C266) and perhaps in other publications. For the circumstances behind the letter, see Janssen 82-90 and Cutrer 213-255.

Type-page 202 (208) x 127 mm, 5 lines = 25 mm; typeface Century. Pale orange-yellow (73) wove paper, no watermark. Edges trimmed. No binding.

Copy: STW.

B32 **1944**

A Vanderbilt Miscellany

[Open face type] A Vanderbilt Miscellany | 1919-1944 | [line drawing of a man holding a rifle and sitting on a fence] | [not open face] Decorated by Marion Junkin | (The Department of Fine Arts) | [open face] Edited by Richmond Croom Beatty | [not open] (The Department of English) | NASHVILLE • VANDERBILT UNIVERSITY PRESS • 1944

Copyright page (4): '[Within a rectangular compartment of floral designs] Copyright, 1944 | By | THE VANDERBILT UNIVERSITY | PRINTED IN THE UNITED STATES OF | AMERICA BY THE PARTHENON PRESS | NASHVILLE, TENNESSEE'.

228 x 150 mm. *1-25*^{8}; 200 leaves. *1-5* 6-7 *8 9 10* 11-27 *28-30* 31-153 *154-156* 157-302 *303-304* 305-395 *396* 397 *398-400* pp.

Contains "A Statement of Principles" (280-288) reprinted from *I'll Take My Stand* (B17); Ransom's essay "Poets without Laurels" (289-302) from *World's Body* (A9); and his poems "Bells for John Whiteside's Daughter" (313), "Janet Waking" (314-315), "Dead Boy" (316), "Spectral Lovers" (317-318), and "Necrological" (319-320). None of the poems appears here for the first time in book form. There are slight variations from previous published texts of the poems. This may be the first time that 'Whiteside's' appears thus rather than as 'Whitesides'. Further examples: the text of "Spectral Lovers" is that of *Southern Treasury* (B23) but without its misprint in line 20 and with 'essence' rather than 'essences' in line 4; in "Dead Boy," what had been 'county' in *Two Gentlemen* (A4) here becomes 'country' (line 2); in "Necrological" 'limbs' is misprinted as 'limps' (line 2).

Type-page 35 lines, 172 (180) x 110 mm, 10 lines = 50 mm (e.g., p. 129); typeface Granjon. White wove paper, no watermark, sheets bulk 38 mm.

Two bindings.

1. Light brown (57) calico cloth over boards, stamped in gold. Front: '[on a background of gold checkmarks] A | VANDERBILT | MISCELLANY'. Spine, running across: 'A | VANDERBILT | MISCELLANY | [20 mm rule] |

EDITED | BY | BEATTY | [publisher's device of a tower, around which are the words 'VANDERBILT UNIVERSITY PRESS']'. Back blank. Yellowish white (92) laid endpapers with vertical chainlines 20 mm apart and watermark '[script] Hamilton | Kilmory'. Edges trimmed.

2. Moderate brown (58) calico cloth over boards; wove endpapers; otherwise the same as binding 1.

Dust jacket of white wove paper coated vivid orange (48) and printed in black. Front: title in horizontally shaded handlettering; drawing of clock tower, trees, buildings, this drawing extending across the spine and on to the back. Back lists contributors. Front flap gives price of $3.50.

Copies: IEN (binding 1), STW (2 copies in binding 1, one with jacket), TNV (binding 2, with jacket). Also in Wright, *Taylor* B2.

Published at $3.50 on 5 May 1944; copyright registration A 180565.

Advertised in *Virginia Quarterly Review* Autumn 1944: xci. Reviewed in *Nashville Banner* 17 May 1944: 14 (Mary Stahlman Douglas); *New York Times Book Review* 28 May 1944: 4 (Marjorie Farber); *Saturday Review of Literature* 17 June 1944: 17-18 (John Gould Fletcher); *Virginia Quarterly Review* Autumn 1944: 624-629 (Herschel Brickell); *Sewanee Review* Winter 1945: 159-164 (Arthur Mizener).

B33 **1947**

The Heritage of the English-Speaking Peoples

THE HERITAGE | OF | THE ENGLISH-SPEAKING PEOPLES | AND | THEIR RESPONSIBILITY | [shield] | ADDRESSES AT THE CONFERENCE | OCTOBER 1946 | KENYON COLLEGE

Copyright page (2): 'Copyright 1947, Kenyon College'.

228 x 150 mm. *1-8*[12]; 96 leaves. *1-7* 8-190 *191-192* pp. (without numbering on opening pages of each address: pp. 17, 32, 38, 48, 66, 78, 95, 114, 130, 140, 157, 170, 177).

Contains Ransom's 5 October 1946 conference address "The Tongue That Shakespeare Spake" (95-113), published here for the first time in book form and with four paragraphs (on literary nationalism) omitted from its publication in the April-June 1947 *Sewanee Review*, where it was entitled "On Shakespeare's Language" (C292). The proceedings of a second conference on the same subject, 26-28 September 1947, include nothing by Ransom, though they do note that he presided at the session devoted to philosophy.

Type-page 34 lines, 156 (165) x 106 mm, 10 lines = 46 mm (e.g., p. 100); typeface Garamond. White wove paper, no watermark, sheets bulk 10 mm.

White wove wrappers printed in black. Front: identical to the title page. Spine, running down: 'KENYON COLLEGE CONFERENCE, 1946'. Back blank. No endpapers. Edges cut.

Copies: ICN (rebound, preserving wrappers), OGK, OO, STW.

Published in May or June 1947 (i.e., between the May 1947 date of the preface and the 26 June 1947 accession date of the Oberlin College copy). Not found in the *Catalog of Copyright Entries*.

B34 **1949**

Lectures in Criticism

[Moderate reddish brown (43)] Lectures | in Criticism | [black] THE JOHNS HOPKINS UNIVERSITY | *R. P. Blackmur • Benedetto Croce • Henri M. Peyre | John Crowe Ransom • Herbert Read • Allen Tate* | Introduction by Huntington Cairns | [Bollingen device in reddish brown] | BOLLINGEN SERIES XVI | [swelled rule] | PANTHEON BOOKS

Copyright page (vi): 'COPYRIGHT 1949 BY BOLLINGEN FOUNDATION INC., NEW YORK, N.Y. | PUBLISHED FOR BOLLINGEN FOUNDATION INC. | BY PANTHEON BOOKS INC. | MANUFACTURED IN THE U.S.A. | PRINTED BY THE MARCHBANKS PRESS, N.Y.'

228 x 151 mm. *1-14*^{8}; 112 leaves. *i-viii* ix-x *1* 2-12 *13-15* 16-42 *43-45* 46-70 *71-73* 74-108 *109* 110-116 *117-119* 120-168 *169-171* 172-183 *184-187* 188-209 *210-214* pp.

Includes Ransom's lecture "The Literary Criticism of Aristotle" (15-42), which had been delivered, along with those of the other contributors, at the Johns Hopkins University Lectures in Criticism held in Baltimore in April 1948 and subsequently printed in *Kenyon Review* (C298). It is published here for the first time in book form.

Type-page 27 lines, 152 (159) x 97 mm, 10 lines = 57 mm (e.g., p. 32); typeface Bodoni Book. White laid paper with vertical chainlines 29 mm apart, watermark 'FOREIGN | AFFAIRS'. sheets bulk 17 mm.

Bound in medium gray (265) calico cloth over boards, with black calico around the spine. Front: Bollingen device in black within a square intersected by two lines, one vertical and one horizontal. Spine, stamped in gold, running down: '[Bollingen device] LECTURES IN CRITICISM [Bollingen device]'. White laid endpapers from the same stock as the text paper. Top and bottom edges cut, fore-edge trimmed.

Dust jacket of white wove paper with lettering and design in black and white on a yellowish gray (93) background on front, spine, and back. Front flap credits jacket design to E. McKnight Kauffer, and back flap lists volumes XII-XVIII in the Bollingen series.

Copies: ICU (rebound), IDeKN, IU, STW, TVN (2 copies, 1 with jacket).

Published at $3.50 on 17 March 1949; copyright registration A31924; renewed 27 May 1976, R632823. Reprinted in 1961 as a paperbound Harper Torchbook (TB 2003), with a revised foreword by Elliott Coleman but without any alteration in Ransom's lecture.

Advertised as *The Johns Hopkins Symposium on Criticism* in *Partisan Review* September 1948 on inside back cover and November 1948 on back cover; advertised as *Lectures in Criticism* in *Publishers' Weekly* 29 January 1949: 428. Listed in "The Weekly Record," *Publishers' Weekly* 26 March 1949: 1468.

Reviewed in *New Yorker* 2 April 1949: 105; *Saturday Review of Literature* 30 April 1949: 12 (Robert Halsband); *New Republic* 6 June 1949: 21-22 (F. O. Matthiessen).

B35 **1950**

The Permanence of Yeats

The Permanence of | YEATS | SELECTED CRITICISM | *Edited* | *by* | JAMES HALL | *and* | MARTIN STEINMANN | *New York* | THE MACMILLAN COMPANY | 1950

Copyright page (iv): '*COPYRIGHT, 1950, BY THE MACMILLAN COMPANY* | [reservation of rights in 5 lines] | First Printing | PRINTED IN THE UNITED STATES OF AMERICA'.

208 x 135 mm. 1^{8} $2\text{-}10^{16}$ 11^{4} $12\text{-}14^{16}$; 212 leaves. *i-v* vi *vii-x* 1-414 pp.

Contains Ransom's essay "Yeats and His Symbols" (95-107), reprinted from the summer 1939 *Kenyon Review* (C242) and published here for the first time in book form.

Type-page 35 lines, 159 (171) x 105 mm, 10 lines = 46 mm (e.g., p. 96); typeface Caledonia. White wove paper, no watermark, sheets bulk 27 mm.

Bound in black calico cloth over boards. Front and back blank. Spine stamped in gold, running across: '[x-like design] | [x-like design] | THE | *Permanence* | OF | YEATS | ◆ | HALL *and* | STEINMANN | [x-like designs as above] | MACMILLAN | [rule]'. Top edge cut, others trimmed. White wove endpapers. Gallup reports a white dust jacket printed in green.

Copies: ICU (rebound), IDeKN (spine taped), InU-Main, TNV (rebound). Also in Gallup, *Eliot* Ba18.

Published at $5.00 on 31 January 1950; copyright registration A4097. Published in a new edition in 1961 by Collier Books (BS11).

Advertised in *Kenyon Review* Spring 1950: 188.

Reviewed in *Library Journal* 1 December 1949: 1817 (Gerald D. MacDonald); *New York Herald Tribune Book Review* 5 February 1950: 3 (Babette Deutsch); *New York Times Book Review* 5 February 1950: 5 (Dudley Fitts); *New Yorker* 11 February 1950:

100; *New Republic* 20 March 1950: 20-21 (Donald A. Stauffer); *Saturday Review* 15 April 1950: 49 (Richard Ellmann); *Commonweal* 2 June 1950: 204-205 (Vivian Mercier); *Poetry* July 1950: 227-229 (Isabel Gamble); *TLS* 25 August 1950: 525-526; *Modern Language Notes* April 1951: 280-281 (Thomas Riggs, Jr.); *Modern Language Review* July-October 1951: 498-499 (M. C. Bradbrook); *Modern Language Quarterly* December 1952: 413-415 (Malcolm Brown).

B36 **1951**

Wordsworth Centenary Studies

[Shaded type] WORDSWORTH | [not shaded] *CENTENARY STUDIES | PRESENTED AT CORNELL AND | PRINCETON UNIVERSITIES* | BY DOUGLAS BUSH, FREDERICK A. POTTLE, | EARL LESLIE GRIGGS, JOHN CROWE RANSOM, B. IFOR EVANS, | LIONEL TRILLING, WILLARD L. SPERRY | [thick-thin double rule, 10 mm] | *EDITED BY GILBERT T. DUNKLIN* | [in grayish olive-green (127), a drawing of trees surrounding a pond with a small building in the background] | [black] PRINCETON, NEW JERSEY | PRINCETON UNIVERSITY PRESS | 1951

Copyright page (iv): 'Copyright, 1951, by Princeton University Press | London: Geoffrey Cumberlege, Oxford University Press | [ornament] | [acknowledgments in 6 lines] | Printed in the United States of America | By Princeton University Press at Princeton, New Jersey'.

215 x 137 mm. *1-12*^{8}; 96 leaves. *i-iv* v-xii *xiii-xvi 1-2* 3-42 *43-44* 45-163 *164* 165-169 *170-176* pp.

Contains Ransom's essay "William Wordsworth: Notes toward an Understanding of Poetry" (91-113), which, like the other essays in this volume, had been "delivered at the Wordsworth Centenary Celebrations held at Cornell and Princeton Universities on April 21 and 22, 1950" (v). The essay was published first in the summer 1950 *Kenyon Review* (C304); it is here published for the first time in book form.

Type-page 35 lines, 163 (174) x 98 mm, 10 lines = 42 mm (e.g., p. 98); typeface Caledonia. White wove paper, watermark 'WARREN'S | OLDE STYLE', sheets bulk 11 mm.

Seen in two bindings.

1. Bound in light grayish olive (109) paper over boards with black calico cloth around the spine. Front: a white paper label with the same drawing as on the title page but in grayish yellow-green (122). Spine, stamped in gold: '[thick-thin double rule, 15 mm] DUNKLIN [running down] WORDSWORTH PRINCETON [thin-thick double rule, 15

mm]'. Back blank. Light olive gray (112) wove endpapers. Edges cut. Top edge stained black.

2. Bound in light bluish gray (191) calico cloth over boards. Front and back blank. Spine like that of binding 1 but printed in black rather than stamped in gold. Yellowish gray (93) wove endpapers. Edges trimmed.

Dust jacket (seen on binding 1) of light yellowish green (135) paper printed in black and dark yellowish green (137). On the front is the same drawing as on the title-page and a list of contributors. Back includes advertisements for Northrop Frye's *Fearful Symmetry* and Joseph E. Baker's *The Reinterpretation of Victorian Literature.*

Copies: ICU (binding 1), IDeKN (binding 2), InU-Lilly (binding 1, with jacket).

Published at $3.00 on 22 June 1951; copyright registration A56916. Published the same year at 20s in England by Cumberlege Reprinted by photo-offset in 1963 by Archon Books, Hamden, CN.

Reviewed in *TLS* 26 October 1951: 672; *Booklist* 1 October 1951: 46; *New York Herald Tribune Book Review* 11 November 1951: 20 (William A. Borst); *Western Humanities Review* Winter 1951-1952: 73-75 (S. B. Neff); *JEGP* January 1952: 114-118 (George Wilbur Meyer); *Poetry* July 1952: 233-241 (R. W. Flint).

B37 **1951**

Case Record from a Sonnetorium

[On facing pages] [verso] CASE [recto] RECORD FROM | [verso] A [recto] SONNETORIUM [verso] BOOKS BY MERRILL MOORE: [list of 9 other books by Moore in 9 lines] [recto] *Cartoons by* EDWARD ST. JOHN GOREY | *Illustrated with Poems by* MERRILL MOORE | *Consultants:* LOUIS UNTERMEYER, *Esq.* | *Professor* JOHN CROWE RANSOM | HENRY W. WELLS, *Ph.D.* | WILLIAM CARLOS WILLIAMS, *M.D.* | TWAYNE PUBLISHERS, *New York*

Copyright page (4): '*Copyright,* 1951, *by Merrill Moore* | [acknowledgment in 4 lines] | M.M. | DESIGNED BY FRED M. KLEEBERG | *Manufactured in the United States of America*'.

228 x 151 mm. *1-2*^{16}; 16 leaves. *1-64* pp.

Contains Ransom's "Consultant's Opinion" (43), a statement on Moore as a poet. This is its only publication.

Type-page of varying number of lines, 168 x 103 mm, 10 lines = 43 mm (e.g., p. 43); typeface Caledonia. White wove paper, no watermark, sheets bulk 5 mm.

Bound in light gray (264) calico cloth over boards, stamped in dark red (16). Front: '[cartoon physician with his chin resting on his left hand] | [printed from hand-drawn lettering] CASE-RECORD | from a | SONNETORIUM | [laurel-wreathed cartoon character]'. Spine, running down: '*Gorey & Moore* Case Record from a Sonnetorium *Twayne*'. Back blank. White wove endpapers. Edges trimmed.

Dust jacket of white wove paper printed in black and deep orange-yellow (69), with two cartoons in black on orange yellow on the front and with an advertisement for Moore's *Clinical Sonnets* and *Illegitimate Sonnets* on the back.

Copies: I, TNV (3 copies, 2 with jackets), STW (3 copies with jackets, one inscribed to Ransom and dated 1951, another to John Ciardi in 1951, and another to Robert Penn Warren in 1952), TxU-HRC, WU-Col. Also in Wallace, *Williams* B59.

Published at $1.50 on 19 November 1951; copyright registration A61448.

B38 **1952**

The Shores of Light

The Shores of Light | *A Literary Chronicle* | *of the Twenties and Thirties* | *By* EDMUND WILSON | FARRAR, STRAUS AND YOUNG, INC. | Publishers New York

Copyright page (iv): '*Copyright 1952 by Edmund Wil-* | *son. All rights reserved, including* | *the right to reproduce this book,* | *or portions thereof, in any form.* | *Manufactured in the U.S.A.*'

187 x 106 mm. *1-26*^{16}; 416 leaves. *i-viii* ix-xii *1-2* 3-793 *794* 795-814 *815-820* pp.

This collection of Edmund Wilson's reviews and essays includes, untitled, Ransom's "The Poet and the Critic" (207-210), along with Edmund Wilson's review to which it was a letter of response and along with Wilson's rejoinder. The letter and rejoinder first appeared in the 22 June 1927 *New Republic* (C159); in introducing the letter, Wilson incorrectly gives the date as 22 July. Ransom's text is unchanged, except for a few matters of spelling and punctuation; Wilson's is revised.

Type-page 34 lines, 148 (153) x 85 mm, 10 lines = 42 mm (e.g., p. 208); typeface Fairfield. White wove paper, no watermark, sheets bulk 37 mm.

Bound in strong red (12) calico cloth over boards. Front and back blank. Spine stamped in gold, running across: 'THE SHORES | OF LIGHT | • | EDMUND WILSON | FARRAR | STRAUS | & YOUNG'. White wove endpapers. Edges trimmed; top edge stained strong red.

Dust jacket of white paper printed in deep red (13) and black on a background of yellowish gray (93) on front and spine, white on back and flaps. Front: author, title, subtitle. The back advertises Wilson's *Classics and Commercials*. Price on front flap: '$6.50'.

Copies: CSA (with jacket), IDeKN, TxU-UG.

Published at $6.50 on 23 October 1952; copyright registration A71779. Sheets printed in the United States were issued in England by W. H. Allen at 25s in November or December 1952. Reprinted in paperback by Vintage Books (V-181) in 1961, by Noonday Press in 1967, and by Northeastern University Press in 1985.

Reviewed in *New York Times Book Review* 26 October 1952: 1 (Charles Poore); *New York Herald Tribune Book Review* 26 October 1952: 1, 29 (Horace Gregory); *New Republic* 10 November 1952: 17-18, 22 (Malcolm Cowley); *New Yorker* 15 November 1952: 181-185 (Alfred Kazin); *Saturday Review* 15 November 1952: 25 (W. T. Scott); *Atlantic* December 1952: 98 (Charles J. Rolo) *Booklist* December 1952: 122; *Commonweal* 12 December 1952: 262 (Frank Getlein); *TLS* 12 December 1952: 811.

B39 **1953**

The New Partisan Reader, 1945-1953

[Open-face type] PR | [not open] THE NEW PARTISAN READER | 1945-1953 | EDITED BY | *William Phillips* | AND | *Philip Rahv* | HARCOURT, BRACE AND COMPANY ■ NEW YORK

Copyright page (iv): 'COPYRIGHT, 1953, BY HARCOURT, BRACE AND COMPANY, INC. | *All rights reserved, including the right to reproduce | this book or portions thereof in any form.* | *first edition* | [acknowledgments in 37 lines] | LIBRARY OF CONGRESS CATALOG CARD NUMBER: 53-7841 | PRINTED IN THE UNITED STATES OF AMERICA'.

204 x 135 mm. *1-20*^{16}; 320 leaves. [2] *i-v* vi-viii *ix* x-xi *xii 1-3* 4-621 (with no numbers on opening page of each work, on part-title pages and their versos, and on blank pages facing part-title pages) *622-626* pp.

Contains Ransom's essay "Blackmur as Critic" (617-621), which had appeared in *Partisan Review* of January-February 1953 (C319) under the title "The Shores of Criticism" and which appears here for the first time in book form.

Type-page 41 lines, 175 (180) x 110 mm, 10 lines = 43 mm (e.g., p. 366); typeface Baskerville. White wove paper, no watermark, sheets bulk 31 mm.

Bound in grayish blue (186) calico cloth over boards, printed in black. Front: '[open type] PR'. Spine, running down: 'THE NEW PARTISAN READER | HARCOURT, BRACE AND COMPANY'. Back blank. White wove endpapers. Top and bottom edge cut; fore-edge trimmed.

Dust jacket of white paper printed in brilliant greenish yellow (98) and moderate greenish blue (173) and with a medium gray (265) background on front and spine. The front lists editors on a panel of yellow and gives the title in blue, yellow, and white, and its list of contributors in white extends across the spine. The back quotes, in blue on white, from the editors' foreword. No jacket design credit given

Copies: I, INS, InU-Main (rebound), IU (2 copies), STW (with jacket), WBB. Also in Bonnell, *Aiken* B68; MacMahon, *Bishop* B14.

Published at $6.00 on 22 October 1953; copyright registration A111586. Published in England at 30s on 24 September 1954 by André Duetsch, who affixed a label with his imprint on the title page.

Reviewed in *Booklist* 1 December 1953: 140; *Commonweal* 11 December 1953: 262-263 (Gerald Weales); *New York Times Book Review* 20 December 1953: 4, 17 (V. S. Pritchett); *TLS* 26 November 1954: 754.

B40 **1954**

The Writer and His Craft

The WRITER *and his* CRAFT | *being the Hopwood Lectures, 1932-1952* | ROBERT MORSS LOVETT • MAX EAST- | MAN • ZONA GALE • HENRY HAZLITT • | CHRISTOPHER MORLEY • WALTER | PRICHARD EATON • CARL VAN | DOREN • HENRY SEIDEL CANBY • | EDWARD WEEKS • JOHN CROWE | RANSOM • MARY M. COLUM • | LOUISE BOGAN • STRUTHERS BURT • | HARLAN HATCHER • ROBERT PENN | WARREN • J. DONALD ADAMS • | F. O. MATTHIESSEN • NORMAN COUSINS • | MARK VAN DOREN • HORACE GREGORY • | *Foreword by* ROY W. COWDEN | Ann Arbor • The University of Michigan Press | 1954

Copyright page (iv): 'COPYRIGHT 1954 BY THE UNIVERSITY OF MICHI- GAN | [42 mm rule] | [acknowledgements for use of quotations, in 33 lines]'.

228 x 150 mm. 1^{8} $2\text{-}8^{16}$ 9^{12} 10^{16} 11^{8}; 156 leaves. [2] *i-iv* v *vi* vii *viii* 1-289 *290* 291-297 *298-302* pp.

Contains Ransom's lecture "Poetry as Primitive Language" (146-157), delivered at the University of Michigan in 1942, first printed that same year in the *Michigan Alumnus Quarterly Review* (C265), and here published for the first time in book form.

Type-page 38 lines, 161 (168) x 101 mm, 10 lines = 43 mm (e.g., p. 147); typeface Granjon. White wove paper, no watermark, sheets bulk 22 mm.

Bound in light grayish olive (109) calico cloth over boards, printed in very dark green (147). Front: *The* WRITER | *and his* CRAFT | *The Hopwood* | *Lectures 1932-1952'*. Spine, running across: '*The* | WRITER | *and his* | CRAFT | *HOPWOOD* | *LECTURES* | *1932-1952* | MICHIGAN'. Back blank. White wove endpapers. Edges trimmed.

Dust jacket of pale greenish yellow (104) wove paper printed in light olive (106) and dark olive green (126). Front has title and publisher in olive green and contributors in greenish yellow on a background of light olive. Back advertises Eugene S. McCartney's *Recurrent Maladies in Scholarly Writing.*

Copies: IDeKN (2 copies), STW (with jacket), TNV (2 copies, 1 with jacket), WBB.

Published at $3.00 on 7 May 1954; copyright registration A138654. Published in England at 24s by Oxford University Press on 30 December 1954. The University of Michigan Press reprinted the book by photo-offset as an Ann Arbor Paperback in 1956.

Reviewed in *TLS* 25 March 1955: 182.

B41 **1954**

The Arts at Mid-Century

The Arts at Mid-Century | EDITED BY ROBERT RICHMAN | HORIZON PRESS NEW YORK 1954

Copyright page (iv): 'Copyright 1954 by Horizon Press Inc. | Library of Congress Catalog Card Number 54-7896 | Manufactured in the United States of America | by H. Wolff, New York | Designed by Marshall Lee'.

234 x 144 mm. *1-10*^{16}; 160 leaves. *i-viii* ix-xi *xii* *1-2* 3-89 *90-92* 93-175 *176-178* 179-205 *206-208* 209-240 *241-242* 243-300 *301-302* 303-306 *307* *308* pp.

Contains Ransom's essays "An Age of Criticism" (24-27) and "Symbolism: American Style" (50-58), both reprinted from *New Republic* (C311, C323) and here published for the first time in book form.

Type-page 37 lines, 184 (191) x 93 mm, 10 lines = 50 mm (e.g., p. 25); typeface Baskerville. White wove paper, no watermark, sheets bulk 22 mm.

Bound in black calico cloth over boards. Front and back blank. Spine stamped in strong yellowish green (131) and silver, running down: '[green] The Arts at Mid-Century | [silver] EDITED BY ROBERT RICHMAN HORIZON'. Light gray (264) wove endpapers. Edges trimmed. Top edge stained strong yellow-green (117).

Dust jacket of white wove paper printed in black and strong yellow-green (117). The front has names of contributors in white on black and the title in white on 4 circular panels of yellow-green. Back advertises other 'Horizon Press Books on the Arts'.

Copies: ICU (top edge not stained), IDeKN, TNV (from Ransom's library, with jacket).

Published at $5.00 on 20 May 1954; copyright registration A140000.

Reviewed in *Booklist* 15 June 1954: 95-96; *New York Herald Tribune Book Review* 18 July 1954: 9.

B42 **1958**

Exercises on the Occasion

[Capitals in swash] *Exercises on the Occasion* | *of the Dedication* | *of the new* | *Phi Beta Kappa Memorial Hall* | [photograph of the hall] | *The College of William and Mary in Virginia* | *Williamsburg* | *Saturday, May the eighteenth* | *nineteenth hundred and fifty-seven*

Copyright page (2): 'COPYRIGHT, 1958 | BY | THE COLLEGE OF WILLIAM | AND MARY IN VIRGINIA | ALL RIGHTS RESERVED'.

228 x 148 mm. *1*[22]; 22 leaves. *1-2* 3-43 *44* pp.

Contains the first publication of Ransom's speech "Our Age among the Ages" (25-42), delivered as the dedicatory address for the new Phi Beta Kappa Hall at William and Mary on 18 May 1957. The speech, with an added prologue and with what Ransom termed "slight revision meant to sharpen it for the printed occasion," subsequently appeared as "The Idea of a Literary Anthropologist and What He Might Say of the *Paradise Lost* of Milton: A Speech with a Prologue" in the winter 1959 *Kenyon Review* (C338).

Type-page 36 lines, 176 (185) x 110 mm, 10 lines = 49 mm (e.g., p. 27); typeface Century. White laid paper blind-embossed with pebble grain, indistinct vertical chainlines 23 and 28 mm apart, partially legible watermark '*Li*[?] *Early Am*[?].' Sheets bulk 4 mm.

Bound in moderate green (145) wove paper wrappers. Front, printed in gold: '[capitals in swash] *Dedication* | *of the* | *Phi Beta Kappa Memorial Hall* | [Phi Beta Kappa seals on a banner with the dates '1776' and '1957'].' Back blank. Edges trimmed.

Copies: IRA, STW.

Published 20 May 1958; copyright registration A340597, listing A. Pelzer Wagener as editor.

B43 **1959**

American Poetry at Mid-Century

American Poetry | at Mid-Century | *by* | *John Crowe Ransom, Delmore Schwartz* | *and John Hall Wheelock* | *Lectures Presented Under the* | *Auspices of the Gertrude Clarke Whittall* | *Poetry and Literature Fund* | [Library of Congress seal] | REFERENCE DEPARTMENT | THE LIBRARY OF CONGRESS | WASHINGTON : 1958

Copyright page (ii): '[catalog card data in 16 lines] | FOR SALE BY THE SUPERINTENDENT OF DOCUMENTS, U.S. GOVERNMENT | PRINTING OFFICE, WASHINGTON 25, D.C. PRICE 25 CENTS'.

Colophon (49): 'U.S. GOVERNMENT PRINTING OFFICE: 1959'.

232 x 145 mm. *1*^{28}; 28 leaves; leaves 5, 9, 13, and 21 are signed 2, 3, 4, and 6. *i-vi* 1-49 *50* pp.

Contains Ransom's lecture "New Poets and Old Muses" (1-14), delivered at the Library of Congress on 13 January 1958 and here published for the first time.

Type-page 44 lines, 192 (201) x 112 mm, 10 lines = 45 mm (e.g., p. 5); typeface Baskerville. Signatures, in the direction line, are preceded by a job number (e.g., '471132-58—2'). White wove paper, no watermark, sheets bulk 3 mm.

Bound in yellowish gray (93) laid paper wrappers with vertical chainlines 23 mm apart (no watermark), printed in dark red (16). Front: '[red] American Poetry at | Mid-Century | *By* JOHN CROWE RANSOM | DELMORE SCHWARTZ | *and* JOHN HALL WHEELOCK | [leaf border] | [in white on red background] *Lectures Presented Under the* | *Auspices of the Gertrude Clarke Whittall* | *Poetry and Literature Fund'*. Back: border and red background extended from the front, otherwise blank. No endpapers. Edges trimmed.

Copies: CSA, IDeKN, INS, InU-Lilly, OGK, STW, TxU-HRC.

Published at $0.25 in January 1959. Listed as entry 907 in the January 1959 *Monthly Catalog of United States Government Publications*. Reviewed in *South Atlantic Quarterly* Summer 1959: 475-477 (Helen Bevington).

B44 **1959**

Fugitives' Reunion

[Shaded triskelion in dark red (16)] | [black] [in the next word, a swash-like J has been mistakenly used for an F] *JUGITIVES' RE- UNION* | *Conversations at Vanderbilt* | *May 3-5, 1956* | Edited by ROB ROY PURDY | Introduction by LOUIS D. RUBIN, JR. | [tower device in black flanked on each side by a 49 mm dark red rule] | VANDERBILT UNIVERSITY PRESS | *Nashville*

Series title page (1): 'FUGITIVES' REUNION | VANDERBILT STUDIES IN THE HUMANITIES | VOLUME III'.

Copyright page (4): 'Copyright 1959 | VANDERBILT UNIVERSITY PRESS | Library of Congress Catalog Card Number: 59-9772'.

Colophon (224): '[publisher's device] | NOTES ON DESIGN: *The triskelion at the top of the* | *title page was drawn from a plaque that hangs in* | *the Vanderbilt English Department commemorat-* | *ing the Fugitives; it is a symbol favored by the* | *group in the early 1920's. The text of this book is* | *in 12-point Linotype Baskerville, with larger sizes* | *of Monotype Bulmer italic used for the headings,* | *on the title page, and for stamping the cover. The* | *book was designed by Robert McGaw. It was set,* | *printed, and bound by the Parthenon Press in* | *Nashville, Tennessee.*'

228 x 148 mm. *1-4*^{16} *5-6*^{8} *7-8*^{16}; 112 leaves. *1-4* 5-7 *8 9 10* 11-83 *84* 85-129 *130* 131-224 pp. One plate, a photograph of assembled Fugitives, inserted as frontispiece.

Contains transcripts of tape recordings of four sessions in which Ransom participated at the Fugitives' reunion at Vanderbilt on 3-5 May 1956. (Ransom also served as moderator at the third session.) The sessions range over a variety of topics, including the state of contemporary poetry, the relation between poetry and politics, the history of the Fugitive group, and the connection of the group to the Agrarian movement. The reunion was made possible by a grant from the Rockefeller Foundation to the American Studies Association. For an account of the event, see Louis D. Rubin, Jr., "The Gathering of the Fugitives." The tapes are located in the Jesse Wills Collection at Vanderbilt.

Type-page 37 lines, 170 (178) x 110 mm, 10 lines = 46 mm (e.g., p. 16); typeface Baskerville. White wove paper, no watermark, sheets bulk 18 mm.

Bound in medium gray (265) calico cloth over boards. Front and back blank. Spine stamped in gold: '[ornament] | [running down within a rule frame on a black panel] [next letter is mistakenly used for an F] *JUGITIVES' REUNION* [floral ornament] *VANDERBILT* [ornament running across outside the panel]'. White wove endpapers. Edges trimmed.

Dust jacket of light yellow (86) wove paper printed in dark red (16) and black. Front has, on the left, the names of the Fugitives in yellow on black and, on the right, a yellow background with a triskelion in red and the title in black. The back advertises Jesse Wills's *Early & Late* (Vanderbilt UP), John M. Bradbury's *The Fugitives* (U of North Carolina P), and Louise Cowan's *The Fugitive Group* (forthcoming from LSU P). The front flap has a photograph of the Fugitives dated 4 May 1956.

Copies: IDeKN, INS, OGK, STW (2 copies with jackets), TNV (2 copies, 1 with jacket), TxU-HRC.

Published at $5.00 on 18 May 1959; copyright registration A399766.

Reviewed in *Journal of Southern History* February 1960: 131-132 (Arlin Turner); *American Quarterly* Spring 1960: 102 (C. Anne Ward Amacher); *South Atlantic Quarterly* Spring 1960: 304 (C. Hugh Holman); *Prairie Schooner* Summer 1960: 95-97 (James E. Miller, Jr.).

B45 **1961**

American Literature: Readings and Critiques

AMERICAN | LITERATURE: | Readings and Critiques | R. W. STALLMAN | University of Connecticut | ARTHUR WALDHORN | The City College of New York | [Putnam device] | G. P. PUTNAM'S SONS, NEW YORK

Copyright page (4): 'Copyright © 1961 by G. P. Putnam's Sons | [reservation of rights in 3 lines] | Library of Congress Catalog Card Number: 61-11080 | Manufactured in the United States of America by American Book-Stratford Press, Inc. | [beginning of acknowledgments]'.

240 x 175 mm. *1*^{8} *2-32*^{16} *33*^{8}; 512 leaves. *1-3* 4-8 *9-10* 11-30 *31-32* 33-71 *72* 73-95 *96* 97-433 *434* 435-1003 *1004* 1005-1020 *1021-1024* pp.

Contains the first book appearance of Ransom's "On Being Modern with Distinction" (874-877), reprinted from the Marianne Moore issue of *Quarterly Review of Literature* (C296); also reprints Ransom's poems "Here Lies a Lady" (899-900), "Philomela" (900-901), "Parting, without a Sequel" (901-902), and "The Equilibrists" (902-903); also an excerpt from "The Poet as Woman" (906-907) reprinted from *World's Body* (A9) and an excerpt on Allen Tate's "The Subway" and Yvor Winters's criticism of it (931-932) reprinted from *New Criticism* (A10).

Type-page 2 columns, 47 lines, 200 (207) x 141 mm (e.g., p. 875); typeface Caledonia. White wove paper, no watermark, sheets bulk 43 mm.

Bound in moderate red (15) calico cloth stamped in gold on front and spine. Front: 'AMERICAN LITERATURE | READINGS AND CRITIQUES [Putnam device]'. Spine: '[running down] AMERICAN LITERATURE | 135 mm rule] | READINGS AND CRITIQUES [running across] [50 mm rule] | STALLMAN | [13 mm rule] | WALDHORN | PUTNAM'. Dark orange-yellow (72) endpapers. Edges trimmed.

Dust jacket of white paper printed in dark red (16) and moderate bluish green (164). Front: eagle on a flag, title, editors. Back: advertisement for *Ten Modern Short Novels* and *Judging Poetry* and a listing of Putnam Capricorn Books. At the foot of the front flap is a device giving jacket credit to J & R.

Copies: IAA, STW (with jacket).

Published at $8.50 on 6 July 1961; copyright registration A513289.

B46 **1961**

Discussions of Poetry

DISCUSSIONS | OF | POETRY: | Rhythm and Sound | *Edited with an Introduction by* | *George Hemphill* | THE UNIVERSITY OF CONNECTICUT | [drawing of books] | [swelled rule, 89 mm] | D. C. Heath and Company | BOSTON

Copyright page (iv): '*Copyright © 1961 by D. C. Heath and Company* | *No part of the material covered by this copyright may be reproduced* | *for any purpose without written permission of the publisher.* | *Printed in the United States of America (6 F 1)*'.

234 x 164 mm. 64 leaves. *i-iv* v *vi* vii-ix *x-xii* 1-112 *112-116* pp.

Contains Ransom's essay "The Strange Music of English Verse" (103-12), reprinted from *Kenyon Review* (C331) and published here for the first time in book form.

Type-page 2 columns, 49 lines, 190 (198) x 131 mm (e.g., p. 105); typeface Bodoni. White wove paper, no watermark, sheets bulk 7 mm.

Perfect bound in white paper printed in moderate reddish orange (37) and light olive brown (94). Front has irregular reddish orange bands at right and left and olive brown between them at top and bottom, leaving a white central space on which appears: '[reddish orange] DISCUSSIONS OF | POETRY: | Rhythm and Sound | [two bands of reddish orange between which are 8 vertical bands resembling book spines] | [band of olive brown] | [reddish orange on white] DISCUSSIONS OF LITERATURE'. Spine: title and publisher. Back: vertical band of reddish orange on the right, the rest olive brown, without lettering. No endpapers.

Copies: CSA, INS, STW, WU.

Published at $1.40 on 5 August 1961 in the Discussions of Literature Series under the general editorship of Joseph H. Summers; copyright registration A532421.

B47 **1961**

Conversations on the Craft of Poetry

Conversations | ON THE CRAFT OF Poetry | CLEANTH BROOKS and ROBERT PENN WARREN | with | ROBERT FROST | JOHN CROWE RANSOM | ROBERT LOWELL | THEODORE ROETHKE | A transcript of the tape recording made to accompany | UNDERSTANDING POETRY, Third Edition | [106 mm rule] | HOLT, RINEHART AND WINSTON • New York

Copyright page (2): 'Copyright © 1961 by Holt, Rinehart and Winston, Inc. | 21096-1021 | Printed in the United States of America | All Rights Reserved | [address for ordering the tape recording, in 5 lines within a rule frame]'.

208 x 134 mm. *1*^{32}; 32 leaves. *1-2* 3-62 *63-64* pp.

Contains a recorded "conversation" with Brooks and Warren (19-32) in which Ransom discusses "Bells for John Whiteside's Daughter," Donne's "Holy Sonnet IX," and Blake's "Sunflower," with particular attention to metrics. For the recording itself, see E13.

Type-page 37 lines, 159 (164) x 101 mm, 10 lines = 42 mm (e.g., p. 21); typeface Times New Roman. White wove paper, no watermark, sheets bulk 4 mm.

The title leaf and final blank leaf are used as wrappers.

Copies: IEuC, InU-Main, OGK, STW. Also in Grimshaw, *Warren* B27.

Published 18 August 1961 at 75¢; copyright registration A536624.

B48 **1961**

New World Writing 19

19 | NEW | WORLD | WRITING | [Lippincott device] | J. B. LIPPINCOTT COMPANY | *Philadelphia & New York*

Copyright page (vi): 'Copyright © 1961 by J. B. Lippincott Company | [copyright notices for works by Marion Montgomery and Theodore Roethke, in 7 lines] | FIRST EDITION | Edited by Stewart Richardson and Corlies M. Smith | [notice to potential contributors, in 6 lines] | Printed in the United States of America | Library of Congress Catalog Card Number 52-1806'.

201 x 135 mm. *1-7*^{16}; 112 leaves. *1-10* 11-219 *220-224* pp.

Contains Ransom's "Essay" (191-201), which is an analysis of Theodore Roethke's poem "In a Dark Time" and which appears with analyses also by Babette Deutsch and Stanley Kunitz and with a response by Roethke as part of "The Poet and His Critics: A Symposium" edited by Anthony Ostroff (189-219). Ostroff later collected the several symposia (D240).

Type-page 39 lines, 165 (170) x 101 mm, 10 lines = 42 mm (e.g., p. 192); typeface Baskerville. White wove paper, no watermark, sheets bulk 14 mm.

Bound in black calico cloth over boards. Front and back blank. Spine, running down, printed in pale orange yellow (73): 'NEW WORLD WRITING 19 [2 mm rule] LIPPINCOTT'. White wove endpapers. Top and bottom edges cut; fore-edge trimmed.

Dust jacket of white paper with lettering in white and black on a background of moderate red (15) and light yellow (86) on front, in white on moderate red on spine, in moderate red and black on white on back, in black on white on flaps. Front has panel of yellow listing the contents. Back advertises the three previous volumes. Front flap lists price as '*$3.50*' and notes that the volume is also available as a paperbound Keystone Book (KB 33) at $1.65. Back flap advertises Keystone short story collections.

Also issued as Keystone Book KB33 in a perfect binding with design and color like those of the hardbound's dust jacket.

Copies: CSA (paperbound), ICU (paperbound), IDeKN, IRo (with jacket), IU (paperbound), STW (2 copies, one with jacket and annotations by Ransom and one paperbound), TxU-PCL.

Published at $3.50 hardbound and $1.65 paperbound on 27 September 1961; copyright registration A531543.

Reviewed in *Chicago Sunday Tribune Magazine of Books* 24 December 1961: 4 (Richard Sullivan); *Library Journal* 1 February 1962: 560 (Frances Burnette).

B49 **1962**

Poet's Choice

POET'S | CHOICE | [46 mm ornamented rule] | EDITED BY | Paul Engle and Joseph Langland | [Dial device] | THE DIAL PRESS NEW YORK 1962

Copyright page (iv): '*Copyright © 1962 by Paul Engle and Joseph Langland* | ALL RIGHTS RESERVED | *Library of Congress Catalog Card Number: 62-17684* | DESIGNED BY ALAN M. HEICKLEN | MANUFACTURED IN THE UNITED STATES OF AMERICA | BY THE HADDON CRAFTSMEN, SCRANTON, PA. | [beginning of acknowledgments in 51 lines]'.

230 x 153 mm. $1\text{-}8^{16}\ 9^{4}\ 10\text{-}11^{16}$; 164 leaves. [2] *i-iii* iv-vii *viii* ix-xi *xii* xiii-xvii *xviii-xx* 1-291 *292* 293-303 *304-306* pp.

Contains Ransom's poem "Prelude to an Evening" (12-13) and the first publication of his untitled comment (13) on why he chose the poem for this anthology.

Type-page 38 lines, 173 (183) x 105 mm, 10 lines = 46 mm (e.g., p. xiv); typeface Electra. White wove paper, no watermark, sheets bulk 19 mm.

Bound in moderate reddish brown (43) calico cloth over boards. Front and back blank. Spine stamped in gold: '[ornament] [running down] | POET'S CHOICE [running across] [ornament] | EDITED BY | ENGLE | AND | LANGLAND | [ornament] | [Dial device] | DIAL'. Moderate reddish orange (37) wove endpapers. Top edge cut; others rough trimmed.

Dust jacket of yellowish white (92) paper printed in gold, black, and dark reddish orange (38). Contributors' signatures appear on back. Front flap lists price as '$6.95'. Back flap credits the jacket design to Jeanyee Wong.

Copies: IDeKN, IRo (with jacket), IU (2 copies), STW (with jacket), TNV, TxU-UG, WBB. Also in Higginson and Williams, *Graves* B60; MacMahon, *Bishop* B20; Stefanik, *Berryman* B19; Wright, *Eberhart* B64; Wright, *Jarrell* B31.

Published at $6.95 on 9 October 1962; copyright registration A587331. Wright's *Jarrell* also records Dial Press publication, at $1.45 on 23 April 1963, of copies in a paper binding resembling the dust jacket of the hardbound copies. Also published paperbound at $1.95 as a Delta Book in January 1966 and paperbound as a Time Reading Program Special Edition in 1966.

Reviewed in *New York Times Book Review* 28 October 1962: 59 (Samuel French Morse); *Christian Century* 31 October 1962: 1328; *Chicago Sunday Tribune Magazine of Books* 9 December 1962: 11 (Margaret H. Carpenter); *Library Journal* 15 January 1963: 109; *Commonweal* 1 February 1963: 496 (Richard Lanham); *Saturday Review* 30 March 1963: 47 (Charles Simmons); *Massachusetts Review* Spring 1963: 614 (D. J. Hughes); *New York Herald Tribune Books* 16 June 1963: 10 (Stephen Stepanchev); *Chicago Review* Summer 1963: 112-118 (Ralph J. Mills, Jr.); *New Yorker* 6 July 1963: 76.

B50 **1963**

The Concise Encyclopedia of English and American Poets and Poetry

The Concise Encyclopedia of | ENGLISH AND AMERICAN | Poets and Poetry | Edited by | STEPHEN SPENDER and | DONALD HALL | HAWTHORN BOOKS INC • *Publishers* • NEW YORK

Copyright page (p. 4): '© Copyright 1963 by George Rainbird Ltd. [reservation of rights in four lines] This book was | designed and produced by George Rainbird Ltd, London. It was printed and | bound by The Garden City Press Ltd, Letchworth, England. The blocks for the | monochrome plates were made by Austin Miles Ltd, London. The endpapers | and the jacket were printed by Garrod and Lofthouse Ltd, London. *The Concise | Encyclopedia of English and American Poets and Poetry* is published simultaneously | in Canada by McClelland & Stewart Ltd, 25 Hollinger Road, Toronto 16. The | Library of Congress has catalogued this book under card number 63-8015. | Suggested decimal classification: 809.1. | First edition 1963 | Printed in England | H-2786.'

247 x 185 mm. 1^8 $2\text{-}26^8$; 208 leaves; $1 signed (e.g., '2-PAP'). *1-6* 7-19 *20* 21-22 *23-24* 25-365 *366* 367-403 *404* 405-407 *408* 409-415 *416* pp. Gatherings 3, 6, 11, 14, 19, and 22 consist of plates of photographs.

Contains Ransom's entries for Thomas Hardy (147-148) and Robert Lowell (191).

Type-page 49 lines, 2 columns, 207 (222) x 152 mm, column width = 74 mm, 10 lines = 42 mm (e.g., p. 286); typeface Bembo. White wove paper (glossy paper for gatherings of plates), no watermark, sheets bulk 35 mm.

Bound in grayish purplish blue (204) calico cloth over boards. Front and back blank. Spine stamped in gold: '[within a rule frame] THE CONCISE | ENCYCLOPEDIA OF | ENGLISH AND | AMERICAN | POETS & POETRY | EDITED BY | STEPHEN SPENDER | AND DONALD HALL | [below the frame] HAWTHORN'. White wove endpapers printed on the paste-down and facing free page with a color photograph of shelves of books. Edges trimmed. Top edge stained grayish purplish blue (204).

Dust jacket of white paper printed on front, spine, and back with the same photograph as the endpapers. On the front and spine, the title and editors are in black on a panel of brilliant greenish yellow (98), and the publisher's imprint appears on a similar panel at the foot of the spine.

Copies: IDeK (with jacket), IDeKN, ICU, STW (with jacket), TNV, WBB.

Published at $15.00 ($12.95 until 31 May) on 6 May 1963; copyright registration AF20975. Also published by Hutchinson, London, at £2 10s. A second edition (London: Hutchinson, 1970) contains the same entries by Ransom; the entries are unrevised, although in a letter of 11 October 1968 Jocelyn Selson of Rainbird Ltd. reminded Ransom of her earlier request for revision (TNV).

Reviewed in *Listener* 1963: 711 (Anthony Thwaite); *Library Journal* 15 May 1963: 1990 (Robert Cayton); *New Leader* 2 September 1963: 18-19 (Howard Nemerov); *New Statesman* 6 December 1963: 844-845 (Christopher Ricks); *TLS* 19 March 1964: 228.

B51 **1963**

Emily Dickinson

EMILY | DICKINSON | A COLLECTION OF CRITICAL ESSAYS | Edited by | *Richard B. Sewall* | [Spectrum Book device] | Prentice-Hall, Inc., *Englewood Cliffs, N.J.*

Copyright page (iv): '© 1963 BY PRENTICE-HALL, INC. | ENGLEWOOD CLIFFS, N.J. | [reservation of rights in 3 lines] | LIBRARY OF CONGRESS CATALOG CARD NO.: 63-9307 | *Printed in the United States of America* | C 20878'.

203 x 140 mm. *1-6*^{16}; 96 leaves. *i-iv* v *vi* 1-177 *178* 179-183 *184-186* pp.

Contains Ransom's essay "Emily Dickinson: A Poet Restored" (88-100), reprinted from the spring 1956 *Perspectives USA* (C330) published here for the first time in book form.

Type-page 45 lines, 175 (181) x 114 mm, 10 lines = 39 mm (e.g., p. 97); typeface Baskerville. White wove paper, no watermark, sheets bulk 14 mm.

Bound in black calico cloth over boards. Front and back blank. Spine stamped in gold, running down: 'EMILY DICKINSON *Edited by* Richard B. Sewall Prentice-Hall'. White wove endpapers. Edges trimmed. Dust jacket of white paper printed in black and pale yellow (89), with a drawing of Dickinson in yellow on black on the front. The back flap credits the drawing to Stanley Wyatt.

Also issued in perfect binding closely resembling the dust jacket of the hardbound copies.

Copies: IDeKN, InU-Main (2 copies), IRo (with jacket), STW (with jacket), WBB, WU (paperbound).

Published at $3.95 ($1.95 paperbound) on 27 June 1963; copyright registration A638962. Reviewed in *New York Times Book Review* 17 November 1963: 67 (DeLancey Ferguson).

B52 **1964**

National Poetry Festival

National | Poetry Festival | HELD IN THE LIBRARY OF CONGRESS | OCTOBER 22-24, 1962 | *PROCEEDINGS* | [Library of Congress seal] | GENERAL REFERENCE AND BIBLIOGRAPHY DIVISION | REFERENCE DEPARTMENT | LIBRARY OF CONGRESS | WASHINGTON : 1964

Copyright page (ii): '[within a rule frame] L.C. card 64-60048 | [without the frame] For sale by the Superintendent of Documents, U.S. Government Printing Office | Washington, D.C., 20402 - Price $1.50'.

Printer's imprint (367): 'U.S. GOVERNMENT PRINTING OFFICE: 1964'.

232 x 147 mm. Gathered *1-10*^{16} *11*^{10} *12*^{16}, but signed *1*^{8} 2-20^{8} 21^{1} 22^{9} 23-24^{8} so that the ninth leaf of gathering 1, the first and ninth leaves of gatherings 2-10 and 12, and the first and second leaves of gathering 11 are signed. 186 leaves. *i-ii* 1-9 *10-12* 13 *14* 15-27 *28* 29-33 *34* 35-53 *54-56* 57-102 *103-104* 105 *106* 107-109 *110* 111-138 *139-140* 141 *142* 143 *144* 145-159 *160* 161-179 *180-182* 183-228 *229-230* 231-259 *260-262* 263 *264* 265-288 *289-290* 291-340 *341-342* 343-367 *368-370*.

Contains Ransom's poem "Prelude to an Evening," his remarks introducing his reading of it, and his comments on its revision (69-74)—these having been presented at the festival's afternoon session on 22 October 1962. The text of the poem is the same as that in the winter 1963 *Kenyon Review* (C347), where he explained at greater length the revision it underwent. (Both poem and explanation were later revised for his 1963 and 1969 *Selected Poems* [A16, A18].) Also contains Ransom's "Introduction of Speakers" for the 24 October morning session entitled "The Problem of Form." His introduction (265-270) presents the topic and the speakers (Allen Tate, Léonie Adams, and J. V. Cunningham). Also printed (284-288) is the subsequent discussion moderated by Ransom. For the tape recording of the festival, see E15.

Type-page 39 lines, 191 (200) x 111 mm, 10 lines = 49 mm (e.g., p. 269); typeface Caslon. Signatures, in the direction line, are preceded by a job number (e.g., '712-081—64—2'). White wove paper, no watermark, sheets bulk 21 mm.

Bound in yellowish white (92) wove paper with faint vertical chainlines 23 mm apart (no watermark). Front: '[white on black] [lyre] | NATIONAL | POETRY | FESTIVAL [running up on the right, in black on white] HELD IN THE LIBRARY OF CONGRESS, OCTOBER 22-24, 1962'. Spine and back blank. Inside covers used for acknowledgements. No endpapers. Edges trimmed.

Copies: IDeKN, STW (3 copies), WU (rebound, preserving front and back covers). Also in Stefanik, *Berryman* BB4; Wright, *Eberhart* B71; Wright, *Jarrell* B39.

Published at $1.50 in January 1964. Listed as entry 13093 in the July 1964 *Monthly Catalog of United States Government Publications*.

Reviewed in *Library Journal* 15 September 1964: 3319 (John R. Willingham); *American Literature* January 1965: 551 (Clarence Ghodes, signed C. G.); *American Book Collector* May 1965: 22 (Julian Lee Rayford).

B53 **1964**

John Crowe Ransom

[Page 3] John Crowe Ransom | Gentleman, Teacher, Poet, Editor | Founder of The Kenyon Review | A Tribute from the | Community of Letters | Edited by | D. David Long and Michael R. Burr | *The* [superimposed on the following C] *Kenyon* [horizontally shaded black-letter type] Collegian | [roman type] A Supplement to Vol. LXXXX, No. 7 | Gambier, Ohio | 1964

Copyright page (p. 2): 'Copyright © 1964 | Kenyon College | All Rights Reserved | Printed by Printing Arts Press, Mount Vernon, Ohio'.

278 x 212 mm. *1*^{28}; 28 leaves. *1-5* 6-56 pp.

Contains Ransom's poem "Painted Head," reproducing a signed autograph manuscript (28) and transcribing it in type (29). The text is that of the 1945 *Selected Poems* (A12) except that it agrees with the 1969 *Selected Poems* (A18) in reading 'The estate of body' in line 29, that it uniquely has a semicolon after 'body' in the same line, and that it uniquely reads 'Calls up this image:' in line 25. Also contains the editors' "Interview with John Crowe Ransom" (7-8), on the founding of *Kenyon Review* and on Ransom's writing of poetry. The volume consists of poems and statements of tribute from 40 or so poets and critics, including W. H. Auden, R. P. Blackmur, R. S. Crane, Lawrence Ferlinghetti, Richard Eberhart, William Empson, Granville Hicks, Randall Jarrell, Robert Lowell, Marianne Moore, Howard Nemerov, Norman Podhoretz, Karl Shapiro, C. P. Snow, Allen Tate, Louis Untermeyer, and Robert Penn Warren. It prints W. D. Snodgrass's explication of "Master's in the Garden Again," which would appear later that same month in *New World Writing* (B54).

Type-page 47 lines, 206 (215) x 162 mm, 10 lines = 45 mm; typeface Century. White wove paper blind-embossed in fine pebble grain, no watermark, sheets bulk 4 mm.

Bound in white wove paper wrapper with title stamped in gold within a gold rule frame on the front. Back blank.

Copies: ICU (rebound), OGK, STW (3 copies, including Ransom's copy in publisher's presentation binding of black half-leather and green cloth with black leather label stamped in gold), TNV, TxU-HRC. Also in Bloomfield and Mendelson, *Auden* B87; Wright, *Eberhart* B70; Wright, *Jarrell* B37.

Published 7 February 1964; copyright registration A746700. Noted in *Publishers' Weekly* 9 March 1964: 28 as available for sale at $2.50. Bloomfield and Mendelson, as well as Wright, give a publication date of 24 January 1964 and report an initial printing of 800 copies (not for sale), followed by additional printings in 1964 (2,000 copies) and 1965 (2,000 copies).

B54 **1964**

New World Writing 22

22 | NEW | WORLD | WRITING | [Keystone device] | J. B. LIPPINCOTT COMPANY | *Philadelphia & New York*

Copyright page (2): 'Copyright © 1964 by J. B. Lippincott Company | FIRST EDITION | Edited by Stewart Richardson | Printed in the United States of America | Library of Congress Catalog Card Number 52-1806 | [acknowledgment in 3 lines]'.

202 x 133 mm. *1-7*^{16}; 112 leaves. [2] *1-6* 7-215 *216* 217 *218-222* pp.

Contains Ransom's poem "Master's in the Garden Again" (185-187) and Ransom's response (208-215) to comments on the poem by Muriel Rukeyser, W. D. Snodgrass, and Léonie Adams—for "The Poet and His Critics: IV, A Symposium" edited by Anthony Ostroff, here published for the first time. The text of the poem is that of *Selected Poems* 1963 (A16). See *The Contemporary Poet as Artist and Critic* (D240), where Ransom's response appears under the title "Now the Grateful Author."

Type-page 38 lines, 161 (167) x 101 mm, 10 lines = 43 mm (e.g., 212); typeface Baskerville. White wove paper, no watermark, sheets bulk 16 mm.

Bound in black calico cloth over boards. Front and back blank. Spine, running down, printed in moderate red (15): 'NEW WORLD WRITING 22 [2 mm rule] LIPPINCOTT'. White wove endpapers. Top and bottom edges cut; fore-edge trimmed.

Dust jacket of white paper printed in black and vivid reddish orange (34). Front: '[on a photograph of a hooded person with a shrub in the foreground and a building in the background] [white] LIPPINCOTT'S | NeW WorLD | WriTiNG [reddish orange] 22 | [white on black] An essay, new poems, short stories and | criticism especially selected for the | adventuresome reader'. Back: list and contents of volumes 21 through 16 in the series, jacket photo credit to Edward Wallowitch. Front flap, in black on white: contents and jacket photo credit again. Back flap: other Keystone books available.

Also issued in a perfect paper binding resembling the jacket of the hardbound copies. At the foot of the front is added in white: '[Keystone device] KEYSTONE BOOKS KB-61 95c'. Back, in black on white: contents, 'Also available in a special clothbound edition', publisher's imprint, cover photo credit. No endpapers. Edges cut.

Copies: ICU (paperbound), IDeKN (paperbound), STW (2 copies, one paperbound, one hardbound with jacket).

Published at $3.50 hardbound and $0.96 paperbound on 13 May 1964; copyright registration A691771.

Reviewed in *New York Times* 18 July 1964: 17 (Charles Poore); *Library Journal* August 1964: 3010 (Richard K. Burns).

B55 **1965**

Poems and Poets

[On facing pages] [recto] *David Aloian* | *Headmaster, Concord Academy* | [verso] POEMS [recto] AND POETS | *Foreword by John Crowe Ransom* | [verso] [design of 9 circular and squarish solids arranged in 3 rows] [recto] WEBSTER DIVISION | MC-GRAW-HILL BOOK COMPANY | *St. Louis New York* | *San Francisco* | *Dallas Toronto London*

Copyright page (iv): '[8-line biographical note on Aloian] | Copyright © 1965 by McGraw-Hill, Inc. | [reservation of rights in 4 lines] | 01397'.

212 x 140 mm. *1-14*^{16}; 224 leaves. *i-iv* v-xxiv *1-2* 3-162 *163-164* 165-424 pp.

Contains Ransom's foreword on "poetic principles" (ix-xii), signed 'JOHN CROWE RANSOM | CHRISTMAS, 1963'; also reprints poems "Blue Girls" (299-300), "Janet Waking" (389), and "Bells for John Whiteside's Daughter" (390).

Type-page varies: Ransom's foreword and the editor's preface have an irregular number of lines, 169 (175) x 101 mm, 10 lines = 35 mm (e.g., p. x); typeface Caledonia. White wove paper, no watermarks, sheets bulk 23 mm.

Bound in moderate brown (58) calico cloth over boards, with black circular and squarish blotches on front spine and back and with lettering printed in white. Front: 'POEMS | AND | POETS'. Spine: 'POEMS | AND | POETS | ALOIAN | WEBSTER | McGRAW-HILL | 01397'. Back without lettering. Top and bottom edges cut; fore-edge trimmed. White wove endpapers.

Copies: IDeKN (lacking gathering 9 and having in its place a duplicate gathering 7), IRo, STW.

Published at $4.96 on 4 January 1965; copyright registration A735315.

B56 **1965**

The Fugitive Poets

MODERN | SOUTHERN POETRY | IN | PERSPECTIVE | *the fugitive poets* | EDITED, | AND WITH AN INTRODUCTION, BY | WILLIAM PRATT | *A Dutton* [Dutton device] *Paperback* | NEW YORK: E. P. DUTTON & CO., INC. | 1965

Copyright page (4): 'Copyright © 1965 by William C. Pratt. / All rights re- | served. Printed in the U.S.A. / [reservation of rights in 6 lines] / First Edition. | [acknowledgments in 46 lines and continued on facing page]'.

184 x 109 mm. 80 leaves. *1-3* 4-5 *6-10* 11-46 *47-48* 49-151 *152* 153-157 *158-160* pp.

Contains Ransom's poems "Bells for John Whiteside's Daughter" (49), "The Vanity of the Blue Girls" (50-51), "The Vanity of the Bright Young Men" (51-52), "Conrad in Twilight" (53), "Necrological" (54-55), "Janet Waking" (55-56), "Piazza Piece" (56), "Old Mansion" (57-58), "Philomela" (58-60), "Amphibious Crocodile" (60-62), "Captain Carpenter" (63-65), "The Equilibrists" (65-67), "Painted Head" (67-68), "Antique Harvesters" (69-70). "The Vanity of the Bright Young Men" appears here in a unique version in many ways intermediate between that of the 1963 edition of *Selected Poems* (A16) and the 1969 edition (A18), where the title (in the "B version") becomes "The Vanity of the Bright Boys." Other of the poems selected by Pratt also appear here in unique versions, notably "Old Mansion." Also, only here does "Blue Girls" become "The Vanity of the Blue Girls." As Pratt indicates in a article in *Mississippi Quarterly* (see C367), he received revisions of the poems from Ransom for this anthology.

Type-page 37 lines, 144 (153) x 88 mm, 10 lines = 39 mm (e.g., p. 14); typeface Garamond. White wove paper, no watermark, sheets bulk 10 mm.

Perfect bound in white paper printed in black and the hues of brown, blue, green, greenish blue, red, yellow, and pink. On the front is a drawing of a tree losing its leaves and another of a pitted and cracked bust of a Civil War soldier on a greenish blue background and partially obscured by green foliage with flowers of red and yellow. The front and spine bear the Dutton book number D161. The back credits the cover design to Paul Davis. No endpapers. Edges cut.

Copies: CSA (2 copies), IDeKN, STW (Ransom's copy in publisher's presentation slipcase of green half-leather and green cloth stamped in gold and inscribed by Pratt in March 1965), TNV (2 copies).

Published at $1.45 ($1.75 in Canada) on 10 March 1965; copyright registration A754012. Reviewed in *Choice* June 1966: 311. A new edition was published in 1991 by J. S. Sanders & Company in its the Southern Classics Series. For this edition, the preface, introduction, and bibliography have been revised, and the contents expanded to include some of the non-Fugitive contributors to the *Fugitive*. There is no change in the selections from Ransom.

B57 **1965**

R. P. Blackmur

[On front wrapper] R. P. Blackmur: | Language as Gesture & | essays by Kenneth Burke | Marianne Moore Conrad Aiken | John Crowe Ransom & others | [abstract line drawing forming a band across the cover]

On p. 1: 'EDITORS: | PAUL BOORSTIN and INTS M. SILINS | DESIGN: JOHN MASON | *Published by The Nassau Literary Magazine in May, 1965.* | Printed by the Princeton Printing Company, 176 Alexander Street, Princeton, | New Jersey. [credits and permissions in 4 lines]'.

355 x 277 mm. *1*^{8}; 8 leaves. *1* 2-16 pp.

Contains Ransom's brief untitled prose tribute to Blackmur (beginning "I cherish the feeling that we were great friends. . .") (8).

Type-page 66 lines, 2 columns, 279 (301) x 209 mm, column width = 98 mm, 10 lines = 42 mm (e.g., p. 4); typeface Bodoni. White wove paper.

Bonnell describes stiff yellowish white (92) laid paper wrappers printed in black. Edges cut.

Copy: NjP (seen only in photocopy). Also in Bonnell, *Aiken* B82.

Published in May 1965.

B58 **1965**

Approaches to the Poem

APPROACHES TO THE *Poem* | *MODERN ESSAYS IN THE ANALYSIS* | *AND INTERPRETATION OF POETRY* | SELECTED AND INTRODUCED BY | *JOHN OLIVER PERRY* | TUFTS UNIVERSITY | [Chandler device] CHANDLER PUBLISHING COMPANY | 124 SPEAR STREET, SAN FRANCISCO, CALIFORNIA 94105

Copyright page (iv): 'COPYRIGHT © 1965 BY CHANDLER PUBLISHING COMPANY | LIBRARY OF CONGRESS CATALOG CARD NO. 65-11377 | PRINTED IN THE UNITED STATES OF AMERICA | [acknowledgements in 45 lines]'.

208 x 136 mm. *1-14*^{16}; 224 leaves. [2] *i-vi* vii-ix *x-xii* 1-35 *36-38* 39-106 *107-108* 109-235 *236-238* 239-273 *274-276* 277-345 *346-348* 349-386 *387-388* 389-433 *434* pp.

Contains Ransom's essay "Poetry: The Formal Analysis" (39-67), first published in two parts in *Kenyon Review* (C293, C295) and published here for the first time in book form.

Type-page 37 lines, 158 (166) x 101 mm, 10 lines = 42 mm (e.g., p. 42); typeface Baskerville. White wove paper, no watermark, sheets bulk 23 mm.

Bound in white paper printed in black and white on a deep orange-yellow (69) background. Front: '[in white on an abstract design in black] APPROACHES | TO THE | POEM | [black on orange] *Modern Essays in the Analysis and* | *Interpretation of Poetry* | [white] JOHN OLIVER PERRY'. Spine: editor, title, publisher. Back: 'Reorder No. 23-10131'. No endpapers. Top and bottom edges cut, fore-edge trimmed.

Copies: IDeKN, INS (rebound, preserving front cover), TNV (rebound, preserving original covers).

Published at $3.75 on 14 May 1965; copyright registration A770299. Reviewed in *Choice* November 1965: 576.

B59 **1966**

Master Poems of the English Language

MASTER | POEMS | OF THE ENGLISH LANGUAGE | [98 mm swelled rule] | *Over one hundred poems* | *together with Introductions* | *by leading poets and critics* | *of the English-speaking world* | EDITED BY | Oscar Williams | [Trident device] | TRIDENT PRESS | *New York 1966*

Copyright page (iv): '*Copyright, ©, 1966, by Trident Press* | [reservation of rights in 6 lines] | *Library of Congress Catalog Card Number: 65-25702* | *Published simultaneously in the United States and Canada* | *Printed in the United States of America*'.

227 x 140 mm. *1-34*^{16}; 544 leaves. *i-v* vi-xiii *xiv* xv-xvi 1-1071 (without numbers on versos preceding each poem and bearing each poet's portrait) *1072* pp.

Reprints Ransom's poem "Captain Carpenter" (983-984) and publishes for the first time his commentary on Wallace Stevens's "Sunday Morning" (893-897). Ransom's poem appears with commentary by John Berryman (985-987).

Type-page 45 lines, 192 (198) x 97 mm, 10 lines = 43 mm (e.g., p. 894); typeface Janson. White laid paper with chainlines 23 mm apart, no watermark, sheets bulk 50 mm.

Bound in black calico cloth over boards. Front and back blank. Spine, stamped in gold and deep orange (51), running across: '[gold] MASTER | POEMS | OF THE | ENGLISH LANGUAGE | [43 mm swelled rule] | [orange] EDITED BY | OSCAR | WILLIAMS | [blind-stamped flourish] | [gold] TRIDENT | PRESS'. Grayish yellow (90) endpapers with a marble-like pattern. Edges cut. Top edge stained very pale green (148). Issued in a box (mentioned by reviews but not seen).

Copies: I, ISy, STW, WBB. Also in Stefanik, *Berryman* B25; Wright, *Eberhart* B83.

Published at $10.00 on 17 January 1966; copyright registration A829032. Wright reports that the book was "reissued in a card cover by Washington Square Press in 1967."

Reviewed in *Best Sellers* 1 April 1966: 7; *Library Journal* 1 April 1966: 1904 (Margaret Beebe); *New York Times* 5 April 1966: 41 (Eliot Fremont-Smith); *Saturday Review* 21 May 1966: 30-31 (Robert J. Clements); *Poetry* February 1967: 345-350 (Ralph J. Mills, Jr.); *Southern Review* October 1968: 1099-1109 (Thomas Vance).

B60 **1966**

T. S. Eliot: The Man and His Work

T. S. ELIOT | THE MAN AND HIS WORK | [100 mm rule] | *A Critical Evaluation by Twenty-six | Distinguished Writers* | EDITED BY | Allen Tate | *A Seymour Lawrence Book* | DELACORTE PRESS | NEW YORK

Copyright page (iv): 'Copyright © 1966 by The University of the South | All rights reserved | Library of Congress catalog card number: 66-20994 | Printed in the United States of America | First printing | [acknowledgments in 18 lines]'.

202 x 136 mm. *1-13*^{16}; 208 leaves. [2] *i-iv* v-vi *vii-viii 1-2* 3-393 (with opening pages of essays unnumbered) *394-395* 396-397 *398-399* 400 *401-406* pp., with 8 leaves of halftone plates after p. 182.

Contains Ransom's essay "Gerontion" (133-158), reprinted from *Sewanee Review* (C354) and published here for the first time in book form.

Type-page 34 lines, 156 (164) x 102 mm, 10 lines = 46 mm (e.g., p. 141); typeface Caslon. Printed by photo-offset, the type-page having been reduced from the typesetting used for the original publication in *Sewanee Review*. White wove paper, no watermark, sheets bulk 24 mm.

Bound in moderate reddish brown (43) calico cloth over boards stamped in gold and black. Front: '[gold] T. S. ELIOT | THE MAN AND HIS WORK | [103 mm rule in black]'. Spine, running across: '[gold] T. S. | ELIOT | THE MAN | AND HIS WORK | [28 mm black rule] | [gold] ALLEN TATE | [publisher's device in black] | [gold] DELACORTE | PRESS'. Back blank. Edges trimmed. Top edge stained moderate orange-yellow (71). Brownish orange (54) wove endpapers.

Dust jacket of white paper lettered in brilliant blue (177) and black. Front: '[blue] T. S. ELIOT: | The Man and His Work | [black] A Critical Evaluation by 26 Distinguished Writers | Edited by Allen Tate | [color portrait of Eliot]'. Spine: title, editor, and publisher's device and imprint. Back: title and contributors.

Front flap: price ('$6.50'), title, blurb. Back flap: blurb continued, jacket portrait credit (to Wyndham Lewis, courtesy of Harvard), publisher's imprint.

Copies: InU-Lilly (with jacket), OGK, STW (with jacket), TNV, WBB, WU. Also in Bonnell, *Aiken* B85; Gallup, *Eliot* B85; Gallup, *Pound* B129.

Published at $6.50 in November 1966. (Not found in *CCE*.) American sheets were published in London in April 1967 by Chatto & Windus at 36s. A photo-offset reprint was published also in April 1967 by Dell Publishing as a paperback (Delta Book 2263, for $2.45); and, according to Gallup's *Pound*, an edition was published in London and Harmondsworth by Penguin in 1971 as a Pelican Book at 50p.

Listed in "Weekly Record," *Publishers' Weekly* 26 December 1966: 247. Advertised at $6.50 in *Kenyon Review* 28.5 (November 1966): 589.

Reviewed in *New York Times Book Review* 27 November 1966 (Hayden Carruth); *Library Journal* 1 December 1966: 5972 (Thomas E. Luddy); *National Review* 7 February 1967: 147, 149 (Hugh Kenner); *New Yorker* 18 March 1967: 195; *New Republic* 20 May 1967: 19-25 (Richard Poirier); *Southwest Review* Summer 1967: 304-307 (Karl Malkoff). Chatto and Windus issue reviewed in *Spectator* 5 May 1967: 524 (C. B. Cox); *Listener* 25 May 1967: 690 (Ian Hamilton); *TLS* 1 June 1967: 485; *Economist* 10 June 1967: 1128.

B61 **1966**

A Symposium on Formalist Criticism

A SYMPOSIUM ON | FORMALIST CRITICISM | [drawing of an open book] | [126 mm rule] | EDITED BY WILLIAM J. HANDY WITH AN INTRODUCTION BY MARK SCHORER | JOHN CROWE RANSOM ELISEO VIVAS | ELDER OLSON KENNETH BURKE | FROM PAPERS DELIVERED ON FEBRUARY 11 AND 12, 1965 | THE UNIVERSITY OF TEXAS, AUSTIN, TEXAS | [126 mm rule]

Copyright page (6): '[126 mm rule] | *Copyright* © 1965 *by The University of Texas* | LIBRARY OF CONGRESS CATALOG NUMBER: 67-63594 | *published by* | THE HUMANITIES RESEARCH CENTER | THE UNIVERSITY OF TEXAS | *Distributed by* | UNIVERSITY OF TEXAS PRESS | AUSTIN, TEXAS 78712 | *Printed and bound in the United States of America* | *Reprint from* THE TEXAS QUARTERLY | [126 mm rule]'.

247 x 170 mm. *1-6*^{8}; 48 leaves. *1-9* 10-92 *93-96* pp.

The text in this book, including that of Ransom's "Theory of Poetic Form" (14-25), is reprinted by offset from the typesetting used for its publication in the spring 1966 issue of *Texas Quarterly* (C353).

Type-page 42 lines, 194 (202) x 127 mm, 10 lines = 46 mm (e.g., p. 15); typeface Garamond. White wove paper, no watermark, sheets bulk 6 mm.

Bound in grayish yellow-green (122) calico cloth over boards, printed in black. Front: drawing of an open book. Spine, running down: 'A SYMPOSIUM ON FORMALIST CRITICISM / THE UNIVERSITY OF TEXAS'. Back: drawing of an open book. Yellowish white (92) wove endpapers. Top and bottom edges cut; fore-edge trimmed. No dust jacket seen.

Copies: IDeKN, INS, TNV.

The spring 1966 issue of *Texas Quarterly* was published on 3 November 1966, and presumably that is the approximate date of publication for this book as well. The publisher and distributor could supply no more precise date.

B62 **1966**

Faulkner:
A Collection of Critical Essays

FAULKNER | A COLLECTION OF CRITICAL ESSAYS | Edited by | *Robert Penn Warren* | Prentice-Hall, Inc. [Spectrum Books device] *Englewood Cliffs, N.J.*

Copyright page (vi): 'To R. W. B. and Nancy Lewis | Copyright © 1966 by Prentice-Hall, Inc., *Englewood Cliffs, New Jersey*. A SPECTRUM | BOOK. All rights reserved. No part of this book may be reproduced in any form or | by any means without permission in writing from the publisher. *Library of Congress* | *Catalog Number 66-28113.* Printed in the United States of America—C. P30820, | C30821 | Current printing (last number): 10 9 8 7 6 5 4 3 2 1'.

202 x 139 mm. *1-10*^{16}; 160 leaves. *i-viii* 1-299 *300-301* 302-311 *312* pp.

Contains Ransom's "William Faulkner: An Impression" (294-295), reprinted from *Harvard Advocate* (C309) but omitting the first two paragraphs and having, in addition to variants in punctuation and spelling, a substantive variant in the final sentence (reading 'for the sense' where the original reads 'in the sense'). The brief essay is published here for the first time in book form.

Type-page 45 lines, 172 (178) x 112 mm, 10 lines = 38 mm (e.g., p. 49); typeface Baskerville. White wove paper, no watermark, sheets bulk 21 mm.

Bound in black calico cloth over boards, stamped in gold. Front blank. Spine, running down: 'FAULKNER *Edited by* Robert Penn Warren Prentice-Hall'. Back: '30821'. White wove endpapers. Edges trimmed.

Dust jacket of white paper printed in black and vivid purplish red (254). Front, in red on black: series title, book title and editor, scene from *The Sound and the Fury*. Back, in black on white: listing of other titles in the series. Blurbs on front and back flaps; jacket credit to Stanley Wyatt on back flap.

Also issued in a paper perfect binding, the covers of which closely resemble the dust jacket of the hardbound issue but with blurbs and cover-design credit on the back.

Copies: CSA (paperbound), IDeK (with jacket), IDeKN, STW (2 copies, one with jacket, the other paperbound), WBB, WU. Also in Grimshaw, *Warren* B30.

Published at $4.95 ($2.45 paperbound) on 23 November 1966; copyright registration A881018, copies deposited 10 January 1967.

Reviewed in *Library Journal* January 1967: 243 (Charles A. Raines), *Critic* April-May 1967: 76-80 (Thomas Merton), *Booklist* 1 April 1976: 831, *American Literature* May 1967: 263, *Saturday Review* 6 May 1967: 27-28 (Granville Hicks), *Choice* July 1967: 535, *Southern Review* Spring 1968: 458-466 (Hyatt H. Waggoner).

B63 **1967**

Years of Protest

YEARS OF | PROTEST | A Collection of American Writings of the 1930's | edited by Jack Salzman | BARRY WALLENSTEIN, ASSISTANT EDITOR | PEGASUS [Pegasus device] NEW YORK

Copyright page (2): '[7-line note on acknowledgments] | LIBRARY OF CONGRESS CATALOG CARD NUMBER: 67-13489 | © COPYRIGHT 1967 BY WESTERN PUBLISHING COMPANY, INC. | [reservation of rights] | DESIGNED AND PRODUCED BY ARTISTS AND WRITERS PRESS, INC. | PRINTED IN THE U.S.A. BY WESTERN PRINTING AND LITHOGRAPHING CO. | PUBLISHED BY PEGASUS, A DIVISION OF WESTERN PUBLISHING COMPANY, INC.'

203 x 134 mm. *1-14*^{16}; 224 leaves. *1-6* 7-8 *9-10* 11-27 *28* 29-74 *75* 76-83 *84* 85-87 *88* 89-100 *101* 102-106 *107* 108-136 *137* 138-199 *200* 201-219 *220* 221-228 *229-230* 231-307 *308* 309-375 *376* 377-448 pp.

Contains Ransom's essay "The South Is a Bulwark" (264-276), reprinted from the May 1936 *Scribner's Magazine* (C219) and published here for the first time in book form.

Type-page 42 lines, 171 (176) x 106 mm, 10 lines = 41 mm (e.g., p. 267); typeface Times New Roman. White wove paper, no watermark, sheets bulk 23 mm.

Bound in pale green (149) calico cloth over boards. Front: Pegasus blindstamped in relief. Spine, stamped in gold, running across: 'YEARS | OF | PROTEST | [14 mm rule] | [Pegasus device] | PEGASUS'. Back blank. White wove endpapers. Edges trimmed.

Dust jacket of white paper printed in black, moderate blue, and strong purplish red (255). Contributors' names on the front create a circular pattern. Book number at head of spine: 'P1001'. On back flap, jacket design credit to Charles & Cuffari.

Also issued in a paper binding resembling the dust jacket (not seen).

Copies: ICU, IDeKN, INS, TNV, WBB, WM (with jacket), WMM, WU.

Published at $7.50 ($2.75 paperbound) on 10 July 1967; copyright registration A949373. Advertised in *PMLA* November 1969: 1858. Reviewed in *Christian Science Monitor* 9 August 1967: 13 (M.M.), *Catholic World* November 1967: 94-95 (John Kearney); *Choice* January 1968: 1246; *Nation* 12 February 1968: 213-214 (Michael B. Folsom).

B64 **1967**

Randall Jarrell, 1914-1965

[Swash first letter] *Randall Jarrell* | [85 mm rule] | 1914-1965 | EDITED BY | Robert Lowell, Peter Taylor, | & Robert Penn Warren | [publisher's device] | *Farrar, Straus & Giroux* | NEW YORK

Copyright page (iv): '*Copyright © 1967 by Farrar, Straus & Giroux, Inc.* | *All rights reserved* | *Library of Congress catalog card number 67-13414* | *First printing, 1967* | *Published simultaneously in Canada by* | *Ambassador Books, Ltd., Rexdale, Ontario* | *Designed by Guy Fleming* | *Printed in the United States of America* | [beginning of acknowledgments in 33 lines]'.

202 x 138 mm. *1-10*^{16}; 160 leaves. *i-vi* vii-xii *1-2* 3-307 *308* pp., and 16 leaves of photographs between pp. 164 and 165 and a reproduction of an engraving tipped-in between pp. 192 and 193.

Contains Ransom's essay "The Rugged Way of Genius" (155-181), reprinted from the spring 1967 *Southern Review* (C355) and here published for the first time in book form.

Type-page 29 lines, 142 (160) x 97 mm, 10 lines = 50 mm (e.g., p. 156); typeface Granjon. White laid paper with vertical chainlines 20 mm apart, no watermark, sheets bulk 23 mm.

Bound in moderate brown (58) calico cloth over boards. Front, blind stamped: '*Randall Jarrell* | [92 mm rule] | 1914-1965'. Spine stamped in gold, running across: '[first letter swash] *Randall* | *Jarrell* | [26 mm rule] | 1914- | 1965 | [26 mm rule] | LOWELL, | TAYLOR, | & | WARREN | [26 mm rule] | [publisher's device] | *Farrar,* | *Straus &* | *Giroux*'. Back blank. Brilliant yellow (83) wove endpapers. Edges trimmed; top edge stained light yellow (86), but top edge of inserted photographs stained light green (144).

Dust jacket of white paper printed in black and brilliant orange-yellow (67). Front: lettered in white on a black background, with a photograph of Jarrell. Back lists contributors. Price on front flap: '$6.50'. Back flap credits photograph to Philippe Halsman and jacket design to Guy Fleming.

Copies: CSA (with jacket), ICU (with jacket), IDeKN (duplicate first gathering bound in at the end), IRo (with jacket), STW (with jacket), WBB, WM (with jacket). Also in Abbott, *Moore* B43; Grimshaw, *Warren* B31; Stefanik, *Berryman* B27; Wright, *Jarrell* B43; Wright, *Taylor* B15.

Published at $6.50 on 28 August 1967; copyright registration A935541. Also published as a Noonday Press paperback on 15 April 1968.

Reviewed in *Saturday Review* 2 September 1967: 26 (Reed Whittemore); *New York Times Book Review* 3 September 1967: 4-5 (Julian Moynahan); *New York Times* 14 September 1967: 45 (Erik Wensberg); *Library Journal* 1 October 1967: 3423 (Ervin J. Gaines); *New York Review of Books* 23 November 1967: 26-31 (Stephen Spender); *Virginia Quarterly Review* Spring 1968: 318-323 (J. C. Levenson); *Poetry* May 1968: 118 (Katherine Hoskins); *Contemporary Literature* Autumn 1968: 567-573 (Samuel French Morse).

B65 **1972**

The Poetry of John Crowe Ransom

The Poetry of | John Crowe Ransom | Miller Williams | [publisher's device] RUTGERS UNIVERSITY PRESS | *New Brunswick, New Jersey*

Copyright page (iv): 'Copyright © 1972 by Miller Williams | Library of Congress Catalogue Number: 78-184566 | ISBN: 0-8135-0712-X | Manufactured in the United States of America by | Quinn & Boden Company, Inc., Rahway, New Jersey | [permissions in 7 lines]'.

Colophon (128): '*The text of this book was set in Baskerville | Linotype and printed by offset on P & S Special | XL manufactured by P. H. Glatfelter Co., Spring | Grove, Pa. Composed, printed and bound by | Quinn & Boden Company, Inc., Rahway, N.J.*'

209 x 138 mm. *1-4*^{8} *5*^{4} *6-9*^{8}; 68 leaves. *i-viii 1-2* 3-59 *60* 61-117 *118* 119-121 *122* 123-125 *126-128* pp.

In addition to generous quotation from Ransom's published poetry, Williams's study contains 9 versions of "The Vanity of the Bright Boys" (80-111), also under the titles "Tom, Tom, the Piper's Son," "The Vanity of the Male," and "The Vanity of the Bright Young Men," including previously unpublished versions that represent what Williams terms "revisions in typescript made after the appearance of the 1963 *Selected Poems*" (79).

Type-page 38 lines, 162 (167) x 100 mm, 10 lines = 43 mm (e.g., p. 5); typeface Baskerville. White wove paper, no watermark, sheets bulk 12 mm.

Bound in dark purplish blue (201) calico cloth over boards. Front and back blank. Spine stamped in gold: '[running down] The Poetry of John Crowe Ransom Miller Williams [running across] [publisher's device]'. Dark orange yellow (72) wove endpapers. Top and bottom edges cut, fore-edge trimmed. Top edge stained brilliant orange yellow (67).

Dust jacket of white paper with a moderate greenish blue (173) background on front and spine. Front: '[white] *The Poetry of* | [black] John | Crowe | Ransom | [65 mm white swelled rule] | [black] *Miller Williams*'. Spine: title in white, author and publisher's device in white. Back: photograph of Ransom credited to Truman Moore, publisher's imprint. Front flap: title, author, blurb, jacket design credit to W. V. Cladek. Back: blurb continued, note on author, ISBN, publisher's imprint.

Copies: CSA (with jacket), IU, OGK, STW (with jacket), TNV (with jacket), TxU-PCL, WBB, WU.

Published at $7.50 on 2 February 1972; copyright registration A314980. Reviewed in *Mississippi Quarterly* Spring 1972: 193-196 (Jean Nosser Biglane); *Library Journal* 1 May 1972: 1719-1720 (Kenyon C. Rosenberg); *Choice* June 1972: 511; *South Atlantic Quarterly* Winter 1973: 169 (Irvin Ehrenpreis); *Georgia Review* Summer 1973: 275-282 (Thomas Daniel Young); *Prairie Schooner* Fall 1973: 281 (W. G. Regier).

B66 **1972**

Allen Tate and His Work

ALLEN TATE | AND HIS WORK | Critical Evaluations | [110 mm wavy rule] | *Edited with an introduction by* | *RADCLIFFE SQUIRES* | UNIVERSITY OF MINNESOTA PRESS ■ MINNEAPOLIS

Copyright page (vi): '© Copyright 1972 by the University of Minnesota. | All rights reserved. | Printed in the United States of America | at Napco Graphic Arts Inc., Milwaukee, Wisconsin. | Published in the United Kingdom and India by the Oxford University | Press, London and Bombay, and in Canada | by the Copp Clark Publishing Co. Limited, Toronto | *Library of Congress Catalog Card Number:* 78-167297 | *ISBN* 0-8166-0627-7 | [acknowledgments in 25 lines]'.

228 x 149 mm. *1-8*^{16} *9-11*^{8} *12-13*^{16}; 184 leaves. *i-viii 1-2* 3-54 *55-56* 57-118 *119-120* 121-148 *149-150* 151-306 *307-308* 309-343 *344-346* 347-355 *356-360* pp.

Contains Ransom's essay "In Amicitia" (11-22), first published in *Sewanee Review* (C341) and here published here for the first time in book form.

Type-page 38 lines, 172 (180) x 110 mm, 10 lines = 46 mm (e.g., p. 13); typeface Baskerville. White wove paper, no watermark, sheets bulk 22 mm.

Bound in moderate purple (223) calico cloth over boards. Front and back blank. Spine, stamped in silver: '[running across] SQUIRES | Editor | [running down] ALLEN TATE | and HIS WORK [running across] Minnesota'. Light blue wove endpapers. Edges trimmed.

Dust jacket of light yellowish brown (76) laid paper printed in black and moderate red. Title and editor on the front.

Copies: CSA, IDeKN, OGK, STW (with jacket), TxU-PCL (2 copies), WBB, WM (with jacket).

Published at $10.75 on 2 May 1972; copyright registration A342818

Reviewed in *Library Journal* 15 January 1972: 199 (Peter A. Dollard); *Choice* October 1972: 973; *Prairie Schooner* Summer 1973: 187 (W. G. Regier); *Virginia Quarterly Review* Summer 1973: cxv.

B67 **1972**

Ezra Pound:
The Critical Heritage

EZRA POUND | *THE CRITICAL HERITAGE* | *Edited by* | ERIC HOMBERGER | School of English and American Studies | University of East Anglia | [101 mm rule] | ROUTLEDGE & KEGAN PAUL: LONDON AND BOSTON

Copyright page (4): '*First published in 1972* | *By Routledge & Kegan Paul Ltd* | [addresses in 4 lines] | © *Eric Homberger 1972* | [reservation of rights in 4 lines] | *ISBN 0 7100 7260 0* | *Printed in Great Britain* | *by W & J Mackay Limited, Chatham*'.

216 x 136 mm. *A-I*^{16} *K-P*^{16} *Q*^{4} *R*^{16}; 260 leaves. *i-viii* ix-xix *xx* 1-32 *33* 34-500 pp.

Contains Ransom's "[Mr.] Pound and the Broken Tradition" (294-296), a review of *ABC of Reading* and *Eleven New Cantos* reprinted from *Saturday Review* (C205) and published here for the first time in book form.

Type-page 40 lines, 168 (179) x 102 mm, 10 lines = 42 mm (e.g., p. 295); typeface Bembo. White wove paper, no watermark, sheets bulk 29 mm.

Bound in moderate blue (182) calico cloth over boards. Front and back blank. Spine stamped in gold: '[running down] EZRA POUND | *THE CRITICAL HERITAGE* | ERIC HOMBERGER [across the foot] ROUTLEDGE & | KEGAN PAUL'. White wove endpapers. The verso of the back free endpaper and recto of the paste-down print a list of 42 titles in the Critical Heritage series. Edges trimmed. Gallup reports a white dust jacket printed in brown and green brown; Wright, in orange and light green.

Copies: IDeKN, InU-Main (2 copies), OGK, STW (with jacket). Also in Gallup, *Pound* B112; Wright, *Eberhart* B112.

Published on 7 December 1972 at £6.50 ($19.50 in the U.S.) in the Critical Heritage series under the general editorship of B. C. Southam; copyright registration AI-13332.

Reviewed in *Economist* 9 December 1972: 64-65; *Spectator* 27 January 1973: 107-108 (Douglas Dunn); *Books & Bookmen* March 1973: 58-59 (Jonathan Meades); *TLS* 16 March 1973: 292; *Choice* June 1973: 619; *Encounter* June 1973: 68 (Hugh Gordon Porteus).

B68 **1973**

E. M. Forster: The Critical Heritage

E. M. FORSTER | *THE CRITICAL HERITAGE* | *Edited by* | PHILIP GARDNER | *Associate Professor of English* | *Memorial University of Newfoundland* | [101 mm rule] | ROUTLEDGE & KEGAN PAUL: LONDON AND BOSTON

Copyright page (iv): '*First published in 1973* | *By Routledge & Kegan Paul Ltd* | [addresses in 4 lines] | *Copyright Philip Gardner 1973* | [reservation of rights in 4 lines] | *ISBN 0 7100 7641 X* | *Library of Congress Catalog Card No. 73-77562* | *Printed in Great Britain by* | *Butler and Tanner Ltd* | *Frome and London*'.

216 x 135 mm. A-I^{16} K-P^{16} Q^4 R^{16}; 260 leaves; $1 signed (- A1, + A5 as 'A*'). *i-vi* vii-xv *xvi* xvii-xx 1-39 *40* 41 *42* 43-491 *492* 493-498 *499-500* pp.

Contains Ransom's "E. M. Forster" (405-410), reprinted from the *Kenyon Review* (C272) and published here for the first time in book form.

Type-page 40 lines, 168 (179) x 101 mm, 10 lines = 42 mm (e.g., p. 408); typeface Bembo. White wove paper, no watermark, sheets bulk 32 mm.

Bound in moderate blue (182) calico cloth over boards. Front and back blank. Spine stamped in gold: '[running down] E. M. FORSTER | *THE CRITICAL HERITAGE* | PHILIP GARDNER [across the foot] ROUTLEDGE & | KEGAN PAUL'. White wove endpapers. The verso of the back free endpaper and recto of the paste-down print a list of 50 titles in the Critical Heritage series. Edges trimmed. Dust jacket not seen.

Copies: IDeKN, TNV, TxU-PCL.

Published in September 1973 at £7.50 ($25.25 in the U.S.) in the Critical Heritage series under the general editorship of B. C. Southam. Reviewed in *TLS* 26 October 1973: 1316; *Library Journal* 1 December 1973: 3560 (Keith Cushman); *Choice* April 1974: 258; *Books and Bookmen* June 1974: 8-11 (Auberon Waugh).

B69 **1977**

The Superfluous Men

The Superfluous Men | Conservative Critics of American | Culture, 1900-1945 | Edited by Robert M. Crunden | University of Texas Press, Austin & London

Copyright page (iv): '[Library of Congress cataloging data in 8 lines] | Copyright © 1977 by the University of Texas Press | All Rights Reserved | Printed in the United States of America | Set in Primer by G&S Typesetters, Inc.'

233 x 153 mm. *1-9*^{16} *10*^{12}; 156 leaves. *i-vii* viii-ix *x-xi* xii-xx *1-3* 4 *5* 6-284 (but without numbers on opening page of each essay, on page preceding an opening page, and on recto and verso of part-title leaves) *285* 286-289 *290-292* pp.

Contains Ransom's "Introduction: A Statement of Principles" (164-170) from *I'll Take My Stand* (B17); his essay "The South Defends Its Heritage" (172-182), reprinted from the June 1929 *Harper's* (C171) and published here for the first time in book form (not counting its incorporation in "Reconstructed but Unregenerate" in *I'll Take My Stand*); and excerpts (262-268) from his *God without Thunder* (A5).

Type-page 47 lines, 183 (193) x 109 mm, 10 lines = 39 mm (e.g., p. 175); typeface Primer. Ragged right margin. White wove paper, watermark 'WARREN'S | OLDE STYLE', sheets bulk 20 mm.

Bound in dark gray (266) calico cloth over boards. Front and back blank. Spine stamped in white: '[running down] The Superfluous Men | Edited by Robert N. Crunden [running across at the foot] [publisher's device] | Texas'. Yellowish white (92) wove endpapers. Edges trimmed. Dust jacket not seen.

Copies: ICU, IDeKN, TNV, TxU-UG (2 copies), WBB.

Published at $14.95 on 5 January 1977; copyright registration A854869.

Reviewed in *Publishers Weekly* 6 December 1976: 57 (for January publication); *Nation* 19 March 1977: 343-345 (John Madison Taylor); *Christian Century* 20 April 1977: 387; *Booklist* 1 May 1977: 1317-1318; *Virginia Quarterly Review* Summer 1977: 104-106; *Modern Age* Fall 1977: 424 (George A. Panichas); *Commonweal* 14 October 1977: 664-666 (Daniel Aaron); *American Literature* November 1977: 475 (William E. Wilson); *Journal of Politics* February 1978: 266 (George F. Brasington); *Virginia Quarterly Review* Spring 1978: 377-380 (Edward S. Shapiro); *Choice* July-August 1977: 663.

B70 **1982**

T. S. Eliot: The Critical Heritage

T. S. ELIOT | *THE CRITICAL HERITAGE* | VOLUME 2 | *Edited by* | MICHAEL GRANT | *Lecturer in English and American Literature* | *The University of Kent at Canterbury* | [101 mm rule] | ROUTLEDGE & KEGAN PAUL | LONDON, BOSTON, MELBOURNE AND HENLEY

Copyright page (iv): '*First published in 1982* | *by Routledge & Kegan Paul Ltd* | [addresses in 6 lines] | *Printed in Great Britain by* | *The Thetford Press Ltd, Thetford, Norfolk* | [copyright note, reservation of rights, and LC cataloging data in 18 lines]'.

215 x 133 mm. *1-12*^{16} *13*^{4} *14*^{16}; 212 leaves. *i-vi* vii-xx 369-769 *770-772* pp.

Contains Ransom's essay "T. S. Eliot as Dramatist" (396-400), reprinted from *Poetry* (C244) and published here for the first time in book form. Volume 1 reprints the essay "Waste Lands" (172-179).

Type-page 49 lines, 175 (185) x 106 mm, 10 lines = 35 mm (e.g., 398). Reproduced by photo-offset from typewritten copy (except that pp. i-xvi are set in Bembo type). White wove paper, no watermark, sheets bulk 29 mm.

Bound in moderate blue (182) paper (resembling calico cloth) over boards. Front and back blank. Spine stamped in gold: '[running down] T. S. ELIOT | *THE CRITICAL HERITAGE* VOLUME 2 | MICHAEL GRANT [across the foot] RKP'. White wove endpapers. Edges cut. Dust jacket not seen.

Copies: IDeKN, INS, OGK, TNV, TxU-PCL.

Published in July 1982, in the Critical Heritage series under the general editorship of B. C. Southam, at £15 (£25 for 2-volume set) and at $33.00 ($55 for set) in the United States.

Reviewed in *Spectator* 7 August 1982: 18 (Peter Ackroyd); *British Book News* March 1983: 190 (John Kelly); *Choice* March 1983: 989.

B71 **1988**

Robert Lowell: Interviews and Memoirs

ROBERT LOWELL | *Interviews and Memoirs* | Edited by | JEFFREY MEYERS | *Ann Arbor The University of Michigan Press*

Copyright page (iv): 'Copyright © by The University of Michigan 1988 | All rights reserved | Published in the United States of America by | The University of Michigan Press | Manufactured in the United States of America | 1991 1990 1989 1988 4 3 2 1 | [LC cataloging-in-publication data in 8 lines] | ISBN 0-472-10089-0 (alk. paper) | [3-line acknowledgement of grant from the University of Colorado]'.

227 x 148 mm. *1-12*^{16}; 192 leaves. *i-vii* viii-ix *x 1* 2-20 *21-22* 23-172 *173-174* 175-359 *360* 361-369 *370-374* pp.

Contains Ransom's "A Look Backwards and a Note of Hope" (175-177), a brief evaluation of Lowell's work, reprinted from its appearance in *Harvard Advocate* (C343) and published here for the first time in book form.

Type-page 39 lines, 172 (185) x 110 mm, 10 lines = 45 mm (e.g., p. 5); typeface Bembo. White wove paper, no watermark, sheets bulk 22 mm.

Bound in grayish purplish blue (204) calico cloth. Stamped in silver on the spine: '[running down] ROBERT LOWELL Meyers [publisher's device running across]'. Front and back blank. White wove endpapers. Edges cut. Dust jacket of white paper printed in black and pale blue (185). Photograph of Lowell on the front (credited to Thomas Victor).

Copies: ICU, IDeKN, INS, STW (with jacket), TxU-PCL, WM (with jacket), WU.

Published at $22.00 in July 1988. Reviewed in *Library Journal* July-August 1988: 82 (John Budd), *American Poetry Review* July 1988: 39-41 (Marianne Boruch), *Choice* November 1988: 493 (D. A. Barton).

Section C
Contributions to Periodicals

1904

C1

Vanderbilt Observer. In *Gentleman,* Young writes: "In the spring semester of his freshman year [spring 1904] Ransom had contributed two or three brief essays to the *Vanderbilt Observer*" (33). I have found nothing appearing over his name, but the *Observer* for 1903-1904 does includes some poems and stories signed Medicus Ransom: 26.1 (October 1903), poem "The Summer Day" (21); 26.2 (November 1903), story "Tossed upon the Deep" (27-30); 26.3 (January 1904), story "Miss Forget-Me-Not" (7-10); 26.5 (March 1904), poem "I Was Happy Once as You" (21-22). I do not know whether these are John Crowe Ransom's.

1908

C2

Vanderbilt Hustler 1 October 1908-3 June 1909. For the school year 1908-1909, Ransom was one of several associate editors of this newspaper published at the time by the Vanderbilt Athletic Association and subtitled *A Weekly Journal of College Life.* The paper featured news and comment on athletic events, club activities, special lectures, and the like. Most items were unsigned, and many are probably Ransom's. For the one item signed by Ransom see C7.

C3

Vanderbilt Observer 31 (November 1908-May 1909). Ransom served as the editor in chief of the *Vanderbilt Observer* for volume 31 (November 1908-May 1909). He regularly wrote the unsigned editorial section, which was devoted primarily to matters of campus life. He may also have written some of the many items that were signed with such pseudonyms as Horatius, U. Rothrock, and Sat. E. Post. The magazine was published by the Dialectic and Philosophic Literary Societies at Vanderbilt.

C4
Vanderbilt Observer 31.1 (November 1908). Unsigned "Editorial" (38-41).

C5
Vanderbilt Observer 31.2 (December 1908). "Editorial" (107-111).

1909

C6
Vanderbilt Observer 31.3 (January 1909). "Editorial" (175-179).

C7
Vanderbilt Hustler 11 February 1909. Editorial "A 'We Sma' Voice from S.W.P.U." (6, 4), responding to a review of the 1908 football season by J. M. Anderson, manager of the team from Southwestern Presbyterian University, Clarksville, Tennessee.

C8
Vanderbilt Observer 31.4 (March 1909). "Editorial" (258-262).

C9
Vanderbilt Observer 31.5 [misnumbered 4] (May 1909). "Editorial" (337-341).

1912

C10
Christian Advocate 73.34 (23 August 1912). "An Interesting Letter" (25), a letter headed "Freiburg, Germany, July 1912, signed "John C. Ransom, and giving an account of his travels. The letter is preceded by a note saying that "the writer is a son of Dr. and Mrs. J. J. Ransom, Nashville, Tennessee." The letter appears in *Selected Letters* (57-59) as addressed to Ransom's mother (Sara Ella Crowe Ransom). The version in the *Advocate* omits all of

the text after the words "an article on Ibsen," and it has variants in spelling and punctuation as well. In a letter to his father on 2 September 1912 Ransom expressed surprise that the editor of the *Advocate* (Thomas N. Ivey) found one of his "private letters available for publication" (*SL* 61-62). The *Christian Advocate,* published in Nashville, was the general organ of the Methodist Episcopal Church, South. Ransom's father, John James Ransom, was himself an occasional contributor.

C11

Christian Advocate 73.36 (6 September 1912). "Tramping through the Black Forest" (25), a letter headed "Frieburg in Griesgan, August 5, 1912," signed "John C. Ransom," and appearing under a note saying that the letter is from Ransom to his father. The letter appears in *Selected Letters* (59-61), where material omitted from the *Advocate,* including a final paragraph, has been restored and where the text differs in other ways (substantive and accidental).

C12

Methodist Quarterly Review 61.4 (October 1912). Essay "Oxford" (760-770), on the university and its students. This essay may be the one Ransom, in a letter to his father on 16 July 1911, mentions sending to him for delivery to the editor of the review, Gross Alexander. In this letter he also wonders whether Alexander would care for an essay on Ibsen (*SL* 32-33), and in another letter to his father, on 19 June 1912, he says that he is writing several articles for Alexander (*SL* 53). "Oxford," however, is the only contribution by Ransom that I have found. (There was an essay on Ibsen in the October 1913 issue, but it was by the Rev. Henry W. Clark.) Members of the Vanderbilt faculty, including Collins Denny, J. H. Kirkland, and Edwin Mims, were frequent contributors to this Nashville-based review. Ransom's father was an occasional contributor.

C13

Oxford Magazine 31.3 (31 October 1912). "The Speckled Band" (41), a review of a 24 October production of a play by that title. Unsigned but attributed to Ransom on the basis of Ransom's 4 November 1912 letter to his sister Ellene (cited in Young's *Gentleman,* p. 62). *Oxford Magazine* was published weekly by the University Press, Oxford, and edited at the time by John Murray,

Ransom's philosophy tutor. Much of its contents (which included articles, book reviews, music and theater reviews, poems, sports news, and the like) appeared unsigned. Thus there may be additional unsigned items contributed by Ransom. I have found no items in volumes 30 (1911-1912) and 31 (1912-1913) that bear his name or initials.

C14
Christian Advocate 73.48 (29 November 1912). "An Oxford Letter" (23-24), under a note indicating that it consists of "extracts" of a letter from Ransom to his mother. The letter was evidently written late in the week of 20-26 October 1912.

1913

C15
Christian Advocate 74.3 (17 January 1913). "T. [i.e., St.] Deiniol's Library, Hawarden" (22), a personal essay or perhaps an extract from a letter about Ransom's visit to the library founded by W. E. Gladstone.

C16
Christian Advocate 74.16 (18 April 1913). "A Home Letter from a Rhodes Scholar" (27), addressed to "Dear Annie" (a sister) and signed "John C. Ransom." The letter appears to have been written in March 1913 while Ransom was at Rosebank, Bear's Hill, near Oxford. In a letter to his father on 10 May 1913, Ransom asked: "Please don't send any more letters to the [*Christian*] *Advocate* as I haven't time to write them properly for publication, and they are much too intimate to go in as they are. I was considerably shocked to find a letter in the last *Advocate*" (*SL* 77).

1914

C17
American Oxonian 1.2 (October 1914). Untitled comment (82-83) for a symposium entitled "The Lack of Competition for the Rhodes Scholarships" (3-83).

1915

C18

Yale Review 4.4 (July 1915). Essay "The Question of Justice" (684-698), on the opposing claims of Germany and England in the war. The essay was reviewed by Frank Aydelotte in *American Oxonian* July 1915: 134-137.

1916

C19

Vanderbilt Alumnus 2.2 (November 1916). "The Alumni Secretaries in Nashville" (35-36), a report on the 5th annual meeting of the National Association of Alumni Secretaries held 26-28 October 1916 in Nashville. Through volume 22 (1936-1937), Ransom served as a member of the editorial committee of the *Alumnus*; it seems likely that, in addition to the signed items I list, he wrote unsigned items that I have not been able to identify as his.

1917

C20

Seven Arts. In a letter to Christopher Morley on 4 June [1917], Ransom said that he had received $50.00 from *Seven Arts*, evidently for a number of his poems that he or Morley had submitted (TxU). On 31 October, however, Morley wrote: "The Seven Arts has gone pop as I feared it eventually would. James Oppenheim says that your poems in his hands were returned to you . . ." (OGK). The magazine's final issue was dated October 1917. Nothing by Ransom appeared in the magazine.

C21

Independent 91 (25 August 1917). Poem "The Swimmer" (270). Signed John Crowe (see C22). While seeking a publisher for Ransom's *Poems about God*, Christopher Morley also submitted individual poems to various magazines, including this one.

C22

Independent 92 (27 October 1917). Poem "What the Old Leaf Said" (180). Signed John Crowe. In a 31 October 1917 letter enclosing this publication, Christopher Morley told Ransom that he was informing the magazine's editors that "in future pieces" they must print his "full name and military designation" (OGK).

1918

C23

Nashville Tennessean In a letter to Christopher Morley, 12 Nov 1918, Ransom referred to the *Nashville Tennessean,* as a paper for which he had he had once "written a certain number of editorials" (*SL* 103). I have not been able to identify these.

C24

Vanderbilt Alumnus 3.3 (January 1918). Letter dated 1 December 1917 from "Somewhere in France" (77), printed with a gathering of letters under the title "From the Boys Overseas." An editorial note says that the letters either "came to the editor" (Charles Cason) or "were handed us by friends and relatives." Ransom's is one of the latter, having evidently been addressed originally to Edwin Mims, chairman of the Vanderbilt English department. In a 29 April 1918 letter to his mother, Ransom complained that he "was mortified" to read his letter to Mims in the *Alumnus,* since it "contained purely private matters for one thing, and sentiments almost unpatriotic for another" (*SL* 99).

C25

Vanderbilt Alumnus 3.6 (April 1918). Letter dated 5 March 1918 (178) and sent to the *Alumnus* at the request of its editor for a gathering of such letters under the title "Letters from Overseas."

C26

Independent 95 (27 July 1918). Poem "One Who Rejected Christ" (116).

C27

Contemporary Verse 6 (December 1918). Poem "Roses" (86).

1919

C28
Independent 97 (22 February 1919). Poem "Sunset" (261).

C29
Independent 98 (12 April 1919). Poem "Noonday Grace" (66).

C30
Current Opinion 66 (May 1919). Poems "Geometry" (324-325) and "The Bachelor" (325), both reprinted from *Poems about God* and accompanied by a brief unsigned review in a section entitled "Voices of Living Poets."

C31
Independent 98 (28 June 1919). Poems "Darkness" and "Under the Locusts" (498), with a note that they are reprinted from *Poems about God.*

1920

C32
New York Evening Post 13 February 1920. Poem "Garden Sonnets: 1. Sweet Will His Sonnet Set Out" (10). For the second in this two-poem sequence, see C33. All of Ransom's contributions to this newspaper appeared in Christopher Morley's column "The Bowling Green," which was printed on the editorial page of the *Evening Post* from 9 February 1920 to 31 December 1923.

C33
New York Evening Post 16 February 1920. Poem "Garden Sonnets: 2. He Burns for Her" (8). See C32.

C34
New York Evening Post 18 February 1920. Poem "Sonnet of a Sure Heart" (8).

C35
New York Evening Post 24 February 1920. Poem "Sonnets of a Selfish Lover I" (first line: "The little cousin is dead, and what subtraction!") (8). This is the first part in a three-sonnet se-

quence. For parts II and III, see C36 and C37. Greatly revised, the sequence became the poem "Dead Boy."

C36
New York Evening Post 1 March 1920. Poem "Sonnets of a Selfish Lover II" (first line: "He was not good nor beautiful nor clever") (8). See C35.

C37
New York Evening Post 6 March 1920. Poem "Sonnets of a Selfish Lover III" (first line: "With low-hung head I step, look left nor right") (10). See C35.

C38
New York Evening Post 12 March 1920. Poem "Sonnets of a Pastoral Pair: I. They Take to the Fields" (10). This is the first part of a four-sonnet sequence. See C39-41. The sequence, especially the fourth sonnet, inspired a sort of poem-in-reply: see J. D. McMaster, "Sunset of a City Couple (Without Apology to John Crowe Ransom)," *New York Evening Post* 2 April 1920: 10.

C39
New York Evening Post 18 March 1920. Poem "Sonnets of a Pastoral Pair: II. They Praise the Sun" (8). See C38.

C40
New York Evening Post 20 March 1920. Poem "Sonnets of a Pastoral Pair: III. They Brave the Night" (10). See C38.

C41
New York Evening Post 25 March 1920. Poem "Sonnets of a Selfish Lover: IV. They Hail the Sunrise" (8). See C38.

C42
New York Evening Post 5 April 1920. Poem "On a Superior Woman" (8). This poem becomes "Triumph" in *Chills and Fever* (A2).

C43
New York Evening Post 24 April 1920. Poem "April Absence" (10).

C44
Vanderbilt Alumnus 6.3 (December 1920). Essay "Memorial Hall as a Social Center" (80-81), one of several articles in this issue on the need to build a memorial hall at Vanderbilt.

C45
Memphis Evening Scimitar. In *Gentleman*, Young writes: Ransom "went to Memphis to spend the summer [of 1920] as a reporter for the *Evening Scimitar*. There he was assigned to write copy for the editorial page, most of which appeared unsigned or over the initials of one of the senior men on the staff" (121). I have examined the *Scimitar* April-June 1920 and have found nothing that I can confidently attribute to Ransom; its editorials are not signed.

1921

C46
Vanderbilt Alumnus 7.1 (October 1921). Review of Donald Davidson's *Ships in Harbor* (18).

1922

C47
Sewanee Review 30.1 (January 1922). Poem "Winter Remembered" (1). Over the six decades during which Ransom made occasional contributions to this quarterly published by the University of the South, the editors were George Herbert Clarke (1920-1925), William S. Knickerbocker (1926-1942), Tudor Seymour Long (1942-1944), Allen Tate (1944-1946), J. E. Parker (1946-1952), Monroe K. Spears (1952-1961), and Andrew Lytle (1961-1973).

C48
Fugitive 1-4 (April 1922-December 1925). For most of its first two years this magazine was "edited" by the Fugitives as a committee. In the third issue, Ransom's editorial explained that they would "gather up the poems that rank the highest, by general consent of the group, and take them down to the publisher" (66). Beginning with the eighth issue (August-September 1923), the masthead listed Donald Davidson as editor and Allen Tate as associate editor. Tate was replaced by Jesse Wills as of the June

1924 issue. Davidson and Wills were replaced for the final volume (1925) by Ransom and Robert Penn Warren. Appearing under pseudonyms in the first two issues and being identified in the third, the first "Board of Editors" (later named simply as Fugitives) consisted of Walter Clyde Curry, Donald Davidson, James M. Frank, Sidney Mttron Hirsch, Stanley Johnson, Merrill Moore, Ransom, Alec Brock Stevenson, Allen Tate, William Yandell Elliott, and William Frierson (the last two listed as Fugitives *in absentia*). There were later additions: Laura Riding Gottschalk (as of June 1925), Alfred Starr (as of September 1925), Robert Penn Warren (as of February 1924), Jesse Wills (as of December 1922), and Ridley Wills (as of December 1922). Beginning with the December 1922 issue, poems by non-Fugitives were admitted, including some by Witter Bynner, Hart Crane, John Gould Fletcher, Robert Graves, David Morton, William Alexander Percy, and Louis Untermeyer. The *Fugitive* was published in Nashville (quarterly in 1922 and 1925, bimonthly in 1923 and 1924). Beginning with the August-September 1923 issue and until the final volume, the masthead bore the subtitle *A Journal of Poetry*. Single copies sold for $0.25; the annual subscription was $1.00 until the issue for June-July 1923, when it increased to $1.50; the subscription price reverted to $1.00 as of the issue for December 1924. Circulation probably never exceeded 500 copies. For reprintings of contemporary reviews and notices of the magazine, see Merrill Moore's *The Fugitive: Clippings and Comment* (B26). For a history of the Fugitives and their magazine, see Louise Cowan's *The Fugitive Group: A Literary History*. See also Allen Tate's "The Fugitive, 1922-1925." The magazine has been reprinted by Johnson Reprint Corporation (New York, 1966) and by Peter Smith (Gloucester, Mass., 1966), with an introduction by Donald Davidson.

C49

Fugitive 1.1 (April 1922). Foreword, unsigned (1); poems "Ego" (3-4), "Night Voices" (10-11), "To a Lady Celebrating Her Birthday" (21-23), "The Handmaidens" (26-32), all signed Roger Prim.

C50

Fugitive 1.2 (June 1922). Editorial "Caveat Emptor" (34), unsigned; poems "Epitaph" (35), "Destitution Raiseth Her Voice" (48), "The Sure Heart" (54), "Necrological" (62-63), all signed Roger Prim.

C51
Fugitive 1.3 (October 1922). Poems "Boris of Britain" (74-75), "The Vagrant" (80), "Poets Have Chanted Mortality" (86), "Fall of Leaf" (94-95); "Editorial," signed J. C. R., on the purpose of the *Fugitive,* also on Robert Graves's *On English Poetry* (66-68). Beginning with this issue, Ransom's poems in the *Fugitive* are signed John Crowe Ransom.

C52
New Republic 127 (6 October 1952). "The Art of Prose" (17-18), a review of Herbert Read's *English Prose Style.*

C53
Double Dealer 4.23 (November 1922). Poem "On the Road to Wockensutter" (233-234).

C54
Fugitive 1.4 (December 1922). Poems "Youngest Daughter" (104), "In Process of a Noble Alliance" (126).

1923

C55
Fugitive 2.5 (February-March 1923). Poems "Philomela" (8-9), "Grandgousier" (12-13), "Conrad at Twilight" (27).

C56
Bookman 57.1 (March 1923). Poem "In Process of a Noble Alliance" (36), which appears in a section edited by David Morton and entitled "The Poems of the Month."

C57
Nashville Tennessean 17 March 1923, sports section. Poem "In Process of a Noble Alliance" (11), which is reprinted in an article on its appearance in *Bookman* (C56). Its textual variants (e.g., 'with' for 'unto' in line 1 and 'than' for 'then' in line 7) are presumably misprints.

C58
Literary Review 3.29 (24 March 1923). Poem "Here Lies a Lady" (545). The *Literary Review* was published by the *New York Evening Post* as a supplement to its Saturday edition.

C59
Fugitive 2.6 (April-May 1923). Poems "April Treason" (36-37), "The Inland City" (53), "*Agitato ma non troppo*" (56).

C60
Fugitive 2.7 (June-July 1923). Poems "Spectral Lovers" (68), "Nocturne" (82), "First Travels of Max" (86-87).

C61
Literary Review 3.46 (14 July 1923). Essay "Waste Lands" (825-826), on Eliot's poem. The 23 June issue, announcing the essay as forthcoming, gave its title as "Waste Lands and Fertile Spirits" (781). A response by Allen Tate appears in the 4 August issue (886); Ransom's rejoinder is in the 11 August issue (C63).

C62
Fugitive 2.8 (August-September 1923). Poems "Blackberry Winter" (107), "Lichas to Polydor" (118).

C63
Literary Review 3.50 (11 August 1923). Letter "Mr. Ransom Replies" (902), a reply to Allen Tate's criticism (4 August 1923) of his essay on *The Waste Land* (C61).

C64
Fugitive 2.9 (October 1923). Poems "Good Ships" (131), "Judith of Bethulia" (140-141), "Spiel of the Three Mountebanks" (146-148), "Rapunzel Has Submitted Herself to Fashion" (151).

C65
Vanderbilt Alumnus 9.2 (November 1923). Poem "Nostri in Memoriam Doctissimi" (40), in memory of Herbert Cushing Tolman.

C66
The Winter Owl November 1923. See B2.

C67
Literary Review 4.10 (3 November 1923). Poem "Emily Hardcastle, Spinster" (201).

C68
Fugitive 2.10 (December 1923). Poems "Number Five" (166), "Vaunting Oak" (174-175), "Old Man Playing with Children" (183).

1924

C69
Fugitive 3.1 (February 1924). Essay "The Future of Poetry," signed J. C. R. (2-4); poems "Bells for John Whitesides' [sic] Daughter" (17), "Captain Carpenter" (18-20), "Prometheus in Straits" (21). Tate's essay "One Escape from the Dilemma," which appears in the next issue, is in part a reply to Ransom's essay.

C70
Nashville Tennessean 10 February 1924, Firing Line section. "Egotistic Canon Neatly Scalped by May Sinclair" (6), a review of *A Cure of Souls*. Like Stanley Johnson, Allen Tate, Jesse Wills, and others associated with the Fugitives, Ransom was among the contributors to "The Tennessean's Book Review and Literary Page" edited by Donald Davidson and appearing in the Sunday *Nashville Tennessean* from February 1924 through November 1930. All of Ransom's reviews in the newspaper appeared on this book page. Through the years, the page itself was generally reckoned in the pagination scheme of various sections of the paper, including the sports section, women's section, and Firing Line (a section devoted to commercial news). In April 1928 the book page was syndicated and carried also by the *Memphis Commercial Appeal* and *Knoxville Journal*. At that point its title was changed to "The Weekly Review: A Page about Books." While Ransom's longer reviews for the page were signed, some shorter ones were not. Because for the first seventeen months of publication reviewers were paid according to the column inches of their reviews, Davidson kept a record of the space each filled. John Tyree Fain's introduction to *The Spyglass: Views and Reviews, 1924-1930*, which reprints Davidson's columns, presents one such record for 27 July through 7 September 1924, and that is the basis on which I attribute unsigned reviews to Ransom. I have not found further records in Davidson's papers at Vanderbilt University.

C71
Nashville Tennessean 17 February 1924. "'Parson's Pleasure,' Morley's Latest Book of Poems, More Philosophical" (12), a review of Christopher Morley's poems.

C72
Nashville Tennessean 24 February 1924, Firing Line section. "Robert Frost's New Poetry Volume Triumph for New England Intellect" (12), a review of *New Hampshire*.

C73
Nashville Tennessean 2 March 1924, Firing Line section. "More Power Given to Arnold Bennett by 'Riceyman Steps,' New London Tale" (9), a review.

C74
Nashville Tennessean 9 March 1924, Firing Line section. "Waldo Frank's Blasts Are of Light Ordnance" (14), a review *Salvos*.

C75
Nashville Tennessean 16 March 1924, Firing Line section. "Edna Ferber Is Her True, Great Self in 'So Big'" (10), a review.

C76
Nashville Tennessean 23 March 1924, Firing Line section. "McLeish's [sic] Poems Rare Distillate to Linger Over" (7), a review of Archibald MacLeish's *The Happy Marriage*; and "Sure Formula for Success Used by Elinor Glyn" (7), a review of *Six Days*.

C77
Literary Review 4.31 (29 March 1924). Essay "The Poet Laureate" (625-626), on Robert Bridges.

C78
Nashville Tennessean 30 March 1924, Firing Line section. "William Y. Elliott Outstanding as Poet at Oxford" (11), a review of Stephen Gwynn's *Collected Poems*, of Edmund Vance Cooke's *Companionable Poems*, and of *Oxford Poetry, 1923*, edited by D. C. Thomson and F. W. Bateson.

C79
Fugitive 3.2 (April 1924). Poems "Ada Ruel" (39), "Old Mansion" (40-41).

C80
Sewanee Review 32.2 (April 1924). Poem "The Dead Boy" (129).

C81
Nashville Tennessean 6 April 1924, Firing Line section. "Kentucky Woman Wins Rank with Her First Book" (6), a review of Mary Lanier MacGruder's *Wages*; and "'Vindication,' by McKenna, Has Post-Bellum Flavor" (6), a review of Stephen McKenna's novel.

C82
Nashville Tennessean 13 April 1924, Firing Line section. "Zona Gale Revives 'Birth' to Toll Sentimental Story of American Life" (6), a review.

C83
Nashville Tennessean 20 April 1924, Firing Line section. "Poetry from Whitman to Sandburg Given Criticism by Bruce Weirick" (7), a review of *From Whitman to Sandburg in American Poetry*.

C84
Nashville Tennessean 27 April 1924, Firing Line section. "'Coast of Folly' Good Despite Its Deceiving Cover" (6), a review of Coningsby Dawson's novel.

C85
Vanderbilt Alumnus 9.7-8 (May-June 1924). "David Morton Issues Book of Poems—'Harvest'" (186), a reprinting of Ransom's review from the *Nashville Tennessean* (C91).

C86
Nashville Tennessean 4 May 1924, Firing Line section. "Vere Hutchinson Adds to Family's Fame in Sea Tale" (9), a review of *Great Waters*.

C87
Nashville Tennessean 11 May 1924, Firing Line section. "Mississipean Is Rated Best Poet of Entire South" (8), a review of William Alexander Percy's *Enzio's Kingdom.*

C88
Nashville Tennessean 18 May 1924. "Owen Johnson's 'Blue Blood' Is Shy Corpuscle," a review of the novel; "Philpotts' Diary of Boy Measures Up with Kipling," a review of Eden Philpotts's *A Human Boy's Diary*; and "Wanted: Lady Reviewer Who Loves Radishes," a review of Louise Driscoll's *Garden Grace*. In this issue of the *Tennessean*, the book page appears not to have been reckoned in the pagination scheme of any section of the paper.

C89
Nashville Tennessean 25 May 1924, Firing Line section. "Wm. Lyon Phelps Reviews Works of Great Writers" (7), a review of *Howells, James, Bryant, and Other Essays.*

C90
Fugitive 3.3 (June 1924). Poems "Blue Girls" (82), "Adventure This Side of Pluralism" (83-86).

C91
Nashville Tennessean 1 June 1924, Firing Line section. "New Volume of Sonnets Puts David Morton among Most Individual of Poets" (7), a review of *Harvest.*

C92
Nashville Tennessean 8 June 1924, unpaged. "Young Boswell Hero Worshipper on a Large Scale," a review of Harold Stark's *People You Know.* In this issue of the *Tennessean*, the book page appears not to have been reckoned in the pagination scheme of any section of the paper.

C93
Nashville Tennessean 15 June 1924, Firing Line section. "'High Road' Is Good Novel of Romantic Type" (7), a review of Janet Ramsey's novel.

C94
Nashville Tennessean 22 June 1924, Firing Line section. "Verse Brings Out a 'Softer Sense' in May Sinclair" (11), a review of *The Dark Night.*

C95
Nashville Tennessean 29 June 1924, Firing Line section. "Two Columnists Show Their Stuff as Fiction Team" (7), a review of Christopher Morley and Don Marquis's *Pandora Lifts the Lid.*

C96
Palms 2.2 (Midsummer 1924). Poem "Applied Eleatics" (53).

C97
Nashville Tennessean 6 July 1924, Firing Line section. "Edith Wharton's 'Old New York' Stories Superb" (11), a review of *Old New York City.*

C98
Nashville Tennessean 13 July 1924, Firing Line section. "'Country People' an Unusual Book and an Able One" (15), a review of Ruth Suckow's novel.

C99
Nashville Tennessean 20 July 1924, Firing Line Annex section. "P. G. Wodehouse Is Accorded Title of Golf's Homer" (5), a review of *Golf without Tears.*

C100
Nashville Tennessean 27 July 1924, Firing Line section. "Dorothy Canfield Lowers Standard in 'Home Maker'" (7), a review of the novel.

C101
Fugitive 3.4 (August 1924). Poems "Parting at Dawn" (99), "Tom, Tom, the Piper's Son" (100-101).

C102
Literary Review 4.49 (2 August 1924). Poem "Miriam Tazewell" (929).

C103
Nashville Tennessean 3 August 1924, Firing Line section. "Danish Author Writes Strange, Powerful Book" (12), a review of Otto Rung's *Shadows That Pass.*

C104
Nashville Tennessean 10 August 1924, Firing Line section. "Frances Keyes' Book on Capital Dreary Reading" (7), a review of Frances Parkinson Keyes's *Letters from a Senator's Wife;* and "'The Saint's Theater' Is Exotic, Romantic Tale" (7), an unsigned review of Horace Fish's novel.

C105
Philadelphia Evening Public Ledger 13 August 1924. Poem "Miriam Tazewell." Not seen but listed in William Stanley Braithwaite's *Anthology of Magazine Verse for 1925 and Yearbook of American Poetry* (Boston: B. J. Brimmer, 1925), 102. Also, in a note in *Chills and Fever,* Ransom acknowledges previous publication in Christopher Morley's column "The Chaffing Dish" in the *Ledger.* A search of the *Ledger* for 13 August 1924 and of an index to the newspaper for 1919-1929 turned up nothing by Ransom (letter, Sandra Owens, The Free Library of Philadelphia, 22 September 1995).

C106
Nashville Tennessean 17 August 1924, Firing Line section. "British Literary Guide Good for Travelers" (7), an unsigned review of Alice Townsend Birdwell and Isabelle Denison Rosentiel's *The Places of English Literature;* "'Darkened Windows' Is a Readable Novel" (7), an unsigned review of Cornelia Kane Rathbone's novel; and "'Golden Bed,' by Wallace Irwin, Is Fine Novel" (7), a review.

C107
Nashville Tennessean 24 August 1924, Firing Line section. "H. D. Dallies with English Meters in 'Heliodora'" (10), a review.

C108
Nashville Tennessean 31 August 1924, Firing Line section. Poem "Bells for John Whiteside's Daughter" (9) reprinted with Donald Davidson's review of *Chills and Fever.*

C109
Nashville Tennessean 7 September 1924, Firing Line section. "Critic Sings Praises of Two English Novels" (10), a review of Richard Dehan's *The Pipers of the Market Place* and Charles Fielding Marsh's *After Harvest.*

C110
Nashville Tennessean 14 September 1924, Firing Line section. "Freud Enters Wider Field in Study of Mind" (13), a review of Sigmund Freud's *Beyond the Pleasure Principle* and *Group Psychology.*

C111
Nashville Tennessean 21 September 1924, Firing Line section. "'Talk' Sets Pace for Realism in Domestic Life" (5), a review of Emanie N. Sachs's *Talk.*

C112
Nashville Tennessean 28 September 1924, Firing Line section. "Great Figures Were Sufferers in Guedalla's Eyes" (8), a review of Philip Guedalla's *Supers and Supermen.*

C113
Saturday Review of Literature 1.10 (4 October 1924). "Freud and Literature" (161-162), a review of Sigmund Freud's *Beyond the Pleasure Principle* and *Group Psychology.* It is not a reprint of Ransom's earlier review of Freud in the *Nashville Tennessean* (C110).

C114
Nashville Tennessean 5 October 1924, Firing Line section. "Girl's Battle for Freedom Ably Depicted" (10), a review of Marian Spitzer's *Who Would Be Free.*

C115
Nashville Tennessean 12 October 1924, Firing Line section. "'Little French Girl' Is Hailed with Acclaim" (5), a review of Anne Douglas Sedgwick's *The Little French Girl.*

C116
Nashville Tennessean 9 November 1924, Firing Line section. "New Phillpotts Novel Follows Antiquated Lives" (10), a review of Eden Phillpotts's *Redcliff.*

C117
Nashville Tennessean 16 November 1924, Firing Line section. "Newest Novel by Miss Sinclair Splendidly Done" (10), a review of May Sinclair's *Arnold Waterlow.*

C118
Nashville Tennessean 30 November 1924, Firing Line section. "'Elsie and the Child' Lags behind Usual Arnold Bennett Standard" (8), a review of Bennett's *Elsie and the Child, and Other Stories.*

C119
Fugitive 3.5 & 6 (December 1924). Poems "The Last Judgment (A Fresco)" (148-150), "Virga" (151-152). The contents page lists the first poem under the title "Day of Judgment: A Fresco."

C120
Nashville Tennessean 14 December 1924, Firing Line section. "'The White Monkey' Is Worthy Addition to Galsworthy Group" (10), a review of John Galsworthy's novel.

1925

C121
Vanderbilt Alumnus 1925. Ransom was a member of the publicity committee for the Vanderbilt semicentennial. Thus he may well have written or had a hand in writing the unsigned news items on the semicentennial appearing in the issues for March, May, and October 1925.

C122
Nashville Tennessean 4 January 1925, Firing Line section. "'Poets of Future' Cites Efforts of College Writers" (12), a review of Henry T. Schnittkind's *The Poets of the Future,* volume 7, and of *The Best Poems of 1924,* edited by L. A. G. Strong.

C123
New York Herald Tribune Books 4 January 1925. "Portraiture and Scandal" (5), a review of Ernest Boyd's *Portraits, Real and Imaginary* and of John Farrar's *The Literary Spotlight.*

C124
Nashville Tennessean 1 February 1925, Firing Line section. "Guedalla Fair in Pen Pictures of Statesmen" (12), a review of Philip Guedalla's *A Gallery.*

C125
Literary Digest 84.6 (7 February 1925). Poem "Here Lies a Lady" (34), reprinted from *Chills and Fever* for the magazine's "Current Poetry" section.

C126
Nashville Tennessean 8 February 1925, sports section. "Swashbuckling Mencken Still Is Battling for Minorities" (5), a review of H. L. Mencken's *Prejudices: Fourth Series.*

C127
Nashville Tennessean 15 February 1925, Firing Line section. "Oxford's Spirit Fills Verse of Rhodes Scholar" (8), a review of Robert P. Tristram Coffin's *Christchurch* and Martha Ostenso's *A Far Land.*

C128
Nashville Tennessean 22 February 1925, Woman's [sic] section. "Notable Treatise on Short Story by Atlanta Woman Wins Praise" (7), a review of Frances Newman's *The Short Story's Mutations.*

C129
Fugitive 4.1 (March 1925). Poems "Piazza Piece" (21), "Eclogue" (22-24); essay "Mixed Modes" (28-29), on poetry, signed J. C. R.

C130
Nashville Tennessean 8 March 1925, Firing Line section. "Rose Macaulay Fails to Thrill in 'Orphan Island'" (8), a review of Macaulay's novel.

C131
Nashville Tennessean 29 March 1925, Firing Line section. "Diversion Author's Chief Goal in Writing Books, Says Cabell" (3), a review of James Branch Cabell's *Straws and Prayers*.

C132
Southwest Review 10.3 (April 1925). Poem "Antique Harvesters" (13-14); also a statement on the poem is quoted in "The Authors in This Issue" (125).

C133
Literary Digest 85.2 (11 April 1925). Excerpt from the poem "Eclogue" (34), reprinted from the *Fugitive* (March 1925) for the "Current Poetry" section.

C134
Nashville Tennessean 12 April 1925, Woman's section. "'Gold by Gold' Is Lacking in Irony Needed in Theme" (8), a review of H. S. Gorman's novel.

C135
Nashville Tennessean 3 May 1925, Woman's section. "Sonnets Give Worth to New Robinson Verse" (9), a review of E. A. Robinson's *Dionysus in Doubt*.

C136
Nashville Tennessean 31 May 1925, Woman's section. "Dreams Are Laid to Secret Desire in Psychic Works" (8), a review of Robert Graves's *The Meaning of Dreams*.

C137
Fugitive 4.2 (June 1925). Poems "The Miller's Daughter" (55-56), "Jack's Letter" (57), "Semi-Centennial" (58-59); essay "Thoughts on the Poetic Discontent" (63-64), on Robert Frost, dualism, and irony, signed J. C. R.

C138
Measure No. 52 (June 1925). Poem "Proud Heart Rained Upon" (11).

C139
Nashville Tennessean 21 June 1925, Firing Line section. "Torrence's Verse Has Fine Rhythms, Fervent Spirit" (7), a review of Ridgely Torrence's *Hesperides.*

C140
Nashville Tennessean 28 June 1925, Firing Line section. "Every Man Has Spark of Genius, Author Contends" (5), a review of Mary Austin's *Everyman's Genius.*

C141
Sewanee Review 33.3 (July 1925). Essay "A Man without a Country" (301-307), on George Moore, with references to Thomas Hardy, James Joyce, and G. B. Shaw.

C142
Calendar of Modern Letters 1.6 (August 1925). Essay "Thoughts on the Poetic Discontent" (461-463). (The text differs from that in the *Fugitive* (C137) only in accidentals.) For a history and evaluation of this precursor of *Scrutiny*, see "A Review in Retrospect," Malcolm Bradbury's essay of introduction (ii-xix) to a 1966 reprinting of the magazine (New York: Barnes & Noble; London: Frank Cass & Co.).

C143
Nashville Tennessean 9 August 1925, Firing Line section. "V. Sackville-West Succeeds in New Type of Fiction" (6), a review of *Seducers in Ecuador.*

C144
Nashville Tennessean 16 August 1925, Firing Line section. "Lloyd George Disguised 'Hero' in Housman's Satire, 'Trimblerigg'" (6), a review of Laurence Housman's *Trimblerigg.*

C145
Nashville Tennessean 23 August 1925, Firing Line section. "Brigham Young's Life Story Work of Great Merit" (5), a review of M. R. Werner's *Brigham Young.*

C146
Fugitive 4.3 (September 1925). Poems "The Two Worthies" (83-84), "Husband Betrayed" (85), "Janet Waking" (86), "History of Two Simple Lovers" (87-88); review-essay "Prose: A Doctrine of Relativity" (93-94), on Robert Graves's *Poetic Unreason*.

C147
Guardian 2.3 (October 1925). Poem "Dog" (440-441).

C148
Fugitive 4.4 (December 1925). Poems "Lady Lost" (119), "Moments of Minnie" (120), "Amphibious Crocodile" (121-123); unsigned editorial "Announcement" (125), on the *Fugitive*'s suspension of "regular publication for an indefinite period."

1926

C149
Calendar of Modern Letters 2.11 (January 1926). Poems "Eclogue" (317-319), "Moments of Minnie" (319-320), "The Miller's Daughter" (320-321).

C150
Literary Digest 88 (13 February 1926). Poem "Lady Lost" (34), reprinted from the *Fugitive* (December 1925) for the "Current Poetry" section.

C151
Nashville Tennessean 11 July 1926, Review of Oswald Spengler's *The Decline of the West*.

C152
New Republic 48.616 (22 September 1926). Poem "Little Boy Blue" (122).

C153
Atlantic Monthly 138.4 (October 1926). Poem "Parting, without a Sequel" (517).

C154
Harper's Magazine 154 (December 1926). "Two Poems": "Ghosts" and "Morning" ("Jane awoke Ralph so gently on one morning") (50). "Ghosts" later becomes, revised, the second part of "Hilda."

1927

C155
Contemporary Verse 22 (February-March 1927). Poem "Morning" ("Jane awoke Ralph so gently on one morning") (21).

C156
Nashville Tennessean 6 March 1927, magazine section. "Old Strains, Sung with Crossed Fingers, Advocated for Poets" (7), a review of I. A. Richards's *Science and Poetry*.

C157
New Republic 50.647 (27 April 1927). Poem "What Ducks Require" (273).

C158
Nashville Tennessean 12 June 1927, magazine section. "Hardy's Sensibility without Parallel" (7), a review of *The Collected Poems of Thomas Hardy* (signed J. C. R.).

C159
New Republic 51.655 (22 June 1927). Letter "The Poet and the Critic" (125-126), responding to Edmund Wilson's "The Muses Out of Work" in the 11 May issue. The letter is followed by Wilson's rejoinder. Writing to Allen Tate on 25 June 1927, Ransom expressed his regret at Wilson's having "cut off the latter third" of his letter (*SL* 175).

C160
Nashville Tennessean 2 October 1927, magazine section. "Donald Davidson's New Volume Offers Poetry Singularly Sustained" (7), a review of *The Tall Men*.

C161
Nashville Tennessean 20 November 1927, magazine section. "Stein's Formula for Arts May Exist for Only One of Them" (7), a review of Leo Stein's *The A.B.C. of Aesthetics.*

C162
New Republic 53.680 (14 December 1927). Letter "The ABC of Aesthetics" (104), a response to Waldo Frank's review of Leo Stein's *The ABC of Aesthetics* in the 2 November issue. The letter is followed by Frank's rejoinder.

1928

C163
American Oxonian 15.1 (January 1928). Obituary "Death of T. T. McCarley" (56).

C164
Nashville Tennessean 5 February 1928, magazine section. "Russell Presents Philosophy from Presumably Unexpected Angle" (7), a review of Bertrand Russell's *Philosophy.*

C165
Nashville Tennessean 4 March 1928, magazine section. "Ethnology of American Indian Admirably Presented for Laymen" (7), a review of Paul Radin's *The Story of the American Indian.*

C166
Sewanee Review 36.2 (April 1928). Essay "The South—Old or New?" (139-147), on industrialization in the South. Portions of the essay were later incorporated in "The South Defends Its Heritage" (C171) and "Reconstructed but Unregenerate" (B17).

C167
Forum 79.5 (May 1928): xxiv. Review of William J. Robertson's *The Changing South.* Not seen.

C168
Nashville Tennessean 15 July 1928, magazine section. "Hibbard's Anthology Suffers in Lack of Conviction and Bias" (7), a review of *The Lyric South,* edited by Addison Hibbard.

1929

C169
New Republic 58.742 (20 February 1929). Poem "Autumn Love (English Sonnet of Italian Parts)" (10).

C170
Nashville Tennessean 17 March 1929, Woman's section. "Jacques Chevalier Seeks Positives in Bergsonianism" (7), a review of Chevalier's *Henri Bergson.*

C171
Harper's Magazine 159 (June 1929). Essay "The South Defends Its Heritage" (108-118). This essay was later revised to become "Reconstructed but Unregenerate" (B17).

C172
Saturday Review of Literature 5.47 (15 June 1929). Poem "Old Man Pondered (English Sonnet of Italian Parts)" (1107).

C173
Sewanee Review 37.3 (July 1929). Review-essay "Flux and Blur in Contemporary Art" (353-366), on Wyndham Lewis's *Time and Western Man.*

C174
New Republic 59.767 (14 August 1929). Poem "The Feasting of Maionides and Stephen Daedalus," accompanied by Ransom's note on the poem (342).

C175
Saturday Review of Literature 6.8 (14 September 1929). Essay "Classical and Romantic" (125-27).

1930

C176
Saturday Review of Literature 6.36 (29 March 1930). "Mr. Babbitt's Dualism" (868), a review of Hugh I'Anson Fausset's *The Proving of Psyche.*

C177
Nashville Tennessean 4 May 1930, Automotive Department. "Deceptive Values of Science as a Philosophy" (9), a review of *The New Economic Order: A Symposium by Twenty-Four Economists,* Michael Pupin's *The Romance of the Machine,* Sir James Jeans's *The Universe around Us,* and Robert A. Millikan's *Science and the New Civilization.*

C178
Nashville Tennessean 20 July 1930, first section. "The Problem of Twins Studied from New Angle" (7), a review of Nathaniel D. Mttron Hirsch's *Twins.*

C179
Nashville Tennessean 28 September 1930, Automotive department. "Christianity" (2), a review of Llewelyn Powys's *An Hour of Christianity.*

C180
Nashville Tennessean ca. October 1930. Open letter by Ransom, Allen Tate, and Donald Davidson responding to criticism by Stringfellow Barr of *I'll Take My Stand.* Not seen but cited in Young's *Gentleman* (218).

C181
Nashville Tennessean 19 October 1930. "John Wesley as Seen by a Southern Biographer" (n.p.), a review of John D. Wade's *John Wesley.*

C182
New Republic 64.829 (22 October 1930). "Santayana's Palm Tree" (262-263), a review of George Santayana's *The Realm of Matter.*

C183
Chattanooga News 22 November 1930. The news article "Whither Dixie?—Mr. Barr and Mr. Ransom in the Great Debate at Richmond" (25) contains substantial quotations from Ransom's debate with Stringfellow Barr, a debate presided over by Sherwood Anderson.

1931

C184

Vanderbilt Alumnus 16.5 (March 1931). Essay "The Rhodes Scholarship" (129, 134), on the scholarship and the men associated with Vanderbilt who have received it.

C185

Proceedings of the Institute of Citizenship, Emory University, Atlanta Georgia, Fourth Annual Session, February 10-13, 1931. Bulletin of Emory University 17.7 (July 1931). Speech "Shall the South Follow the East and Go Industrial?" (47-55), delivered 11 February 1931 in a "debate" with W. D. Anderson, whose speech also appears.

1932

C186

New Republic 70.898 (17 February 1932). Essay "The State and the Land" (8-10), on Agrarianism. See note at C187.

C187

Harper's Magazine 165 (July 1932). Essay "Land! An Answer to the Unemployment Problem" (216-224). In the September 1932 issue, the editor's column "Personal and Otherwise" notes receipt of many letters "which have sharply challenged Professor Ransom's contentions" and then quotes a lengthy letter of response by Rose Wilder Lane. The column appears on pages 4 and 5 of an unpaginated section following page 512. Ransom's essay and an earlier one in *New Republic* (C186) were part of a book manuscript (entitled *Land!*) for which he was unsuccessful in finding a publisher and which he evidently consigned to the incinerator (see Young's *Gentleman* 238-241).

1933

C188

Sewanee Review 41.2 (April-June 1933). Essay "Shall We Complete the Trade?" (182-190), on war debts. A brief unsigned editorial on Ransom's essay appears in "Topics of the Times," *New York Times* 9 April 1933: sec. 4, p. 4.

C189
Vanderbilt Alumnus 18.6 (April 1933). Essay "Shall We Complete the Trade?: A Proposal for the Settlement of Foreign Debts of the United States" (173-175), reprinted from *Sewanee Review* (C188).

C190
American Review 1.2 (May 1933). Essay "A Poem Nearly Anonymous" (179-203), on Milton's "Lycidas." See also C192. In the first issue of this monthly (April 1933), its editor, Seward Collins, stated its purpose: "The *American Review* is founded to give greater currency to the ideas of a number of groups and individuals who are radically critical of conditions prevalent in the modern world, but launch their criticism from a traditionalist basis. . ." (122). The magazine was to be an instrument of alliance between New Humanists, Agrarians, and Distributists. Among the contributors to the early issues were Hilaire Belloc, Dorothea Brande, Donald Davidson, G. K. Chesterton, T. S. Eliot, Norman Foerster, Allen Tate, and Robert Penn Warren. See Albert E. Stone, Jr., "Seward Collins and the American Review," and Paul K. Conkin, *The Southern Agrarians* (106-113).

C191
Review of Reviews 88.2 (August 1933). "Trading Culture for War Debts" (53), an excerpt reprinted from the essay "Shall We Complete the Trade?" (C188). Signed John Crowne [sic] Ransom.

C192
American Review 1.4 (September 1933). Essay "A Poem Nearly Anonymous: The Poet and His Formal Tradition," on Milton's "Lycidas" (444-467). Editorial note: "Part I appeared in the May issue" (144). See C190.

C193
American Review 1.5 (October 1933). Review-essay "Happy Farmers" (513-535), on Louis M. Hacker's *The Farmer Is Doomed*.

C194
American Review 2.2 (December 1933). Essay "A Capital for the New Deal" (129-142).

1934

C195

American Review 2.3 (January 1934). Essay "The Aesthetic of Regionalism" (290-310).

C196

American Review 2.5 (March 1934). Essay "Hearts and Heads" (554-571), responding to Aubrey Starke's "The Agrarians Deny a Leader," which appears in the same issue (534-553) and which is a response to Allen Tate's and Robert Penn Warren's reviews of Starke's biography of Sidney Lanier.

C197

Saturday Review of Literature 10.36 (24 March 1934). "T. S. Eliot on Criticism" (574), a review of Eliot's *The Use of Poetry*.

C198

American Review 3.2 (May 1934). Essay "Poetry: A Note in Ontology" (172-200), on types of poetry. Poem "Prelude to an Evening" (262-263). Both of these appear in "Poetry Supplement," edited by Allen Tate (171-265).

C199

New Mexico Quarterly 4.2 (May 1934). Essay "Regionalism in the South" (108-113), missigned John Crowe Ransome.

C200

New Verse No. 10 (August 1934). Poem "Prelude to an Evening" (9-10).

C201

Saturday Review of Literature 11.11 (29 September 1934). Poem "Autumn Grief of Margaret" (137).

C202

Saturday Review of Literature 11.12 (6 October 1939). "520 Public Appearances without Predictability" (182), a letter in a group of letters under the collective title "Twenty-Six Estimates of Our First Ten Years."

C203
American Review 4.2 (December 1934). "Sociology and the Black Belt" (147-154), a review of Charles S. Johnson's *Shadow of the Plantation.*

C204
New Republic 81.1047 (26 December 1934). Poem "Painted Head" (185). The poem appears in "Seven Southern Poets," edited by Robert Penn Warren.

1935

C205
Saturday Review of Literature 11.27 (19 January 1935). "Mr. Pound and the Broken Tradition" (434-435), a review of Ezra Pound's *ABC of Reading* and *Eleven New Cantos.*

C206
Yale Review 24.3 (March 1935). Essay "Poets without Laurels" (503-518), on modern poetry.

C207
Virginia Quarterly Review 11.2 (April 1935). Essay "Modern with the Southern Accent" (184-200), on Southern writers—James Branch Cabell, Erskine Caldwell, William Faulkner, DuBose Heyward, Ellen Glasgow, Julia Peterkin, Stark Young, and others.

C208
American Review 5.3 (Summer 1935). Review-essay "The Cathartic Principle" (287-300), on Arthur Quiller-Couch's *The Poet as Citizen.*

C209
Saturday Review of Literature 12.13 (27 July 1935). "Poetic Strategy" (6), a review of William Rose Benét's *Golden Fleece.*

C210
Saturday Review of Literature 12.18 (31 August 1935). "Thomism and Esthetic Experience" (17), a review of F. W. Bateson's *English Poetry and the English Language* and Thomas Gilby's *Poetic Experience.*

C211
Southern Review 1.2 (Autumn 1935). Essay "The Tense of Poetry" (221-238). Initially, Charles W. Pipkin, was editor and Cleanth Brooks and Robert Penn Warren were managing editors of this quarterly published by Louisiana State University. For its history see Thomas W. Cutrer's *Parnassus on the Mississippi,* and, especially for the review's relation to Ransom's *Kenyon Review,* see G. A. M. Janssens's *The American Literary Review* (192-247); also see Lewis P. Simpson's "The *Southern Review* and a Post-Southern American Letters."

C212
American Review 5.5 (October 1935). Essay "The Mimetic Principle" (536-551).

C213
Virginia Quarterly Review 11.4 (October 1935). Essay "The Psychologist Looks at Poetry" (575-592), on I. A. Richards.

1936

C214
Vanderbilt Alumnus 22 (1936-1937). For this volume of the *Alumnus* Ransom served as chairman of the editorial board. It seems likely, then, that during this year he contributed at least some of the many unsigned items appearing in the magazine, especially in view of a letter he wrote Edwin Mims on 8 June 1937. In the letter Ransom says that the offer for him to join the faculty at Kenyon includes the proposal that he continue his own writing but "not write for the alumni publication" (*SL* 223), the implication being that one of his duties at Vanderbilt was to write for such a publication—and to write more than the two signed items that appeared in this volume of the *Alumnus* (C224, C227).

C215

Southern Review 1.3 (Winter 1936). "Autumn of Poetry" (609-623), a review of Forrest Anderson's *Sea Pieces*, T. S. Eliot's *Murder in the Cathedral*, Archibald Fleming's *The Island Called Pharos*, D. W. Hicky's *Call Back the Spring*, Edgar Lee Masters's *Invisible Landscapes*, Ruth Pitter's *A Mad Lady's Garland*, E. A. Robinson's *King Jasper*, Muriel Rukeyser's *Theory of Flight*, Ann Winslow's *Trial Balances*. The portion on Eliot later becomes the essay "A Cathedralist Looks at Murder" (A9).

C216

American Review 6.3 (January 1936). Essay "Characters and Character: A Note on Fiction" (271-288), on Edith Wharton and, to a lesser extent, Joseph Conrad, Henry James, George Meredith, George Moore, Booth Tarkington, and Leo Tolstoy.

C217

Southern Review 1.4 (Spring 1936). Essay "The Making of a Modern: The Poetry of George Marion O'Donnell" (864-874).

C218

Virginia Quarterly Review 12.2 (April 1936). Essay "What Does the South Want?" (180-194).

C219

Scribner's Magazine 99.5 (May 1936). Essay "The South Is a Bulwark" (299-303), responding to V. F. Calverton's essay "The Bankruptcy of Southern Culture" in the same issue (294-298). In the following issue (June 1936), the editors note that "Calverton's essay has drawn fire from many quarters," and they print a telegram from Donald Davidson and Chard Powers Smith (p. 10 of advertising section).

C220

American Review 7.3 (Summer 1936). Essay "The Content of the Novel: Notes toward a Critique of Fiction" (301-318).

C221

Yale Review 26.1 (September 1936). "Gestures of Dissent" (181-183), a review of E. M. Forster's *Abinger Harvest*.

C222
Nashville Banner Magazine 20 September 1936. "Allen Tate's New Poetry" (6), a review of *The Mediterranean and Other Poems.*

C223
Southern Review 2 (Autumn 1936). Review-essay "Fiction Harvest" (399-418), on novels by Anthony Bertram, Phyllis Bentley, Ethel Boileau, Arna Bontemps, Alec Brown, James Saxon Childers, Walter Edmonds, Mildred Burcham Hart, Winifred Holtby, Aldous Huxley, Halldor Laxness, Andrew Lytle, André Malraux, Margaret Mitchell, Charles Morgan, L. H. Myers, Vincent Sheean, Olaf Stapleton, S. M. Steward, Sylvia Thompson, Alexei Tolstoi, Rebecca West, and Sophus Keith Winther.

C224
Vanderbilt Alumnus 22.2 (November 1936). Excerpts from Ransom's *Nashville Banner* review of Tate's *The Mediterranean and Other Poems* (9). See C222.

C225
Yale Review 26.1 (December 1936). Essay "Sentimental Exercise" (353-368), on sentiment and the arts.

1937

C226
Scholastic (High School Teacher Edition) 30 (6 February 1937). Poems "Bells for John Whiteside's Daughter" and "Piazza Piece" (12) in Dorothy Emerson's "Poetry Corner."

C227
Vanderbilt Alumnus 22.5 (March 1937). Review of David Morton's *Spell against Time* (9); and editorial "Why Students Fail" (24), signed J. C. R.

C228
Southern Review 2.4 (Spring 1937). Review-essay "The Poet as Woman" (783-806), on Elizabeth Atkins's *Edna St. Vincent Millay and Her Times.*

C229
Virginia Quarterly Review 13.3 (Summer 1937). Essay "Art and Mr. Santayana" (420-436).

C230
Virginia Quarterly Review 13.4 (Autumn 1937). Essay "Criticism, Inc." (586-602).

C231
New York Herald Tribune Books 21 November 1937. "A Fine Poet Experiments" (20), a review of Mark Van Doren's *The Last Look.*

C232
Saturday Review of Literature 17.8 (18 December 1937). "The Unequal Sections" (6-7), a review of Walter Prescott Webb's *Divided We Stand.*

1938

C233
Southern Review 3.3 (Winter 1938). Essay "Shakespeare at Sonnets" (531-553).

C234
Southern Review 4.2 (Autumn 1938). Essay "Mr. Empson's Muddles" (322-339).

C235
Hika 5.1 (October 1938). Untitled letter to the editor (1) by Ransom, Philip Blair Rice, and Norman Johnson, on the founding of the *Kenyon Review. Hika* is the student-edited magazine of Kenyon College.

C236
Yale Review 28.2 (December 1938). "The Teaching of Thinking" (410-412), a review of I. A. Richards's *Interpretation in Teaching.*

1939

C237

Kenyon Review 1-21 (Winter 1939-Autumn 1959). This quarterly published by Kenyon College, in Gambier, Ohio, was founded by Ransom and edited by him through volume 21 (1959). Philip Blair Rice was the managing editor (and later, as of 1945 and until his death on 25 January 1956, the associate editor). The advisory editors were R. P. Blackmur, Paul Rosenfeld, Roberta Teale Swartz, Allen Tate, Philip Timberlake, Mark Van Doren, and Eliseo Vivas. They were replaced, as of the autumn 1942 issue, by Cleanth Brooks and Robert Penn Warren after the demise of the *Southern Review* in April 1942. These two were joined by Lionel Trilling as of the next issue, by Eric Bentley as of summer 1945, and by Peter Taylor in 1953 (and Roger Sessions served briefly in 1945). The initial subscription rate was $2.00 a year and the newsstand price for a single issue was 50¢. The circulation as 31 July 1939 was about 600 copies, a figure that was almost doubled by September 1941. By 1946 the circulation had grown to about 2,000 and after that remained more or less steady between 2,000 and 3,000 during Ransom's editorship. For a history and evaluation of the review, see Marian Janssen's The Kenyon Review, *1939-1970*. See also Gordon Hutner's "Reviewing America." The review has been reprinted by AMS Reprint Co., New York, which also published in 1964 Elizabeth Browne's index for the years 1939-1963.

C238

Kenyon Review 1.1 (Winter 1939). Review-essays "Was Shakespeare a Philosopher" (75-80), on Walter Clyde Curry's *Shakespeare's Philosophical Patterns*; and "The Teaching of Poetry" (81-83), on Cleanth Brooks and Robert Penn Warren's *Understanding Poetry*. Both are signed J. C. R. and appear in a section entitled "Editorial Notes."

C239

Hika 5.5 (March 1939). Essay "Joyce Kilmer's 'Trees': A Criticism" (9-10, 21-24). Within the essay, Ransom rewrites Kilmer's poem—the poem "Kilmer intended"—using the title "The Two Trees."

C240

Kenyon College Bulletin Spring 1939: 4. Statement by Ransom on the *Kenyon Review*—its purposes at founding. Not seen; cited in Young, *Gentleman* 336.

C241

Kenyon Review 1.2 (Spring 1939). Review-essay "The Arts and the Philosophers" (194-199), on the *International Encyclopedia of Unified Science,* signed J. C. R. and appearing in "Editorial Notes"; "One Thousand Sonnets," a review of Merrill Moore's *One Thousand Autobiographical Sonnets* (229-231).

C242

Kenyon Review 1.3 (Summer 1939). Essay "Yeats and His Symbols" (309-322).

C243

Mesures 5.3 (15 July 1939). Poems "Captain Carpenter" (321-325) translated by A.-M. Petitjean, and "Painting: A Head" (326-328) translated by Marc Le Templier; in English and French on the same pages. The form of the title of the second poem (a variation on "Painted Head") implies that the source of its text was Louis Untermeyer's *Modern American Poetry* (B19).

C244

Poetry 54.5 (August 1939). Review-essay "T. S. Eliot as Dramatist" (264-271), on *The Family Reunion.*

C245

Kenyon Review 1.4 (Autumn 1939). Poem "Address to the Scholars of New England" (406-408); essay "The Aesthetic of *Finnegans Wake*" (424-428) signed J. C. R. and appearing in "Editorial Notes."

1940

C246

Kenyon Review 2.1 (Winter 1940). Essay "The Pragmatics of Art" (76-87); also "Editorial Notes": "The Cover" (92), on the review's cover designed by Norris Rahming; "Mr. Blackmur's Essay" (92-93), on R. P. Blackmur's essay on Henry Adams and

Henry James (in the same issue); and "Andre Malraux' Novels" (93)—all signed J. C. R. In the spring 1940 issue there is a letter from Haakon M. Chevalier responding to Ransom's comments on Malraux.

C247

Free America 4 (January 1940). "Book Review" (19-20), of Bernard Smith's *Forces in American Criticism*. For a history of this Distributist-Agrarian magazine, see William E. Leverette, Jr., and David E. Shi's "Herbert Agar and *Free America*." See also B22.

C248

Kenyon Review 2.2 (Spring 1940). "Apologia for Modernism" (247-251), a review of Cleanth Brooks's *Modern Poetry and the Tradition*.

C249

Hika 6 (May 1940). Essay "The Thing about Poetry" (9-11), an essay later incorporated in "Wanted: An Ontological Critic."

C250

Kenyon Review 2.3 (Summer 1940). "Editorial Notes": "Old Age of a Poet" (345-347), on Yeats; "Mr. Tate and the Professors" (348-350)—both signed J. C. R.

C251

Southern Review 6.1 (Summer 1940). Essay "Honey and Gall" (2-19), on Thomas Hardy and A. E. Housman, for a special issue on Hardy.

C252

Kenyon Review 2.4 (Autumn 1940). "Concerning the Symposium" (476-477), an editorial note on the symposium entitled "Literature and the Professors" and appearing jointly in the autumn issues of *Kenyon Review* and *Southern Review*. Signed "J. C. R."

C253

Southern Review 6 (Autumn 1940). Essay "Strategy for English Studies" (226-235), on scholarship and criticism, for "Literature and the Professors: A Symposium," the other contributors being

Joe Horrell, Harry Levin, Allen Tate, and Wright Thomas. The other "half" of the symposium appears in the autumn 1940 issue of *Kenyon Review* (C252).

1941

C254
Kenyon Review 3.1 (Winter 1941). Essay "Ubiquitous Moralists" (95-100), on R. P. Blackmur, signed J. C. R. and appearing in "Editorial Notes."

C255
Southern Review 6.3 (Winter 1941). Essay "Yvor Winters: The Logical Critic" (558-583). Editorial note: "This essay is in abridgment of a much longer chapter on Yvor Winters in *The New Criticism*, to be published shortly by New Directions" (558).

C256
Accent 1.3 (Spring 1941). Essay "Eliot and the Metaphysicals" (148-156). Editorial note: "This essay is part of Mr. Ransom's book, *The New Criticism*, to be published soon by New Directions" (148).

C257
Kenyon Review 3.2 (Spring 1941). Essay "Muses and Amazons" (240-242), on the treatment of the arts in *Decision*, *New Republic*, and *Kenyon Review*, signed J. C. R. and appearing in "Editorial Notes."

C258
Furioso 1 (Summer 1941). "Lyrics Important, Sometimes Rude" (68-70), a review of Richard Eberhart's *Song and Idea*.

C259
Kenyon Review 3.3 (Summer 1941). Essay "Moholy-Nagy's New Arts" (372-374), signed J. C. R. and appearing in "Editorial Notes"; "Constellation of Five Young Poets" (377-380), a review of *Five Young American Poets* (Mary Barnard, John Berryman, Randall Jarrell, W. R. Moses, and George Marion O'Donnell).

C260
Kenyon Review 3.4 (Autumn 1941). "Editorial Notes": "The Younger Poets" (491-494), on John Ciardi, Jean Garrigue, Ruth Herschberger, Elizabeth Lee, Howard Moss, Howard Nemerov, John Nerber, John Pauker, and Reed Whittemore; "The Aesthetics of Music" (494-497)—both signed J. C. R. Also "Indefatigable Tommy" (519-520), a review of Denis Mackail's *Barrie*.

C261
Hika 9.3 (December 1941). Essay "All Verse Is Not Poetry" (22-25), on Latin poems by Frederick LaMotte Santee and on the distinction between scientific and nonscientific discourse.

1942

C262
Southern Review 7.3 (Winter 1941 [so dated but actually 1942]). Essay "The Irish, the Gaelic, the Byzantine" (517-546), on W. B. Yeats.

C263
Partisan Review 9.1 (January-February 1942). Statement "On the Brooks-MacLeish Thesis" (40-41), on Van Wyck Brooks and Archibald MacLeish's thesis that there are no great modern writers.

C264
Kenyon Review 4.2 (Spring 1942). "War and Publication" (218-220), on the announcement that the *Southern Review* will cease publication and on the need for funds to continue the *Kenyon Review*, signed J. C. R. and appearing in "Editorial Notes"; review-essay "An Address to Kenneth Burke" (219-237), on Burke's *The Philosophy of Literary Form*.

C265
Michigan Alumnus Quarterly Review 48 (Summer 1942). Essay "Poetry as Primitive Language" (278-284).

C266
American Oxonian 29.3 (July 1942). "War Letter" (151), a letter dated 5 June 1942 and signed by Ransom, Philip Blair Rice, and Robert A. Weaver, Jr., on the discontinuation of the *Southern Review* and on a promotion campaign to raise funds for the continued publication of *Kenyon Review*. The letter appears, under the title "The Kenyon Review," with an editorial headnote mentioning the Rhodes scholars who have been associated with the reviews. See also B31.

C267
Kenyon Review 4.4 (Autumn 1942). "Editorial Notes": "We Resume" (405-406) on continuation of *Kenyon Review* after omission of the summer 1942 issue, signed The Editors; "Mr. Russell and Mr. Schorer" (406-407), signed J. C. R. Also "Bright Disorder" (430-432), a review of Harry Levin's *James Joyce: A Critical Introduction*.

C268
American Scholar 12.1 (Winter 1942-1943). Donald A. Stauffer's "Critical Principles and a Sonnet" (52-56) reports, in dialogue form, on a group reading of Shakespeare's Sonnet 146 by Dan Aaron, Ben Brower, Elizabeth Drew, and Ransom.

1943

C269
Kenyon Review 5.2 (Spring 1943). Essay "The Inorganic Muses" (278-300), on Eliot's poetry, published as "Editorial Comment." See C271 for Ransom's reply to a response to this essay.

C270
Modern Language Notes 58.4 (April 1943). Review of Frederick. A. Pottle's *The Idiom of Poetry* (321).

C271
Kenyon Review 5.3 (Summer 1943). Essay "Positive and Near-Positive Aesthetics" (443-447), replying to Ruth Herschberger's "The Structure of Metaphor," which appears in the same issue (433-443) and which was itself a response to Ransom's "The Inorganic Muses" in the spring 1943 issue (C269).

C272
Kenyon Review 5.4 (Autumn 1943). Review-essay "E. M. Forster" (618-623), on American editions of Forster and on a study of Forster by Lionel Trilling, signed J. C. R. and appearing in "Editorial Notes."

1944

C273
Kenyon Review 6.1 (Winter 1944). Essay "Art Needs a Little Separating" (114-122), in part a commentary on Van Meeter Ames's essay "Art and Science" in the same issue (101-113) and appearing with Ransom's essay in a section entitled "Discussion."

C274
Kenyon Review 6.2 (Spring 1944). "Editorial Notes: "Announcement to Contributors" (275), an unsigned note on the review's receipt of "a considerable three-year benefaction" and on increased payment to contributors; essay "Artists, Soldiers, Positivists" (276-281), quoting and responding to a letter from an unnamed soldier. The benefactor, not named in the announcement, was the Rockefeller Foundation. Ransom's essay and the letter it quotes seem to have prompted Wallace Stevens's poem "Esthétique du Mal," which appeared in the autumn 1944 issue (see Marian Janssen 134-135).

C275
Saturday Review of Literature 27.21 (20 May 1944). "The Inklings of 'Original Sin'" (10-11), a review of Robert Penn Warren's *Selected Poems.*

C276
Kenyon Review 6.3 (Summer 1944). "Essays of Horace Gregory" (469-473), a review of Gregory's *The Shield of Achilles.*

C277
Sewanee Review 52.4 (October-December 1944). Essay "The Bases of Criticism" (556-571), responding to Hoyt Trowbridge's "Aristotle and the 'New Criticism'" in the same issue (537-555).

1945

C278

Kenyon Review 7.1 (Winter 1945). Essay "The Severity of Mr. Savage" (114-117), signed J. C. R. and appearing in "Editorial Notes" as a response to D. S. Savage's essay "The Aestheticism of W. B. Yeats," which appears in the same issue (118-134).

C279

Kenyon Review 7.2 (Spring 1945). Essay "Art Worries the Naturalists, Who in Turn Worry the Arts with Organism, Fusion, Funding" (282-292).

C280

New York Times Book Review 10 June 1945. Poem "Blue Girls" (2).

C281

Kenyon Review 7.3 (Summer 1945). "Beating the Naturalists with the Stick of Drama" (515-520), a review of S. C. Bethell's *Shakespeare and the Popular Dramatic Traditions;* also "Brief Comment" reviews of Alex Comfort's *The Power House* (522-523), José Ortega y Gasset's *Mission of the University* (524-525), John Steinbeck's *Cannery Row* (526-527). All are signed J. C. R.

C282

Kenyon Review 7.4 (Autumn 1945). Essay "Speculation III: Art and the Human Economy" (683-688) on W. P. Southard's "Speculation I: The Religious Poetry of Robert Penn Warren" (653-676) and on T. W. Adorno's "Theses upon Art and Religion Today" (677-682) in the same issue. For Southard's response, see his "Escape to Reality" in the winter 1946 issue (136-139).

1946

C283

Kenyon Review 8.1 (Winter 1946). "Short Notice" reviews of Kenneth Patchen's *Memoirs of a Shy Pornographer* (171) and Fred B. Millett's *The Rebirth of Liberal Education* (176-177), signed J. C. R.

C284
Sewanee Review 54.1 (January-March 1946). "Descartes's Angels" (153-156), a review of Jacques Maritain's *The Dream of Descartes.*

C285
New Republic 114.7 (18 February 1946). "Mr. Burke's Dialectic" (257-258), a review of Kenneth Burke's *A Grammar of Motives.*

C286
Kenyon Review 8.2 (Spring 1946). "Brief Notices" reviews of Jerome Hamilton Buckley's *William Ernest Henley* (338-339), Tennessee Williams's *27 Wagons Full of Cotton and Other One Act Plays* (344-345).

C287
Kenyon Review 8.3 (Summer 1946). Review of Eudora Welty's *Delta Wedding* (503-507).

C288
American Scholar 15.4 (Autumn 1946). Essay "These Little Magazines" (550-551), as a contribution to "American Scholar Forum: The Misery and Necessity of the Quarterly" (550-554). The other contributors are Paul Bixler and Delmore Schwartz.

C289
Nation 162.23 (7 December 1946). "American Aesthete" (650, 652), a review of Henry James's *The American Scene,* ed. W. H. Auden.

1947

C290
New York Times Book Review 19 January 1947. "On a New England Lyre" (7, 28), a review of Yvor Winters's *Edwin Arlington Robinson.* For information on the matter of permission fees raised by Ransom in the review, see the column "People Who Read and Write" in the 16 February 1947 issue (p. 8).

C291
Nation 164.13 (29 March 1947). "Political Anthology" (368), a review of *Discovery of Europe*, ed. Philip Rahv.

C292
Sewanee Review 55.2 (April-June 1947). Essay "On Shakespeare's Language" (181-198). Editorial note: "The substance of this paper was delivered as an address at the Conference on the Heritage of the English-Speaking Peoples and Their Responsibility at Kenyon College, October 5, 1946" (181). For Ransom's response to criticism of his essay, see C294. For publication of the conference proceedings, see B33.

C293
Kenyon Review 9.3 (Summer 1947). Essay "Poetry: I. The Formal Analysis" (436-456).

C294
Sewanee Review 55.3 (July-September 1947). Answer to a letter in the same issue by Richmond C. Beatty (536-537), on a passage from Shakespeare's *Tempest*. See C292.

C295
Kenyon Review 9.4 (Autumn 1947). Essay "Poetry: II, The Final Cause" (640-658). Although a parenthetical concluding note reads, "To be continued in the Winter issue," it was not thus continued, although portions were revised for *Beating the Bushes* (A21), where they appear as "The Iconography of the Master."

1948

C296
Quarterly Review of Literature 4.2 (1948), Marianne Moore issue. Essay "On Being Modern with Distinction" (136-142), on Moore.

C297
Quarterly Review of Literature 4.3 (1948). Blurb (inside front cover) on Pound's *Cantos* for New Directions advertisement of *The Cantos* and *The Pisan Cantos*.

C298
Kenyon Review 10.3 (Summer 1948). Essay "The Literary Criticism of Aristotle (Reconsiderations, No. 10)" (382-402). A note reads: "This paper was read at the symposium on 'The Great Critics' at Johns Hopkins University on April 13" (382).

C299
Partisan Review 15.8 (August 1948). Answers to questions (879-883), for a symposium entitled "The State of American Writing, 1948: Seven Questions" (855-893).

C300
Kenyon Review 10.4 (Autumn 1948). "The New Criticism" (682-688) a review of R. P. Blackmur's "A Burden for Critics" and Kenneth Burke's "The Imagery of Killing" in the *Hudson Review* (Summer 1948) and of Stanley Edgar Hyman's *The Armed Vision*.

1950

C301
Kenyon Review 12.1 (Winter 1950). Unsigned editorial announcement of critical essays to appear in *Kenyon Review* during 1950 (188).

C302
Kenyon Review 12.2 (Spring 1950). Review-essay "The Understanding of Fiction" (189-218), on Philip Rahv's *Image and Idea*. For Rahv's response, see his "Fiction and the Criticism of Fiction" in spring 1956 issue (276-299).

C303
Folio 15 (May 1950). 2-22. Brief sketch of Robert Penn Warren's career (2-3), as a contribution to "*All the King's Men*: A Symposium."

C304
Kenyon Review 12.3 (Summer 1950). Essay "William Wordsworth: Notes toward an Understanding of Poetry" (498-519).

C305
Partisan Review 17.6 (July-August 1950). Quotation (529) from "The Understanding of Fiction" (C302) in an advertisement for Philip Rahv's *Image and Idea.*

1951

C306
St. Louis Post-Dispatch 4 February 1951. Poems "Here Lies a Lady," "Parting at Dawn," "Bells for John Whitesides' Daughter," reprinted from *Chills and Fever* (A2) on the occasion of Ransom's receiving the Bollingen award. Seen only as a clipping.

C307
ELH: A Journal of English Literary History 18.2 (June 1951). Essay "The Poetry of 1900-1950" (155-162). Editorial note: "This paper was read, in a slightly different form, at a meeting of the Ohio College English Association, April 6, 1951. It is printed here by courtesy of *The Kenyon Review,* by whom it is copyrighted" (155).

C308
Kenyon Review 13.3 (Summer 1951). Essay "The Poetry of 1900-1950" (445-454). Note: "A paper read before the Ohio English Association on April 6, among others sketching the literary achievement of the half-century just gone" (445).

C309
Harvard Advocate 135.2 William Faulkner issue (November 1951). Essay "William Faulkner: An Impression" (17).

1952

C310
Kenyon Review 14.1 (Winter 1952). "Poets and Flatworms" (157-162), a review of Max Eastman's *The Enjoyment of Poetry, with Anthology for the Enjoyment of Poetry.*

C311
New Republic 126.13 (31 March 1952). Essay "An Age of Criticism" (18-19). Ransom was carried on the masthead as one of the magazine's "Contributing Critics" from 17 March 1952 through 4 October 1954.

C312
Kenyon Review 14.2 (Spring 1952). Review-essay "Why Critics Don't Go Mad," on Cleanth Brooks and John Edward Hardy's *Poems of Mr. John Milton* (331-339).

C313
Proceedings of the American Academy of Arts and Letters and the National Institute of Arts and Letters 2nd series, no. 2 (1952). Speech of acceptance of the Russell Loines Award for Poetry (14-16). The award was presented by William Carlos Williams.

C314
New Republic 126.19 (12 May 1952). Essay "Hardy—Old Poet" (16, 30-31), on Thomas Hardy.

C315
Shenandoah 3.2 (Summer 1952). Responses to questions posed by the editor for "A Symposium: The Agrarians Today: Five Questions" (14-16). The other participants are Donald Davidson, Andrew Lytle, Herman C. Nixon, Frank L. Owsley, Allen Tate, and John D. Wade (14-33).

C316
Kenyon Review 14.4 (Autumn 1952). Announcement "Kenyon Review Fellowships" (facing p. 535), signed The Editors, on three fellowships to be funded by the Rockefeller Foundation; essay "Humanism at Chicago" (647-659), on neo-Aristotelianism at the University of Chicago and in part reviewing *Critics and Criticism*, edited by R. S. Crane. See C320 for Ransom's rejoinder to a response by Wayne Booth.

C317
Confluence 1.4 (December 1952). Essay "The Communities of Letters" (86-92), appearing as part of a series on "The Social Role of Art and Philosophy." There are also summaries of the essay: in French by Lee Van Horn and Paul De Man (115), in German

by Ernst M. Oppenheimer (120), in Italian by Arnolfo B. Ferruolo (124). The periodical was directed by William Yandell Elliott, who had been one the Fugitives; edited by Henry A. Kissinger. Beginning with the September 1952 issue, Ransom was listed among the members of its "advisory board."

C318
New Republic 127.23 (8 December 1952). Essay "The Poems of T. S. Eliot: A Perspective" (16-17), a review of Eliot's *Complete Poems and Plays.*

1953

C319
Partisan Review 20.1 (January-February 1953). Review-essay "The Shores of Criticism" (108-111), on R. P. Blackmur's *Language as Gesture;* also the first paragraph of "Ubiquitous Moralists" (8) quoted in a advertisement for Blackmur's *Language as Gesture.*

C320
Kenyon Review 15.2 (Spring 1953). "A Reply by the Author" (301-04), a response to a letter from Wayne Booth ("On the Aristotelian Front," 299-301) objecting to Ransom's treatment of the Chicago critics (C316); "Alienation a Century Ago" (335-336), a review of E. D. H. Johnson's *Alien Vision of Victorian Poetry.*

C321
Sewanee Review 61.2 (April-June 1953). "Responsible Criticism" (300-303), a review of F. O. Matthiessen's *The Responsibilities of the Critic.*

C322
Kenyon Review 15.4 (Autumn 1953). "Empirics in Politics" (648-650, 652-654), a review of Russell Kirk's *The Conservative Mind: From Burke to Santayana.*

C323
New Republic 129.14 (2 November 1953). Review-essay "Symbolism: American Style" (18-20), on Charles Feidelson Jr.'s *Symbolism and American Literature.*

1954

C324
Hika 18.1 (Spring 1954). Ransom is listed as a faculty advisor of *Hika* in this issue.

C325
Kenyon Review 16.4 (Autumn 1954). Essay "The Concrete Universal: Observations on the Understanding of Poetry" (554-564), in part a review of W. K. Wimsatt's *The Verbal Icon*. For part II, see C327.

1955

C326
Kenyon Review 17.2 (Spring 1955). Blurb (303) in an advertisement for Howard Nemerov's *The Salt Garden*, published by Little, Brown & Company.

C327
Kenyon Review 17.3 (Summer 1955). Essay "The Concrete Universal: Observations on the Understanding of Poetry. II." (383-407). The essay ends with the note "to be continued"; it was continued in *Beating the Bushes* (A21). For Part I, see C325.

1956

C328
Hika Winter 1956. Poems "Spectral Lovers" (iv) and "Painted Head" (vi). This issue of the magazine is dedicated to Ransom.

C329
Kenyon Review 18.2 (Spring 1956). Memorial tribute "Philip Blair Rice" (facing p. 169). Rice, associate editor of *Kenyon Review*, died 25 January 1956.

C330
Perspectives USA 15 (Spring 1956). Essay "Emily Dickinson: A Poet Restored" (5-20). Ransom is listed as a member of the advisory board of this quarterly published by James Laughlin and with support from the Ford Foundation. Not seen but

presumably publishing translations of the essay are the foreign editions: *Perspektiven* (Frankfurt), *Profils* (Paris), and *Prospetti* (Florence).

C331
Kenyon Review 18.3 (Summer 1956). Essay "The Strange Music of English Verse" (460-477), which appears with essays by Seymour Chatman, Arnold Stein, and Harold Whitehall under the collective title "English Verse and What It Sounds Like" (411-477). A letter from Chatman responding to Ransom's essay appears in the autumn 1956 issue (648).

1957

C332
New York Times Book Review 24 November 1957. Poems "Blue Girls" (2), "Dead Boy" (2).

C333
New York Times Book Review 8 December 1957. Poem "Piazza Piece" (2).

1958

C334
Kenyon Review 20.1 (Winter 1958). Unsigned editorial "Announcement" [iv], on Ransom's retirement as editor as of June 1958. But his retirement was delayed (see C340).

C335
Kenyon Review 20.2 (Spring 1958). Editorial "Announcement" [iv], on appointment of Robie Macauley as editor, Edgar Bogardus as managing editor.

C336
Kenyon Review 20.3 (Summer 1958). "Edgar Collins Bogardus" [vi], notice of his death, followed by an unsigned note stating that Irving Kreutz has been appointed managing editor.

C337
Kenyon Review 20.4 (Autumn 1958). Blurb (649) in an advertisement for *An Anthology of French Poetry*, edited by Angel Flores and published by Doubleday Anchor Books.

1959

C338
Kenyon Review 21.1 (Winter 1959). Speech "The Idea of a Literary Anthropologist and What He Might Say of the *Paradise Lost* of Milton: A Speech with a Prologue" (121-140). The speech itself is entitled "Our Age among the Ages" and had been delivered at the dedication of the Phi Beta Kappa Society hall at the College of William and Mary in May 1958. See B42.

C339
Johns Hopkins Magazine 10.4 (January 1959). Poem "Prelude to an Evening" (23). The poem appears without title in a feature by Elliott Coleman entitled "The Meaning of Poetry" (17-29), which presents photographs of and poems by six poets participating in the Johns Hopkins Poetry Festival.

C340
Kenyon Review 21.4 (Autumn 1959). Editorial "Announcement" [vii], on this the last issue of *Kenyon Review* under Ransom's editorship and on the return of his successor, Robie Macauley, from a year's leave of absence abroad.

C341
Sewanee Review 67.4 (October-December 1959). Essay "In Amicitia" (528-539), on Allen Tate for a special Tate issue of the review.

1960

C342
Kenyon Review 22.2 (Spring 1960). Essay "Thomas Hardy's Poems, and the Religious Difficulties of a Naturalist" (169-193).

1961

C343

Harvard Advocate 145 (November 1961). Prose comment "A Look Backwards and a Note of Hope" (22-23), on Robert Lowell.

1962

C344

Vanderbilt Alumnus 47.4 (March-April 1962). "Upon Returning" (14-15, 45), an interview by Robert L. Welker.

C345

Sewanee Review 70.2 (April-June 1962) (the contents page misidentifies the issue as number 1 [January-March]). "The Most Southern Poet" (202-207), a review of Donald Davidson's *The Long Street.*

C346

Kenyon Review 24 (Summer 1962). Poem "Master's in the Garden Again" (439-440).

1963

C347

Kenyon Review 25.1 (Winter 1963). "Prelude to an Evening: A Poem Revised and Explicated" (70-80), consisting of the poem "Prelude to an Evening" (70-71) and of Ransom's comments on his revision of it.

C348

American Oxonian 50.2 (April 1963). Report "The Gordon Keith Chalmers Memorial Library at Kenyon" (91-93), on the dedication of the library at Kenyon College and on his and Chalmers's relations with Robert Frost, portions of whose dedicatory address for the occasion are quoted preceding Ransom's piece.

1964

C349

Kenyon Review 26.1 (Winter 1964). Essay "The Planetary Poet" (233-264), on Wallace Stevens.

C350

Sewanee Review 72.3 (July-September 1964). "Acceptance Speech: The National Book Award for Poetry, March 10, 1964" (548-550). Ransom received the award for his 1963 *Selected Poems* (see A16.1).

1965

C351

Vanderbilt Alumnus 51.2 (September-October 1965). The column "Words of Our Years" reprints Ransom's letter of 1 December 1917 (C24).

1966

C352

Hika 28.3 (Spring-Summer 1966). Poem "The Vanity of the Bright Young Men" (32-33).

C353

Texas Quarterly 9.1 (Spring 1966). Essay "Theory of Poetic Form" (190-201), printed along with essays by Kenneth Burke, Elder Olson, and Eliseo Vivas and an introduction by Mark Schorer as part of a Symposium on Formalist Criticism held at the University of Texas on 11-12 February 1965.

C354

Sewanee Review 74.2 (April-June 1966). Essay "Gerontion" (389-414), on T. S. Eliot's poem of that title. An editorial note in the January-March issue, an issue devoted to Eliot and edited by Allen Tate, says that Ransom's essay "was delayed, and could not be included in this special issue" and that it will appear in the spring issue instead ([xii]).

1967

C355
Southern Review n.s. 3.2 (Spring 1967). Essay "The Rugged Way of Genius: A Tribute to Randall Jarrell" (263-281).

C356
Southern Review n.s. 3.3 (Summer 1967). Poem "The Vanity of the Bright Young Men" (634-635).

1968

C357
Kenyon Review 30.4 (1968). Essay "A Postscript on Shakespeare's Sonnets" (523-531).

C358
Life 64.19 (10 May 1968). Poem "Piazza Piece" (109), reprinted to accompany an unsigned article, entitled "To Pay a Poet Honor," on the celebration of Ransom's eightieth birthday (109-110).

C359
Southern Review 4.3 (Summer 1968). Essay "T. S. Eliot: A Postscript" (579-597), presenting second thoughts on his review of Eliot's *Murder in the Cathedral* (A9, C215).

1969

C360
Kenyon Review 31.1 (1969). Poem "Two Gentlemen Scholars (A Pastoral)" (54-56).

C361
New York Review of Books 13.7 (23 October 1969). "Blake Triumphant" (4-5), a review of K. Raine's *Blake and Tradition;* and poem "*Agitato ma non troppo*" (5).

1970

C362

American Oxonian 57.3 (July 1970). Obituary "Edward Henry Eckel (1890-1969)" (421-423).

1971

C363

Sewanee Review 79.1 (January-March 1971). Poem "Kingdom Come" ("Angered with a braggart kind") (26). An editorial note (29) says that the poem has been revised from the "original version," entitled "Adventure This Side of Pluralism," in *Chills and Fever* (A2). Actually, the earliest published version appeared in the *Fugitive* (C90), its text there differing from that in *Chills*. The poem also appeared, under the early title, in *Grace after Meat* (A3). The title "Kingdom Come" had previously been used, in the 1969 *Selected Poems* (A18), for a distinctly different poem that had before that been entitled "Disappointment of a Thrall" (A4, B8).

C364

Michigan Quarterly Review 10.3 (Summer 1971). Poems "Farmer Husband" (164) and "Grim Wedlock" (165). These are revisions of, respectively, "Husband Betrayed" and "In Process of a Noble Alliance," both of which had first appeared in the *Fugitive* (C146, C54).

1973

C365

Sewanee Review 81.3 (July-September 1973). Poem "Four Threesomes; or Three Foursomes?" (387-388). The poem is a revision of "Old Man Pondered," which had first appeared in *Saturday Review of Literature* (C172), had been collected in the 1963 *Selected Poems* (A16), and had been omitted from the 1969 *Selected Poems* (A18). The poem later appears as "The Eye Can Tell," in *Southern Review* (C368) and *Selected Letters* (A24), where it is said, on the authority of Robert Penn Warren, to have been written in late winter 1973.

1976

C366

Southern Review 12.4 (October 1976). "Art as Adventure in Form: Letters of John Crowe Ransom, 1923-1927" (776-797) edited by Thomas Daniel Young and George Core and consisting of a brief introduction by the editors and six letters to Allen Tate dated 17 December 1922 [sic], 15 April 1924, 22 April 1924, 6 May 1924, 5 September 1926, and 20 February 1927

C367

Mississippi Quarterly 30.1 (Winter 1976-1977). William Pratt's article "Metamorphosis of a Poem" (29-58) prints 14 versions of "The Vanity of Bright Young Men" (also entitled "Tom, Tom, the Piper's Son," "The Vanity of the Male," and "The Vanity of the Bright Boys"), including a previously unpublished version (version 12) that Ransom sent Pratt in 1964 for inclusion in *The Fugitive Poets* (B56) but that was later replaced by another (version 7).

1983

C368

Southern Review n.s. 19.4 (October 1983). Poem "The Eye Can Tell" (836-837). Editorial note: "John Crowe Ransom's 'The Eye Can Tell,' according to Thomas Daniel Young, is the last poem the poet wrote. In the spring of 1973, when Ransom was nearly 85, he read it to Robert Penn Warren at Gambier, Ohio, and later sent Warren the copy that is printed in this issue" (vii, ix). "*The Southern Review* is grateful to Helen Ransom Forman for permission to publish 'The Eye Can Tell'" (837). For previous versions of the poem, see the note at C365.

1985

C369

Southern Review 21.2 (April 1985). Letter from Ransom to William Alexander Percy, 8 May [1923] (424-425), included with letters by Donald Davidson, Percy, and Allen Tate in a group of letters edited by Jo Gulledge under the title "William Alexander Percy and the Fugitives: A Literary Correspondence, 1921-1923" (415-427).

1989

C370

Kenyon Review 11.1 (Winter 1989). Announcement "War and Publication" (179-180); essays "Ubiquitous Moralists" (126-129), "Muses and Amazons" (130-131), "Artists, Soldiers, Positivists" (203-207). All are reprinted from *Kenyon Review* (C264, C254, C257, C274).

Section D
Contributions to Books

1913

D1
American Rhodes Scholars, Oxford, 1910-1913. 1913. See B1.

1923

D2
Anthology of Magazine Verse for 1923 and Yearbook of American Poetry. 1923. See B4.

D3
Armageddon by John Crowe Ransom, A Fragment by William Alexander Percy, Avalon by Donald Davidson. 1923. See B3.

D4
The Winter Owl. 1923. See B2.

1924

D5
Anthology of Magazine Verse for 1924 and Yearbook of American Poetry. Ed. William Stanley Braithwaite. Boston: B. J. Brimmer, 1924. Published 24 December 1924; copyright registration A814938 (copies deposited 5 February 1925). Poems "Bells for John Whitesides' Daughter" (216) and "Captain Carpenter" (217-219). The poems are reprinted from the *Fugitive* with slight textual variation evidently from misprinting: for example, in "Bells" (line 5) 'window,' for 'window.' and in "Captain" (line

17) 'Corpenter' for 'Carpenter'. Described in Hogan, *Robinson* pp. 68-69.

D6
The Best Poems of 1924. 1924. See B7.

D7
Bowling Green. 1924. See B5.

D8
Modern Essays (Second Series). 1924. See B6.

D9
The Year Book of the Poetry Society of South Carolina. [Volume 2, number 2 (October 1924).] Ed. John Bennett, DuBose Heyward, Henrietta Kollock, and Josephine Pinckney. Charleston: Poetry Society of South Carolina, 1924. Poem "Bells for John Whitesides' Daughter" (32), reprinted from the *Fugitive* with no textual alteration.

1925

D10
American Poetry, 1925: A Miscellany. 1925. See B8.

D11
Anthology of Magazine Verse for 1925 and Yearbook of American Poetry. 1925. See B11.

D12
The Best Poems of 1925. 1925. See B10.

D13
The Home Book of Modern Verse: An Extension of The Home Book of Verse, *Being a Selection from American and English Poetry of the Twentieth Century*. Ed. Burton Egbert Stevenson. New York: Henry Holt, 1925. Poems "Triumph" (130), "Here Lies a Lady" (536-537).

D14
Modern American Poetry. 3rd rev. ed. See B9. Ransom does not appear in the 1st (1919) and 2nd (1921) editions.

D15
Poems for Youth: An American Anthology. Ed. William Rose Benét. New York: E. P. Dutton, 1925. Poem "The Swimmer" (461-463).

1926

D16
The Best Poems of 1926. 1926. See B13.

D17
In Memoriam: Herbert Cushing Tolman. 1926. See B12.

1927

D18
The Third Book of Modern Verse: A Selection from the Work of Contemporaneous American Poets. Ed. Jessie B. Rittenhouse. Boston: Houghton Mifflin, 1927. Poems "Blue Girls" (80-81), "Piazza Piece" (204-205), "Here Lies a Lady" (293-294).

1928

D19
Anthologie de la nouvelle poésie américaine. By Eugene Jolas. Paris: Kra, 1928. Poem "Blackberry Winter" (181-182) translated into French.

D20
Fugitives: An Anthology of Verse. 1928. See B14.

D21
The Lyric South: An Anthology of Recent Poetry from the South. Ed. Addison Hibbard. New York: Macmillan, 1928. Poems "Judith of Bethulia" (89-91), "Under the Locusts" (91-92), "Noonday Grace" (134-137), "Our Two Worthies" (138-140), "Sur-

vey of Literature" (169-170), "Morning" ("Jane awoke Ralph so gently on one morning") (191), "The Lover" (192), "The Equilibrists" (193-195), "Bells for John Whitesides' Daughter" (203-204), "Dead Boy" (204-205), "Emily Hardcastle, Spinster" (205-206).

D22
Modern American and British Poetry. Revised and enlarged. Ed. Louis Untermeyer. New York: Harcourt, Brace, 1928. (This anthology is not to be confused with Untermeyer's combined editions that bind up together his *Modern American Poetry* and *Modern British Poetry.*) Poem "Lady Lost" (227-228).

D23
New Voices: An Introduction to Contemporary Poetry. By Marguerite Wilkinson. New edition revised and enlarged. Macmillan, 1928. Poems "The Vagrant" (486-487) and "Emily Hardcastle, Spinster" (487).

1929

D24
American Poetry, 1671-1928: A Comprehensive Anthology. Ed. Conrad Aiken. New York: Modern Library, 1929. Poems "Blue Girls" (347), "Antique Harvesters" (347-349), "Captain Carpenter" (349-351). Described in Bonnell, *Aiken* B25.

D25
The Noise That Time Makes. 1929. See B15.

D26
Twentieth-Century Poetry. Ed. John Drinkwater, Henry Seidel Canby, and William Rose Benét. Cambridge: Houghton Mifflin, 1929. Poems "Spectral Lovers" (567-568), "Number Five" (568-569). Described in Gallup, *Eliot* Ba5.

1930

D27
I'll Take My Stand. 1930. See B17.

D28
Lyric America: An Anthology of American Poetry. Ed. Alfred Kreymborg. New York: Coward-McCann, Inc., 1930. Poems "Janet Waking" (518-519), "Amphibious Crocodile" (519-521), "The Equilibrists" (522-523), "Here Lies a Lady" (523-524), "Parting at Dawn" (524). The revised "editions" of 1935 and 1941 merely add supplements with additional poets, making no changes in the earlier selections.

D29
Modern American Poetry: A Critical Anthology. 4th rev. ed. 1930. See B16.

1932

D30
American Poets, 1630-1930. Ed. Mark Van Doren. Boston: Little, Brown, and Company, 1932. (Also published in 1936 by Garden City Publishing as *Masterpieces of American Poets.*) Poems "Bells for John Whitesides'Daughter" (541), "Here Lies a Lady" (541-542), "Necrological" (542-543), "Epitaph" (543), "Captain Carpenter" (543-545), "Piazza Piece" (545), "Miller's Daughter" (545-546), "Two in August" (546-547), "Antique Harvesters" (547-548), "The Equilibrists" (548-550).

D31
The New Poetry: An Anthology of Twentieth-Century Verse in English. New ed., rev. and enlarged. Ed. Harriet Monroe and Alice Corbin Henderson. New York: Macmillan, 1932. Poems "Bells for John Whitesides' Daughter" (466), "Parting, without Sequel [sic]" (467), "Blue Girls" (467-468). Ransom does not appear in the 1917 and 1923 editions.

D32
Shorter Modern Poems, 1900-1931, American—Irish—English. Ed. David Morton. New York: Harper & Brothers, 1932. Poems "In Process of a Noble Alliance" (43), "Here Lies a Lady" (44).

1933

D33
The Albatross Book of Living Verse: English and American Poetry from the Thirteenth Century to the Present Day. Ed. Louis Untermeyer. London: The Albatross, 1933. Poems "Parting, without a Sequel" (586-587), "Piazza Piece" (587).

D34
An American Omnibus. Intro. Carl Van Doren. Garden City: Doubleday, Doran, 1933. Poem "Here Lies a Lady" (23). The poem appears in a section entitled "An Anthology of Modern American Poetry Especially Selected for *An American Omnibus* by Mark Van Doren."

D35
A Book of Poems for Every Mood. Ed. Harriet Monroe and Morton Dauwen Zabel. Racine: Whitman Publishing, 1933. Poems "Blue Girls" (44-45), "Bells for John Whitesides' Daughter" (128).

D36
Contemporary Trends: American Literature since 1914. Ed. John Herbert Nelson. New York: Macmillan, 1933. Poems "Piazza Piece" (307-308), "Somewhere Is Such a Kingdom" (308).

1934

D37
Daemon in the Rock. By Edwin Richardson Frost. 1934. See B18.

D38
The Modern Muse: Poems of To-Day, British and American. London: Oxford University Press, for the English Association, 1934. "The association would like to express its deep sense of obligation to John Gould Fletcher and the late John Freeman for the very valuable help they gave in the compilation" (viii). Poems "Antique Harvesters" (192-194), "Judith of Bethulia" (194-195).

1936

D39

Announcement to Persons Interested in Agrarian, Distributist and Homestead Principles. 1936. See B22.

D40

An Anthology of World Poetry. Rev. & enl ed. Ed. Mark Van Doren. New York: Harcourt, Brace, 1936. Poems "Here Lies a Lady" (1407), "Two in August" (1408-1409).

D41

An Approach to Literature: A Collection of Prose and Verse with Analyses and Discussions. By Cleanth Brooks, Jr., John Thibaut Purser, and Robert Penn Warren. Baton Rouge: Louisiana State University Press, 1936. Poem "Bells for John Whitesides' Daughter" (468-469). Described in Grimshaw, *Warren* B7

D42

The Borzoi Reader. Ed. Carl Van Doren. New York: Alfred A Knopf, 1936. Poems "Bells for John Whitesides' Daughter" (693-694), "Here Lies a Lady" (694), "Epitaph" (694-695), "Two in August" (695-696).

D43

Great Poems of the English Language: An Anthology, with a Supplement of Recent Poetry Selected by William Rose Benét. Ed. Wallace Alvin Briggs. New York: Tudor, 1936. Poem "Here Lies a Lady" (1422).

D44

An Introduction to Poetry. Rev. ed. Ed. Jay B. Hubbell and John O. Beaty. New York: Macmillan, 1936. Poem "Bells for John Whiteside's Daughter" (418-419).

D45

Modern American Poetry: A Critical Anthology. 5th rev. ed. 1936. See B19.

D46
Modern English Readings. Rev. ed. [i.e., 2nd ed.] Ed. Roger Sherman Loomis and Donald Leman Clark. New York: Farrar & Rinehart, 1936. Essay "Happy Farmers" (193-199), reprinted from *American Review,* with portions omitted.

D47
The New Republic Anthology, 1915-1935. Ed. Groff Conklin. New York: Dodge Publishing, 1936. Poem "What Ducks Require" (259-260). Described in Bonnell, *Aiken* B42; Gallup, *Eliot* Ba11.

D48
Southern Poets: Representative Selections. 1936. See B20.

D49
Who Owns America? A Declaration of Independence. 1936. See B21.

1937

D50
Literary Opinion in America: Essays Illustrating the Status, Methods, and Problems of Criticism in the United States since the War. 1937. See B24.

D51
Southern Treasury of Life and Literature. 1937. See B23.

1938

D52
America through the Essay: An Anthology for English Courses. 1938. See B25.

D53
American Sketchbook. Ed. Tremaine McDowell et al. New York: Macmillan, 1938. Essay "Reconstructed but Unregenerate" (339-350).

D54

M: One Thousand Autobiographical Sonnets. By Merrill Moore. New York: Harcourt, Brace, 1938. Uses a quotation from *World's Body* (A9) as an epigraph (i) and reprints Ransom's foreword (1006-1009) to Moore's *The Noise That Time Makes* (B15).

D55

The Modern Poet: An Anthology. Ed. Gwendolen Murphy. London: Sidgwick & Jackson, 1938. Poems "Wrestling" (62-63), "Southern Mansion" (63-64), reprinted from *Grace after Meat* (A3). Described in Higginson and Williams, *Graves* B27.

D56

A New Anthology of Modern Poetry. Ed. Selden Rodman. New York: Modern Library, 1938. Poem "Here Lies a Lady" (276).

D57

The Oxford Anthology of American Literature. Ed. William Rose Benét and Norman Holmes Pearson. New York: Oxford University Press, 1938. Poems "Spectral Lovers" (1512-1513), "Old Man Playing with Children" (1513), "Philomela" (1513-1514). Described in Abbott, *Moore* B11; Bonnell, *Aiken* B45; Boughn, *H.D.* B14; Wallace, *Williams* B34.

D58

Understanding Poetry: An Anthology for College Students. By Cleanth Brooks, Jr., and Robert Penn Warren. New York: Henry Holt, 1938. Poems "Winter Remembered" (349), "The Equilibrists" (485-486). Described in Grimshaw, *Warren* B10.

1939

D59

An Approach to Literature: A Collection of Prose and Verse with Analyses and Discussions. Rev. ed. By Cleanth Brooks, John Thibaut Purser, and Robert Penn Warren. New York: F. S. Crofts, 1939. Poem "Bells for John Whitesides' Daughter" (468-469).

D60
Foreword by John Crowe Ransom to The Noise That Time Makes, *a First Volume of 101 Sonnets by Merrill Moore and Some Reviews of This Book.* N.p.: n.d. [1939?]. Reprints, with some substantive textual variation, Ransom's foreword (3-5) to Moore's *Noise* (B15).

D61
The Fugitive: Clippings and Comments about the Magazine and the Members of the Group That Published It. 1939. See B26.

D62
This Generation: A Selection of British and American Literature from 1914 to the Present with Historical and Critical Essays. By George K. Anderson and Eda Lou Walton. Chicago: Scott, Foresman, 1939. Poems "Spectral Lovers" (346), "The Tall Girl" (346-347), "April Treason" (347), "Two in August" (347-348), "Survey of Literature" (348), "Here Lies a Lady" (348-349).

1940

D63
Contemporary Southern Prose. 1940. See B27.

D64
A Voyage to the British Isles. By Charles McKinley. 1940. See B28.

1941

D65
The Intent of the Critic. 1941. See B30.

D66
A Little Book of Modern Verse. Ed. Anne Ridler, preface by T. S. Eliot. London: Faber and Faber, 1941. Poem "Captain Carpenter" (73-75). Described in Gallup, *Eliot* B41.

D67
New Poems 1940: An Anthology of British and American Verse. 1941. See B29.

D68
The Prose and Poetry of Today: Regional America. Ed. Harriet Marcella Lucas and Elizabeth Frances Ansorge. Syracuse: L. W. Singer, 1941. Poem "Lady Lost" (110).

D69
Reading Poems: An Introduction to Critical Study. By Wright Thomas and Stuart Gerry Brown. New York: Oxford University Press, 1941. Poems "Janet Waking" (508-509), "Here Lies a Lady" (509).

D70
The Viking Book of Poetry of the English-Speaking World. Ed. Richard Aldington. New York: Viking Press, 1941. Poem "Tom, Tom, the Piper's Son" (1167-1168).

1942

D71
American Harvest: Twenty Years of Creative Writing in the United States. Ed. Allen Tate and John Peale Bishop. New York: L. B. Fischer, 1942; Garden City: Garden City Publishing, 1943. Poems "Captain Carpenter" (431-433), "Blue Girls" (433-434).

D72
Modern American Poetry: A Critical Anthology. 6th ed. Ed. Louis Untermeyer. New York: Harcourt, Brace, 1942. Poems "Bells for John Whitesides' Daughter" (446), "Lady Lost" (447), "Blue Girls" (447), "Here Lies a Lady" (448), "Janet Waking" (448-449), "Spiel of the Three Mountebanks" (449-450), "First Travels of Max" (450-451), "Antique Harvesters" (451-452), "Piazza Piece" (452-453), "Captain Carpenter" (453-454), "Old Man Pondered" (454-455), "Parting, without a Sequel" (455), "Prelude to an Evening" (456), "Painting: A Head" (456).

D73
Song and Idea, by Richard Eberhart. New York: Oxford University Press, 1942. Quotation from Ransom's review in *Furioso* ("Lyrics Important, Sometimes Rude," C258) used a blurb on the front flap of the dust jacket. Described in Wright, *Eberhart* A3b.

D74
A Treasury of Great Poems, English and American, from the Foundations of the English Spirit to the Outstanding Poetry of Our Own Time, with the Lives of the Poets and Historical Settings. Ed. Louis Untermeyer. New York: Simon and Schuster, 1942. Poems "Lady Lost" (1157-1158), "Piazza Piece" (1158).

D75
War Letter. 1942. See B31.

1943

D76
Chief Modern Poets of England and America. 3rd ed. Ed. Gerald DeWitt Sanders and John Herbert Nelson. New York: Macmillan, 1943. Poems "Bells for John Whitesides' Daughter" (763-764), "Here Lies a Lady" (764), "Miss Euphemia" (765), "Emily Hardcastle, Spinster" (766), "Inland City" (766), "Blue Girls" (766-767), "Somewhere Is Such a Kingdom" (767-768), "The Equilibrists" (768-770). Ransom is not represented in the 1929 and 1936 editions.

D77
Great Modern Reading: W. Somerset Maugham's Introduction to Modern English and American Literature. Garden City: Nelson Doubleday, 1943. Poem "Blue Girls" (417).

D78
The Penguin Book of Sonnets. Ed. Carl Withers. New York: Penguin Books, 1943. Poem "The Tall Girl" (228).

D79
The Triumph of Life: Poems of Consolation for the English Speaking World. Ed. Horace Gregory. New York: Viking Press, 1943. Poem "Spectral Lovers" (280-281).

D80
W. Somerset Maugham's Introduction to Modern English and American Literature. New York: Home Library, 1943. Poem "Blue Girls" (417).

1944

D81
Antología de excritores contemporáneos de los Estados Unidos. Vol. 2. Ed. John Peale Bishop and Allen Tate. Santiago: Editorial Nascimento, 1944. Poems "Captain Carpenter" (196-201) translated by Francisco Aguilera, and "Blue Girls" (202-203) translated by Angel Flores; in Spanish on versos, English on rectos.

D82
A Comprehensive Anthology of American Poetry. Ed. Conrad Aiken. New York: Modern Library, 1944. Poems "Blue Girls" (388-389), "Antique Harvesters" (389-390), "Captain Carpenter" (390-392), "Bells for John Whiteside's Daughter" (392-393), "Lady Lost" (393), "Here Lies a Lady" (394). Described in Bonnell, *Aiken* B55, which gives a publication date of 20 February 1945.

D83
Twentieth-Century American Poetry. Ed. Conrad Aiken. New York: Modern Library, 1944. Poems "Bells for John Whiteside's Daughter" (217-218), "Lady Lost" (218), "Blue Girls" (219), "Here Lies a Lady" (219-220), "Captain Carpenter" (220-222), "Husband Betrayed" (222-223), "Little Boy Blue" (223). Described in Bonnell, *Aiken* B56, which gives a publication date of 20 March 1945.

D84
A Vanderbilt Miscellany, 1919-1944. 1944. See B32.

1945

D85
An Anthology of Famous English and American Poetry. Ed. William Rose Benét and Conrad Aiken. New York: Modern Library, 1945. Poems "Blue Girls" (841), "Antique Harvesters" (841-843), "Captain Carpenter" (843-845), "Bells for John Whiteside's Daughter" (845), "Lady Lost" (845-846), "Here Lies a Lady" (846). Described in Bonnell, *Aiken* B57.

D86
Écrivains et poètes des Etats-Unis d'Amérique. Ed. Jean Wahl. Paris: Fontaine, 1945. (This is an edition of the double number of *Fontaine* for June-July 1943.) Poem "Vision by Sweetwater" (190) translated into French by Hélène Bokanowski.

D87
North, East, South, West: A Regional Anthology of American Writing. Ed. Charles Lee et al. Southern section ed. Struthers Burt. New York: Howell, Soskin, 1945. Poem "Blue Girls" (308).

1946

D88
A Little Treasury of Modern Poetry, English and American. Ed. Oscar Williams. New York: Charles Scribner's Sons, 1946. Poems "Here Lies a Lady" (136), "The Equilibrists" (350-352), "Captain Carpenter" (497-499), "Little Boy Blue" (524).

D89
Love. Ed. Walter de la Mare. N.p.: William Morrow, 1946. Poem "Yea" (596) appearing untitled and reprinted from the sequence "Two Sonnets" in *Chills and Fever.*

D90
A New Anthology of Modern Poetry. Rev. ed. Ed. Selden Rodman. New York: Modern Library, 1946. Poem "Here Lies a Lady" (212).

D91
Entry canceled.

1947

D92
American Poetry and Prose. 3rd ed. Ed. Norman Foerster. Boston: Houghton Mifflin, 1947. Poems "Bells for John Whiteside's Daughter" (1515), "Address to the Scholars of New England" (115-116). Ransom did not appear in the previous edition (1934).

D93
The Heritage of the English-Speaking Peoples and Their Responsibility: Address at the Conference, October 1946, Kenyon College. 1947. See B33.

D94
Little Treasury of Great Poetry, English and American, from Chaucer to the Present Day. Ed. Oscar Williams. New York: Charles Scribner's Sons, 1947. Poems "Captain Carpenter" (176-178), "Painted Head" (193-194).

D95
World Literature: An Anthology of Human Experience. Ed. Arthur E. Christy and Henry W. Wells. New York: American Book, 1947. Poem "Antique Harvesters" (426-427).

1948

D96
Criticism: The Foundations of Modern Literary Judgment. Ed Mark Schorer, Josephine Miles, and Gordon McKenzie. New York: Harcourt, Brace, 1948. Essay "A Poem Nearly Anonymous" (333-342). Described in Gallup, *Eliot* Ba15.

D97
A Little Treasury of American Poetry: The Chief Poets from Colonial Times to the Present Day. Ed. Oscar Williams. New York: Charles Scribner's Sons, 1948. Poems "Survey of Literature" (505-506), "Dog" (506-507), "Painted Head" (507-508), "Captain Carpenter" (509-511), "Dead Boy" (511), "Bells for John Whiteside's Daughter" (512), "Blue Girls" (512-514), "Judith of Bethulia" (513-514), "Armageddon" (515-517), "Somewhere Is Such a Kingdom" (517-518). Described in Wright, *Eberhart* B25.

D98
Losses. By Randall Jarrell. New York: Harcourt, Brace, 1948. Blurb on dust jacket back. Described in Wright, *Jarrell* (A3a).

D99
100 American Poems: Masterpieces of Lyric, Epic and Ballad from Colonial Times to the Present. Ed. Selden Rodman. New York: Mentor Book-New American Library, 1948. Poem "Philomela" (142-143).

D100
Readings for Liberal Education. Vol. 2: *Introduction to Literature.* Ed. Louis G. Locke, William M. Gibson, and George Arms. New York: Rinehart, 1948. Poem "Here Lies a Lady" (174-175).

D101
T. S. Eliot: A Selected Critique. Ed. Leonard Unger. New York: Rinehart, 1948. Sections 1-3 and 6 from the essay "T. S. Eliot: The Historical Critic" (92-208), reprinted from *The New Criticism* (A10).

1949

D102
American Literature: A Brief Anthology. Ed. Charles S. Bouslog and Alfons L. Korn. Honolulu: University of Hawaii, 1949. Poems "Dead Boy" (128), "Janet Waking" (128-129), "Here Lies a Lady" (129), "Survey of Literature" (129).

D103
Contemporary Trends: American Literature since 1900. Rev. ed. Ed. John Herbert Nelson and Oscar Cargill. New York: Macmillan, 1949. Poems "Captain Carpenter" (744-745), "Miss Euphemia" (745-746), "Piazza Piece" (746), "Somewhere Is Such a Kingdom" (746-747).

D104
The Critical Reader: Poems, Stories, Essays. Ed. Wallace Douglas, Roy Lamson, and Hallett Smith. New York: W. W. Norton, 1949. Poem "Here Lies a Lady" (75).

D105
Critiques and Essays in Criticism, 1920-1948, Representing the Achievement of Modern British and American Critics. Ed. Robert Wooster Stallman. Foreword by Cleanth Brooks. New York: Ronald Press, 1949. Essay "Poetry: A Note on [sic] Ontology" (30-46). Described in Gallup, *Eliot* Ba17.

D106
Lectures in Criticism: The Johns Hopkins University. 1949. See B34.

D107
A Little Treasury of American Prose: The Major Writers from Colonial Times to the Present Day. Ed. George Mayberry. New York: Charles Scribner's Sons, 1949. Essay "Wanted: An Ontological Critic" (645-662).

D108
100 Modern Poems. Ed. Selden Rodman. New York: Pellegrinni & Cudahy, 1949. Poem "Blackbery Winter" (140-141). (This book was also published by New American Library as a Mentor Book in 1951, with the poem appearing on p. 157.) Described in Wallace, *Williams* B55.

D109
Panorama y antología de la poesía norteamericana. Trans. José Coronel Urtecho. Madrid: Seminario de Problemas Hispanoamericanos, 1949. Poem "Piazza Piece" (245) translated into Spanish.

D110
This Generation: A Selection of British and American Literature from 1914 to the Present, with Historical and Critical Essays. Rev. ed. By George K. Anderson and Eda Lou Walton. Chicago: Scott, Foresman, 1949. Poems "Spectral Lovers" (281), "The Tall Girl" (281-282), "April Treason" (282), "Two in August" (282-283), "Survey of Literature" (283), "Here Lies a Lady" (283).

1950

D111
A Little Treasury of Modern Poetry, English and American. Rev. ed. Ed. Oscar Williams. New York: Charles Scribner's Sons, 1950. Poems "Captain Carpenter" (301-302), "The Equilibrists" (303-304), "Little Boy Blue" (305), "Here Lies a Lady" (305-306), "Judith of Bethulia" (306-307), "Bells for John Whiteside's Daughter" (308), "Her Eyes" (308-309), "Painted Head" (309-310), "Man without Sense of Direction" (311-312), "Address to the Scholars of New England" (313-314).

D112
Milton Criticism: Selections from Four Centuries. Ed. James Thorpe. New York: Rinehart, 1950. Essay "A Poem Nearly Anonymous" (225-238).

D113
Modern American Poetry. Mid-Century edition [i.e., 7th ed.]. Ed. Louis Untermeyer. New York: Harcourt, Brace, 1950. Poems "Bells for John Whiteside's Daughter" (427), "Lady Lost" (428), "Blue Girls" (428), "Here Lies a Lady" (429), "Janet Waking" (429-430), "Spiel of the Three Mountebanks" (430-431), "First Travels of Max" (431-432), "Antique Harvesters" (432-433), "Piazza Piece" (433-434), "Captain Carpenter" (434), "Old Man Pondered" (435), "Parting, without a Sequel" (436), "Prelude to an Evening" (437), "Painting: A Head" (437). Described in Wallace, *Williams* B58.

D114
The New Modern American and British Poetry. Mid-Century ed. Ed. Louis Untermeyer. New York: Harcourt, Brace, 1950. Poems "Lady Lost" (190-191), "Piazza Piece" (191), "Here Lies a Lady" (191-192).

D115
The Oxford Book of American Verse. Ed. F. O. Matthiessen. New York: Oxford University Press, 1950. Poems "*Agitato ma non troppo*" (835-836), "Bells for John Whiteside's Daughter" (836), "Winter Remembered" (837), "Vaunting Oak" (837-839), "Conrad in Twilight" (839-840), "Blackberry Winter" (840-841), "Old Mansion" (841-842), "Philomela" (843-844), "Captain Carpenter" (844-846), "Piazza Piece" (846), "Vision by

Sweetwater" (847-848), "Persistent Explorer" (848-849), "Dead Boy" (850), "Parting, without a Sequel" (850-851), "Two in August" (851-852); "Antique Harvesters" (853-854), "Man without Sense of Direction" (854-856), "The Equilibrists" (856-858), "Prelude to an Evening" (859-860), "Painted Head" (860-861).

D116
The Permanence of Yeats: Selected Criticism. 1950. See B35.

D117
Reading Poetry: A Method of Analysis, with Selections for Study. By Fred B. Millett. New York: Harper & Brothers, 1950. Poem "Here Lies a Lady of Beauty and High Degree [sic]" (193-194).

D118
Understanding Poetry: An Anthology for College Students. Rev. ed. By Cleanth Brooks and Robert Penn Warren. New York: Henry Holt, 1950. Poems "Bells for John Whiteside's Daughter" (170), "Winter Remembered" (191), "The Equilibrists" (261-262).

1951

D119
Achievement in American Poetry. By Louise Bogan. Chicago: Henry Regnery, 1951. Poem "Piazza Piece" (133).

D120
The American Genius: An Anthology of Poetry with Some Prose. Ed. Edith Sitwell. London: John Lehmann, 1951. Poem "Captain Carpenter" (152-154). Described in Fifoot, *Sitwell* EB30.

D121
American Literary Criticism, 1900-1950. Ed. Charles I. Glicksberg. New York: Hendricks House, 1951. Essay "Criticism, Inc." (453-467).

D122
Case Record from a Sonnetorium. Cartoons by Edward St. John Gorey and poems by Merrill Moore. 1951. See B37.

D123
Enjoying Poetry. By Mark Van Doren. New York: William Sloane, 1951. Poems "Here Lies a Lady" (492), "Bells for John Whiteside's Daughter" (493), "Piazza Piece" (493-494), "Two in August" (494-495), "Antique Harvesters" (495-496).

D124
The Faber Book of Modern Verse. 2nd ed. Ed. Michael Roberts, with a supplement of poems chosen by Anne Ridler. London: Faber and Faber, 1951. Poems "Vision by Sweetwater" (195), "Captain Carpenter" (195-197), "Judith of Bethulia" (198-199), "What Ducks Require" (200).

D125
The Great Critics. Ed. James Harry Smith and Edd Winfield Parks. 3rd ed. New York: W. W. Norton, 1951. Essay "Poetry: A Note in Ontology" (769-787).

D126
Literary Opinion in America: Illustrating the Status, Methods, and Problems of Criticism in the United States in the Twentieth Century. Revised ed. Ed. Morton Dauwen Zabel. New York: Harper and Brothers, 1951. Essay "Criticism as Pure Speculation" (639-654). Editor's note: "This essay was presented as a lecture at Princeton University in the winter of 1940-4. . . . The first two paragraphs, referring to the local occasion of the discussion, have here been condensed into the present first paragraph by the editor, with the author's permission" (639). The first edition of *Literary Opinion* (B24) printed a different essay by Ransom.

D127
Modern Poetry, American and British. Ed. Kimon Friar and John Malcolm Brinnin. New York: Appleton-Century-Crofts, 1951. Poems "Painted Head" (163-164), "Prelude to an Evening" (164-165), "The Equilibrists" (165-166), "Two in August" (166-167), "Judith of Bethulia" (167-168). Described in Wallace, *Williams* B61.

D128
Wordsworth: Centenary Studies Presented at Cornell and Princeton Universities. 1951. See B36.

1952

D129
An Approach to Literature. 3rd ed. By Cleanth Brooks, John Thibaut Purser, and Robert Penn Warren. New York: Appleton-Century-Crofts, 1952. Poems "Philomela" (341), "Bells for John Whiteside's Daughter" (343).

D130
Essays in Modern Literary Criticism. Ed. Ray B. West, Jr. New York: Rinehart, 1952. Essay "Criticism as Pure Speculation" (228-245).

D131
Immortal Poems of the English Language: British and American Poetry from Chaucer's Time to the Present Day. Ed. Oscar Williams. New York: Washington Square Press, 1952. Poem "Captain Carpenter" (543-545).

D132
The Literature of the South. Ed. Richmond Croom Beatty, Floyd C. Watkins, Thomas Daniel Young, and Randall Stewart. Chicago: Scott, Foresman, 1952. Poems ""Bells for John Whiteside's Daughter" (751-752), "Janet Waking" (752-753), "Dead Boy" (753-754), "Spectral Lovers" (754-755), "Necrological" (755-756), "Prelude to an Evening" (756-757); essay "Poets without Laurels" (757-766).

D133
Poetry and Experience. By Norman C. Stageberg and Wallace L. Anderson. New York: American Book Company, 1952. Poem "Dead Boy" (26).

D134
Readings for Liberal Education. Rev. ed. Vol. 2: *Introduction to Literature.* Ed. Louis G. Locke, William M. Gibson, and George Arms. New York: Rinehart, 1952. Poems "Here Lies a Lady" (232-233), "Blue Girls" (235).

D135
The Shores of Light: A Literary Chronicle of the Twenties and Thirties. By Edmund Wilson. 1952. See B38.

1953

D136
A Concise Treasury of Great Poems, English and American. Ed. Louis Untermeyer. Garden City: Permabooks-Doubleday, 1953. Poems "Lady Lost" (488-489), "Piazza Piece" (489-490).

D137
F. T. Palgrave's The Golden Treasury of the Best Songs and Lyrical Poems: A Modern Edition. Ed. Oscar Williams. New York: Mentor Book-New American Library, 1953. Poem "Captain Carpenter" (437-439).

D138
The Faber Book of Children's Verse. Ed. Janet Adam Smith. London: Faber and Faber, 1953. Poem "Survey of Literature" (34-35).

D139
Fugitive Sonnets. By Merrill Moore. Aldington, Kent: Hand and Flower Press, 1953. Reprints as its foreword (7-9) Ransom's foreword to Moore's *Noise That Time Makes* (B15).

D140
The Home Book of Modern Verse: An Extension of The Home Book of Verse, *Being a Selection from American and English Poetry of the Twentieth Century.* 2nd ed. Ed. Burton Egbert Stevenson. New York: Henry Holt, 1953. Poems "Triumph" (130), "Here Lies a Lady" (536-537).

D141
The New Partisan Reader, 1945-1953. 1953. See B39.

1954

D142
The Arts at Mid-Century. 1954. See B41.

D143
The Creative Reader: An Anthology of Fiction, Drama, and Poetry. By R. W. Stallman and R. E. Watters. New York: Ronald Press, 1954. Poems "Philomela" (686-687), "Here Lies a Lady" (713-714), "Piazza Piece" (718).

D144
The Golden Treasury of the Best Songs and Lyrical Poems in the English Language. Ed. Francis Turner Palgrave, with additional selections by C. Day Lewis. London: Collins, 1954. Poem "Bells for John Whiteside's Daughter" (493-494).

D145
The Pocket Book of American Poems: From the Colonial Period to the Present Day. Ed. Louis Untermeyer. New York: Pocket Books, 1948. Poem "Bells for John Whiteside's Daughter" (269)

D146
A Pocket Book of Modern Verse: English and American Poetry of the Last Hundred Years from Walt Whitman to Dylan Thomas. Revised ed. Ed. Oscar Williams. New York: Washington Square Press, 1954. Poems "Blue Girls" (350), "Here Lies a Lady" (350-351), "Man without Sense of Direction" (351-352), "Captain Carpenter" (353-355), "Painted Head" (355-356), "Philomela" (356-357). Described in Wright, *Eberhart* B33.

D147
The Writer and His Craft, Being the Hopwood Lectures, 1932-1952. 1954. See B40.

1955

D148
American Heritage: An Anthology and Interpretative Survey of Our Literature. Vol. 2. Ed. Leon Howard, Louis B. Wright, and Carl Bode. Boston: D. C. Heath, 1955. Essay "Introduction: A Statement of Principles" (751-755) from *I'll Take My Stand* (B17); poems "Miriam Tazewell" (755), "Captain Carpenter" (755-756), "The Tall Girls" (756), "The Equilibrists" (756-757), "Dead Boy" (757), "Two in August" (757); essay "Poets without Laurels" (758-764).

D149
The American Treasury, 1455-1955. Ed. Clifton Fadiman, assisted by Charles Van Doren. New York: Harper & Row, 1955. Poem "Here Lies a Lady" (605); excerpt from poem "Survey of Literature" (631-632).

D150
The College Omnibus. 8th ed. Ed. Leonard F. Dean. New York: Harcourt, Brace & World, 1955. Poems "Bells for John Whiteside's Daughter" (1084), "Equilibrists" (1084-1085).

D151
Exploring Poetry. By M. L. Rosenthal and A. J. M. Smith. New York: Macmillan, 1955. Poem "Janet Waking" (6).

D152
Lirici americani. By Alfredo Rizzardi. Rome: Edizioni Salvatore Sciascia, 1955. Poem "Miller's Daughter" (132-135), in English on versos, Italian on rectos, translated by Rizzardi.

D153
Modern American and Modern British Poetry. Revised, shorter ed. Ed. Louis Untermeyer in consultation with Karl Shapiro and Richard Wilbur. New York: Harcourt, Brace, 1955. Poems "Bells for John Whiteside's Daughter" (232), "Blue Girls" (232-233), "Lady Lost" (233), "Here Lies a Lady" (234), "Janet Waking" (234-235), "Spiel of the Three Mountebanks" (235-237), "Antique Harvesters" (237-238), "Piazza Piece" (238-239), "Captain Carpenter" (239-241), "Parting, without a Sequel" (241), "Vision by Sweetwater" (241), "Winter Remembered" (242), "The Equilibrists" (243-244), "Prelude to an Evening" (244-245), "Painting: A Head [sic]" (245-246).

D154
The New Pocket Anthology of American Verse from Colonial Days to the Present. Ed. Oscar Williams. New York: Pocket Library, 1955. Poems "Bells for John Whiteside's Daughter" (403), "Captain Carpenter" (403-405), "Her Eyes" (406), "Two in August" (407), "Prelude to an Evening" (408-409), "Judith of Bethulia" (409-410), "The Equilibrists" (410-412), "Address to the Scholars of New England" (412-414). (This selection also appears in the World Publishing Company edition published under the same title in 1955.) Described in Bonnell, *Aiken* B70; Wright *Eberhart* B39.

D155
Reading Modern Poetry. By Paul Engle and Warren Carrier. Glenview: Scott, Foresman, 1955. Poems "Blue Girls" (71), "Painted Head" (72-73). Described in Wright, *Eberhart* B38.

D156
A Southern Reader. By Willard Thorp. New York: Alfred A Knopf, 1955. Poems "Dead Boy" (709-710), "Judith of Bethulia" (710-711), "Two in August" (711-712).

D157
A Treasury of Great Poems, English and American, from the Foundations of the English Spirit to the Outstanding Poetry of Our Own Time, with the Lives of the Poets and Historical Settings. Ed. Louis Untermeyer. New York: Simon and Schuster, 1955. Poems "Lady Lost" (1157-1158), "Piazza Piece" (1158).

1956

D158
Anthologie de la poésie américaine des origines a nos jours. By Alain Bosquet. Paris: Librairie Stock, 1956. Poems "Parting, without a Sequel" (172), "Blue Girls" (173), "Here Lies a Lady" (173-174), in English on versos, French on rectos (each recto repeating the page number of its preceding verso).

D159
The Faber Book of Modern American Verse. Ed. W. H. Auden. London: Faber and Faber, 1956. Poems "Vision by Sweetwater" (131), "Bells for John Whiteside's Daughter" (131-132), "Antique Harvesters" (132-134), "Judith of Bethulia" (134-135), "Painted Head" (135-136). This anthology was published in the United States as *The Criterion Book of Modern American Verse* (New York: Criterion Books, 1956). Described in Bloomfield and Mendelson, *Auden* B60.

D160
The Critical Performance: An Anthology of American and British Literary Criticism of Our Century. Ed. Stanley Edgar Hyman. New York: Vintage Books, 1956. Essay "Yeats and His Symbols" (191-204).

D161
Invitation to Poetry: A Round of Poems from John Skelton to Dylan Thomas. By Lloyd Frankenberg. Garden City: Doubleday, 1956. Poem "Here Lies a Lady" (367-368).

D162
Poet's Gold: Poems for Reading Aloud. Ed. David Ross. New York: Devin-Adair, 1956. Poem "Piazza Piece" (343).

D163
Theme and Form: An Introduction to Literature. Ed. Monroe Beardsley, Robert Daniel, and Glenn Leggett. Englewood Cliffs: Prentice-Hall, 1956. Poem "Dead Boy" (559).

D164
This Way, Delight: A Book of Poetry for the Young. Ed. Herbert Read. New York: Pantheon, 1956. Poem "Janet Waking" (21).

1957

D165
Form and Value in Modern Poetry. By R. P. Blackmur. Garden City: Doubleday Anchor Books, 1957. Quotation of the first paragraph of Ransom's "Ubiquitous Moralists" used as a blurb on the back cover of this paperback.

D166
Image and Idea: Twenty Essays on Literary Themes. By Philip Rahv. Rev. ed. Norfolk: New Directions, 1957. Quotation from "The Understanding of Fiction" used as a blurb on the back paper cover.

D167
Literary Criticism in America. Ed. Albert D. Van Nostrand. American Heritage Series, 16. New York: Liberal Arts Press, 1957. Essay "Poets without Laurels" (273-287).

D168
Modern Poet's World. Poetry Book Shelf. Ed. James Reeves. London: Heinemann, 1957. Poems "Old Man Playing with Children" (77-78), "Winter Remembered" (78), "Piazza Piece" (79), "Blue Girls" (79-80), "Dead Boy" (80).

D169
Seven Centuries of Verse, English and American, from the Early English Lyrics to the Present Day. 2nd ed. Ed. A. J. M. Smith. New York: Charles Scribner's Sons, 1957. Poem "Captain Carpenter" (664-665). Ransom does not appear in the first edition (1947).

D170
The Silver Treasury of Light Verse. Ed. Oscar Williams. New York: Mentor Books-New American Library, 1957. "Survey of Literature" (98-99).

1958

D171
The Atlantic Book of British and American Poetry. Ed. Edith Sitwell. Boston: Atlantic Monthly Press-Little, Brown, 1958. Poem "Captain Carpenter" (882-884). Described in Fifoot, *Sitwell* EB45.

D172
A College Book of Modern Verse. Ed. James K. Robinson and Walter B. Rideout. Evanston: Row, Peterson, 1958. Poems "Bells for John Whiteside's Daughter" (337), "Here Lies a Lady" (338), "Captain Carpenter" (338-340), "Vision by Sweetwater" (340-341), "Piazza Piece" (341), "Antique Harvesters" (341-343), "The Equilibrists" (343-344), "Prelude to an Evening" (345), "Painted Head" (346).

D173
Criticism: The Foundations of Modern Literary Judgment. Rev. ed. Ed. Mark Schorer, Josephine Miles, and Gordon McKenzie. New York: Harcourt, Brace, 1948. Essay "A Poem Nearly Anonymous" (333-342).

D174
Exercises on the Occasion of the Dedication of the New Phi Beta Kappa Memorial Hall. 1958. See B42.

D175
The Faber Book of English Verse. Ed. John Hayward. London: Faber and Faber, 1958. Poem "Antique Harvesters" (429).

D176
Modern Verse in English, 1900-1950. Ed. David Cecil and Allen Tate. New York: Macmillan Company, 1958. Poems "Bells for John Whiteside's Daughter" (306), "Piazza Piece" (307), "Philomela" (307-308), "The Equilibrists" (308-310), "Blue Girls" (310), "Parting, without a Sequel" (310-311), "Painted Head" (311-312), "Prelude to an Evening" (312-313), "Captain Carpenter" (313-314).

D177
The Viking Book of Poetry of the English-Speaking World. Revised, Mid-Century edition. Ed. Richard Aldington. New York: Viking Press, 1958. Poem "Tom, Tom, the Piper's Son" (1186-1188).

1959

D178
American Poetry at Mid-Century. 1958 [1959]. See B43.

D179
Anthology of Magazine Verse for 1958 and Anthology of Poems from the Seventeen Previously Published Braithwaite Anthologies. Ed. William Stanley Braithwaite and Margaret Haley Carpenter. New York: Schulte Publishing, 1959. Poems "Here Lies a Lady" (346-347), "Bells for John Whitesides' Daughter" (347-348). Described in Wright, *Eberhart* B50.

D180
The Cherry-Tree: A Collection of Poems. Ed. Geoffrey Grigson. London: Phoenix House; New York: Vanguard Press, 1959. Poems "Blue Girls" (51), "Philomela" (106-107).

D181
Fugitives' Reunion: Conversations at Vanderbilt, May 3-5, 1956. 1959. See B44.

D182
Heads. A collection of 24 prints by Joseph Low. Newtown, CN: Eden Hill Press, December 1959. 24 linocuts. Epigraph by Ransom. Listed in Cave and Rae (12).

D183
How Does a Poem Mean? By John Ciardi. Part 3 of *An Introduction to Literature.* Boston: Houghton Mifflin, 1959. Poem "Blue Girls" (802).

D184
Looking Glass Book of Verse. Ed. Janet Adam Smith. New York: Looking Glass Library, 1959. Poem "Survey of Literature" (36-38).

D185
The Poem: A Critical Anthology. Ed. Josephine Miles. Englewood Cliffs: Prentice-Hall, 1959. Poem "Piazza Piece" (137).

1960

D186
American Poetry. Ed. Karl Shapiro. New York: Thomas Y. Crowell, 1960. Poems "Bells for John Whiteside's Daughter" (179), "Philomela" (179-180), "The Equilibrists" (180-181), "Janet Waking" (181-182), "Blue Girls" (182).

D187
The Arts of Reading. By Ralph Ross, John Berryman, and Allen Tate. New York: Thomas Y. Crowell, 1960. Excerpt from essay "A Poem Nearly Anonymous" (171-172); poem "The Equilibrists" (329-331). Described in Stefanik, *Berryman* A10.

D188
The Britannica Library of Great American Writing. Vol. 2. Ed. Louis Untermeyer. Chicago: Britannica Press, 1960. Poems "Here Lies a Lady" (1410), "Janet Waking" (1411), "Bells for John Whiteside's Daughter" (1411-1412), "Lady Lost" (1412-1413), "Parting, without a Sequel" (1413).

D189

A Library of Literary Criticism: Modern American Literature. Ed. Dorothy Nyren. New York: Frederick Ungar, 1960. Excerpts from "Poetry I: The Formal Analysis" (77), on Cleanth Brooks; "An Address to Kenneth Burke" (84-88); "T. S. Eliot as Dramatist" (161); "Art and Mr. Santayana" (425).

D190

Literary Types and Themes. By James E. Cronin and Joseph A. Rogers. New York: Holt, Rinehart and Winston, 1960. Poems "Bells for John Whiteside's Daughter" (571), "Dead Boy" (571-572).

D191

Literature: An Introduction. By Hollis Summers and Edgar Whan. New York: McGraw-Hill, 1960. Poems "Blue Girls" (331-332), "Two in August" (337), "Survey of Literature" (355), "Dead Boy" (385).

D192

Poeti del novecento: Italiani e stranieri. Ed. Elena Croce. Turin: Einaudi, 1960. Poems "Janet Waking" (582-585) translated by Carlo Izzo and "Dead Boy" (586-587) and "The Equilibrists" (588-593) translated by Lea Oppenheim. In English on versos, Italian on rectos.

D193

Poetry for Pleasure: The Hallmark Book of Poetry. Selected and arranged by the editors of Hallmark Cards, Inc. Garden City: Doubleday, 1960. Poem "Her Eyes" (111-112).

D194

Understanding Poetry. 3rd ed. By Cleanth Brooks and Robert Penn Warren. New York: Holt, Rinehart and Winston, 1960. Poems "Bells for John Whiteside's Daughter" (236), "Winter Remembered" (260).

D195

The Written Word: Forms of Writing. By Robert W. Daniel and Glenn Leggett. Englewood Cliffs: Prentice-Hall, 1960. Poems "Antique Harvesters" (664-665), "Winter Remembered" (671-672).

1961

D196

American Literature: A College Survey. By Clarence A. Brown and John T. Flanagan. New York: McGraw-Hill, 1961. Poems "Bells for John Whiteside's Daughter" (703), "Blackberry Winter" (703), "Captain Carpenter" (703-704).

D197

American Literature: Readings and Critiques. 1961. See B45.

D198

The Complete Reader. Ed. Richard S. Beal and Jacob Korg. Englewood Cliffs: Prentice-Hall, 1961. Poem "Blue Girls" (605).

D199

The Continuity of American Poetry. By Roy Harvey Pearce. Princeton: Princeton UP, 1961. Statement used as a blurb on the back cover of paperbound copies (seen on second Princeton paperback printing, 1967).

D200

Conversations on the Craft of Poetry. 1961. See B47.

D201

Discovering Modern Poetry. By Elizabeth Drew and George O'Connor. New York: Holt, Rinehart and Winston, 1961. Poems "Janet Waking" (54-55), "Captain Carpenter" (82-83), "The Equilibrists" (253-254), "Winter Remembered" (254-255), "Bells for John Whiteside's Daughter" (255-256).

D202

Discussions of Poetry: Rhythm and Sound. 1961. See B46.

D203

F. T. Palgrave's The Golden Treasury of the Best Songs and Lyrical Poems. Centennial edition. Ed. Oscar Williams. New York: Mentor Book-New American Library, 1961. Poem "Captain Carpenter" (437-439).

D204
Literature for Interpretation. By Wallace A. Bacon and Robert S. Breen. New York: Holt, Rinehart and Winston, 1961. Poems "Blue Girls" (246-247), "Bells for John Whiteside's Daughter" (247).

D205
Milton's "Lycidas": The Tradition and the Poem. Ed. C. A. Patrides. New York: Holt, Rinehart and Winston, 1961. Essay "A Poem Nearly Anonymous" (64-81).

D206
Modern Poetry. 2nd ed. Ed. Maynard Mack, Leonard Dean, and William Frost. Vol. 7 of *English Masterpieces: An Anthology of Imaginative Literature from Chaucer to T. S. Eliot.* Englewood Cliffs: Prentice-Hall, 1961. Poems "Bells for John Whitesides' Daughter" (319), "The Equilibrists" (320-321).

D207
New World Writing 19. 1961. See B48.

D208
The Ways of the Poem. Ed. Josephine Miles. Englewood Cliffs: Prentice-Hall, 1961. Poem "Piazza Piece" (113).

1962

D209
American Literature Survey. Vol. 4: *The Twentieth Century.* Ed. Milton R. Stern and Seymour L. Gross. New York: Viking Press, 1962. Poems "Piazza Piece" (507), "Bells for John Whiteside's Daughter" (508), "Antique Harvesters" (508-510), "The Equilibrists" (510-511).

D210
Chief Modern Poets of England and America. 4th ed. Ed. Gerald DeWitt Sanders, John Herbert Nelson, and M. L. Rosenthal, 1962. [Vol. 2.] New York: Macmillan, 1962. Poems "Bells for John Whitesides' Daughter" (256), "Here Lies a Lady" (256-257), "Miss Euphemia" (257-258), "Philomela" (258-259), "Emily Hardcastle, Spinster" (259), "Inland City" (259-260), "Blue Girls" (260),

"Somewhere Is Such a Kingdom" (260-261), "The Equilibrists" (261-263), "Dead Boy" (263-264), "Janet Waking" (264), "Vision by Sweetwater" (265).

D211
The Creative Reader: An Anthology of Fiction, Drama, Poetry. 2nd ed. By R. W. Stallman and R. E. Watters. New York: Ronald Press, 1962. Poems "Here Lies a Lady" (688-689), "Philomela" (704-705), "Piazza Piece" (775).

D212
The Critical Reader: Essays, Stories, Poems. Rev. ed. Ed. Roy Lamson et al. New York: W. W. Norton, 1962. Poem "Here Lies a Lady" (687-688).

D213
Idea and Image: Reading for College English. By Hans P. Guth. Belmont, CA: Wadsworth, 1962. Poems "Bells for John Whiteside's Daughter" (2: 735), "The Equilibrists" (2: 735-737).

D214
Literary Opinion in America: Illustrating the Status, Methods, and Problems of Criticism in the United States in the Twentieth Century. 2 vols. 3rd ed. Ed. Morton Dauwen Zabel. New York: Harper Torch Books-Harper & Row, 1962. Essay "Criticism as Pure Speculation" (1: 639-654).

D215
The Mentor Book of Major American Poets from Edward Taylor and Walt Whitman to Hart Crane and W. H. Auden. Ed. Oscar Williams and Edwin Honig. New York: Mentor Book-New American Library, 1962. Poems "Winter Remembered 388), "Necrological" (388-389), "Bells for John Whiteside's Daughter" (389-390), "Dead Boy" (390), "Good Ships" (391), "Emily Hardcastle, Spinster" (391), "Here Lies a Lady" (391-392), "Conrad in Twilight" (392), "Armageddon" (393-395), "Judith of Bethulia" (395), "Blue Girls" (396), "Old Man Playing with Children" (397), "Captain Carpenter" (397-399), "Old Mansion" (399-400), "Piazza Piece" (400), "Vision by Sweetwater" (401), "Her Eyes" (401-402), "Parting, without a Sequel" (402), "Janet Waking" (403), "Two in August" (403-404), "Our Two Worthies" (404-406), "Man without Sense of Direction" (406-407), "Survey of Literature" (407-408),

"The Equilibrists" (408-410), "Painted Head" (410), "Address to the Scholars of New England" (411-413).

D216

Modern American Poetry. Ed. Louis Untermeyer. New and enlarged [i.e., 8th] ed. New York: Harcourt, Brace & World, 1962. Poems "Bells for John Whiteside's Daughter" (408), "Lady Lost" (409), "Blue Girls" (409), "Here Lies a Lady" (410), "Janet Waking" (410-411), "Spiel of the Three Mountebanks" (411-412), "First Travels of Max" (412-413), "Antique Harvesters" (413-414), "Piazza Piece" (414-415), "Captain Carpenter" (415-416), "Old Man Pondered" (416-417), "Parting, without a Sequel" (417), "Prelude to an Evening" (418), "Painting: A Head" (418). Described in Wright, *Eberhart* B63.

D217

The Modern Critical Spectrum. Ed. Gerald Jay Goldberg and Nancy Marmer Goldberg. New York: Prentice-Hall, 1962. Essay "On Shakespeare's Language" (48-57).

D218

A Poetry Sampler. Ed. Donald Hall. New York: Franklin Watts, 1962. Poems "Lady Lost" (69-70), "Blue Girls" (183).

D219

Poetry II. Ed. R. Stanley Peterson. New York: Macmillan, 1962. Poem "Bells for John Whiteside's Daughter" (129).

D220

Poet's Choice. 1962. See B49.

D221

Theme and Form: An Introduction to Literature. Ed. Monroe Beardsley, Robert Daniel, and Glenn Leggett. Englewood Cliffs: Prentice-Hall, 1962. Poem "Dead Boy" (526).

1963

D222
Anthology of Modern Poetry. Ed. John Wain. London: Hutchinson Educational, 1963. Poem "Old Man Playing with Children" (129-130).

D223
Antologia de la poesia norteamericana. Trans. José Coronel Urtecho and Ernesto Cardenal. Madrid: Aguilar, 1963. Poem "Piazza Piece" (183) translated into Spanish.

D224
The Concise Encyclopedia of English and American Poets and Poetry. 1963. See B50.

D225
Dylan Thomas's Choice: An Anthology of Verse Spoken by Dylan Thomas. Ed. Ralph Maud and Aneirin Talfan Davies. New York: New Directions, 1963. Poems "Judith of Bethulia" (139-140), "Parting, without a Sequel" (141), "Bells for John Whiteside's Daughter" (142).

D226
Emily Dickinson: A Collection of Critical Essays. 1963. See B51.

D227
An Introduction to Literature. 2nd ed. By Sylvan Barnet, Morton Berman, and William Burto. Boston: Little Brown, 1963. Poems "Piazza Piece" (381), "Bells for John Whiteside's Daughter" (426).

D228
An Introduction to Literature: Poems. Ed. Lynn Altenbernd and Leslie L. Lewis. New York: Macmillan, 1963. Poems "Bells for John Whiteside's Daughter" (463), "Prelude to an Evening" (463).

D229
Modern Criticism: Theory and Practice. Ed. Walter Sutton and Richard Foster. New York: Odyssey Press, 1963. Essay "Poetry: A Note on [sic] Ontology" (221-233).

D230
The Modern Poets: An American-British Anthology. Ed. John Malcolm Brinnin and Bill Read. New York: McGraw-Hill, 1963. Poems "Survey of Literature" (274-275), "Dead Boy" (275), "Captain Carpenter" (276-278).

D231
Poems for Pleasure. Ed. Herman M. Ward. New York: Hill and Wang, 1963. Poem "Janet Waking" (113-114).

D232
Poesia americana del '900. Ed. Carlo Izzo. Collana Fenice 4. Parma: Guanda, 1963. Poems "Piazza Piece" (220-221), "Janet Waking" (222-225), "Vision by Sweetwater" (226-227), "Winter Remembered" (228-229), "Bells for John Whiteside's Daughter" (230-231), in English on versos, Italian on rectos; translated by Izzo.

D233
Poetry: A Closer Look, Programmed Instruction with Selected Poems. By James M. Reid, John Ciardi, and Laurence Perrine. New York: Harcourt, Brace & World, 1963. Poem "Bells for John Whiteside's Daughter" (86).

D234
Poetry in English. Ed. Warren Taylor and Donald Hall. New York: Macmillan, 1963. Poems "Bells for John Whiteside's Daughter" (600), "Captain Carpenter" (600-602), "Janet Waking" (602-603), "Painted Head" (603-604).

D235
Sound and Sense: An Introduction to Poetry. 2nd ed. By Laurence Perrine. New York: Harcourt, Brace, 1963. Poems "Parting, without a Sequel" (157), "Piazza Piece" (292).

D236
Twentieth-Century American Poetry. Ed. Conrad Aiken. New York: Modern Library, 1963. Poems "Bells for John Whiteside's Daughter" (213), "Lady Lost" (213-214), "Blue Girls" (214-215), "Here Lies a Lady" (215), "Captain Carpenter" (215-217), "Husband Betrayed" (217-218), "Little Boy Blue" (218-219). Described in Bonnell, *Aiken* B77.

1964

D237
Adventures in Poetry. Ed. Edwin C. Custer. New York: Harcourt Brace and World, 1964. Poems "Piazza Piece" (520), "Janet Waking" (520-521).

D238
American Lyric Poems: From Colonial Times to the Present. Ed. Elder Olson. New York: Appleton-Century-Crofts, 1964. Poems "Bells for John Whiteside's Daughter" (110), "Janet Waking" (110-111).

D239
An Approach to Literature. 4th ed. By Cleanth Brooks, John Thibaut Purser, and Robert Penn Warren. New York: Appleton-Century-Crofts, 1964. Poems "Philomela" (338-339), "Bells for John Whiteside's Daughter" (341).

D240
The Contemporary Poet as Artist and Critic: Eight Symposia. Ed. Anthony Ostroff. Boston: Little Brown and Company, 1964. Essay "On Theodore Roethke's 'In a Dark Time'" (26-35); poem "Master's in the Garden Again" (112-113); and essay "Now the Grateful Author" (134-140) responding to criticism of poem by Léonie Adams, Muriel Rukeyser, and W. D. Snodgrass. Described in Wright, *Eberhart* B73. When the poem earlier appeared as part of Ostroff's "symposium" in *New World Writing* 22 (B54), line 4 of section 3 had the reading 'Who hurt'; here the reading is 'Who harmed'.

D241
Introducing Poetry: An Anthology. Ed. Alice C. Coleman and John R. Theobald. New York: Holt, Rinehart and Winston, 1964. Poem "Janet Waking" (282-283).

D242
John Crowe Ransom, Gentleman, Teacher, Poet, Editor, Founder of The Kenyon Review: *A Tribute from the Community of Letters.* 1964. See B53.

D243
National Poetry Festival. 1964. See B52.

D244
A New Directions Reader. Ed. Hayden Carruth and J. Laughlin. Norfolk: New Directions, 1964. "Ontological Unity in Poetry" (28-31), which is an excerpt from "Wanted: An Ontological Critic" in *The New Criticism* (A10).

D245
New World Writing 22. 1964. See B54.

D246
Reading Literature. Part 4: *Reading Poetry.* By Joseph Satin. Boston: Houghton Mifflin, 1964. Poems "Survey of Literature" (1110-1111), "Miriam Tazewell" (1303-1304), "Here Lies a Lady" (1304), "Piazza Piece" (1304-1305).

D247
A Second Book of Poetry. By R. Stanley Peterson and Brother Francis Emery. New York: Macmillan, 1964. Poem "Bells for John Whiteside's Daughter" (137).

D248
The Variety of Poetry: An Anthology. Ed. Edward A. Bloom, Charles H. Philbrick, and Elmer M. Blistein. New York: Odyssey Press, 1964. Poems "Bells for John Whiteside's Daughter" (130), "Here Lies a Lady" (183).

1965

D249
American Poetry. By Gay Wilson Allen, Walter B. Rideout, and James K. Robinson. New York: Harper & Row, 1965. Poems "Winter Remembered" (820-821), "Bells for John Whiteside's Daughter" (821), "Captain Carpenter" (822-824), "Vision by Sweetwater" (824), "Piazza Piece" (824-825), "Antique Harvesters" (825-826), "The Equilibrists" (826-828), "Painted Head" (828-829), "Master's in the Garden Again" (829-831), "Prelude to an Evening" (831-832).

D250
Approaches to the Poem: Modern Essays in the Analysis and Interpretation of Poetry. 1965. See B58.

D251
The Case for Poetry: A Critical Anthology. 2nd ed. Ed. Frederick L. Gwynn, Ralph W. Condee, and Arthur O. Lewis, Jr. Englewood Cliffs: Prentice-Hall, 1965. Poems "Winter Remembered" (234), "Bells for John Whitesides' Daughter" (235), "The Equilibrists" (236-237).

D252
The Cassell Book of English Poetry. Ed. James Reeves. New York: Harper & Row, 1965. Poems "Piazza Piece" (poem 984), "Winter Remembered" (poem 985).

D253
The Faber Book of Modern Verse. 3rd ed. Ed. Michael Roberts, with a supplement of poems chosen by Donald Hall. London: Faber and Faber, 1965. Poems "Vision by Sweetwater" (168), "Captain Carpenter" (168-170), "Dead Boy" (170-171), "Judith of Bethulia" (171-172).

D254
The Fugitive Poets: Modern Southern Poetry in Perspective. 1965. See B56.

D255
Fifty Years: Being a Retrospective Collection of Novels, Novellas, Tales, Drama, Poetry, and Reportage and Essays (Whether Literary, Musical, Contemplative, Historical, Biographical, Argumentative, or Gastronomical), All Drawn from Volumes Issued during the Last Half-Century by Alfred and Blanche Knopf over This Sign and Device [Borzoi device]. Ed. Clifton Fadiman. New York: Alfred A Knopf, 1965. Poems "Here Lies a Lady" (1043), "Captain Carpenter" (1044-1045).

D256
A Grammar of Literary Criticism: Essays in Definition of Vocabulary, Concepts, and Aims. By Lawrence Sargent Hall. New York: Macmillan, 1965. Essays "Criticism as Pure Speculation" (514-533), "A Poem Nearly Anonymous" (586-598).

D257
Introduction to the Poem. By Robert W. Boynton and Maynard Mack. New York: Hayden Book Co., 1965. Poems "Bells for John Whiteside's Daughter" (17-18), "Piazza Piece" (30).

D258
Literature: Form and Function. By P. Albert Duhamel and Richard E. Hughes. Englewood Cliffs: Prentice-Hall, 1965. Essay "A Poem Nearly Anonymous" (74-83).

D259
Modern Poetics. Ed. James Scully. New York: McGraw-Hill, 1965. Essays "Poetry: A Note in Ontology" (83-102).

D260
101 Poemas: Antología bilingüe de la poesia norteamericana moderna. Ed. Salvador Novo. Mexico, D.F.: Editorial Letras, 1965. Poem "Blue Girls" (314-317), in English on versos, Spanish on rectos, translated by Nuria Parés.

D261
Poems and Poets. 1965. See B55.

D262
Poems: Wadsworth Handbook and Anthology. Ed. C. F. Main and Peter J. Seng. Belmont, CA: Wadsworth, 1965. Poem "Captain Carpenter" (252-253).

D263
Portrait of a Publisher, 1915-1965. Vol. 2: *Alfred A. Knopf and the Borzoi Imprint: Recollections and Appreciations.* Typophile Chap Book 43. New York: The Typophiles, 1965. Prose appreciation "The Poets Go Along" (228-231).

D264
R. P. Blackmur: Language as Gesture and Essays by Kenneth Burke, Marianne Moore, Conrad Aiken, John Crowe Ransom, and Others. 1965. See B57.

D265
Réflexions sur la poésie américaine. By Louise Bogan. Collection Vent d'Ouest 8, a translation of Bogan's *Achievement in American Poetry, 1900-1950* (D119). Paris: Seghers, 1965. Poem "Piazza Piece" (168-169), in English on verso and French on recto, translated by Laurette Véza.

D266
The Sonnet: A Comprehensive Anthology of British and American Sonnets from the Renaissance to the Present. Ed. Robert M. Bender and Charles L. Squier. New York: Washington Square Press, 1965. Poems "The Tall Girl" (431), "Piazza Piece" (432).

D267
Sprints and Distances: Sports in Poetry and the Poetry in Sport. Ed. Lillian Morrison. New York: Thomas Y. Crowell, 1965. Poem "The Swimmer" (98-99).

D268
Studying Poetry: A Critical Anthology. By Karl Kroeber and John O. Lyons. New York: Harper & Row, 1965. Poems "Captain Carpenter" (144-146) and "Bells for John Whiteside's Daughter" (192).

D269
Trio: A Book of Stories, Plays, and Poems. 2nd ed. Ed. Harold P. Simonson. New York: Harper & Row, 1965. Poems "Bells for John Whiteside's Daughter" (627), "Two Sonnets: I. Yea, II. Nay" (628-629), "Nocturne" (629).

D270
Twentieth Century American Writing. Ed. William T. Stafford. New York: Odyssey Press, 1965. Poems "Bells for John Whiteside's Daughter" (615), "Here Lies a Lady" (616), "Blue Girls" (616).

1966

D271
Beginning with Poems: An Anthology. Ed. Rueben Brower, Anne Ferry, and David Kalstone. New York: W. W. Norton, 1966. Poems "Here Lies a Lady" (362), "Piazza Piece" (363).

D272
The Cry of Rachel: An Anthology of Elegies on Children. Ed. Sister Mary Immaculate. New York: Random House, 1966. Poems "Dead Boy" (88) and "Bells for John Whiteside's Daughter" (109).

D273
The Distinctive Voice: Twentieth-Century American Poetry. Ed. William J. Martz. Glenview: Scott, Foresman, 1966. Poems "Winter Remembered" (113), "Captain Carpenter" (114-115), "Old Mansion" (115-116), "Hilda" (116-117).

D274
English Meter. Bobbs-Merrill Reprint Series in Language and Linguistics, 97. Indianapolis: Bobbs-Merrill, 1966. Essay "The Strange Music of English Verse." Not seen.

D275
Észak-Amerikai költök Antológiája. Budapest: Kozmosz Könyvek, 1966. Poems "Bells for John Whiteside's Daughter" (260-261), translated into Hungarian by Végh György, and "Her Eyes" (261-262), translated by Weöres Sándor.

D276
Faulkner: A Collection of Critical Essays. 1966. See B62.

D277
The Force of a Few Words: An Introduction to Poetry. By Jacob Korg. New York: Holt, Rinehart and Winston, 1966. Poem "Parting, without a Sequel" (344-345).

D278
The Form of Poetry. By Thomas R. Arp. New York: Macmillan, 1966. Poems "Here Lies a Lady" (268), "Janet Waking" (268-269).

D279
An Introduction to Literature. Ed. Ralph H. Singleton and Stanton Millet. Cleveland: World Publishing, 1966. Poem "Janet Waking" (253).

D280
An Introduction to Poetry. By X. J. Kennedy. Boston: Little Brown, 1966. Poems "Janet Waking" (237), "Bells for John Whiteside's Daughter" (334).

D281
Literature: Introduction to Short Stories, Drama, and Poetry. 4th ed. By Walter Blair, John Gerber, and Eugene Garber. Glenview: Scott, Foresman, 1966. Poem "Bells for John Whiteside's Daughter" (806-807).

D282
Literature for Understanding. Ed. B. Bernard Cohen. Chicago: Scott, Foresman, 1966. Poem "The Equilibrist" (102-103).

D283
Master Poems of the English Language: Over One Hundred Poems Together with Introductions by Leading Poets and Critics of the English-Speaking World. 1966. See B59.

D284
Modern Poets: British and American. Dayton: George A. Pflaum, 1966. Poem "Dead Boy" (67).

D285
100 American Poems of the Twentieth Century. Ed. Laurence Perrine and James M. Reid. New York: Harcourt Brace, 1966. Poems "The Equilibrists" (135-136), "Blue Girls" (137-136), "Parting, without a Sequel" (139).

D286
The Province of Poetry. Ed. Edwin B. Benjamin. New York: American Book Co., 1966. Poem "Bells for John Whiteside's Daughter" (105-106).

D287
The Silver Swan: Poems of Romance and Mystery. Ed. Horace Gregory and Marya Zaturenska. New York: Holt, Rinehart and Winston, 1966. Poem "Piazza Piece" (122).

D288
A Symposium on Formalist Criticism. 1966. See B61.

D289
T. S. Eliot, the Man and His Work: A Critical Evaluation by Twenty-Six Distinguished Writers. 1966. See B60.

1967

D290
Art and Craft in Poetry. By James T. Lape and Elizabeth Baymore Lape. Boston: Ginn, 1967. Poems "Judith of Bethulia" (451-462), "Captain Carpenter" (513-514).

D291
The Discovery of Poetry. By Thomas E. Sanders. Glenview: Scott, Foresman, 1967. Poem "Piazza Piece" (213).

D292
Essays on the Language of Literature. Ed. Seymour Chatman and Samuel R. Levin. Boston: Houghton Mifflin, 1967. Excerpt from essay "Wanted: An Ontological Critic" (269-282).

D293
The Experience of Literature: A Reader with Commentaries. By Lionel Trilling. New York: Holt, Rinehart and Winston, 1967. Poems "Here Lies a Lady" (1258-1259), "Bells for John Whiteside's Daughter" (1259), "Blue Girls" (1259).

D294
Literature for Writing: An Anthology of Major British and American Authors. 2nd ed. Ed. Martin Steinmann and Gerald Willen. Belmont, CA: Wadsworth, 1967. Poems "Bells for John Whiteside's Daughter" (673), "Her Eyes" (673), "The Equilibrists" (673-674).

D295
New Choices. Ed. John Colmer and Dorothy Colmer. Melbourne: F. W. Cheshire, 1967. Poem "Blue Girls" (144).

D296
The Pattern of Poetry: The Poetry Society Verse-Speaking Anthology. Ed. William Kean Seymour and John Smith. New York: Franklin Watts, 1967. Poem "Janet Waking" (66).

D297
Poems to Read Aloud. Rev. ed. Ed. Edward Hodnett. New York: W. W. Norton, 1967. Poems "Here Lies a Lady" (273-274), "Blackberry Winter" (274).

D298
Poems to Remember. Ed. Dorothy Petitt. New York: Macmillan, 1967. Poem "Blue Girls" (40).

D299
Randall Jarrell, 1914-1965. 1967. See B64.

D300
The Range of Literature: An Introduction to Prose and Verse. 2nd ed. Ed. Elisabeth W. Schneider, Albert L. Walker, and Herbert E. Childs. New York: American Book Company, 1967. Poems "Bells for John Whiteside's Daughter" (311-312), "Blue Girls" (326).

D301
12 Poets. Alternate ed. Ed. Glenn Leggett and Henry-York Steiner. New York: Holt, Rinehart and Winston, 1967. Poems "Winter Remembered" (219), "Miriam Tazewell" (219-220), "Dead Boy" (220-221), "Spectral Lovers" (221-222), "Necrological" (222-223), "Bells for John Whiteside's Daughter" (223-224), "Here Lies a Lady" (224), "Judith of Bethulia" (224-226), "Blue Girls" (226), "Captain Carpenter" (226-228), "Piazza Piece" (228-229), "Parting, without a Sequel" (229), "Janet Waking" (230), "Little Boy Blue" (231), "Two in August" (231-232), "Survey of Literature" (232-233), "The Equilibrists" (233-235).

D302
Years of Protest: A Collection of American Writing of the 1930's. 1967. See B63.

1968

D303
The American Literary Anthology 1: The First Annual Collection of the Best from the Literary Magazines. New York: Farrar, Straus & Giroux, 1968. Essay "Gerontion" (288-310).

D304
American Literature. Ed. Mark Schorer et al. Boston: Houghton Mifflin, 1968. Poems "Blue Girls" (688), "Here Lies a Lady" (688-689).

D305
Amerikanske stemmer. Ed. and trans. Jens Nyholm. Copenhagen: Arne-Frost Hansens, 1968. Poems "Blue Girls" (105), and "Here Lies a Lady" (106), translated into Danish.

D306
A Collection of Critical Essays on The Waste Land. Ed. Jay Martin. Englewood Cliffs: Prentice-Hall, 1968. Excerpt from essay "Gerontion" (15).

D307
Essays of Four Decades. By Allen Tate. Chicago: Swallow Press, 1968. Blurb on front dust-jacket flap.

D308
An Introduction to Literature. By Mary Rohrberger, Samuel H. Woods, Jr., and Bernard F. DuKore. New York: Random House, 1968. Poems "Here Lies a Lady" (537-538), "Philomela" (538) accompanied by Woods's explication, "Captain Carpenter" (542-543), "Piazza Piece" (543-544), "Janet Waking" (544-545), "Survey of Literature" (545-546), "Of Margaret" (546).

D309
The Literature of the South. Rev. ed. By Thomas Daniel Young, Floyd C. Watkins, and Richard Croom Beatty. Glenview: Scott, Foresman, 1968. Poems "Bells for John Whiteside's Daughter" (711-712), "Janet Waking" (712-713), "Spectral Lovers" (714-715), "Necrological" (715-716), "Blue Girls" (716), "Here Lies a Lady" (716-717), "Captain Carpenter" (717-719), "Prelude to an Evening" (719); essay "Poets without Laurels" (720-729).

D310
Patterns in Poetry. By Harry M. Brown and John Milstead. Glenview: Scott, Foresman, 1968. Poems "Janet Waking" (30-31), "Parting, without a Sequel" (140).

D311
Perspectives on Poetry. Ed. James L. Calderwood and Harold E. Toliver. New York: Oxford University Press, 1968. Essays "Poetry: A Note on [sic] Ontology" (34-50), "The Strange Music of English Verse" (184-190).

D312
The Poem: An Anthology. Ed. Stanley B. Greenfield and A. Kingsley Weatherhead. New York: Appleton-Century-Crofts, 1968. Poems "Winter Remembered" (343), "Bells for John Whiteside's Daughter" (343-344).

D313
Poems of Protest Old and New: A Selection of Poetry. Ed. Arnold Kenseth. New York: Macmillan, 1968. Poem "Bells for John Whiteside's Daughter" (31).

D314
Poetry: An Introductory Anthology. Ed. Hazard Adams. Boston: Little, Brown, 1968. Poems "Bells for John Whiteside's Daughter" (295), "Captain Carpenter" (295-297).

D315
Poetry: Premeditated Art. By Judson Jerome. Boston: Houghton Mifflin, 1968. Poems "Janet Waking" (193-194), "The Equilibrist" (447-448), "Blue Girls" (448-449).

D316
Reading Modern Poetry. [Rev. ed.] By Paul Engle and Warren Carrier. Glenview: Scott, Foresman, 1968. Poems "Bells for John Whitesides' Daughter" (41), "Blue Girls" (44), "Painted Head" (45-46), "The Equilibrists" (46-48). The first poem is accompanied by Robert Penn Warren's analysis that appeared in his "Pure and Impure Poetry," *Kenyon Review* 5 (Spring 1943): 228-254.

D317
Reading Poetry. 2nd ed. Ed. Fred B. Millet, Arthur W. Hoffman, and David R. Clark. New York: Harper & Row, 1968. Poems "Here Lies a Lady of Beauty and High Degree [sic]" (236-237), "The Tall Girl" (416), "Winter Remembered" (416-417), "Bells for John Whiteside's Daughter" (417-418).

D318
Wonders and Surprises: A Collection of Poems. Ed. Phyllis McGinley. Philadelphia: J. B. Lippincott, 1968. Poem "Blue Girls" (75).

1969

D319
Agrarianism in American Literature. Ed. M. Thomas Inge. New York: Odyssey Press, 1969. Essay "Twelve Southerners: A Statement of Principles" (183-189); poems "Antique Harvesters" (316-317), "Captain Carpenter" (318-320).

D320
The Critical Temper: A Survey of Modern Criticism on English and American Literature from the Beginnings to the Twentieth Century. Ed. Martin Tucker. 3 vols. New York: Frederick Ungar, 1969. Excerpts from essays "A Poem Nearly Anonymous" (2: 132) and "William Wordsworth: Notes toward and Understanding of Poetry" (2: 514-515), and excerpt from the introduction to *Selected Poems of Thomas Hardy* (3: 110).

D321
Formalismo Americano. By John Crowe Ransom, Elder Olson, Eliseo Vivas, and Kenneth Burke. Intro. Mark Schorer. Bari: De Donato, 1969. A translation into Italian, by Valerio Fantinel, of *A Symposium on Formalist Criticism* (B61), including Ransom's "Theory of Poetic Form" (13-29).

D322
Marianne Moore: A Collection of Critical Essays. Ed. Charles Tomlinson. Englewood Cliffs: Prentice-Hall, 1969. Essay "On Being Modern with Distinction" (101-106).

D323
The Many Worlds of Poetry. Ed. Jacob Drachler and Virginia R. Terris. New York: Knopf, 1969. Poems "Janet Waking" (50), "Her Eyes" (104), "Captain Carpenter" (183-184), "Survey of Literature" (229).

D324
Philosophy and Literature: Truth, Beauty, Goodness, Commitment. Ed. Cameron Thompson. New York: Harcourt, Brace, 1969. Poems "Piazza Piece" (215).

D325
Poetry: Meaning and Form. Ed. Joseph Schwartz and Robert C. Roby. New York: McGraw Hill, 1969. Poems "Bells for John Whiteside's Daughter" (28), "Captain Carpenter" (81-82), "Piazza Piece" (171).

D326
The Survival Years: A Collection of American Writings of the 1940's. Ed. Jack Salzman. New York: Pegasus, 1969. Excerpt from essay "Criticism as Pure Speculation" (235-241).

D327
To Play Man Number One. Ed. Sara Hannum and John Terry Chase. New York: Atheneum, 1969. Poem "Good Ships" (53-54).

1970

D328
A Book of Modern American Poetry. By Jane McDermott and Thomas V. Lowery. New York: Harcourt Brace Jovanovich, 1970. Poems "Bells for John Whiteside's Daughter" (121-122), "Janet Waking" (123-124), "Piazza Piece" (125).

D329
A Casebook on "Gerontion." Ed. E. San Juan, Jr. The Merrill Literary Casebook Series. Columbus, OH: Charles E. Merrill Publishing, 1970. Essay "Gerontion" (90-109).

D330
Chief Modern Poets of Britain and America. 5th ed. Vol. 2: *Poets of America.* Ed. Gerald DeWitt Sanders, John Herbert Nelson, and M. L. Rosenthal. New York: Macmillan, 1970. Poems "Bells for John Whitesides' Daughter" (247), "Here Lies a Lady" (247-248), "Miss Euphemia" (248-249), "Philomela" (249-250), "Emily Hardcastle, Spinster" (250), "Inland City" (250-251), "Blue Girls" (251), "Somewhere Is Such a Kingdom" (251-252), "The

Equilibrists" (252-254), "Dead Boy" (254-255), "Janet Waking" (255), "Vision by Sweetwater" (256).

D331
Discovery and Response: Drama, Fiction, and Poetry. Ed. Martha Banta and Joseph N. Slatterwhite. New York: Macmillan, 1970. Poem "Bells for John Whiteside's Daughter" (348).

D332
Mandala: Literature for Critical Analysis. Ed. Wilfred L. Guerin et al. New York: Harper & Row, 1970. Poems "Blue Girls" (302-303), "Bells for John Whiteside's Daughter" (303), "The Equilibrists" (304-305).

D333
The Illustrated Treasury of Poetry for Children. Ed. David Ross. New York: Grosset & Dunlap, 1970. Poem "Blue Girls" (311).

D334
Moderne englische und amerikanische Literaturkritik. Ed. Willi Erzgräber. Darmstadt: Wissenschaftliche Buchgesellschaft, 1970. Section 4 through the end of the essay (in English only) "Wanted: An Ontological Critic" (65-90). See also A19.

D335
The Norton Anthology of Poetry. Ed. Arthur M. Eastman et al. New York: W. W. Norton, 1970. Poems "Bells for John Whiteside's Daughter" (1019), "Emily Hardcastle, Spinster" (1020), "Vaunting Oak" (1020-1021), "Dead Boy" (1021), "Persistent Explorer" (1021-1022), "Antique Harvesters" (1022-1023), Man without Sense of Direction" (1023-1024), "The Equilibrists" (1024-1025), "Of Margaret" (1025-1026).

D336
The Norton Anthology of Poetry. Shorter ed. Ed. Arthur M. Eastman et al. New York: W. W. Norton, 1970. Poems "Bells for John Whiteside's Daughter" (511), "Dead Boy" (511-512).

D337
The Premier Book of Major Poets: An Anthology. Ed. Anita Dore. New York: Fawcett Premier, 1970. Poem "Janet Waking" (234-235).

D338
Readings in American Criticism. Ed. Thomas Elliott Berry. N.p.: Odyssey Press, 1970. Excerpt from essay "Criticism as Pure Speculation" (232-241).

D339
Sounds and Silences: Poetry for Now. Ed. Richard Peck. New York: Dell, 1970. Poems "Janet Waking" (32), "Bells for John Whiteside's Daughter" (159).

D340
A Third Treasury of the Familiar. Ed. Ralph L. Woods. New York: Macmillan, 1970. Poems "Blue Girls" (255), "Bells for John Whiteside's Daughter" (560), "Piazza Piece" (602).

D341
The Total Experience of Poetry. Ed. Ruth Thompson and Marvin Thompson. New York: Random House, 1970. Poems "Bells for John Whiteside's Daughter" (193-194), "Blue Girls" (194), "Piazza Piece" (194-195).

D342
Toward Composition: Readings for Freshman English. Ed. Members of the Freshman English Staff, University of Minnesota. Dubuque: Kendall/Hunt, 1970. Poem "Blue Girls" (529).

D343
Twentieth-Century Poetry: American and British (1900-1970), an American-British Anthology. Ed. John Malcolm Brinnin and Bill Read. New York: McGraw-Hill, 1970. (Also published in a textbook edition in the same year under the title *The Modern Poets*, 2nd ed.) Poems "Survey of Literature" (335-336), "Dead Boy" (336-337), "Captain Carpenter" (337-339).

D344
The Voice That Is Great within Us: American Poetry of the Twentieth Century. Ed. Hayden Carruth. New York: Bantam Books, 1970. Poems "Winter Remembered" (147-148), "Bells for John Whiteside's Daughter" (148), "Vaunting Oak" (148-150), "Here Lies a Lady" (150), "Blue Girls" (150-151), "Survey of Literature" (151-152).

D345
Voices of Poetry. Ed. Allen Kirschner. New York: Dell-Laurel, 1970. Poems "Blue Girls" (37), "Bells for John Whiteside's Daughter" (111).

1971

D346
Hero's Way: Contemporary Poems in the Mythic Tradition. Ed. John Alexander Allen. Englewood Cliffs: Prentice-Hall, 1971. Poem "Captain Carpenter" (18-20).

D347
An Introduction to Poetry. By X. J. Kennedy. 2nd ed. Boston: Little Brown, 1971. Poems "Janet Waking" (292-293), "Bells for John Whiteside's Daughter" (420-421).

D348
Invitation to Poetry. By Janet M. Cotter. Cambridge, MA: Winthrop, 1971. Poems "Piazza Piece" (243), "Bells for John Whiteside's Daughter" (312), "Janet Waking" (314-315).

D349
Literature in America: The Modern Age. Ed. Charles Kaplan. New York: Free Press, 1971. Poem "Survey of Literature" (565-566).

D350
Muses of Fire: Approaches to Poetry. By H. Edward Richardson and Fred B. Shroyer. New York: Knopf, 1971. Poems "Janet Waking" (86-87), "Bells for John Whiteside's Daughter" (159).

D351
The Pleasures of Poetry. By Donald Hall. New York: Harper & Row, 1971. Poem "Captain Carpenter" (285-287).

D352
Synthesis: Responses to Literature. Ed. Charles Sanders, Robin R. Rice, and Watt J. Cantillon. New York: Alfred A. Knopf, 1971. Poems "Winter Remembered" (659), "Good Ships" (659-660), "Judith of Bethulia" (660-661), "Prelude to an Evening" (661).

1972

D353
Allen Tate and His Work: Critical Evaluations. 1972. See B66.

D354
An Anatomy of Literature. By Robert Foulke and Paul Smith. New York: Harcourt Brace Jovanovich, 1972. Poem "Captain Carpenter" (1017-1018).

D355
Beowulf to Beatles: Approaches to Poetry. Ed. David R. Pichaske. New York: Free Press, 1972. Poem "Bells for John Whiteside's Daughter" (133).

D356
The College Anthology of British and American Poetry. 2nd ed. Ed. A. Kent Hieatt and William Park. Boston: Allyn and Bacon, 1972. Poem "Janet Waking" (568-569). Ransom does not appear in the earlier edition (1964).

D357
Critics on Emily Dickinson: Readings in Literary Criticism. Ed. Richard H. Rupp. Coral Gables: University of Miami Press, 1972. "Dickinson's Poetic Personality" (30-33), which is an excerpt from the essay "Emily Dickinson: A Poet Restored."

D358
Ezra Pound: The Critical Heritage. 1972. See B67.

D359
An Introduction to Poetry. 2nd ed. Ed. Louis Simpson. New York: St. Martin's Press, 1972. Poems "Bells for John Whiteside's Daughter" (299), "Dog" (299-300).

D360
The Liberating Form: A Handbook-Anthology of English and American Poetry. By Bert C. Bach, William A. Sessions, and William Walling. New York: Dodd, Mead, 1972. Poems "Blue Girls" (320), "Captain Carpenter" (95-96), "Piazza Piece" (131).

D361
Minorities: Good Poems by Small Poets and Small Poems by Good Poets. By T. E. Lawrence. Ed. J. M. Wilson. Garden City: Doubleday, 1972. Poem "The Lover" (193). According to the editor's introduction, this collection is based on a "private anthology" that Lawrence had compiled in a small notebook (17).

D362
The Poem: An Anthology. 2nd ed. Ed. Stanley B. Greenfield and A. Kingsley Weatherhead. New York: Appleton Century, 1968. Poems "Winter Remembered" (403), "Bells for John Whiteside's Daughter" (404), "Piazza Piece" (404).

D363
Poetry and Its Conventions: An Anthology Examining Poetic Forms and Themes. Ed. Frederick R. Lapides and John T. Shawcross. New York: Free Press, 1972. Poems "Bells for John Whiteside's Daughter" (242-243), "Piazza Piece" (493).

D364
Poetry and the Age, by Randall Jarrell. New York: Noonday Press, 1972. Blurb on back of paper binding. Also on back of paper binding of Ecco Press impression (New York, 1980). Described in Wright, *Jarrell* A5d, A5e.

D365
The Poetry of John Crowe Ransom. By Miller Williams. 1972. See B65.

D366
20th Century Literary Criticism: A Reader. Ed. David Lodge. London: Longman, 1972. Essay "Criticism, Inc." (228-239).

D367
The Ways of the Poem. [Rev. ed.] Ed. Josephine Miles. Englewood Cliffs: Prentice-Hall, 1972. Poem "Piazza Piece" (210).

D368
Words in Flight: An Introduction to Poetry. By Richard Abcarian. Belmont, CA: Wadsworth, 1972. Poem "Bells for John Whiteside's Daughter" (82).

1973

D369
Accent: An Anthology, 1940-60. Ed. Daniel Curley, George Scouffas, and Charles Shattuck. Urbana: University of Illinois Press, 1973. Essay "Eliot and the Metaphysicals" (442-451). Described in Bonnell, *Aiken* B92.

D370
E. M. Forster: The Critical Heritage. 1973. See B68.

D371
The Faber Book of Love Poems. Ed. Geoffrey Grigson. London: Faber and Faber, 1973. Poems "Blue Girls" (56-57), "Spectral Lovers" (91-92).

D372
Literary Lectures Presented at the Library of Congress. Washington, DC: Library of Congress, 1973. Essay "New Poets and Old Muses" (229-243).

D373
Literature: The Human Experience. Ed. Richard Abcarian and Marvin Klotz. New York: St. Martin's, 1973. Poem "Bells for John Whiteside's Daughter" (817).

D374
The Norton Anthology of Modern Poetry. Ed. Richard Ellmann and Robert O'Clair. New York: W. W. Norton, 1973. Poems "Bells for John Whiteside's Daughter" (435), "Here Lies a Lady" (435-436), "Judith of Bethulia" (436-437), "Philomela" (437-438), "Captain Carpenter" (438-439), "Piazza Piece" (439-440), "Blue Girls" (440), "Janet Waking" (440-441), "Dead Boy" (441), "The Equilibrists" (442-443), "Painted Head" (443-444), "Master's in the Garden Again" (444-445).

D375
The Norton Introduction to Literature: Poetry. Ed. J. Paul Hunter. New York: W. W. Norton, 1973. Poems "Bells for John Whiteside's Daughter" (34-35), "The Equilibrists" (108-109).

D376
The Poet in America, 1650 to the Present. Ed. Albert Gelpi. Lexington, MA: D. C. Heath, 1973. Poems "Dead Boy" (489), "Spectral Lovers" (489-490), "Necrological" (491-492), "Bells for John Whiteside's Daughter" (492), "Judith of Bethulia" (493-494), "Piazza Piece" (494), "Janet Waking" (495), "Persistent Explorer" (496-497), "Painted Head" (497-498).

D377
Poetry: An Introduction through Writing. By Lewis Turco. Reston, VA: Reston Publishing, 1973. Poem "Bells for John Whiteside's Daughter" (200-201).

1974

D378
American Literature: The Makers and the Making. Book D: *1914 to the Present*. By Cleanth Brooks, R. W. B. Lewis, and Robert Penn Warren. New York: St. Martin's, 1974. Poems "Persistent Explorer" (2642-2643), "Morning" (Jane awoke Ralph so gently on one morning") (2643), "Antique Harvesters" (2645-2646), "*Agitato ma non troppo*" (2649), "Judith of Bethulia" (2650-2651), "Captain Carpenter" (2651-2652), "Vision by Sweetwater" (2652), "Spiel of the Three Mountebanks" (2653), "Bells for John Whiteside's Daughter" (2654), "Janet Waking" (2654), "Two in August" (2656), "The Equilibrists" (2656), "Painted Head" (2658). Essay "Poetry: A Note in Ontology" (2843-2853). The poems are accompanied by Brooks, Lewis, and Warren's commentary. Described in Grimshaw, *Warren* B36.

D379
The American Tradition in Literature. 4th ed. Ed. Sculley Bradley, Richmond Croom Beatty, E. Hudson Long, and George Perkins. Vol. 2. New York: Grosset & Dunlap (distributed by W. W. Norton & Company), 1974. Poems "Winter Remembered" (1431-1432), "Bells for John Whiteside's Daughter" (1432), "Blue Girls" (1432-1433), "Antique Harvesters" (1433-1434), "The Equilibrists" (1434-1436).

D380
Amerikanische Lyrik. Vol. 17: *Jahrhundert bis zur Gegenwart*. Ed. Franz Link. Trans. Annemarie Link and Franz Link. Stuttgart: Philipp Reclam, 1974. Poem "Antique Harvesters" (308-311); in English on versos, German on rectos.

D381
A Book of Love Poetry. Ed. Jon Stallworthy. New York: Oxford University Press, 1974. Poem "Piazza Piece" (90-91).

D382
An Introduction to Poetry. By X. J. Kennedy. 3rd ed. Boston: Little Brown, 1974. Poems "Janet Waking" (251), "Bells for John Whiteside's Daughter" (373).

D383
Literature: Structure, Sound, and Sense. 2nd ed. By Laurence Perrine. New York: Harcourt Brace Jovanovich, 1974. Poems "Parting, without a Sequel" (726-727), "Bells for John Whiteside's Daughter" (801-802).

D384
The Lyric Potential. By James E. Miller, Robert Hayden, and Robert O'Neal. Glenview: Scott Foresman, 1974. Poem "Parting, without a Sequel" (93), "Bells for John Whiteside's Daughter" (152), "Blue Girls" (398).

D385
Mirrors: An Introduction to Literature. Ed. John R. Knott, Jr., and Christopher R. Reaske. San Francisco: Canfield Press, 1975. Poem "Here Lies a Lady" (265).

D386
New Coasts and Strange Harbors: Discovering Poems. Ed. Helen Hill and Agnes Perkins. New York: Thomas Y. Crowell, 1974. Poem "Janet Waking" (137).

D387
Twentieth Century Criticism: The Major Statements. Ed. William J. Handy and Max Westbrook. New York: Free Press, 1974. Essay "Poetry: A Note on [sic] Ontology" (43-58).

D388
Viewpoints in Literature. Ed. Stoddard Malarkey et al. New York: Holt, Rinehart, and Winston, 1974. Poem "Janet Waking" (238).

1975

D389
An Approach to Literature. 5th ed. By Cleanth Brooks, John Thibaut Purser, and Robert Penn Warren. Englewood Cliffs: Prentice-Hall, 1975. Poems "Bells for John Whiteside's Daughter" (383-384), "Philomela" (466).

D390
The Heath Introduction to Poetry. By Joseph de Roche. Lexington: D. C. Heath, 1975. Poems "Piazza Piece" (325), "Spectral Lovers" (325-326), "Bells for John Whiteside's Daughter" (326-327).

D391
How Does a Poem Mean?. 2nd ed. By John Ciardi and Miller Williams. Boston: Houghton Mifflin, 1975. Poems "Captain Carpenter" (41-42), "Bells for John Whiteside's Daughter" (229).

D392
Love's Aspect: The World's Great Love Poems. Ed. Jean Garrigue. Garden City: Doubleday, 1975. Poems "Spectral Lovers" (72-73), "Parting at Dawn" (247), "The Equilibrists" (252-254).

D393
The Norton Anthology of Poetry. Rev. ed. Ed. Alexander W. Allison et al. New York: W. W. Norton, 1975. Poems "Bells for John Whiteside's Daughter" (1052), "Vaunting Oak" (1052-1053), "Dead Boy" (1053), "Antique Harvesters" (1054-1055), "The Equilibrists" (1055-1056).

D394
The Uses of Poetry. Ed. Agnes Stein. New York: Holt, Rinehart, & Winston, 1975. Poems "Piazza Piece" (51), "Survey of Literature" (153), "Vision by Sweetwater" (317).

D395
Ways to Poetry. By Stanley A. Clayes and John Gerrietts. New York: Harcourt Brace Jovanovich, 1975. Poems "Janet Waking" (10-11), "Dead Boy" (125), "Bells for John Whiteside's Daughter" (137-138), "The Equilibrists" (319-320).

1976

D396
American Poetry of the Twentieth Century. Ed. Richard Gray. Cambridge: Cambridge University Press, 1976. Poems "Winter Remembered" (101), "Dead Boy" (101-102), "Bells for John Whiteside's Daughter" (102), "Parting at Dawn" (103), "Blue Girls" (103), "Captain Carpenter" (104-105), "Vision by Sweetwater" (105-106), "Antique Harvesters" (106-107), "Painted Head" (107-108). The editor provides substantial notes on each poem (206-213).

D397
The Faber Book of Sonnets. Ed. Robert Nye. London: Faber and Faber, 1976. Also published as *A Book of Sonnets* (New York: Oxford University Press, 1976). Poem "Piazza Piece" (203).

D398
Literature and Liberalism: An Anthology of Sixty Years of The New Republic. Ed. Edward Zwick. Washington, DC: New Republic Book Company, 1976. Poem "Painted Head" (103-104).

D399
Modern Poems: An Introduction to Poetry. Ed. Richard Ellmann and Robert O'Clair. New York: W. W. Norton, 1976. Poems "Bells for John Whiteside's Daughter" (164), "Here Lies a Lady" (165), "Captain Carpenter" (165-167), "Piazza Piece" (167), "Janet Waking" (167-168), "The Equilibrists" (168-169).

D400
New Oxford Book of American Verse. Ed. Richard Ellmann. New York: Oxford University Press, 1976. Poems "Bells for John Whiteside's Daughter" (575-576), "Judith of Bethulia" (576-577), "Winter Remembered" (577-578), "Captain Carpenter" (578-580), "Philomela" (580-581), "Old Mansion" (581-582), "Piazza Piece"

(582-583), "Vision by Sweetwater" (583), "The Equilibrists" (583-585), "Painted Head" (585-586).

D401
Structure and Meaning: An Introduction to Literature. Ed. Anthony Dubé et al. Boston: Houghton Mifflin, 1976. Poems "Bells for John Whiteside's Daughter" (418), "Piazza Piece" (530), "Here Lies a Lady" (664).

D402
Understanding Poetry. 4th ed. By Cleanth Brooks and Robert Penn Warren. New York: Holt, Rinehart and Winston, 1976. Poems "Bells for John Whiteside's Daughter" (180-181), "Winter Remembered" (183), "Lady Lost" (365).

1977

D403
The Crystal Image. Ed. Paul Janeczko. New York: Dell, 1977. Poems "Parting, without a Sequel" (90-91), "Bells for John Whiteside's Daughter" (146-147), "Janet Waking" (153).

D404
The Superfluous Men: Conservative Critics of American Culture, 1900-1945. 1977. See B69.

1978

D405
College English: The First Year. 7th ed. By Alton C. Morris et al. New York: Harcourt Brace Jovanovich, 1978. Poems "Captain Carpenter" (543), "Bells for John Whiteside's Daughter" (573).

D406
English and American Surrealist Poetry. Ed. Edward B. Germain. Harmondsworth: Penguin Books, 1978. Poem "Prelude to an Evening" (78-79).

D407
Fine Frenzy: Enduring Themes in Poetry. 2nd ed. By Robert Baylor and Brenda Stokes. New York: McGraw-Hill, 1978. Poem "Bells for John Whiteside's Daughter" (295).

D408
Life Hungers to Abound: Poems of the Family. Ed. Helen Plotz. New York: Greenwillow Books, 1978. Poems "Dead Boy" (113), "Old Man Playing with Children" (115).

D409
Literature: The Human Experience. 2nd ed. Ed. Richard Abcarian and Marvin Klotz. New York: St. Martin's, 1978. Poem "Bells for John Whiteside's Daughter" (965).

D410
The Treasury of American Poetry. Ed. Nancy Sullivan. Garden City: Doubleday, 1978. Poems "Bells for John Whiteside's Daughter" (457), "Piazza Piece" (458), "Here Lies a Lady" (458-459), "Blue Girls" (459), "Janet Waking" (459-460), "Survey of Literature" (460-461), "The Equilibrists" (462-463).

1979

D411
Goodbye, Farewell, and Adieu: Three Songs of Parting for Medium Voice and Piano, Op. 33, Nos. 1, 2, 3. By Kirke Mechem. New York: Carl Fischer, 1979. Poem "Parting, without a Sequel" (1), set to music as Opus 33, Number 2 (8-13). Also set to music are Michael Drayton's "Since There's No Help" and Sara Teasdale's "Let It Be Forgotten."

D412
The Literary South. By Louis D. Rubin, Jr. New York: John Wiley & Sons, 1979. Poems "Bells for John Whiteside's Daughter" (436), "Blue Girls" (437), "Janet Waking" (437-438), "Conrad in Twilight" (438-439), "Philomela" (439-440), "Captain Carpenter" (440-441), "The Equilibrists" (442-443), "Antique Harvesters" (443-444); essay "Poets without Laurels" (435-455); excerpt from essay "Introduction: A Statement of Principles" (478-483).

D413
Literature as Experience: An Anthology. Ed. Irving Howe, John Hollander, and David Bromwich. New York: Harcourt Brace Jovanovich, 1979. Poem "Captain Carpenter" (438-439).

D414
The Norton Anthology of American Literature. Vol 2. By Ronald Gottesman et al. New York: W. W. Norton, 1979. Poems "Dead Boy" (1264-1265), "Spectral Lovers" (1265-1266), "Bells for John Whiteside's Daughter" (1266), "Here Lies a Lady" (1266), "Philomela" (1267-1268), "Captain Carpenter" (1268-1270), "Old Mansion" (1270-1271), "Piazza Piece" (1271), "Janet Waking" (1272), "Two in August" (1272-1273), "Antique Harvesters" (1273-1274), "Dog" (1274-1276), "The Equilibrists" (1276-1277), "Painted Head" (1277-1278), "Address to the Scholars of New England" (1278-1280).

D415
The Oxford Book of American Light Verse. Ed. William Harmon. New York: Oxford University Press, 1979. Poems "Amphibious Crocodile" (343-345), "Philomela" (345-346), "Her Eyes" (344), "Our Two Worthies" (347-349), "Dog" (349-350), "Survey of Literature" (350-351).

1980

D416
Poetry: An Introduction. By Ruth Miller and Robert A. Greenberg. New York: St. Martin's, 1980. Poems "Piazza Piece" (33-34), "Bells for John Whiteside's Daughter" (190).

D417
The Practical Imagination: Stories, Poems, Plays. Ed. Northrop Frye, Sheridan Baker, and George Perkins. New York: Harper & Row, 1980. Poems "Bells for John Whiteside's Daughter" (805-806), "Blue Girls" (806), "Winter Remembered" (807).

D418
Robert Penn Warren Talking: Interviews, 1950-1978. Ed. Floyd C. Watkins and John T. Hiers. New York: Random House, 1980. "Fugitives' Reunion: Conversations at Vanderbilt" (9-26), which is an excerpt from *Fugitives' Reunion* (B70).

1981

D419
Beowulf to Beatles and Beyond: The Varieties of Poetry. By David R. Pichaske. New York: Macmillan, 1981. Poem "Bells for John Whiteside's Daughter" (480).

D420
The Harper Anthology of Poetry. By John Frederick Nims. New York: Harper & Row, 1981. Poems "Winter Remembered" (552), "Here Lies a Lady" (553), "Bells for John Whiteside's Daughter" (553), "The Equilibrists" (554-555).

D421
Tygers of Wrath: Poems of Hate, Anger, and Invective. Ed. X. J. Kennedy. Athens: University of Georgia Press, 1981. Poem "Miriam Tazewell" (226-227).

1982

D422
The Faber Book of Modern Verse. Ed. Michael Roberts. 4th ed. revised by Peter Porter. London: Faber and Faber, 1982. Poems "Vision by Sweetwater" (198), "Captain Carpenter" (198-200), "Dead Boy" (201), "Judith of Bethulia" (201-203).

D423
Literature. By James H. Pickering and Jeffrey Hoeper. New York: Macmillan, 1982. Poems "Bells for John Whiteside's Daughter" (864), "Winter Remembered" (864-865), "Piazza Piece" (865), "Two in August" (865-866).

D424
Poetry: Sight and Insight. By James W. Kirkland and F. David Sanders. New York: Random House, 1982. Poem "Bells for John Whiteside's Daughter" (121).

D425
T. S. Eliot: The Critical Heritage. 1982. See B70.

1983

D426
The Heath Guide to Poetry. By David Bergman and Daniel Mark Epstein. Lexington, MA: D. C. Heath, 1983. Poems "Here Lies a Lady" (73-74), "Piazza Piece" (89-90), "Winter Remembered" (186-187).

D427
Milton's "Lycidas": The Tradition and the Poem. Rev. ed. Ed. C. A. Patrides. Columbia: University of Missouri Press, 1983. Essay "A Poem Nearly Anonymous" (68-85).

D428
The Poem in Question. By Robert E. Bourdette, Jr., and Michael Cohen. New York: Harcourt Brace Jovanovich, 1983. Poem "Bells for John Whiteside's Daughter" (70-71).

D429
The World's Best Poetry: The Granger Anthology. Series 1, supplement 1: *The Twentieth Century English and American Verse, 1900-1929*. Ed. Editorial Board, Granger Book Co. Great Neck, NY: Granger, 1983. Poems "Spectral Lovers" (258-259), "Number Five" (259-260), "Piazza Piece" (260).

1984

D430
Fifty Years of American Poetry: Anniversary Volume for the Academy of American Poets. New York: Harry N. Abrams, 1984. Poem "Judith of Bethulia" (37-38).

D431
The Heath Introduction to Literature. 2nd ed. By Alice S. Landy. Lexington, MA: D. C. Heath, 1984. Poem "Bells for John Whiteside's Daughter" (573).

1985

D432 seen
The Oxford Book of Short Poems. Ed. P. J. Kavanagh and James Michie. Oxford: Oxford University Press, 1985. Poem "Emily Hardcastle, Spinster" (209).

1986

D433
British and American Poets: Chaucer to the Present. Ed. W. Jackson Bate and David Perkins. San Diego: Harcourt Brace Jovanovich, 1986. Poems "Bells for John Whiteside's Daughter" (772), "Here Lies a Lady" (772), "Dead Boy" (773).

D434
Literature: An Introduction to Reading and Writing. By Edgar V. Roberts and Henry E. Jacobs. Englewood Cliffs: Prentice-Hall, 1986. Poem "Bells for John Whiteside's Daughter" (987).

D435
Literature: Reading Fiction, Poetry, Drama, and the Essay. By Robert DiYanni. New York: Ransom House, 1986. Poems "Bells for John Whiteside's Daughter" (659-660), "Piazza Piece" (660), "Blue Girls" (660-661), "Winter Remembered" (661).

D436
A Modern Southern Reader: Major Stories, Drama, Poetry, Essays, Interviews and Reminiscences from the Twentieth-Century South. Ed. Ben Forkner and Patrick Samway. Atlanta: Peachtree Publishers, 1986. Poems "Bells for John Whiteside's Daughter" (297), "The Equilibrists" (297-299), "Antique Harvesters" (299-301), "Vision by Sweetwater" (301), "Two in August" (301-302).

D437
The Norton Book of Light Verse. Ed. Russell Baker and Kathleen Leland Baker. New York: W. W. Norton, 1986. Poem "Survey of Literature" (90-91).

D438
100 Poems by 100 Poets: An Anthology. Ed. Harold Pinter, Geoffrey Godbert, and Anthony Astbury. New York: Grove Press, 1986. Poems "Piazza Piece" (124).

D439
Survey of Modern Poetry. Vol. 8: *Interval between World Wars, 1920-1939*. Prepared by the Editorial Board, Roth Publishing. Great Neck, NY: Poetry Anthology Press, 1986. Poems "Dead Boy" (99), "Bells for John Whiteside's Daughter" (99-100), "Blue Girls" (100), lines 33-70 of "Address to the Scholars of New England" (101-102), "Here Lies a Lady" (102), "Captain Carpenter" (102-104), "Piazza Piece" (105), "Janet Waking" (105-106), "Antique Harvesters" (107-109), "Dog" (109-110), "The Equilibrists" (110-112), "Painted Head" (112-113).

1987

D440
An Invitation to Poetry. By Jay Parini. Englewood Cliffs: Prentice-Hall, 1987. Poems "Janet Waking" (55), "Blue Girls" (133-134), "Bells for John Whiteside's Daughter" (219).

D441
Literature: Art and Artifact. By William Heffernan, Mark Johnston, and Frank Hodgins. New York: Harcourt Brace Jovanovich, 1987. Poem "Bells for John Whiteside's Daughter" (585-586).

D442
Modern American Poets: Their Voices and Visions. By Robert DiYanni. New York: Random House, 1987. Poems "Piazza Piece" (79), "Bells for John Whiteside's Daughter" (550), "Here Lies a Lady" (551), "Blue Girls" (551), "Janet Waking" (552).

D443
Sound and Sense: An Introduction to Poetry. 7th ed. By Laurence Perrine, with Thomas R. Arp. San Diego: Harcourt Brace Jovanovich, 1987. Poems "Parting, without a Sequel" (164), "Bells for John Whiteside's Daughter" (234-235).

1988

D444
The Amis Anthology. Ed. Kingsley Amis. London: Hutchinson, 1988. Poem "Captain Carpenter" (222-224).

D445
The Heath Introduction to Literature. 3rd ed. By Alice S. Landy. Lexington, MA: D. C. Heath, 1984. Poem "Bells for John Whiteside's Daughter" (605).

D446
The Norton Anthology of Modern Poetry. 2nd ed. Ed. Richard Ellmann and Robert O'Clair. New York: W. W. Norton, 1988. Poems "Bells for John Whiteside's Daughter" (469-470), "Here Lies a Lady" (470), "Judith of Bethulia" (470-471), "Philomela" (471-472), "Captain Carpenter" (473-474), "Piazza Piece" (474), "Blue Girls" (475), "Janet Waking" (475-476), "Dead Boy" (476), "The Equilibrists" (476-478), "Painted Head" (478-479).

D447
Robert Lowell: Interviews and Memoirs. 1988. See B71.

1989

D448
The Art of the Critic: Literary Theory and Criticism from the Greeks to the Present. Vol. 9: *Middle Twentieth Century.* Ed. Harold Bloom. New York: Chelsea House, 1989. Essays "The Cathartic Principle" (5-13), "The Mimetic Principle" (14-22).

D449
The Kenyon Poets: Celebrating the Fiftieth Anniversary of the Founding of the Kenyon Review. Ed. Galbraith M. Crump. Gambier: Kenyon Review, 1989. Poems ""Bells for John Whiteside's Daughter" (3), "Piazza Piece" (4), "Blue Girls" (4-5), "Vision by Sweetwater" (5), "Winter Remembered" (6), "Philomela" (7-8), "Antique Harvesters" (8-10), "The Equilibrists" (10-12), "To the Scholars of Harvard" (12-14).

D450
Literature: An Introduction to Reading and Writing. 2nd ed. By Edgar V. Roberts and Henry E. Jacobs. Englewood Cliffs: Prentice-Hall, 1989. Poem "Bells for John Whiteside's Daughter" (965).

D451
Modern Poems: A Norton Introduction. 2nd ed. Ed. Richard Ellmann and Robert O'Clair. New York: W. W. Norton, 1989. Poems "Bells for John Whiteside's Daughter" (265), "Here Lies a Lady" (266), "Captain Carpenter" (266-267), "Piazza Piece" (268), "Dead Boy" (268), "The Equilibrists" (269-270).

D452
The Norton Anthology of American Literature. 3rd ed. Vol. 2. By Nina Baym et al. New York: W. W. Norton, 1989. Poems "Bells for John Whiteside's Daughter" (1377-1378), "Here Lies a Lady" (1378), "Philomela" (1378-1379), "Piazza Piece" (1380), "Janet Waking" (1380-1381), "The Equilibrists" (1381-1382).

1990

D453
The Chatto Book of Love Poetry. Ed. John Fuller. London: Chatto & Windus, 1990. Poem "Winter Remembered" (314).

D454
The Heath Anthology of American Literature. Vol. 2. Ed. Paul Lauter et al. Lexington, MA: D. C. Heath, 1990. Poems "Here Lies a Lady" (1682-1683), "Philomela" (1683-1684), "Piazza Piece" (1684), "The Equilibrists" (1685-1686), "Crocodile" (1686-1688).

D455
Literature: Reading Fiction, Poetry, Drama, and the Essay. 2nd ed. By Robert DiYanni. New York: McGraw-Hill, 1990. Poems "Blue Girls" (718), "Piazza Piece" (718).

D456
A New Treasury of Poetry. Ed. Neil Philip. New York: Stewart, Tabori, & Chang, 1990. Poem "First Travels of Max" (32-33).

D457
Poetry. By Jill P. Baumgaertner. San Diego: Harcourt Brace Jovanovich, 1990. Poems "Bells for John Whiteside's Daughter" (525-526), "Piazza Piece" (526), "Janet Waking" (527).

D458
Southern Voices for Mezzo Soprano. By Lee Hoiby. Commissioned by Lester Senter. Long Eddy, NY: Aquarius Music, 1990. Poem "Bells for John Whiteside's Daughter" (11-17) set to music. Also set to music are A. R. Ammons's "Butterflies," Robert Penn Warren's "Lullaby," and Carson McCullers's "Berenice Sadie Brown."

D459
T. S. Eliot: Critical Assessments. Ed. Graham Clarke. 4 vols. London: Christopher Helm, 1990. Essays "Waste Lands" (2: 96-102), "T. S. Eliot as Dramatist" (3: 346-349), "T. S. Eliot: A Postscript" (3: 599-613).

1991

D460
Criticism: Major Statements. 3rd ed. Ed. Charles Kaplan and William Anderson. New York: St. Martin's, 1991. Essay "Criticism as Pure Speculation" (469-487).

1992

D461
Critical Theory since Plato. Rev. ed. Ed. Hazard Adams. New York: Harcourt Brace Jovanovich, 1992. Essays "Poetry: A Note in Ontology" (866-874), "Criticism as Pure Speculation" (874-887).

D462
One Hundred and One Poems of Romance. Ed. Christine Benton. Chicago: Contemporary Books, 1992. Poems "Blue Girls" (27), "Winter Remembered" (92-93).

D463
The Top 500 Poems. Ed. William Harmon. New York: Columbia University Press, 1992. Poems "Bells for John Whiteside's Daughter" (995-996), "Piazza Piece" (997). This collection presents the poems that, according to *The Columbia Granger's Index to Poetry,* "have been most often anthologized" (1). In order of publication frequency, "Bells" ranked 101st; "Piazza Piece," 332nd.

1993

D464
Chapters into Verse: Poetry in English Inspired by the Bible. Vol. 2: *Gospels to Revelation.* Ed. Robert Atwan and Laurance Wieder. Oxford: Oxford University Press, 1993. Poem "Armageddon" (352-354).

D465
Discovering Poetry. By Hans P. Guth and Gabriele L. Rico. Englewood Cliffs: Prentice Hall, 1993. Poems "Bells for John Whiteside's Daughter" (233-234) and "Janet Waking" (452).

D466
The McGraw-Hill Book of Poetry. By Robert DiYanni and Kraft Rompf. New York: McGraw-Hill, 1993. Poems "Bells for John Whiteside's Daughter" (671-672), "Piazza Piece" (672).

D467
More Light: Father and Daughter Poems: A Twentieth-Century American Selection. Ed. Jason Shinder. New York: Harcourt Brace, 1993. Poem "Bells for John Whiteside's Daughter" (3).

D468
Poetry: A HarperCollins Pocket Anthology. By R. S. Gwynn. New York: HarperCollins, 1993. Poem "Bells for John Whiteside's Daughter" (194-195).

D469
Poetry Out Loud. Ed. Alden Rubin. Chapel Hill: Algonquin Books, 1993. Poem "Janet Waking" (133-134).

1994

D470
An Introduction to Poetry. 8th ed. By X. J. Kennedy and Dana Gioia. New York: HarperCollins, 1994. Poem "Bells for John Whiteside's Daughter" (400).

D471
Modern American Poets: Their Voices and Visions. 2nd ed. By Robert DiYanni. New York: McGraw-Hill, 1994. Poems "Bells for John Whiteside's Daughter" (655-656), "Blue Girls" (656), "Janet Waking" (656-657).

D472
The Norton Anthology of American Literature. 4th ed. Vol. 2. By Nina Baym et al. New York: W. W. Norton, 1994. Poems "Bells for John Whiteside's Daughter" (1368-1369), "Here Lies a Lady" (1369), "Philomela" (1369-1370), "Piazza Piece" (1371), "Janet Waking" (1371-1372), "The Equilibrists" (1372-1373).

1995

D473
The Columbia Anthology of American Poetry. Ed. Jay Parini. New York: Columbia University Press, 1995. Poems "Bells for John Whiteside's Daughter" (397), "Piazza Piece" (397-98), "Blue Girls" (398), "Janet Waking" (399).

Section E
Recordings

Included here, in addition to published recordings, are tapes in the Library of Congress archive of recorded poetry, a collection begun in 1943 when Allen Tate was Consultant in Poetry to the library. The tapes themselves were not published but copies may be purchased from the library, and some recordings have been issued as phonograph discs.

E1

John Crowe Ransom reading his poems, with comment, to the Writers' Club of the Library of Congress, 29 January 1945. Library of Congress tape T 6117-42, side A. Poems: "Winter Remembered," "Necrological," "Bells for John Whiteside's Daughter," "Here Lies a Lady," "Captain Carpenter," "Parting, without a Sequel," "Janet Waking," "Survey of Literature," "The Equilibrists," "Of Margaret," "Address to the Scholars of New England," "What Ducks Require," "Painted Head."

E2

John Crowe Ransom reading his poems in the Library of Congress recording laboratory, 30 January 1945. Library of Congress tape T 6117-42, side B. Poems: "Winter Remembered," ""Bells for John Whiteside's Daughter," "Necrological," "Miriam Tazewell," "The Tall Girl," "Here Lies a Lady," "Number Five," "Captain Carpenter," "Blue Girls," "Here Lies a Lady" (reread), "Tom, Tom, the Piper's Son," "Philomela," "Lady Lost," "Janet Waking," "Parting, without a Sequel," "Puncture," "Antique Harvesters," "Survey of Literature," "The Equilibrists," "Painted Head," "Prelude to an Evening."

E3
John Crowe Ransom reading his poems in the Coolidge Auditorium, 12 April 1948. Library of Congress tape T 6117-43, side A. Poems "Winter Remembered," "Miriam Tazewell," "Necrological," "Here Lies a Lady," "Tom, Tom, the Piper's Son," "Captain Carpenter," "Janet Waking," "Puncture," "Survey of Literature," "What Ducks Require," "Painted Head," "Address to the Scholars of New England," "The Equilibrists," "Blue Girls."

E4
John Crowe Ransom reading his poems in the Library of Congress recording laboratory, 16 April 1948. Library of Congress tape T 6117-43, side B. Poems "Dead Boy," ""Bells for John Whiteside's Daughter," "Here Lies a Lady," "Tom, Tom, the Piper's Son," "Conrad in Twilight," "Vision by Sweetwater," "Judith of Bethulia," "Captain Carpenter," "Old Mansion," "Janet Waking," "Prelude to an Evening," "Of Margaret," "Painted Head," "What Ducks Require."

E5
John Crowe Ransom Reading His Own Poems. Record P 21 of the series entitled Twentieth Century Poetry in English: Contemporary Recordings of the Poets Reading Their Own Poems Selected and Arranged by the Consultants in Poetry in English at The Library of Congress and Issued under a Grant from The Bollingen Foundation. 12 inch, 78 rpm. Accompanied by 2 pages with a biographical note and texts of the poems. Library of Congress, 1949. Based on the 1948 recording (see E4). Poems "Bells for John Whiteside's Daughter," "Janet Waking," "Here Lies a Lady," "Captain Carpenter." Also listed in Gallup's *Eliot* (E5g-h).

E6
Poets Reading Their Own Poems: Theodore Spenser, John Crowe Ransom, E. E. Cummings, Robinson Jeffers. Record PL 5 of the 8-record series entitled Twentieth Century Poetry in English: Contemporary Recordings of the Poets Reading Their Own Poems Selected and Arranged by the Consultants in Poetry in English at The Library of Congress and Issued under a Grant from The Bollingen Foundation. 12 inches, 33 1/3 rpm. Library of Congress, 1953. Side B includes Ransom's reading "Bells for

John Whiteside's Daughter," "Janet Waking," "Here Lies a Lady," "Captain Carpenter."

E7

John Crowe Ransom reading his poems, with comment, at his home in Gambier, Ohio, 1-2 March 1957. Library of Congress tape T 2588-2 and 3. Poems "Miriam Tazewell," "Dead Boy," "Spectral Lovers," "Necrological," "Bells for John Whiteside's Daughter," "The Tall Girl," "Good Ships," "Here Lies a Lady," "Judith of Bethulia," "Captain Carpenter," "Janet Waking," "Survey of Literature," "The Equilibrists," "What Ducks Require," "Our Two Worthies," "Lady Lost," "Prelude to an Evening," "Vision by Sweetwater," "Piazza Piece," "Painted Head," "Parting, without a Sequel," "Antique Harvesters," "Address to the Scholars of New England."

E8

John Crowe Ransom delivering his paper "New Poets and Old Muses" in the lecture series entitled "American Poetry at Mid-Century," in the Coolidge Auditorium, 13 January 1958. Library of Congress tape T 2609. For original publication in print, see B43.

E9

John Crowe Ransom reading his poems and discussing them with Randall Jarrell in the Library of Congress recording laboratory, 14 January 1958. Library of Congress tape T 2628. Poems "Vision by Sweetwater," "Judith of Bethulia," "Puncture," "Prelude to an Evening," "Tom, Tom, the Piper's Son," "Piazza Piece," "Captain Carpenter," "Here Lies a Lady," "Old Mansion."

E10

Johns Hopkins Poetry Festival. Library of Congress tape T 3905-1-10. Poets delivering lectures and reading their poems, with comment, at the first Johns Hopkins Poetry Festival, Baltimore, Maryland, 5-11 November 1958. Reel 4 includes Ransom's reading, on 8 November, these poems: "Bells for John Whiteside's Daughter," "Janet Waking," "Necrological," "Her Eyes," "Our Two Worthies," "Survey of Literature," "The Equilibrists," "Prelude to an Evening," "Painted Head."

E11

An Album of Modern Poetry: An Anthology Read by the Poets. Ed. Oscar Williams. Twentieth Century Poetry in English series. Washington, D.C.: Library of Congress Recording Laboratory, 1959. Three 12 inch, 33 1/3 rpm records (PL 20, 21, and 22) issued with a 42-page leaflet containing the printed texts. Record PL 20, side A, includes Ransom's reading of "Captain Carpenter." Edelstein's *Stevens* (G7) notes a reissue in 1964 by Record Collectors Guild, New York. See also the re-engineered version listed below (E16).

E12

Voices of Kenyon. Vol. 3: *John Crowe Ransom Reading and Commenting on His Own Poems.* Produced by Franklin Miller, Jr. 12-inch 33 1/3 rpm record, sides numbered XTV 60670, XTV 60671. Gambier: Kenyon College, ca. 1959. Side 1: poems "Bells for John Whiteside's Daughter," "Here Lies a Lady," "Judith of Bethulia," "Piazza Piece," "Janet Waking," "Survey of Literature." Side 2: poems "The Equilibrists," "Painted Heads"; also "The Early Days of the *Kenyon Review*," an interview by Franklin Miller, Jr. The poems, accompanied by Ransom's commentary and an introduction of Ransom by Frank E. Bailey, were recorded on 25 March 1957 at Kenyon on the occasion of the third Larwill Lecture of the 1956-57 series. The interview was recorded in June 1959. The recordings were re-issued as cassettes in 1995, with distribution by the Kenyon College Bookstore.

E13

Conversations on the Craft of Poetry. By Cleanth Brooks and Robert Penn Warren. New York: Holt, Rinehart and Winston, 1961. Two 7-inch, 2-track tape reels, 3 3/4 ips. Recorded to accompany the 3rd edition of Brooks and Warren's *Understanding Poetry.* For the transcript, see B47. On reel 1, Ransom discusses the composition of "Blue Girls."

E14

John Crowe Ransom Reads His Works (title on the record). Yale Series of Recorded Poets. Produced by the Yale University Department of English and Audio Visual Center. Ed. Alvin B. Kernan. Carillion YP 306, 1961. 12-inch, 33 1/3 rpm record. "This is a field recording made in the poet's own locale" (back of record jacket). In 1966 the recording was also issued as Decca DL

9147. Side 1: "Miriam Tazewell," "Dead Boy," "Spectral Lovers," "Bells for John Whiteside's Daughter," "Good Ships," "Here Lies a Lady," "Judith of Bethulia," "Captain Carpenter," "Piazza Piece," "Lady Lost," "Two in August." Side 2: "Antique Harvesters," "Our Two Worthies," "Survey of Literature," "The Equilibrists," "What Ducks Require," "Painted Head," "Address to the Scholars of New England." Reviewed by Anthony Ostroff in *Kenyon Review* 23.2 (Spring 1961): 343-51. The Yale Series of Recorded Poets ıdvertised in *Kenyon Review* 23.1 (Winter 1961): [iv]—sol subscription for $95.00 for 22 albums or at $5.98 each.

E15

National Poetry Festival. Library of Congress tapes T 3868, 3869, and 3870. The recording was made in the library's Coolidge Auditorium, 22-24 October 1962. For the published transcript, see B52. Tape T 3868-2, recorded on 22 October, includes Ransom's reading of and commentary on his poem "Prelude to an Evening." Tape T 3870 includes Ransom's introduction of the topic and speakers for a 24 October session entitled "The Problem of Form."

E16

An Album of Modern Poetry, British and American: An Anthology Read by the Poets. Ed. Oscar Williams. 3 "volumes" (records AA3308, 3309, 3310; and in 1966 also in a boxed set GR902-3-4). Audio Arts Library. New York: Gryphon Records, 1963. 12-inch, 33 1/3 rpm record. Record AA3308 ("volume" 1), side 1, includes Ransom's reading of "Captain Carpenter." The record is accompanied by an 8-page leaflet with the printed texts of the poems. This is a re-engineered version of the album published by Library of Congress in 1959 (E11). It was re-issued as a cassette by Listening Library, Old Greenwich, Connecticut, in 1970.

E17

A Modern Classicist Discusses Wit and Irony in Poetry. N. Hollywood, CA: Center for Cassette Studies, ? 1970, 1979. 1 sound cassette (29 min.), 1 7/8 ips. Series: American Poets. #10170. Also, listed in OCLC, is another cassette of 29 min, entitled *A Distinguished Poet Discusses Validity of Varied Interpretations,"* evidently in the same series. Not seen.

E18

The Spoken Arts Treasury of 100 Modern American Poets. Vol. 4: *Robinson Jeffers, Marianne Moore, John Crowe Ransom, T. S. Eliot, and Conrad Aiken Reading Their Poems.* Produced by Arthur Luce Klein. Ed. Paul Kresh. New Rochelle, NY: Spoken Arts, 1970. 12-inch, 33 1/3 rpm, record SA 1043. Side 2 includes Ransom's reading of "Prelude to an Evening," "Captain Carpenter," "Here Lies a Lady." Also issued by Spoken Arts as a cassette (SAC 1043) in 1985.

Section F
Ghosts

F1

Poems in the *Liberator* (1919). Ransom's 1919 *Poems about God* (A1) listed the *Liberator* among the magazines in which some of its poems were originally published. In a letter to Christopher Morley, 11 March 1918, Ransom said that he was sending three poems—"The Resurrection," "Roses," and "The Power of God"—to the *Liberator*, the little magazine superseding *Masses* and edited at the time by Max Eastman. If the *Liberator* accepted any of Ransom's work, however, it did not publish it.

F2

Emily Dickinson (1941). In an advertisement in *New Directions in Prose and Poetry* [6] (1941): 738, Ransom was listed as the author of this future volume in the Makers of Modern Literature series published by New Directions; the volume was also advertised on the dust jacket of *New Criticism* (A10). In "Checklist of New Directions Books in Print," *New Directions* 7 (1942): 498, no author was given for the volume on Dickinson or for other volumes "in preparation" for the Makers series. Ransom had in fact signed a contract with New Directions, dated 17 June 1940, for the volume on Dickinson, the manuscript to be delivered by 1 January 1943 and, contradictorily, the book to be published before 1 April 1941 (STW). Although Ransom did not have a volume appear in the Makers series, he continued to have an interest in preparing a pamphlet on Dickinson. In fact, he signed a contract with the University of Minnesota, dated 2 November 1960, for "a Manuscript now entitled EMILY DICKINSON" to be delivered to the university in summer 1961 (STW), presumably for the University of Minnesota Pamphlets on American Writers series. This project too did not come to publication.

F3

Poetics (1942). This ghost was listed for sale at $2.00 in "Checklist of New Directions Books in Print," *New Directions* 7 (1942): 498, and was advertised in *PMLA* December 1942, part 2: 35. It was listed as published in 1942 at $2.00 in the *Cumulative Book Index, 1943-1948* (New York: Wilson, 1950), 1871. The book was not included in "A List of Books Published by New Directions, 1936-1963," *A New Directions Reader*, ed. Hayden Carruth and James Laughlin (Norfolk: New Directions, 1964). However, it was subsequently listed in several reference works: *Contemporary Authors: A Bio-Bibliographical Guide to Current Authors and Their Works*, ed. Barbara Harte and Carolyn Riley, first revision, vols. 5-8 (Detroit: Gale, 1969), 930; in *Dictionary of Literary Biography*, vol. 45 (Detroit: Gale, 1986), 344; in *Dictionary of Literary Biography*, vol. 63 (Detroit: Gale, 1988), 237; in *First Printings of American Authors*, vol. 5, ed. Philip B. Eppard (Detroit: Gale Research, 1987), 266; and in *Dictionary of American Biography*, Supplement 9 (New York: Scribner's, 1994), 644. It does appear that in fact a volume under the title *Poetics* or *Essays in Poetics* (F4) was planned for publication. In a letter to Allen Tate on 19 November 1940, Ransom said that adding the final chapter to *New Criticism* had "*almost* saved" him from having to write "another book" on his "own doctrine" (qtd. in Young, *Gentleman* 345), implying that such a volume was still needed. In a letter to Ransom on 30 June 1971, however, Frederick Martin (managing editor of New Directions) asked about a title for a collection of his essays (which would become *Beating the Bushes*, A21) and referred to "Poetics: A Study of Language" as "the title of the book that never was" (TNV). There may have been, however, a pamphlet with the title *Poetics* issued by New Directions as publicity for the aborted volume and containing a short essay by Ransom and brief comments on his work by other critics (letter, Karen L. Rood, Bruccoli Clark Layman, Inc., to T. H. Howard-Hill, 6 February 1996).

F4

Essays in Poetics (1945). The biographical blurb on back flap of the dust jacket for the first impression of Ransom's 1945 *Selected Poems* (A12) included this sentence: "At the time of writing, New Directions has in press a fourth volume of prose, *Essays in Poetics*." The sentence is omitted from the jacket of the second impression. See also *Poetics* (F3).

F 5

Preface to *The Making of a Modern,* by George Marion O'Donnell (1948). In "John Crowe Ransom: A Checklist," R. W. Stallman noted that Ransom's essay on O'Donnell in *Southern Review* (C217) was to appear in a revised form as a preface to this volume to be published by Alcestis Press. The volume evidently was never published.

F 6

Poetic Sense: A Study of Problems in Defining Poetry by Content (1971). This title, with a publication date of 1971, was listed among Ransom's books in the bibliographical section of *The Norton Anthology of Modern Poetry* (D374, D446). Evidently, the editors mistakenly attributed to Ransom the Ph.D. dissertation that his son David Reavill Ransom completed at Vanderbilt in 1964 and that was actually entitled "The Poetic Sense: A Study of Problems in Defining Poetry by Content and a Suggestion toward the Criteria of Presence and Finality in Language."

F 7

An edition of Paul Valéry (n.d.). In his 1989 anthology *The Art of the Critic* (D448) Harold Bloom said that Ransom had edited Valéry (9: 3). Bloom's statement may have been based on an a pre-publication announcement or advertisement for the multi-volume edition of Valéry published by Princeton University Press in the Bollingen Series. On 24 May 1957 Jackson Matthews, its general editor, asked Ransom to contribute an introduction to the volume devoted to Valéry's essays on Descartes, Goethe, and others (TNV). Ransom agreed but, despite repeated reminders from Matthews, never sent him the introduction. Instead, Joseph Frank wrote the introduction to the volume: *Masters and Friends,* trans. Martin Turnell, vol. 9 of *Collected Works of Paul Valéry,* Bollingen Series XLV (Princeton: Princeton UP, 1968).

Works Cited

Abbott, Craig S. "John Crowe Ransom's Ghosts." *PBSA* 90 (1996): 217-221.

—. *Marianne Moore: A Descriptive Bibliography.* Pittsburgh: University of Pittsburgh Press, 1977.

Agner, Dwight. *The Books of WAD: A Bibliography of the Books.* Baton Rouge: Press of the Night Owl, 1974.

Bloomfield, B. C., and Edward Mendelson. *W. H. Auden: A Bibliography, 1924-1969.* 2nd ed. Charlottesville: University Press of Virginia for the Bibliographical Society of the University of Virginia, 1972.

Bonnell, F. W., and F. C. Bonnell. *Conrad Aiken: A Bibliography (1902-1978).* San Marino: Huntington Library, 1982.

Boughn, Michael. *H. D.: A Bibliography, 1905-1990.* Charlottesville: University Press of Virginia for the Bibliographical Society of the University of Virginia, 1993.

Bowers, Fredson. *Principles of Bibliographical Description.* Princeton: Princeton University Press, 1949.

Browne, Elizabeth. Kenyon Review *Index: 25 Year Cumulative Compilation, 1939-1963.* New York: AMS, 1964.

Cave, Roderick, and Thomas Rae. *Private Press Books, 1960.* Pinner: Private Libraries Association, 1961.

Conkin, Paul K. *The Southern Agrarians.* Knoxville: University of Tennessee Press, 1988.

Cowan, Louise. *The Fugitive Group: A Literary History.* Baton Rouge: Louisiana State University Press, 1959.

Cutrer, Thomas W. *Parnassus on the Mississippi: The* Southern Review *and the Baton Rouge Literary Community, 1935-1942.* Baton Rouge: Louisiana State University Press, 1984.

Davidson, Donald. "*I'll Take My Stand*: A History." *American Review* 5 (Summer 1935): 310-321.

Edelstein, J. M. *Wallace Stevens: A Descriptive Bibliography.* Pittsburgh: University of Pittsburgh Press, 1973.

Fain, John Tyree, ed. The Spyglass*: Views and Reviews, 1924-1930.* By Donald Davidson. Nashville: Vanderbilt University Press, 1963.

Fifoot, Richard. *A Bibliography of Edith, Osbert, and Sachevrell Sitwell.* 2nd ed. London: Rupert Hart-Davis, 1971.

Gallup, Donald. *Ezra Pound: A Bibliography.* Charlottesville: University Press of Virginia for the Bibliographical Society of the University of Virginia and St. Paul's Bibliographies, 1983.

—. *T. S. Eliot: A Bibliography.* Rev. ed. New York: Harcourt, 1969.

Gilbert, Ellen D. *The House of Holt, 1866-1946: An Editorial History.* Metuchen: Scarecrow, 1993.

Graves, Robert. *In Broken Images: Selected Letters of Robert Graves, 1914-1946.* Ed. Paul O'Prey. London: Hutchinson, 1982.

Grimshaw, James A., Jr. *Robert Penn Warren: A Descriptive Bibliography, 1922-79.* University Press of Virginia for the Bibliographical Society of the University of Virginia, 1981.

Higginson, Fred H., and William Proctor Williams. *A Bibliography of the Writings of Robert Graves.* Winchester: St. Paul's Bibliographies, 1987.

Hogan, Charles Beecher. *A Bibliography of Edwin Arlington Robinson.* New Haven: Yale University Press, 1936.

Hohenberg, John. *The Pulitzer Prizes: A History of the Awards in Books, Drama, Music, and Journalism Based on the Private Files over Six Decades.* New York: Columbia University Press, 1974.

Hutner, Gordon. "Reviewing America: John Crowe Ransom's *Kenyon Review.*" *American Quarterly* 44 (1992): 101-114.

Janssen, Marian. The Kenyon Review, *1939-1970: A Critical History.* Baton Rouge: Louisiana State University Press, 1990.

Janssens, G. A. M. *The American Literary Review: A Critical History, 1920-1950*. The Hague: Mouton, 1968.

Jaspert, W. Pincus, W. Turner Berry, and A. F. Johnson. *The Encyclopedia of Typefaces*. 4th ed. London: Blanford, 1990.

Lewis, Randolph, Heather Moore, and Michael Winship, eds. *The Knopf Archive at Texas*. A special issue of *Library Chronicle* 22.4 (1992): 1-161.

Leverette, William E., Jr., and David E. Shi. "Herbert Agar and *Free America*: A Jeffersonian Alternative to the New Deal." *Journal of American Studies* 16 (1982): 189-206.

Linton, Cecelia Lampp. "A Textual Variorum of John Crowe Ransom's *Selected Poems*." Ph.D. diss. Catholic University of America, 1991.

MacMahon, Candace W. *Elizabeth Bishop: A Bibliography, 1927-1979*. Charlottesville: University Press of Virginia for the Bibliographical Society of the University of Virginia, 1980.

Peters, Mildred Brooks. "Bibliography." *John Crowe Ransom: Critical Essays and a Bibliography*. Ed. Thomas Daniel Young. Baton Rouge: Louisiana State University Press, 1968.

Ransom, John Crowe. *Selected Letters of John Crowe Ransom*. Ed. Thomas Daniel Young and George Core. Baton Rouge: Louisiana State University Press, 1985.

Rhein, Donna E. *The Handprinted Books of Leonard and Virginia Woolf at the Hogarth Press, 1917-1932*. Ann Arbor: UMI Research Press, 1985.

Richmond, Mary L. "The Cummington Press," *Books at Iowa* 7 (November 1967): 9-31.

Rock, Virginia. "The Making and Meaning of *I'll Take My Stand*: A Study in Utopian Conservatism." Ph.D. diss. University of Minnesota, 1961.

Rubin, Louis D., Jr. "The Gathering of the Fugitives: A Recollection." *Southern Review* 30 (Autumn 1994): 658-673.

—. *The Wary Fugitives: Four Poets and the South*. Baton Rouge: Louisiana State University Press, 1978.

Simpson, Lewis P. "The *Southern Review* and a Post-Southern American Letters." *The Little Magazine in America: A Modern Documentary History*. Ed. Elliott Anderson and Mary Kinzie. Yonkers: Pushcart, 1978

Stallman, R. W. "John Crowe Ransom: A Checklist." *Sewanee Review* 56 (July-September 1948): 442-476.

Stefanik, Ernest C., Jr. *John Berryman: A Descriptive Bibliography.* Pittsburgh: University of Pittsburgh Press, 1974.

Stone, Albert E., Jr. "Seward Collins and the *American Review*: Experiment in Pro-Fascism, 1933-37." *American Quarterly* 12 (1960): 3-19.

Tanselle, G. Thomas. "A Sample Bibliographical Description with Commentary." *Studies in Bibliography* 40 (1987): 1-30.

Tate, Allen. "*The Fugitive*, 1922-1925." *Princeton University Library Chronicle* 3 (April 1942): 75-84.

Wallace, Emily Mitchell. *A Bibliography of William Carlos Williams.* Middletown: Wesleyan University Press, 1968.

Willis, J. H., Jr. *Leonard and Virginia Woolf as Publishers: The Hogarth Press, 1917-41.* Charlottesville: University Press of Virginia, 1992.

Woolmer, J. Howard. *A Checklist of the Hogarth Press, 1917-1946.* Revere, Pennsylvania: Woolmer/Brotherson, 1986.

Wright, Stuart. *Peter Taylor: A Descriptive Bibliography, 1934-87.* Charlottesville: University Press of Virginia for the Bibliographical Society of the University of Virginia, 1988.

—. *Randall Jarrell: A Descriptive Bibliography, 1929-1983.* Charlottesville: University Press of Virginia for the Bibliographical Society of the University of Virginia, 1986.

—. *Richard Eberhart: A Descriptive Bibliography, 1921-1987.* Westport: Meckler, 1989.

Young, Thomas Daniel. *John Crowe Ransom: An Annotated Bibliography.* New York: Garland, 1982.

—. *Gentleman in a Dustcoat: A Biography of John Crowe Ransom.* Baton Rouge: Louisiana State University Press, 1976.

—. *Waking Their Neighbors Up: The Nashville Agrarians Rediscovered.* Mercer University Lamar Memorial Lectures, No. 24. Athens: University of Georgia Press, 1982.

Title Index: Poems

Title Index: Prose

General Index